Urban Heritage, Development and Sustainability

More than half of the world's population now live in urban areas and cities provide the setting for contemporary challenges such as population growth, mass tourism and unequal access to socio-economic opportunities. *Urban Heritage, Development and Sustainability* examines the impact of these issues on urban heritage considering innovative approaches to managing developmental pressures and focusing on how taking an ethical, inclusive and holistic approach to urban planning and heritage conservation may create a stronger basis for the sustainable growth of cities in the future.

This volume is a timely analysis of current theories and practises in urban heritage with particular reference to the conflict between, and potential reconciliation of, conservation and development goals. A global range of case studies detail a number of distinct practical approaches to heritage on international, national and local scales. Chapters reveal the disjunctions between international frameworks and national implementation and assess how internationally agreed concepts can be misused to justify unsustainable practices or to further economic globalisation and political nationalism. The exclusion of many local communities from development policies and the subsequent erosion of their cultural heritage is also discussed, with the collection emphasising the importance of 'grass roots' heritage and exploring more inclusive and culturally responsive conservation strategies.

Contributions from an international group of authors, including practitioners as well as leading academics, deliver a broad and balanced coverage of this topic. Addressing the interests of both urban planners and heritage specialists, *Urban Heritage, Development and Sustainability* is an important addition to the field that will encourage further discourse.

Sophia Labadi is Senior Lecturer in Heritage Studies and co-Director of the Centre for Heritage at the University of Kent, UK and consultant on heritage for international organizations. She is also co-editor of *Heritage and Society.* Her latest publication *UNESCO, Cultural Heritage, and Outstanding Universal Value* was published in 2013.

William Logan is Professor Emeritus in the Cultural Heritage Centre for Asia and the Pacific at Deakin University, Melbourne, Australia. He is a fellow of the Academy of Social Sciences in Australia and was formerly a member of the Heritage Council of Victoria and president of Australia ICOMOS. He is co-editor of the Routledge *Key Issues in Cultural Heritage* book series.

Key Issues in Cultural Heritage
Series Editors: William Logan and Laurajane Smith

Urban Heritage, Development and Sustainability

International frameworks, national and local governance

Edited by Sophia Labadi and William Logan

Routledge
Taylor & Francis Group

LONDON AND NEW YORK

First published 2016
by Routledge
2 Park Square, Milton Park, Abingdon, Oxon OX14 4RN

and by Routledge
711 Third Avenue, New York, NY 10017

Routledge is an imprint of the Taylor & Francis Group, an informa business

British Library Cataloguing-in-Publication Data
A catalogue record for this book is available from the British Library

Library of Congress Cataloging-in-Publication Data
Urban heritage, development and sustainability: international frameworks, national and local governance/edited by Sophia Labadi and William Logan.
     pages cm. – (Key issues in cultural heritage)
     Includes index.
     1. Cultural property–Protection. 2. Historic preservation–International cooperation. 3. City planning. 4. Urbanization–Social aspects. 5. Sustainable urban development. I. Labadi, Sophia, editor.
     CC135.U73 2015
     363.6'9–dc23   2015014371

ISBN: 978-1-138-84573-2 (hbk)
ISBN: 978-1-138-84575-6 (pbk)
ISBN: 978-1-315-72801-8 (ebk)

Typeset in Times New Roman and Gill Sans
by Sunrise Setting Ltd, Paignton, UK

In memoriam:
Dr Ron Van Oers (1965–2015)

Contents

Illustrations

Figures

Tables

Series editors' foreword

The interdisciplinary field of Heritage Studies is now well established in many parts of the world. It differs from earlier scholarly and professional activities that focused narrowly on the architectural or archaeological preservation of monuments and sites. Such activities remain important, especially as modernisation and globalisation lead to new developments that threaten natural environments, archaeological sites, traditional buildings and arts and crafts. But they are subsumed within the new field that sees 'heritage' as a social and political construct encompassing all those places, artefacts and cultural expressions inherited from the past which, because they are seen to reflect and validate our identity as nations, communities, families and even individuals, are worthy of some form of respect and protection.

Heritage results from a selection process, often government-initiated and supported by official regulation; it is not the same as history, although this, too, has its own elements of selectivity. Heritage can be used in positive ways to give a sense of community to disparate groups and individuals or to create jobs on the basis of cultural tourism. It can be actively used by governments and communities to foster respect for cultural and social diversity and to challenge prejudice and misrecognition. But it can also be used by governments in less benign ways, to reshape public attitudes in line with undemocratic political agendas or even to rally people against their neighbours in civil and international wars, ethnic cleansing and genocide. In this way there is a real connection between heritage and human rights.

This is time for a new and unique series of books canvassing the key issues dealt with in the new Heritage Studies. The series seeks to address the deficiency facing the field identified by the Smithsonian in 2005 – that it is 'vastly undertheorized'. It is time to look again at the contestation that inevitably surrounds the identification and evaluation of heritage and to find new ways to elucidate the many layers of meaning that heritage places and intangible cultural expressions have acquired. Heritage conservation and safeguarding in such circumstances can only be understood as a form of cultural politics and that this needs to be reflected in heritage practice, be that in educational institutions or in the field.

It is time, too, to recognise more fully that heritage protection does not depend alone on top-down interventions by governments or the expert actions of heritage industry professionals, but must involve local communities and communities of interest. It is critical that the values and practices of communities, together with traditional management systems where such exist, are understood, respected and incorporated in heritage management plans and policy documents so that communities feel a sense of 'ownership' of their heritage and take a leading role in sustaining it into the future.

This series of books aims then to identify interdisciplinary debates within Heritage Studies and to explore how they impact on not only the practices of heritage management and conservation, but also the processes of production, consumption and engagement with heritage in its many and varied forms.

William Logan
Laurajane Smith

Contributors

Dr Janet Blake is a Reader in Law at the University of Shahid Beheshti (Tehran) where she teaches International, Environmental and Human Rights Law. She is a member of both the UNESCO Chair for Human Rights, Peace and Democracy and the Centre for Excellence in Education for Sustainable Development, based at the university. She is also a member of the Cultural Heritage Law Committee of the International Law Association and she has acted as an International Consultant to UNESCO since 1999 in the field of cultural heritage and endangered languages. She has published three books on safeguarding intangible cultural heritage as well as several articles on safeguarding cultural heritage, environmental protection law and justice, human and cultural rights, cultural diversity and sustainable development. Her next book, *International Cultural Heritage Law*, has recently been published by Oxford University Press.

Kristal Buckley AM is a Lecturer in Cultural Heritage at Deakin University's Cultural Heritage Centre for Asia and the Pacific in Melbourne, Australia. Her work has a focus on evolving forms of global cultural heritage practice, with emphases on cultural diversity, community processes, the cultural values of nature and cultural landscapes. Kristal has served as an international Vice-President of ICOMOS since 2005 and she has been a member of the ICOMOS delegation to the World Heritage Committee since 2007.

Dr Elisabete Cidre is Principal Teaching Fellow in Urban Design at UCL's Bartlett School of Planning and Director of the BSc Planning Programmes. Elisabete was educated as an architect and urban designer in Portugal and as a planner in the UK and she has worked in practice in both countries. Her PhD in Town Planning looked at planning for public realm conservation in the World Heritage cities of Portugal and her current research, practice and teaching interests focus on urban design (policy, practice and education), urban heritage conservation, public space and place making, and reflective learning practice and procedures in built environment academia. She is also the Book Reviews and Practice Notes Editor for the *Journal of Urban Design*.

Dr Steven Cooke is a cultural and historical geographer who has published widely on issues relating to the memorial landscapes of war and genocide, museums and national identity and heritage and urban redevelopment. He is Course Director for the Cultural Heritage and Museum Studies programmes at Deakin University, Melbourne, Australia, where he is a Senior Lecturer in Cultural Heritage, and he is an honorary research fellow in the Faculty of Humanities and Social Sciences, University of Winchester, UK.

Dr Lynne D. DiStefano, an architectural historian by training, is currently the Adjunct Professor and Academic Advisor of the Division of Architectural Conservation Programmes at the University of Hong Kong.

Susan Fayad is the Coordinator Heritage Strategy at the City of Ballarat, Victoria, Australia, and she is managing the roll out of UNESCO's Recommendation on the Historic Urban Landscape pilot programme through a Strategic Cooperation Agreement with the World Heritage Institute of Training and Research in Asia and the Pacific (WHITR-AP) in Shanghai. She was instrumental in developing the City of Ballarat's 'Preserving Ballarat's Heritage Strategy' that addresses heritage management challenges using a preventive change management approach. The strategy has been recognised with awards for innovation from the Heritage Council of Victoria and Planning Institute of Australia (Vic).

Dr Matthew J. Hill is a Senior Research Fellow at the Center for Heritage and Society at the University of Massachusetts Amherst and Lecturer in the Department of Anthropology at the University of Massachusetts Amherst. His research examines the use of historic urban landscapes as a resource for urban and social development in Cuba and the Spanish-speaking Caribbean as well as North America. At UMass, he teaches courses on international heritage policy and urban heritage management as well as the Caribbean region. He has also worked as an applied anthropologist with city governments on the sustainable redevelopment of historic park systems and downtowns.

Pham Thi Thanh Huong has qualifications in International Economics (BA) from Vietnam's Institute for International Relations, Hanoi, and in Public Policy, Media and Communications (MA) from Swinburne University of Technology, Melbourne, Australia. She is a Cultural Specialist at the UNESCO Field Office in Hanoi where she manages the UNESCO Program Building Capacity for World Heritage Site Professionals and the Sustainable Tourism Program in Vietnam. Pham applies her cross-disciplinary background to investigating the political economy of World Heritage, traditional crafts innovation and heritage tourism.

Stacey Jessiman is currently a Visiting Scholar and Lecturer in Law, Stanford Law School, where she teaches 'Stolen Art' and 'Indigenous Cultural Heritage: Protection, Practice, Repatriation'. Prior to completing graduate studies in law, Stacey practised as an international transactional and dispute resolution lawyer in New York and Paris. She received BA degrees in Art History (Honours) and International Relations from Stanford, her JD degree from the University of Toronto and an LLM from The University of British Columbia Faculty of Law. Her most recent publications are 'The Edgy State of Decolonization at the Canadian Museum of History', *UBC L Rev* (2014), 47(3), 889 and 'The Repatriation of the G'psgolox Totem Pole: A Study of its Context, Process and Outcome', *International Journal of Cultural Property* (2011), 18, 365–91.

Albino Jopela is a Lecturer in Archaeology and Heritage Studies at the Department of Archaeology and Anthropology at the Eduardo Mondlane University in Mozambique and a PhD candidate at the School of Geography, Archaeology and Environmental Studies at the University of the Witwatersrand in South Africa. He is also a researcher at Kaleidoscopio (Research in Public Policy and Culture) in Mozambique and Vice-President of the PanAfrican Archaeological Association. His research interests include heritage management systems (traditional custodianship systems), rock art conservation, heritage socio-politics and liberation heritage in Mozambique and southern Africa.

Dr Sophia Labadi is currently Senior Lecturer in Heritage Studies and co-Director of the Centre for Heritage at the University of Kent and consultant on heritage for international organizations. She is also co-editor of Heritage and Society. She previously worked for UNESCO, in the Secretariat of the 1972 World Heritage Convention and the 2003 Intangible Cultural Heritage Convention and participated in the strategic planning and drafting of the 2009 UNESCO World Report on Cultural Diversity. Her latest publication, *UNESCO, Cultural Heritage, and Outstanding Universal Value*, was published in 2013 by AltaMira.

Professor William Logan is Professor Emeritus in the Cultural Heritage Centre for Asia and the Pacific at Deakin University, Melbourne, Australia. He is a fellow of the Academy of Social Sciences in Australia and was formerly a member of the Heritage Council of Victoria and president of Australia ICOMOS. He is co-editor of the Routledge *Key Issues in Cultural Heritage* book series and the *Blackwell Companion to Heritage Studies*. His research interests include World Heritage, heritage and human rights and Asian heritage, especially the urban heritage of Vietnam and Myanmar and the management of intangible cultural heritage in Southeast Asia's borderlands with China.

Dr Yamini Narayanan is Australian Research Council DECRA Fellow at Deakin University, Melbourne, Australia. Her research explores the vital role that religion has in inclusive urban planning in India, especially as regards women and minorities. More recently, her work has also begun to explore trans-species feminist urban planning – examining the significant and yet invisible role of animals in city building and the complicity of urban religion in enabling animal exploitation for urban development. Her book *Religion, Heritage and the Sustainable City: Hinduism and Urbanisation in Jaipur* (Routledge) was published in 2015.

Bianca Maria Nardella has trained as an architect, urbanist and social scientist in Italy, the USA and the UK. She combines professional practice in architecture and urban conservation with university teaching and policy analysis research. Her consulting experience includes management and technical expertise for 'heritage and development' projects financed by the World Bank, EuropeAid and the Inter-American Development Bank, which are often centred around UNESCO World Heritage sites. Her geo-cultural area of speciality is the Mediterranean region, including the Middle East and North Africa. In parallel, she tutors students for urban design studios at the Bartlett Faculty of the Built Environment, University College London. She is currently completing her PhD dissertation 'Interrogating communities of expertise on urban conservation and development: How do you mean "public and open spaces" in Tunis?' at the Bartlett Development Planning Unit, UCL.

Professor Robert Pickard is Emeritus Professor in Built Environment and Heritage Conservation at Northumbria University, UK. He has been a technical consultant to the Council of Europe on cultural heritage issues since 1994, including coordinating a European expert group – the Legislative Support Task Force – for legal, policy and institutional reform, the integration of planning and heritage protection, heritage-led urban rehabilitation and funding mechanisms to support the built heritage. His most recent work has been through the Council of Europe's Regional Programme for South-East Europe (in the Balkans), including legal and institutional capacity building activities through the Ljubljana Process II, a jointly funded programme with the European Commission for 'Rehabilitating our Common Heritage' and the Regional Programme for the Black Sea and South Caucasus (Kyiv Initiative: Pilot Project on the Rehabilitation of Culture Heritage in Historic Towns) involving the development of a Town Reference Plan for sustaining historic towns, with initial application in 23 priority intervention towns. Other recent work has included acting as co-investigator to an Arts and Humanities Research Council-funded international research network on the implementation of procedures for the preservation of World Heritage Sites in national contexts. He is also author and editor of several books, including *Conservation in the Built Environment* (1996), *Policy and Law in Heritage Conservation* (2001), *Management of Historic Centres* (2001), *European Cultural Heritage: Volume II: A Review of Policy and Practice* (2002), three books in a European Heritage Series: *Analysis and Reform of Cultural Heritage Policies in South-East Europe* (2008), *Integrated Management Tools in the Heritage of South-East Europe* (2008) and *Sustainable Development Strategies* (2008) – and also *Funding the Architectural Heritage: A Guide to Policies and Examples* (2009), *Guidance on the Development of Legislation and Administration Systems in the Field of Cultural Heritage* (2011) and author/co-author of many journal papers, most recently 'Reconstruction: The Need for Guidelines' (2013).

Dr Eduardo Rojas is an independent consultant on urban development and a Lecturer on Historic Preservation at the School of Design at the University of Pennsylvania, USA. He works regularly with the World Bank, the Organization for Economic Cooperation and Development (OECD), the Lincoln Institute of Land Policy of Cambridge, USA, and the Wold Bank Institute. He is a former Principal Specialist in Urban Development and Housing at the Inter-American Development Bank where he worked in the appraisal and implementation of housing, municipal and urban development loans and technical cooperation projects. He also formulated sector policies and strategies for the Bank and did good practices research and dissemination in the urban sector including housing sector reform and low income housing programmes, urban heritage preservation and integrated urban development. Eduardo also worked at the Regional Development Department of the Organization of American States, lectured at the Masters Degree Programme in Urban Studies at the Catholic University of Chile and worked with the Urban Development Corporation of the Government of Chile. He holds a degree in Architecture from the Catholic University of Chile, an MPhil in Urban and Regional Planning from the University of Edinburgh, UK, an MBA from Johns Hopkins University in the USA and a Doctorate in City Planning from Universidade Lusofona in Portugal.

Dr Kearrin Sims recently completed his PhD at the University of Western Sydney's Institute for Culture and Society. With a background in Sociology, International Relations and Development Studies, Kearrin's current research explores the impact of East Asia on the development landscape of Laos. Kearrin has travelled extensively throughout Southeast Asia and he has published across a number of different mediums.

Dr Maki Tanaka earned her PhD in socio-cultural anthropology at the University of California, Berkeley in 2011. She conducted her ethnographic fieldwork in Cuba and her dissertation focused on the contradictions of heritage preservation, tourism and Cuban late socialism in the World Heritage site of Trinidad, Cuba. Her interests include urban heritage, built environment, UNESCO World Heritage, tourism, post-socialism and Cuba. Maki currently works in international development consulting and is based in Tokyo, Japan.

Dr Tim Winter is Research Professor at the Cultural Heritage Centre for Asia and the Pacific, Deakin University, Melbourne, Australia. He has published widely on heritage, development, modernity, urban conservation and tourism in Asia. He is co-editor of *The Routledge Handbook of Heritage in Asia* and editor of *Shanghai Expo: An International Forum on the Future of Cities* (Routledge 2013).

Dr Celia Martínez Yáñez is a Lecturer in the Art History Department at the University of Granada and the Master on Historic Heritage and Architecture (MARPH) at the University of Seville, the Andalusian Institute of Historic

Heritage (IAPH) and the Council of Alhambra and Generalife. She is also an expert member of the ICOMOS International Scientific Committees on Cultural Routes (CIIC) and Cultural Tourism (ICTC), Editor of ERPH, Revista Electrónica de Patrimonio Histórico, and author of many international contributions on new approaches to cultural heritage identification, protection and management.

Dr Lee Ho Yin, an architect by training, is currently an Associate Professor and the Head of the Division of Architectural Conservation Programmes at the University of Hong Kong.

Chapter 1

Approaches to urban heritage, development and sustainability

Sophia Labadi and William Logan

More than half of the world's population now live in urban areas (UN-Habitat 2008). Cities provide the locale for many of the great issues of our time – exponential population growth due to high in-migration and birth rates, rapid urban development and re-development, the engulfing of surrounding agricultural and recreational land, uncontrolled mass tourism and social exclusion and unequal access to socio-economic opportunities. These issues impact dramatically on the conservation and management of urban heritage. Yet, at the same time, the sensitive management of urban heritage may be part of the solution to these city problems. This volume of commissioned papers discusses these two aspects of the heritage versus development dilemma. It focuses on innovative approaches to managing the developmental pressures faced by urban heritage, as well as the ways in which taking an ethical, inclusive and holistic approach to urban planning and heritage conservation may create a stronger basis for the sustainable growth of cities into the future.

The volume will analyse, first, how these two concepts – urban heritage and development – have been theorised and used by international intergovernmental organisations such as the United Nations Educational Scientific and Cultural Organisation (UNESCO), the World Bank and UN-Habitat. The strengths and weaknesses in these theoretical approaches and international frameworks are canvassed. The volume explores how conservation and development come together in the notion of 'balance', which is an oft-heard planning objective, but in fact, one of the chief conundrums bedevilling contemporary heritage theory and practice as well as urban planning and management. This applies especially in urban contexts where a long history has resulted in a rich legacy of the past, both tangible and intangible, and where pressures to create new environmental conditions, claimed to be better suited to the needs of modern economic activities, are concentrated. It is, of course, not a new dilemma; indeed, the modern heritage movement in many countries and internationally flowed out of earlier manifestations of the same concern about the lack of balance, notably with heritage being neglected in favour of development. More recent versions of the issue have led to more integrated approaches, balancing heritage protection with urban development, as seen in UNESCO's Historic Urban Landscape (HUL).

The volume notes the contradictions within international narratives and guidance; the inadequacy of internationally agreed concepts, such as sustainable development, and their operationalisation as well as the exclusionary nature of policies and programmes for urban conservation and development. Too often heritage destruction is carried out in the name of modernity and progress and against the wishes of local communities for whom the heritage is a valued part of their living environment and a manifestation of their identity. Local people are left out of discussions about the future of their places and innovative grassroots approaches to the development pressures faced by urban heritage are seldom considered. These negatives notwithstanding, the volume argues that the conservation of heritage can assist the achievement of sustainable economic growth and social justice. Social exclusion and unequal access to socio-economic opportunities are common threads in the book. In addition, efforts are directed towards identifying by whom and for whom conservation and development policies and programmes are established.

Early approaches to urban heritage conservation and development

Urban heritage conservation in Europe extends back to the mid-nineteenth century (Siravo 2011). It emerged in response to the destruction of ancient and medieval buildings in the French Revolution and other European revolutions and insurrections and to the wider scale destruction of whole historic quarters in modernisation campaigns that aimed to open them up to new economic activities and transport systems as well as improving standards of hygiene (Bandarin and Van Oers 2012: 3). The revolutionary wave of destruction principally attacked aristocratic and religious buildings, while the wave of modernisation primarily targeted vernacular buildings. In France, the response to the ravages of the 1789 Revolution led to the emergence, a generation later, of the first national heritage protection system with the appointment of the first inspector general of historical monuments in 1831 – Prosper Mérimée, mostly remembered by the world as the author of the novella on which Bizet's opera *Carmen* is based. Eugène Viollet-le-Duc's contribution to the development of a national heritage system is better known. Appointed by Mérimée in 1839, Viollet-le-Duc did an enormous amount of work over the next 35 years, from the abbey church of La Madeleine in Vézelay to the Notre Dame cathedral in Paris and the fortress of Carcassonne.

Much of this early French work has been criticised as representative of an approach that focused on iconic and monumental buildings that were presented in their full glory and beauty but protected in an isolated manner, divorced from their wider urban context (Glendinning 2013: 90). This is the case, for instance, with the Gothic Notre Dame in Paris, which was subsequently cleared of the mazes of medieval streets and houses for the construction of its forecourt by the Baron Georges Haussmann as part of his reshaping of Paris between 1848 and 1870. While Haussmann's approach turned Paris into a more unified, beautified and ventilated capital, with open avenues and streets, it was also an exercise in 'civic cleansing'. It had a political dimension in that the wide avenues were supposed to be more secure, to prevent, among other things, the construction of barricades (easier to erect in small streets) and to facilitate the movement of army troops.

Local communities were totally excluded from this contradictory process of conservation and destruction. The values these communities might have seen in individual monuments or more vernacular parts of cities were not taken into account. A number of prominent intellectuals of the time strongly objected to this approach to urban heritage conservation, the most renowned and vehement being Victor Hugo. In his pamphlet *La Guerre aux Démolisseurs* (1832), Hugo condemned speculators who destroyed medieval quarters for profit-making activities, resulting in the loss of priceless intangible and vernacular heritage. Across the channel in the United Kingdom, initial critics, such as John Ruskin, disliked the French 'imaginative restoration' and preferred a more Romantic approach that kept ruins as ruins. Ruskin's *The Stones of Venice* (three volumes 1851–3) set a British pattern that was reinforced in 1877 by William Morris' Society for the Protection of Ancient Buildings. Both Ruskin and Morris were social reformers, particularly in criticising the workings of industrial capitalism and in advocating greater status for craftsmen; nevertheless, taking note of local community views of heritage was not among their priorities.

The end of the nineteenth century saw a more decisive move away from urban heritage conservation understood as single monumental buildings, detached from their surroundings and disconnected from local communities. The Austrian architect Camillo Sitte, for instance, adopted a global understanding of the urban fabric as an aesthetic entity, through focusing on urban morphologies (Sitte 1965; Choay 1969). He thus condemned an approach that would focus on individual urban monuments. He also criticised an approach to urban planning and landscaping that would lead to regular and grid plans, detached from their socio-economic histories, preferring more organic cities, built according to social, economic and cultural necessities and opportunities. This was more in line with the Garden City Movement in the UK that sought to break down the distinction between built urban and organic rural (Hardy 1991).

Also in Britain, the Scottish biologist and town planner Patrick Geddes introduced his holistic approach to urban planning and heritage conservation in his *Cities in Evolution: An Introduction to the Town Planning Movement and to the Study of Civics* (1915). The book contained some pioneering ideas on the relationship between urban heritage, development and sustainability. For him, before any development could take place, the city as a whole needed to be understood through surveys and mappings of its economic, social and cultural functions. His approach was strongly influenced by Darwinism and the theory of evolution. Indeed, he believed that any development project should respect and conserve the 'urban ecosystem' of the whole city, paying particular attention to the connections between spaces for work, places for cultural and social uses as well as local communities.

In other words, Geddes believed in the protection of the historic urban environment as a whole and the harmonious integration of any development project within this urban ecosystem. He also believed that urban development projects should be seen in the broader context of the surrounding countryside, considered as an integral part of the ecosystem. Finally, and making a distinct break with what had come before, Geddes argued that local communities and their intangible attachments to places should be at the heart of urban heritage conservation and urban planning interventions. Geddes can thus be considered as a visionary, who introduced, before his time, the idea of a sustainable approach to development that should take account of the existing urban landscape in all its complexities. His writings seem to have been a major inspiration for the 2011 UNESCO Recommendation on the Historic Urban Landscape (Veldpaus *et al.* 2013: 5–6).

International and national heritage management approaches after World War II

The conditions created by World War II – death and displacement of peoples, unsettling of colonial empires, destruction of cities and national economies – led to a variety of responses affecting urban and heritage management principles and practice. Reacting to the need for economic and social recovery, in the United Kingdom, the *Town and Country Planning Act 1947*, in conjunction with a parallel piece of legislation in Scotland, established a new national system that, although revised many times, continues to define how the management of land, and hence development and conservation, can be carried out today. It established the rule, for instance, that ownership of land alone does not confer the untrammelled right to develop the land but that planning permission is required for land development. Under the 1947 Act, local authorities were also given power to redevelop land themselves or compulsorily acquire and lease it to private developers. Already anxious about urban sprawl and its impact on villages and the countryside, the Act also allowed local authorities to control outdoor advertising and to preserve woodland and buildings of architectural or historic interest.

This marked the start of the British listed building system, a rather eclectic system based on the personal preferences of a band of heritage professionals rather than on a clear set of significance criteria and attributes, but one that has been influential in other parts of the world, notably in former British colonies. The decolonisation processes occurring after World War II saw many new countries becoming both independent and 'newly developing', with huge demands for improved standards of living and the lowering of environmental protection standards in the bid to attract industrial investment and development. Heritage was, understandably, low on the agenda of governments in such countries. Other countries bent on post-war recovery and improved living standards, such as Japan, rushed into industrial and urban developments, with dire consequences for urban environments and an urge to re-construct lost heritage monuments a generation later.

In response to some insensitive infrastructure developments in the 1950s and inner city urban renewal in the 1960s, the United States also took steps to protect its heritage. This meant, in the American social and political context where private property rights are particularly strong, that the protection focus was on natural rather than cultural heritage. Even so, many cities adopted preservation regulations. According to Gustavo Araoz:

> The will to conserve and monumentalize such sites did not issue from either the central or the local government, but rather, from local citizen groups who valued the cultural, historic and patriotic sites that lay in their immediate community. For decades, the government offered little interest, no assistance, and no official recognition to any of these sites. Thus, from its very origin, the preservation movement in the United States has been characterized by being a grassroots effort driven at the local level and one that evolved in isolation from outside influences, responding only to perceived local needs.
>
> (Araoz 2015)

Nevertheless, public pressure did lead to the *National Historic Preservation Act 1966*, which covers districts as well as site, buildings, structures and artefacts, requires assessment of the potential impact on heritage of all federally funded development projects and provides a range of grants, loans and tax incentives to encourage individuals to restore and maintain their properties.

In France, the urban redevelopment pressures on heritage came to a head in the Marais district in Paris in the early 1960s. Here, rather than allow the demolition of the *hôtels* (townhouses) built by noble families in the *ancien régime* and smaller medieval houses, André Malraux, the French Minister for Culture, established a set of planning regulations in 1962 that came to be known as the *loi Malraux*. From this beginning, the planning treatment of urban heritage around the world has sought to protect broad areas of historic, aesthetic, architectural or scientific interest, rather than simply focusing on individual monuments. It is rather remarkable that about the same time – 1964 – when a group of conservation architects working to restore buildings in war-torn cities, mostly in Europe, met in Venice and decided to formalise a set of principles to guide conservation practice, they kept to the old focus on monuments and sites and ignored the broader, more modern concepts of historic precincts, villages, towns and townscapes. This same group was behind the creation in 1965 of the International Council on Monuments and Sites (ICOMOS) that adopted the so-called Venice Charter (Second ICATHM 1964) as its foundational doctrine and it is now positioned under the UNESCO World Heritage Convention as an official advisory body to the World Heritage Committee on matters relating to cultural heritage.

It had been the creation of UNESCO in 1945 that led to the internationalisation of the debate about, and approaches to, the protection of urban heritage and the connection between heritage, development and sustainability. The adoption of the 1972 *Convention Concerning the Protection of the World Cultural and Natural*

Heritage (the World Heritage Convention), in particular, can be understood as reflecting concerns for unsustainable models of development and their impacts on heritage, chiefly cultural in Europe and natural in North America. This legal instrument reflects many of the dominant ideas of the 1970s related to the adverse environmental consequences of growth – pollution, wasteful resource use, spoiled rural landscapes and inhospitable urban environments. These concerns about unbridled growth are clearly spelt out at the beginning of the Preamble of the Convention, which highlights that:

> The cultural heritage and natural heritage are increasingly threatened with destruction not only by the traditional causes of decay, but also by changing social and economic conditions which aggravate the situation with even more formidable phenomena of damage and destruction.
>
> (UNESCO 1972)

The Convention also reflects the need to take better account and care of non-renewable resources, including cultural heritage. It is revealing that the book *The Limits to Growth* (Meadows 1972), commissioned by the Club of Rome, which clearly warns against unsustainable growth trends, was released in the year the World Heritage Convention was adopted. The promotion of 'spaceship earth' (Ward 1966) and ZPG (zero population growth) helped popularise the awareness of resource sustainability concerns. At the heart of the notion of sustainable development, is the notion of intergenerational equity. This is clear from Article 4 of the Convention, which recognises that heritage should be identified, protected and transmitted to future generations. The idea of protecting finite resources for future generations, of intergenerational equity, was echoed, 12 years later, in the iconic definition of sustainable development in the Brundtland Report: 'sustainable development is development that meets the needs of the present without compromising the ability of future generations to meet their own needs' (UNWCED 1987: Paragraph 27).

Into the twenty-first century

The late 1960s to early 1970s was a period of political turmoil in both the communist and non-communist world centring on the Vietnam War, as well as intellectual excitement associated with the appearance of new theoretical positions in sociology and philosophy. It was the right time for the emergence and consolidation of global organisations with idealist, universalist and environmental principles such as UNESCO and its advisory bodies. It proved to be a short-lived time, however, soon to be overtaken in the 1980s by Reaganomics, Thatcherism and other forms of neo-liberal economics and politics in many Western countries. At the philosophical level, a shift was seen from the idealism and universalism of the mid-century modernists to a greater emphasis on individualism, while the growing strength of multinational corporations produced a nationalist reaction that eventually came to impact on the workings of the World Heritage Committee (Logan 2013; Meskell 2013). Economic growth was clearly the main objective of governments, especially when the long boom from the 1970s was brought to a sharp halt by the Global Financial Crisis (GFC) of 2007 to 2008 that hit Europe, Asia and North America badly. Heritage has dropped lower in the list of government concerns. Except where it plays a crucial role in nation-building, cultural heritage in particular is not seen as a priority; business people enjoy it on their vacation travels but tend to see it as not relevant in considering the development of their home cities. Notions such as the 'public good' that were once central to planning interventions have been set aside, while belief in the primacy of private property ownership has become more entrenched. Private property ownership is seen as a 'right' and confused with human rights. Governments will not and, often, cannot pay for comprehensive and effective conservation systems and taxpayers resist paying more to make them possible. In short, urban heritage protection is reaching a crisis point in many cities, even including Venice.

Thus, while the World Heritage Convention was adopted in 1972 amid calls for more sustainable approaches to growth and new models of development, the momentum has been lost now for several decades. The impact of the changing global context is seen in the fact that it was not until 2002, 30 years after the adoption of the Convention, that the World Heritage Committee adopted the Budapest Declaration, the first official document to mention heritage and sustainable development in the same breath. The Declaration expresses the need to

> ensure an appropriate and equitable balance between conservation, sustainability and development, so that World Heritage properties can be protected through appropriate activities contributing to the social and economic development and the quality of life of our communities.
>
> (UNESCO 2002)

This Declaration clearly refers to sustainable development in terms of economic growth and social equity. It has been followed by many meetings, documents and statements on World Heritage and sustainable development. These have adopted a similar definition of sustainable development as the Budapest Declaration. Among the statements is the important Vienna Memorandum (UNESCO 2005), which calls for a harmonious integration of new urban development projects within the existing historic urban landscape (for a summary of these initiatives and documents, see Labadi forthcoming).

Unfortunately, these activities have not been followed by any real effort to transform the Convention into a sustainable development tool. An agreement was reached at the 2008 World Heritage Committee meeting to adopt an Australian proposal to hold a workshop (in fact, a series of meetings held both within and outside the Committee's annual meetings) to reflect on the Convention in view of the approaching fortieth anniversary of the World Heritage Convention in 2012, as well as the inscription of the thousandth property to the World Heritage List

(Logan 2012: 124–5). The meetings identified five key issues: imbalances within the World Heritage List; public perception and maximisation of the brand value of World Heritage; current focus on inscription to the detriment of conservation; governance structures that are not participatory and are overloaded; and financing the implementation of the Convention. This was a largely bureaucratic response (Logan 2012: 125) and sustainability was not highlighted. This was a lost opportunity to come to terms with the escalation of development projects, primarily in urban contexts, that pose threats to the Outstanding Universal Value of World Heritage properties – a trend that is reflected in the growing number of State of Conservation reports on the potential or recognised harmful impacts of urban development projects (Bandarin and Labadi 2007: 184; Van Oers 2010: 7).

Nevertheless, several more positive events have occurred. First, flowing out of the Budapest and Vienna discussions about the impact of development on urban heritage, in 2005 the World Heritage Committee called for a Recommendation on the subject of conservation of the historic urban landscape to be drawn up. Following large-scale consultations (Van Oers 2010: 12), the Recommendation on the Historic Urban Landscape was adopted by UNESCO's General Conference in 2011. The Recommendation, which is discussed in this volume in the chapters by Jessiman, by Buckley, Cooke and Fayad as well as by Hill and Tanaka, drew some of its ideas and concepts from the writings of Geddes and the reflections of the Brundtland Report. It calls for an approach that aims to balance urban heritage conservation and socio-economic development (Article 11). In doing so, it considers urban heritage in its broader urban and historical contexts and geographical settings (Article 8), including through taking into account land use patterns and spatial organisations, social and cultural practices and values, economic processes and the intangible dimension of heritage. The Recommendation also offers a number of tools to help achieve such a holistic and balanced approach between urban heritage conservation and socio-economic development. These tools deal with civic engagement, knowledge and planning, and regulatory systems as well as finance (Article 24). The Recommendation also provides conceptual tools for a better consideration of the limits of acceptable change in significant heritage areas and for finding a balance between urban heritage conservation, socio-economic development and sustainability.

Second, in parallel with these reflections on the historic urban landscape, another approach has increasingly been promoted at international levels; that is, the fundamental role played by urban heritage towards the achievement of sustainable development. More precisely, this approach claims *inter alia* that heritage conservation leads to poverty reduction through economic growth, tourism and job creation and it leads to the reduction of social inequalities through the provision of new opportunities and access to basic goods and services, as well as increased security and health, through better provision of shelter, clean air, water, food and other key resources. The approach has been endorsed by the Florence Declaration on Heritage and Landscape as Human Values (ICOMOS 2014) adopted by ICOMOS at its eighteenth General Assembly in October 2014. While focusing mostly on the traditional intangible of local communities and Indigenous peoples, the Declaration nevertheless recommends broadly that intergovernmental organisations, national and local authorities and all organisations and specialists should link heritage conservation and sustainable local socio-economic development and ensure that heritage conservation contributes to sustainable development objectives (ICOMOS 2014: Art 4.3a). The World Bank has been a keen supporter and developer of this approach and it has argued that heritage conservation leads to major social and economic improvements (Cernea 2001). One of the key projects implemented during the first decade of the twenty-first century by the World Bank has been the wide-scale rehabilitation of urban heritage, including medinas in the Middle East and North African region (Bigio and Licciardi 2010; World Bank 2012). The aim of the World Bank project was to manage urban heritage quarters in a holistic manner rather than focusing on individual and iconic monuments and to focus on projects that would lead to high economic returns, as well as to employment creation and poverty reduction in local communities (Lafrenz 2006: 2).

The Florence Declaration flows out of the push emanating in ICOMOS Norway towards strengthening the human rights basis of World Heritage management (see Ekern *et al.* 2012, 2014). Very similar intentions are held by Farida Shaheed, a Pakistani sociologist, who, in 2015, completed six years as Independent Expert/Special Rapporteur on cultural rights at the Office of the UN High Commissioner for Human Rights (OHCHR) in Geneva. Across 2010 to 2011, Ms Shaheed chose to focus on access to and enjoyment of cultural heritage as a human right (see United Nations Human Rights Council 2011). Her other reports cover the cultural rights of women; historical and memorial narratives in divided societies; history teaching and memorialisation processes; copyright policy and the right to science and culture; and the impact of advertising and marketing practices on the enjoyment of cultural rights.

All of these moves are brought together in respect of the World Heritage system, which now contains more than 1,000 sites in 161 countries, in the work of a UNESCO working group across 2013 to 2015 to draft a policy for the integration of a sustainable development perspective into the processes of the World Heritage Convention. The draft policy will go to the General Assembly of States Parties in November 2015 for adoption. It commences by recognising that the World Heritage Convention is an integral part of UNESCO's overarching mandate to foster equitable sustainable development and to promote peace and security and that, as part of the United Nations family of organisations, UNESCO and the States Parties to the World Heritage Convention should adhere to the post-2015 UN sustainable development agenda, existing international humanitarian standards and other multilateral environmental agreements. This text reiterates the Budapest Declaration and requests States Parties to 'ensure an appropriate and equitable balance between conservation, sustainability and development' (UNESCO 2002). In addition, this draft policy sees clearly the reciprocal nature of the relationship between heritage and sustainability:

> By protecting cultural and natural heritage places of Outstanding Universal Value (OUV), the World Heritage Convention, in itself, contributes significantly to sustainable development and the wellbeing of people. At the same

time, strengthening various dimensions of sustainable development, such as environmental sustainability, inclusive social and economic development, and the fostering of peace and security, may bring benefits to World Heritage and enhance the OUV of properties, if carefully integrated within conservation and management systems for World Heritage properties.

Implementing international frameworks at the national level

The States Parties to the World Heritage Convention will no doubt respond in various ways to these moves to reconceptualise the connection between heritage, development and sustainability. Some of these ways are suggested in the chapters in this volume. In addition, these chapters also show the disjunctions that commonly occur between the international frameworks and their implementation at the national level. Often, too, internationally agreed concepts such as sustainable development are distorted and misused to justify unsustainable economic, social and environmental practices or to further economic globalisation and political nationalism. Kearrin Sims and Tim Winter, for instance, portray the situation in the Lao People's Democratic Republic in Southeast Asia where respect for and involvement of local communities in heritage management is still lacking. Their chapter focuses on the town of Luang Prabang, a World Heritage property that is a site of rapid modernisation. Centred on the prioritisation of the needs of tourism development and the upgrading of the Luang Prabang airport, this chapter provides often sad accounts, based on personal interviews, of forced displacements. It details the detrimental impacts of these displacements on the wellbeing of those affected, as they are accompanied by new forms of marginalisation, social, cultural and economic disadvantages, as well as livelihood constraints. This infringement of people's rights continues despite it becoming standard UNESCO policy since the 2003 Amsterdam conference on 'Linking Universal and Local Values' that heritage protection does not depend alone on top-down interventions by governments or the expert actions of heritage industry professionals, but must involve local communities.

In his chapter, Albino Jopela also portrays an administrative system that relies on regulatory frameworks but seems to care little for the wellbeing and rights of the local community. Using the example of the Island of Mozambique in the Republic of Mozambique, he details how UNESCO and its World Heritage Centre have adopted and implemented an approach to urban heritage conservation for sustainable development. He provides a detailed account of the different initiatives, most of them funded by international or regional development agencies, to reverse the increasing degradation of the island's built heritage, to reduce poverty and improve the living conditions of the inhabitants. Critically analysing the power relations and dynamic processes involving key stakeholders who have influenced and shaped decision-making about the island, Jopela shows that the implementation of these initiatives has been undermined by weak governance structures in which heritage conservation policy and implementation sit.

In their chapter for this volume, Bianca Maria Nardella and Elisabete Cidre also critically assess administrative systems and regulatory frameworks. They focus on the medina of Tunis as well as the Tunisia Cultural Heritage Project (2002 to 2012) that was funded by the World Bank to 'ensure the sustainable management of the country's cultural heritage with a view to developing cultural tourism' (World Bank 2012: iii). This project also aimed to implement a set of proposed actions to reform both institutions and management practices while delivering physical improvements at key heritage sites. A key component of this project was to strengthen the operationalisation of the country's policies on cultural heritage and the operating capacities of the institutions in charge of cultural heritage conservation and management. Nardella and Cidre look at the challenges facing this and other international projects for the medina of Tunis, including the lack of coherence between the programmes and their implementation on the ground, as well as the lack of human resources and political and community goodwill.

Turning to analyses of the implementation of UNESCO's Recommendation on the Historic Urban Landscape, Stacey Jessiman's chapter analyses a case study on Aboriginal stakeholders in Canada. Focusing on controversial legal decisions relating to the Musqueam Nation's Marpole midden in metropolitan Vancouver and the Tsilhqot'in Nation's land claim, also in British Columbia, she draws out the implications for implementing the Historic Urban Landscape (HUL) Recommendation in Canada. She highlights the limits of the Recommendation's text and accompanying tools, arguing that they do not demonstrate adequate sensitivity to colonial harms and so do little to encourage Aboriginal stakeholders in Canada to facilitate implementation of the Recommendation. In particular, Jessiman explains that the Recommendation does not adequately address the problem of ongoing grievances of Indigenous peoples relating to land title and urban planning and development.

With the intention of illustrating what introducing the Historic Urban Landscape concept into local government means on the ground in terms of existing planning arrangements, Kristal Buckley, Steven Cooke and Susan Fayad introduce a case study of the City of Ballarat in Victoria, Australia. Ballarat is the state's third largest urban area and one of its most significant 1850s gold-rush boom towns noted for its historic urban fabric. A projected 50 per cent increase of the existing population over the next 15 to 25 years will put significant pressure on the existing urban form. In an Australian local government context, heritage is often seen through the lens of planning controls and as a problem to be solved, rather than an economic and social resource and a key component of individual and collective identities. As the authors argue, heritage 'battles' are either won or lost as the result of local councils attempting to 'balance' competing values. In this governance context, the chapter explores the first stage of Ballarat's experimental use of the HUL approach to guide the city's strategic planning. The HUL programme in Ballarat has challenged practitioners and council officers but it has shown the importance of 'continually moving between theorisation, experimentation and applied learning – even in such constrained and pragmatic processes as local city planning and development'.

Intangibility is a vital component of urban heritage, as highlighted by the Recommendation on the Historic Urban Landscape, echoing Geddes, especially important for local communities and for understanding urban contexts, histories and morphologies. This category of heritage has taken increasing prominence since the adoption of the 2003 UNESCO Convention for the Safeguarding of the Intangible Cultural Heritage. Intangible heritage in urban settings, as living traditions, know-how or cultural practices, is an important marker of identity, social cohesion and conviviality. The safeguarding of intangible heritage manifestations is the subject of Janet Blake's chapter, where she argues that intangible heritage is, in fact, the key to equipping people with tools that help them to live better in urban settings and to overcome any potential sense of social and cultural dislocation. Conversely, Blake highlights the threats posed by increased migrations to the transmission and safeguarding of intangible heritage manifestations, particularly in urban settings, as well as the potential issues of major transformations to these manifestations when transposed to an urban context.

Reconciling urban heritage conservation and development?

The previous section has detailed the approach supported by international and regional organisations that suggests urban heritage contributes to sustainable development, as well as referring to the limits of this approach. One of the recurrent criticisms is that urban heritage conservation and sustainable development, defined as entailing both economic growth and increasing social equity, are paradoxical aggregations that attempt to bring together fields with contradictory objectives and methods (Flipo 2005: 1; Labadi 2013: 99). These concepts have also been criticised as impractical and as not applicable to actual, concrete cases. Meskell (2011: 27), for instance, criticises the notion of intergenerational equity, which is one of the core principles of sustainable development. Indeed, in an unequal world, how can those who are already deprived of resources bequeath them to future generations? How can this principle of intergenerational equity work in a global context where instant profit is so valued to the detriment of long-term benefits? Certainly, there are difficulties, too, in reaching widespread understanding of sustainability when the concept is applied to the cultural realm. The concept was taken from the natural sciences, where the 'natural environment' and its need for protection are well understood. However, the need to protect the cultural environment is often not seen as relevant and the safeguarding interventions are regarded as not workable for some forms of cultural heritage. In the context of the built environment, it is commonly argued that people are infinitely creative and can always build something better in place of the monument destroyed.

Despite the failings outlined previously in applying international normative statements at the national and local levels, there are some good news stories in which cultural heritage has been valorised socially and economically in urban settings and effectively protected through urban planning policies and programmes. New concepts and mechanisms are now available as part of the urban planner's and heritage conservationist's toolkits, such as corporate social responsibility, social capital formation, urban regeneration and tourism development, as well as heritage impact assessment. The approach that claims that urban heritage conservation can lead to sustainable social and economic development has been adopted and implemented by a number of regional institutions in Europe. In his chapter, Robert Pickard analyses the Council of Europe's programme entitled 'Town Reference Plan', which aims to use urban heritage rehabilitation to revitalise downgraded areas or town centres. He also outlines the European Union's 'Heritage as Opportunity' (HerO) programme that aims to safeguard heritage for the benefit of local communities. He provides different examples where the use of these programmes has helped to create the means for managing the urban environment as well as allowing urban development to be monitored and the cultural heritage to be safeguarded. Importantly, these two approaches are based on local stakeholder involvement, particularly to gain political and community support from the beginning of the project. The strength of these initiatives is that they are based on historic towns exchanging information and expertise through consolidated networks and facilitating bilateral cooperation between historic towns and the participation of investors and funders.

Several of the chapters in this volume demonstrate that, despite the innovative ideas debated and projects disseminated at the international level, post-World War II monuments-based approaches to urban heritage conservation and development are still a reality in many countries in the twenty-first century. In the case of Hong Kong, Lee and DiStefano describe a situation where officially designated urban monuments are not always valued by local communities. These individual monuments and antiquities are protected in isolation from their surrounding precincts, reflecting the entrenched views of heritage bureaucrats and influential professionals. Vernacular sites, precincts and objects, valued by local communities because they use them or have personal connections with them, such as the local diner or the old tramway systems, have faced difficulty in being officially recognised as heritage. Lee and DiStefano argue that the balance between conservation and development is shifting and they outline the transformation process that is bringing the two polarised interests to a relationship based on compromise.

The reconciliation path, however, remains difficult as Sophia Labadi shows in her chapter in this volume. She analyses the widely held belief that urban heritage regeneration brings major economic and social benefits to local communities (Roberts and Sykes 2000: 296; Bowitz and Ibenholt 2009: 1–8). Using Liverpool in the UK and Lille in France as examples, she focuses on the common strategy of trying to transform run-down cities with a significant industrial past through comprehensive culture- and heritage-led regeneration programmes, tapping into international and regional heritage and funding programmes and soft law. She finds that the economic and social impacts of urban heritage regeneration are in reality not as significant as they are officially claimed to be. This image of success is a catalyst to attract bigger investments. Labadi also explains that gentrification might be intrinsically embedded within regeneration programmes, as the transformation of the city through heritage-led regeneration is usually associated with a change in the original population with the arrival of more affluent, dynamic and creative residents.

In her chapter for this volume, Celia Martínez Yáñez focuses on the promotional activities of private corporations and their visual impacts on urban heritage sites. In spite of the rules in many countries dealing with both cultural heritage and the historic urban landscape, cultural properties are too frequently hidden by overlapping posters, advertising and ancillary facilities that devalue, distort and sometimes annihilate the environmental, historical and aesthetic values of the urban landscape. This is especially evident in cities, where all these evils come together, reducing the quality of life and environment. Drawing on existing scientific research and comparative analysis of the visual impact of corporate brand design and advertising, she assesses the negative impact of corporate promotional and branding activities, which include loss of authenticity and local cultural identity. She finds that almost no multinational corporations have included visual impact on heritage within their corporate social responsibility strategy, although most of them report on issues concerning sustainability and environmental responsibility. This suggests that corporations do not consider heritage when developing their strategies. Heritage policy makers at local, national and international levels (including UNESCO and ICOMOS) have not addressed this topic sufficiently, but it is clear, Martínez Yáñez argues, that awareness about visual impact needs to be raised and principles developed to foster a more visually compatible and ethically responsible approach towards historic urban landscape management.

Hill and Tanaka's chapter reveals the workings of governments and government agencies in the heritage field in a socialist context. They examine how the transformation in UNESCO's policy towards urban conservation – from a narrow emphasis on architectural conservation to a broader focus on the management of historic urban landscapes – has played out in the context of Old Havana, a UNESCO World Heritage site. In particular, they argue that this policy shift in the Cuban case has given rise to a new form of governance that encourages the creation of a new type of 'socialist man' (*hombre novisimo*) through the disciplining of and shaping of the participation in the cultural production of heritage. This new form of governance is particularly pronounced in the Cuban context given the centralisation of power with the state controlling all of the patrimony in Cuba. It means that the national heritage agency is able to govern and dispose of territory and population in ways that are complicated in liberal polities that have to negotiate with the demands of private developers and property owners and publicly accountable institutions. In Cuba, national culture has become a major resource for socio-economic development as part of a post-Soviet service economy based on tourism and the competitive marketing of cultural goods. Historic centres, such as Old Havana, play an increasingly significant role in Cuba's tourism-oriented development strategy. Old Havana is of particular note because of the experiment being made to combine urban landscape conservation with a dynamic form of urban development that is known officially as 'comprehensive development' (*desarrollo integral*). According to Hill and Tanaka, Old Havana as a Historic Urban Landscape, when incorporated into these dynamic urban heritage development processes, also becomes a site of biopolitical management of culture that they refer to as 'entrepreneurial heritage'. This is yet another way in which nation states have learnt to organise urban space, encourage development and at the same time manage their heritage in keeping with UNESCO and the notion of Outstanding Universal Value.

Grassroots heritage and bottom-up approaches

Numerous contributions to this volume have referred to the lack of engagement that local communities have had in the past and continue to have in many countries around the world in the identification and interpretation, listing and management of the cultural heritage to which they have particular attachment. This is now routinely deplored in UNESCO statements, including recent editions of the *Operational Guidelines for the Implementation of the World Heritage Convention* (UNESCO 2013). The need for meaningful engagement of the local community in heritage decision-making has also been taken up strongly by ICOMOS in its Florence Declaration (2014), notably in Article 4 that deals with 'Community-driven conservation and local empowerment'. Article 4.2 recommends use of a 'bottom-up approach for effective conservation and management of heritage', with local communities having an active role in formal planning and management systems, while the role of heritage professionals is one of 'providing technical advice in community-led conservation initiatives and being that of a facilitator when a community's engagement with its heritage is fragmented'.

The third group of chapters take up the notions of a 'grassroots' definition of heritage and 'bottom-up' approaches to its management. They present theoretical arguments for, and case studies of, culturally responsive strategies that offer an alternative to imported solutions and manage change in ways that both respond to the need to conserve urban heritage and strengthen the social and cultural rights of local communities whose heritage is being conserved. In his chapter, Eduardo Rojas outlines the still widespread arguments that heritage conservation stands against urban development and that urban land occupied by heritage buildings should be used according to real estate market demand. However, as he explains, governments and concerned communities have a key role to play to ensure that part of the urban heritage is conserved for the future generations because of its important non-economic values. In some cases, this does not prevent developers from opting to demolish heritage buildings in order to develop the land beneath, relying on the slowness and leniency of the planning enforcement mechanisms. Rojas puts the argument for wide stakeholder involvement as a precondition for the sustainable conservation of urban heritage, although he notes that harmonising the often-conflicting aims and expectations of the various stakeholders can become a major governance problem in many cities. He concludes, however, that more inclusive governance approaches to urban heritage preservation can mobilise more resources and are capable of sustaining the conservation efforts longer.

William Logan's chapter uses a case study of Myanmar, a developing country that is coming out of 50 years of isolation under a military junta and reconnecting with the global economy, and Yangon, which was once the capital and is still the largest city, to show the ways in which cultural heritage is being used in the development of political, social, economic and physical planning strategies by various levels of government. Myanmar as a state, and Yangon, the city, have two narratives that do not fit well together but manage to co-exist because they operate at different governmental levels. The former narrative is imposed top-down over all of Myanmar; the latter is upheld from below. In the absence of a specific government authority adequately funded and staffed to conserve the city's historic places, an NGO – the Yangon Heritage Trust – has stepped in with a mission to protect Yangon's urban heritage within a cohesive urban plan. Its view is that 'Yangon is for all' and efforts are starting to be made to take into account the views of local Indian and Chinese communities, as well as ethnic minorities who have moved in from the outlying States. The inclusive approach that the city government and the Trust have taken to urban planning and heritage conservation offers the hope that Yangon will achieve more sustainable growth into the future. On the basis of his Yangon case study, Logan questions whether local people's voices will really be heard on heritage issues in countries without strong representative democratic structures except through progressive, if elite, civil society organisations such as the Trust – still effectively a form of top-down heritage management. In Myanmar, as in many countries, opportunities for bottom-up approaches to urban heritage management are limited. Moreover, while there can be considerable grassroots heritage conservation activity by the local people and communities themselves, this may not be sufficient to establish inclusive and meaningful decision-making processes at the official level. He suggests that the chances for creating effective, efficient and fair planning systems are best where decisions are made openly and decision-makers are accountable to the citizenry through democratic processes.

Pham Thi Thanh Huong's chapter shifts the focus to the ancient town of Hoi An on the coast of central Vietnam and to the 'living heritage' approach that was developed initially by ICCROM and moves heritage conservation practice from materials to the role of heritage in the lives of the people to whom the heritage belongs. She demonstrates how, in combination with participatory decision-making processes, the living heritage approach can contribute to strategic policies for achieving sustainable development at World Heritage sites. In the context of site degradation and the undermining of its OUV due to rapid tourism growth and economic development pressures following Hoi An's 1999 World Heritage inscription, policy discussions at the municipal level began to question the existing development priorities, the roles and the right of local communities and the importance of heritage preservation to the sustainability of the town and its inhabitants' wellbeing. A wide consultation planning process resulted that redefined the concepts of development, reset the targets for local economic growth and drew up a comprehensive heritage tourism strategy for the entire Quang Nam province. The Hoi An experience leads Huong to conclude that the living heritage approach is a prerequisite for community-based heritage preservation, a conclusion that is relevant to World Heritage sites across Asia and beyond.

In another heritage-rich Asian country, Yamini Narayanan argues for a reconceptualisation of the 'sustainable cities' notion by exploring ways in which conventional Indian planning approaches to historic cities and urban heritage can be reframed. Her chapter uses the case of Hauz Khas village in New Delhi, one of the best-preserved sites of the second incarnation of the ancient capital built in the thirteenth century CE. Villagers had maintained Hauz Khas's heritage for more than 700 years before the Delhi Development Authority formally took over the preservation and development of the area in 1954. Taking advantage of its historic environment, Hauz Khas is now an affluent suburb, an elitist enclave of Delhi's celebrity fashion designers, Michelin star restaurants and art galleries. Hauz Khas also faces pressing issues of traffic congestion, the steady marginalisation and eviction of the poor, unsustainably high living densities and one of the highest rates of air pollution in Delhi. Clearly, the mid-twentieth-century planning approach failed here, as in other Indian cities, and attention has turned towards the concept of 'sustainable development' as something of a panacea. The concept, with its three components of ecological preservation, heritage conservation and a growth-oriented economy, has also run into trouble. Criticised in the West for excluding the poor, minorities and women, in India, these issues are accentuated as they undermine the 'rights to the city' of the majority of urban citizens.

Narayanan's study demonstrates the limited, and even retrogressive, impact that the concept has had to date on Hauz Khas and, by extension, on urban areas across India. She argues that urban heritage has a significant role in influencing social organisation, equity and environmental sustainability in Indian cities, and therefore, must play a central part in urban planning approaches in India. Planning must accommodate the informal sector and new development should take inspiration from indigenous forms of urbanism in order to establish a more inclusive, ethical and effective basis for sustainable urbanism, not merely in Hauz Khas but also in other Indian historic towns and cities. However, Narayanan's conclusion has a much wider application, well beyond India. Sustainability is more than the current buzzword in the field of heritage protection – it is the key to heritage survival. It should serve as a fundamental principle for negotiating an acceptable balance between development and conservation in all societies. This means applying a long-term perspective to all processes of decision-making about heritage and development, with a view to fostering intergenerational equity, justice and cities fit for future generations.

References

Araoz, G. (2015). *Historic Preservation in the United States.* Available at: http://www. usicomos.org/preservation (accessed 26 March 2015).

Bandarin, F. and Labadi, S. (eds) (2007). *World Heritage: Challenges for the Millennium.* Paris: UNESCO.

Bandarin, F. and Van Oers, R. (2012). *The Historic Urban Landscape.* Oxford: Wiley-Blackwell.

Bigio, A. and Licciardi G. (2010). *The Urban Regeneration of Medinas: The World Bank Experience in the Middle East and North Africa.* Washington, D.C.: The World Bank.

Bowitz, E. and Ibenholt, K. (2009). Economic impacts of cultural heritage: research and perspectives, *Journal of Cultural Heritage,* 10, 1–8.

Cernea, M.M. (2001). *Cultural Heritage and Development: A Framework for Action in the Middle East and North Africa.* Washington, D.C.: The World Bank.

Choay, F. (1969). *The Modern City: Planning in the 19th Century.* New York: George Braziller.

Ekern, S., Logan, W., Sauge, B. and Sinding-Larsen, A. (2012). Human rights and World Heritage: preserving our common dignity through rights-based approaches to site management. *International Journal of Heritage Studies,* 18(3), 213–25.

Ekern, S., Logan, W., Sauge, B. and Sinding-Larsen, A. (eds) (2014). *World Heritage Management and Human Rights,* London: Routledge.

Flipo, F. (2005). Les tensions constitutives du 'développement durable'. In: Ministère Délégué à l'Aménagement du Territoire (ed.), *Développement Durable et Territoires. Dossier de séance,* Paris: DATAR, 1–6.

Geddes, P. (1915). *Cities in Evolution: An Introduction to the Town Planning Movement and to the Study of Civics,* London: Williams and Norgate.

Glendinning, M. (2013). *The Conservation Movement: A History of Architectural Preservation,* London: Routledge.

Hardy, D. (1991) *From Garden Cities to New Towns: Campaigning for Town and Country Planning,* Volume 1: 1899–1946. London: Spon.

Hugo, V. (1832). Guerre aux démolisseurs. *Revue des Deux Mondes,* 1(5), 607–22.

ICOMOS (2014). *The Florence Declaration on Heritage and Landscape as Human Values: declaration on the principles and recommendations on the value of cultural heritage and landscapes for promoting peaceful and democratic societies,* Paris: ICOMOS. Available at: http://www.icomos.org/images/DOCUMENTS/Secretariat/2015/GA_2014_results/ GA2014_Symposium_FlorenceDeclaration_EN_final_20150318.pdf (accessed 3 April 2015).

Labadi, S. (2013). *UNESCO, Cultural Heritage, and Outstanding Universal Value.* Plymouth: AltaMira Press.

Labadi, S. (forthcoming). UNESCO, heritage and sustainable development: international discourses and local impacts. In: P. Gould and A. Pyburn (eds), *Promise and Peril: Archaeology Engaging with Economic Development.* New York: Springer.

Lafrenz, K. (2006). *The World Bank's Cultural Heritage Management. Draft for 'Cultures of Contact' Conference.* Available at: http://metamedia.stanford.edu/projects/culturesof contact/ (accessed 21 February 2015).

Logan, W. (2012). States, governance and the politics of culture: World Heritage in Asia. In: P. Daly and T. Winter (eds), *Routledge Handbook of Heritage in Asia.* Abingdon: Routledge.

Logan, W. (2013). Australia, indigenous peoples and world heritage from Kakadu to Cape York: state party behaviour under the World Heritage Convention. *Journal of Social Archaeology,* 13(2), 153–276.

Meadows, D.H., Meadows, D.L., Randers, J. and Behrens III, W.W. (1972). *The Limits to Growth: A Report of the Club of Rome's Project on the Predicament of Mankind.* New York: Universe Books.

Meskell, L. (2011). *The Nature of Heritage: The New South Africa.* Oxford: Wiley-Blackwell.

Meskell, L.M. (2013). UNESCO's World Heritage Convention at 40: challenging the economic and political order of international heritage conservation'. *Current Anthropology,* 54(4), 483–94.

Roberts, P. and Sykes, H. (2000). Current challenges and future prospects. In: P. Roberts and H. Sykes (eds), *Urban Regeneration: A Handbook.* London: Sage.

Ruskin, J. (1851–3). *The Stones of Venice,* 3 vols. London: Smith, Elder and Co.

Second ICATHM (Second International Congress of Architects and Technicians of Historic Monuments) (1964). *International Charter for the Conservation and Restoration of Monuments and Sites* (The Venice Charter). ICATHS, Venice.

Siravo, F. (2011). Conservation planning: the road less traveled. Conservation perspectives. *The GCI Newsletter,* 26(2).

Sitte, C. (1965). *City Planning According to Artistic Principles.* London: Collins.

The World Bank (2012). *Tunisia Cultural Heritage Project. Implementation Completion and Results Report.* Washington, D.C.: The World Bank.

UNESCO (1972). *Convention Concerning the Protection of the World Cultural and Natural Heritage.* Paris: UNESCO. Available at: http://whc.unesco.org/en/conventiontext/ (accessed 3 April 2015).

UNESCO (2002). *Budapest Declaration on World Heritage.* Paris: UNESCO. Available at: http://whc.unesco.org/archive/02budapest-decl.htm (accessed 18 February 2015).

UNESCO (2003). *Convention for the Safeguarding of the Intangible Cultural Heritage.* Paris: UNESCO. Available at: http://www.unesco.org/culture/ich/en/convention (accessed 3 April 2015).

UNESCO (2005). *Vienna Memorandum on 'World Heritage and Contemporary Architecture – Managing the Historic Urban Landscape'.* Available at: http://whc.unesco.org/archive/2005/whc05-15ga-inf7e.pdf (accessed 3 April 2015).

UNESCO (2011). *Recommendation on the Historic Urban Landscape.* Paris: UNESCO. Available at: http://whc.unesco.org/en/activities/638 (accessed 3 April 2015).

UNESCO (2013). *Operational Guidelines for the Implementation of the World Heritage Convention.* Paris: UNESCO. Available at: http://whc.unesco.org/archive/opguide13-en.pdf (accessed 3 April 2015).

UN-Habitat (2008). *State of the World's Cities 2008/2009: Harmonious Cities.* London: Earthscan.

United Nations Human Rights Council (2011). *Access to Cultural Heritage as a Human Right (A/HRC/17/38).* Available at: http://www.unesco.org/new/fileadmin/MULTIMEDIA/HQ/CLT/images/Report%20of%20Farida%20Shaheed.pdf (accessed 2 April 2015).

United Nations World Commission on Environment and Development (UNWCED) (1987). *Our Common Future (The Brundtland Report).* Available at: http://www.un-documents.net/our-common-future.pdf (accessed 3 April 2015).

Van Oers, R. (2010). Managing cities and the historic urban landscape initiative – an introduction. In: R. van Oers and S. Haraguchi (eds), *Managing Historic Cities*, World Heritage Papers 27. Paris: World Heritage Centre.

Veldpaus, L., Pereira Roders, A.R. and Colenbrander, B.J.F. (2013). Urban heritage: putting the past into the future. *Historic Environment,* 4(1), 3–18.

Ward, B. (1966). *Spaceship Earth*. New York: Columbia University Press.

Part I

Implementing international frameworks at the local level

Chapter 2

In the slipstream of development

World Heritage and development-induced displacement in Laos

Kearrin Sims and Tim Winter

International focus concerning heritage conservation governance is rapidly consolidating around the discourses and paradigms of sustainability. This can be seen in attempts to include culture as one of the pillars of the post-2015 Sustainable Development Goals and in the move to incorporate sustainable development into recent World Heritage Committee meetings. In Doha, in July 2014, for example, considerable discussion occurred about initiatives that support 'conservation for human well-being', such that economic empowerment and the social sustainability of communities are now seen as priority areas for the World Heritage Committee. Multiple cases from developing countries around the world vividly testify as to why the need to better integrate conservation with development is long overdue.

All too often, a lack of attention has been paid to the profound social and economic change experienced by those living in or around places designated for World Heritage protection. Such issues remain particularly charged in the fast developing economies of Asia, and nowhere more so than in the remote site of Luang Prabang in Laos. Long recognised as an important place in the country's Buddhist culture, Luang Prabang has fast emerged as a key node for greater regional integration. Given its location, the expansion of the airport has become a critical development project for a state seeking to capitalise upon the rapid growth of its regional neighbours, most notably China. This chapter asks questions about accountability towards those invisible communities of World Heritage: those residents who live beyond core zones and boundaries, and whose welfare and livelihoods are threatened not by the need to conserve and resist modernisation, but by developmental projects that arise on the back of heritage-driven tourism. To achieve this, the chapter is centred on the upgrading of the Luang Prabang airport and draws on a series of personal interviews conducted by Kearrin Sims in 2012 with residents living in the area that focused on the issue of forced displacement.

Heritage place making in the Asian century

Luang Prabang is the former royal capital of Laos and a UNESCO World Heritage site since 1995. It is one of the best-known historic urban landscapes in Southeast Asia and has been, to date, Laos' key tourist attraction (Reeves and Long 2011).

A fusion of traditional Lao and French colonial design, Luang Prabang's protection from the forces of modernisation has, for some, led to the creation of a nostalgiascape (Berliner 2011: 235); one that draws on an 'orientalised' colonial imagining of the country and region.

With its 34 Buddhist temples and many young monks wandering about its streets, Luang Prabang has come to be seen as the quintessential 'authentic' and 'romantic' Asia. Lonely Planet (Burke and Vaisutis 2010: 134) describes the town as a place with 'hundreds of monks' and 'resplendent gold and claret wats' that will captivate 'even the most jaded travellers' and lull them 'into a somnambulant bliss'. Yet, somewhat contradictorily, such narratives and framings exist alongside global connectivity. Today, it is a place where wealthy tourists fly in from faraway destinations to drink imported wine and check emails while discussing 'untouched' and 'remote' beauty. To be sure, Luang Prabang tourism continues to bring change, both physical and socio-cultural.

The past two decades have seen the number of tourist arrivals to Laos grow rapidly. For the period spanning 1995 to 2009, the country experienced close to a 500 per cent increase in visitor numbers, reaching the landmark figure of 2 million (Lao National Tourism Administration 2009: 5; United Nations 2010: 37). But where it was once the realm of adventurous Western tourists searching for authentic, 'off the beaten track' experiences, in recent years, much of the growth in tourism in Laos has been the result of growing regional tourist markets, most notably from China, South Korea and ASEAN nations.[1] Indeed, visitors from these countries now account for more than three-quarters of all inbound tourism (United Nations 2010: 39). Of the 2 million visitors in 2009, over 1.7 million came from within the region. While Western tourists typically spend more than day-trippers or weekend tourists from Thailand or Vietnam, the sheer number of visitors from within the region means that more than 90 per cent of tourism revenue now comes from within Asia-Pacific (Lao National Tourism Administration 2009: 6–7). In light of this shift, Winter has previously argued there is a need to better account for how the ongoing rise of intra-regional Asian tourism 'is emerging as a powerful force of social transformation for a series of heritage landscapes' (2010: 116). This growth in intra-regional tourism has also been well noted by the Lao Association of Travel Agents, such that marketing efforts have turned towards prioritising the Asian market (Laovoices 2011).

As the visitor base shifts increasingly towards East Asia and ASEAN countries, new investors from Thailand, Hong Kong, Singapore, South Korea and Vietnam are reconfiguring the city's landscape in accordance with the desires of intraregional tourists (see Figures 2.1 and 2.2). For the most part, these desires do not entirely break away from longstanding representations of Luang Prabang as an untouched Buddhist Shangri-La. Many Thai tourists, for example, come to Laos to 'see' a romanticised version of how Thailand once 'was'. Crucially however, and as Berliner (2011) points out, important shifts have occurred concerning how these tourists seek to inhabit and engage with the urban heritage landscape. Whereas European tourists seek out their own imaginaries of 'authentic' Laos

Figure 2.1 Hotel signs in Luang Prabang (photos by K. Sims).

Figure 2.2 Hotel signs in Luang Prabang (photos by K. Sims).

through the discursive practices of eco-tourism, by lodging in colonial-style guesthouses, eating street food and searching for Eastern spiritual encounters, the package tours of many Asian tourists mean they experience Luang Prabang and other sites in Laos via the fairways of golf courses, the balconies of luxury hotels or the seats of large tour buses.

Some of the biggest forces of modernisation stem from China. Chinese-run hotels and restaurants are opening in increasing numbers on the city's periphery. Luang Prabang now has its own Chinese market selling imported goods, while many stalls within the local 'Lao' markets are also owned by Chinese entrepreneurs who often work alongside their Lao employees. A number of Chinese health-care centres also now exist in the city and the provincial hospital, with all its furnishings and equipment built with aid from China. Although Chinese investment into Luang

Prabang has primarily taken place outside the heritage zone, an increasing number of hotels within the old city are also being bought by Chinese operators, who have invested in businesses selling tourism-related goods imported from China.

The biggest long-term investment associated with tourism development, however, might well come from South Korea. Just across the river from the World Heritage zone, plans to develop a South Korean megaproject known as Diamond City have long been mooted. This US$2 billion joint-investment, if undertaken, will incorporate around 3,000 hectares of land (Voice of Asia 2008). This new urban area has been conceived to serve as a comprehensive tourist, trading, financial and recreational centre, which will be linked by road, and potentially rail, to China and Thailand. While speculation surrounded its viability in July 2014, if completed, the project will include five-star hotels, shopping malls, a 36-hole golf course, residential areas, business service and tourism centres (Voice of Asia 2008). This will be the second South Korean golf course to be built in the area.

Aero-urbanism

At the heart of this pathway towards development is the local airport. With a continual growth in the number of inbound tourists, the Government of Laos has deemed the upgrading and expansion of the city's current airport facilities as a priority development project. In technical terms, the plans for the airport upgrade include improving the runway to an 'International Civil Aviation Organization (ICAO) Code 4C Category I precision approach instrument runway', effectively enabling the airport to receive the larger B737 and A320 aircraft (Asian Development Bank 2008). According to the Department of Civil Aviation, Luang Prabang is the second busiest airport in the country. Serving as a regional hub with scheduled international flights to Bangkok, Chiang Mai and Siem Reap, it is also a major domestic centre for other northern cities in Laos, with scheduled connections to Houay Xai, Phongsaly, Vientiane and Xieng Khuang (Asian Development Bank 2006; Vaenkeo 2010b). At present, the airport is only served by three airlines operating short-haul services (up to 1,500 km), with no more than 80 passengers per flight.

Upgrading the runway and other airport facilities would enable both medium-haul services and a doubling of capacity. The possibility to serve aircraft of longer range will allow for more non-stop destinations, thus accessing new markets, with the potential of flights from Seoul, Tokyo and Taipei, amongst others. A longer runway will also bring Luang Prabang within range of Asia's other key hubs. Presently, only Vietnam Airlines can provide network traffic through connections at their hub in Hanoi. However, it is expected that with a longer runway, Thai Airways will seek to enter the market, creating the capability to feed traffic from its extensive network, as well as from its Star Alliance partners. Other new airlines expected to commence direct flights include China Eastern Airlines: outbound from Kunming and Jinghong, Yunnan. Such developments mean that projections for inbound arrivals are in the order of increases from 3,973 in 2006 to 11,655 in

2032, with the total number of arrivals increasing by almost 400 per cent over the next 20 years (Asian Development Bank 2008).

At a cost of approximately US$83.6 million, the airport's construction has been 75 per cent financed by the China-Exim Bank, with construction led by China CAMC Engineering (CAMCE), a company also headquartered in China.[2] Laos' aviation sector has received considerable support from China, through both government aid and foreign direct investment (FDI). CAMCE is undertaking a US$38 million renovation of Vientiane international airport and is currently in the planning stages of a US$77 million upgrade to Xieng Khuang airport (Pansivongsay 2010). Both these projects have been funded with Chinese aid and further extend long-term airline industry links with China, a story that includes the 1992 Yunnan airlines' purchase of 60 per cent of Lao Airways and the 2010 Lao Airlines' purchase of two aeroplanes from the Commercial Aircraft Corporation of China Ltd (Evans 2000: 166).

Whilst it is easy to see that the airport upgrade will deliver significant financial opportunities for some – most notably foreign investors and the domestic elite – for others, it is delivering a range of unforeseen challenges and existential questions. Golf courses, integrated resort facilities, casinos and other tourism-related projects have been the source of considerable wealth creation for an elite few in recent years. In the context of Luang Prabang however, among those marginalised by tourism were the 420 households living immediately behind the airport. Their subsequent displacement – our focus here – was undertaken by the provincial government, a process that also involved resettlement to a new village site. Brick factories, educational institutions, religious sites, private homes, businesses, agricultural plots and fruit-bearing trees have all been demolished for the airport expansion and the costs for resettlement and environmental mitigation and compensation have been estimated to be around US$14.5 million (Asian Development Bank 2008).

Experiencing displacement

The case of Luang Prabang reveals that heritage preservation is not necessarily the key force driving medium- to large-scale urban displacement, as is often presumed. Instead, rapid modernisation has placed the greatest pressures on land access, residents and their resources. New donors and investors are rapidly modernising the city beyond its heritage core, delivering new challenges for local residents – especially for those who have been dispossessed and displaced from their land. With respect to the airport displacement, the experiences of those living in the area are captured below via five key points of focus.

The first and perhaps most important consequence of the rapid modernisation of the city's periphery is increasing competition over land access. At the airport relocation site, almost all residents were allocated the same 15×20 m^2 land parcel, irrespective of how much land they previously owned. The majority of family allotments were substantially smaller than their former landholdings and the size and quality of land was an issue of real concern.[3] Much of the resettlement village was located on rice paddies that required landfill before they could be built on, an expense that would be borne by the villagers themselves. As one informant explains:

> (Tshua)[4] They gave me land that was a fish farm. I had to pay for fifty deliveries of soil [at a cost of US$23 per carload] to fill my land so that I could build on it.

Faced with such unsuitable land, many villagers resisted their resettlement and employed various forms of protest to gain better allotments. At least 51 families resisted relocation and were living illegally in the resettlement site on land owned by other residents. To provide just one example, Mr Blia Lor lives in a tent on land that he shares with three other families. Despite owning a 29×32 m^2 plot in the former village site, Blia Lor had been provided with just 10×18 m^2 of steep, dry land in the resettlement site. Unhappy with this allocation, he repeatedly applied for land elsewhere. While he undertook protracted negotiations with the government, however, his land had since been re-allocated to another family, leaving him with no land at all.

In an attempt to provide property to those who had previously lived in their own house on shared family land, the government also allocated non-landowners their own holdings. This strategy largely proved unsuccessful, however, as villagers were only provided with 10×18 m^2 plots that were located on a dirt hillock behind the two areas allocated for resettlement. Littered with grey stone, the land was dry and dusty for prolonged periods of the year and lacked piped water. In the wet season, it became a slippery, muddy space that carried the risk of landslide. Relocated families complained the plots were too small and that the land was unsuitable for building or farming:

> (Neng Lee) I do not want to move to this land. Nobody has moved there yet because it is not good land . . . it is not good for farming because the soil is dry and hard. There is no water there and it will be hard to carry water [to that place].

> (Xee Her) We will not move there until the government says we will kill you if you do not move!

Finally, for those who owned land at the former village site, but had not embarked upon any form of construction, no compensation was provided. Space in the resettlement site was limited and one of the means through which the government had accounted for the limited availability of land was by providing new plots only to those who intended to immediately live in the area. As one landowner explained:

> (Seng Hung) In the old village site I owned 20×17 m^2 of land. I owned that land for more than ten years. But the only people who have been given money for land [without a house on it] are those who pay the government five million

kip [as a bribe]. I used to be a lawyer so I am fighting hard to get more land but the government will not speak to me. Before they took away my land I had a place where I could build a house for my son to live and to study. Now I cannot give this [the land] to them.

In these responses, we can see that the removal of land and resettlement undermined hopes for upward social mobility and a sense of confidence in the prospects of children. Such complaints over insufficient land compensation following resettlement are common in Laos and represent state-supported acts of accumulation by dispossession (Harvey 2005).

A second concern that is common amongst forcibly displaced residents in situations such as Luang Prabang is the insufficient financial compensation for housing and other lost assets. As with land reparations, every resident expressed frustration about receiving less financial recompense than it would cost them to rebuild their former homes:

(Tshua) We received 18,900,000 kip (*c.* US$2,380) for our old home, but it will cost us around 70 million kip (*c.* US$8,780) to rebuild.

(Blia Lor) I only received 9 million kip (*c.* US$1,400) for my house, but it will cost me twice that to rebuild . . . and I have already spent 5 million kip on rice and my children's school fees since we were relocated.

(Sheng Lor) Our land at the old village was worth 60 million kip (*c.* US$7,560). My husband is a singer who has travelled to America and so we had very nice land. But we were only given 5.5 million kip (*c.* US$690) in compensation.

In addition to these housing construction costs, the resettlement also required numerous additional expenses such as buying soil to landfill flooded land and costs for water and electricity connection. No compensation was given for fruit trees and other lost assets or the time lost from income generation caused by the need to construct new homes. For those who had been allocated land on the dusty hillock behind the village, piped water and electricity had still not been provided more than a year after they were first relocated. As a result, these residents had to purchase these amenities from their neighbours, who often sold water at inflated prices in order to make a profit.

One of the more common justifications for the forced resettlement of rural residents in Laos has been the need to bring them closer to state services and infrastructure (Evrard and Goudineau 2004; Petit 2008). However, in the case of urban displacement, residents are often relocated in order to make space for the construction of new infrastructure and built environments. In other words, they are often pushed away from state services. As a result, the new opportunities for increased mobility that infrastructure upgrades provide to migrants and tourists frequently come at the expense of existing residents. At Luang Prabang airport, the disruptions of the resettlement made it difficult for some residents to continue employment as they had in the past or to continue growing crops on their land. Residents were expected to build their own homes and this time-intensive task had limited people's ability to engage in income-generating activities. In the initial 2 months of the displacement period, residents also lacked electricity and piped water and had to travel 20 minutes each day to collect fresh water.

One critical implication of the time lost from generating household income was the associated loss in physical mobility. For those living in a tent, the resettlement substantially limited people's ability to work, visit friends or travel for other everyday activities such as shopping, doctor visits and schooling:

> (Blia Lor) I am angry because me and my wife cannot go anywhere . . . we have no door and we cannot lock our tent. If I leave the tent my wife must stay here and if she leaves I must stay here. Otherwise people can come and steal from us and I am worried people will take our rice . . . . It is also a problem because we [he and his wife] used to work together and could earn 50,000 kip (US$6.30) per day. Now only I can work. We also cannot visit our friends and we cannot spend much time together as one person must always be here [at the tent].

Here, he also explained to me that he does not own a motorbike and that, in the past, if he and his wife found employment far from their home they would stay at the worksite together for several days. Not being able to do this now, he needed to travel more frequently and this was time consuming and expensive. Consequently, as a result of the resettlement, his family income had been halved.

While prevailing discourses of development within the country present new infrastructure as a sign of increased progress and mobility, large-scale infrastructure development at the local scale involves both increased mobility for some and a 'tying to place', or a restriction of mobility, for others (Bauman 2000). For those families – some of whom had returned to villages that were more than 1.5 days, walk from the nearest road – the new regional connectivity provided by the airport upgrade forced them to withdraw to a location that was further disconnected from their existing infrastructure and the potential opportunities that would arise through tourism and a growing economy. As one resident explained:

> (Gikong Lau) I am worried about my children going to school. There is no school here [in his rural village] but I cannot afford to live in the city anymore. I want to raise some cattle and sell them so I can take my family back to the city.

Such concerns over their families' futures, trying to negotiate better compensation agreements and living in makeshift homes while new houses were built, had also placed a great deal of stress and physical discomfort on displaced residents. In the interim period, while displaced residents tried to rebuild their homes, they were provided with green canvas tents to live in that provided limited protection from the weather. Given that it was monsoon season many villagers complained rain would often blow in on them and their belongings. Villages also lacked access to piped water and electricity at this time and many had lost food and personal belongings due to flooding. More specifically, some families lost up to 50 bags of rice, leading them to cut back on food consumption, especially expensive items such as meat:

> (Gong Gue) It has been very difficult since the relocation. My family does not have enough food . . . we are given rice [by a South Korean NGO] but without this my children would be hungry.

Laos is a country where chronic malnutrition rates for children under the age of five remain around 50 per cent and, as many observers have noted, this figure has persisted over the past decade despite strong economic growth (Howe and Sims 2011). Although primarily a problem for the country's rural population, large-scale urban displacements, rising living expenses and the loss of arable land are also seeing threats to food security within urban environments.

At the lower end of the socio-economic spectrum of displaced residents, many villagers continued to live in tents more than a year after being relocated. These individuals still lacked access to plumbed water and ongoing discomfort had become an unavoidable part of their everyday lives. Tents were only about 4 sqm in length and, despite a small plastic window on each side, remained permanently dark inside. Faced with such limited living space, villagers often stored their belongings in large nylon bags and spent much of their time outside, where they were constantly exposed to the natural elements. As two residents described it:

> (Neng) We live the same as the chickens. When it is hot we are hot and when it is cold we are cold. When it rains we get wet.

> (Blia Lor) Just this morning it was raining and the rain came in on us and we could not sleep.

Indeed, in many ways the living conditions of the families in the relocation site were much worse than in more remote villages located alongside dirt roads several hours from the city. For residents, the lack of access to proper infrastructure created significant everyday problems:

> (Blia Lor) We even have to dig for our water. We have to pour the water through a cloth so we can use it.

For those who were able to quickly rebuild and move out from their tents, over-crowding of housing was common, with many families sharing small temporary homes until they could afford to build larger dwellings. To give just one example, Mr Chor Her's home of thatched timber and straw above an uneven dirt floor was more basic and considerably smaller, at around 8×5 m^2, than his previous dwelling. He shares this basic space with his parents, three brothers, his brother's wife and three children. The family aspires to build a bigger, more durable dwelling. However, Chor Her estimates it will be another two years before his family can afford to complete the larger concrete and brick house that stands unfinished beside their current home.

Beyond physical discomforts, face-to-face interviews revealed numerous signs of emotional fatigue, frustration and anger amongst displaced residents. Cracked voices, hunched posture, staring at the ground and direct exclamations of frustration were common. Stress and fatigue were most evident amongst those who had been forced to live in a tent for more than a year. For some the threat of eviction remained ever present, even for the wealthier members of the village:

> (Par Yee) There were five families who would not move from the old village. We stayed there for twenty days [after everyone else had been relocated] but then the police came and said to me 'if you do not move by this afternoon you will be taken to jail'. So we all have to move on this day but we are very angry with this.

Finally, for the Hmong community at least, the impact of the resettlement also had important cultural implications. The residents who were relocated were from three ethnic groups (Hmong, Khmu and Laotian) that have their own languages and socio-cultural practices. While there did not appear to be any major tensions between these neighbours of more than six years, the location of the new village site and housing provided compromised the cultural practices of the Hmong residents. The issue of living in a tent for a prolonged period of time posed particular, culturally specific challenges:

> (Blia Lor) One of my biggest worries now is if someone dies or gets sick. I cannot afford to take them to the hospital but I also cannot call the Shaman because I have no house to bring them to. The tent has no windows and no back door.

Typically, Hmong households have a front door for people to enter and a back door for the comings and goings of spirits. When a spiritual ceremony is undertaken, such as when a shaman is present, this back door must be opened. The tents provided thus violated the spiritual and cultural practices of Blia Lor and his family:

> Now it is September already and Hmong New Year is soon (December) and I need a house for the New Year celebrations when there are many spiritual ceremonies.

While it can be argued that these dwellings were only temporary and that there were no restrictions on how Hmong villagers rebuilt their new homes, many residents ended up having to reside under canvas for more than a year. Furthermore, the land that many villagers had been allocated – on the dusty hillock behind the relocation village – was not suitable for traditional Hmong architecture, which traditionally employs flat earth floors and requires flat ground.

As these various examples highlight, the airport resettlement programme had a detrimental impact on the wellbeing of many of the town's residents. Although the improvements to the airport will position the resettled community directly beside expanding regional connectivity networks, many people continue to face social, cultural and economic disadvantages that have prevented them from benefiting from this development project. Pre-existing inequalities have informed the manner in which the airport displacement was conducted and – accompanied by new forms of marginalisation and disadvantage – have resulted in the emergence of new livelihood constraints. By implication, this new 'connective' infrastructure has seen many local residents brushed aside within an agenda that prioritises the needs of tourism development.

Conclusion: heritage landscapes beyond the buffer zones

Fears that Luang Prabang's historic charm will be damaged by the tourism industry and the new infrastructure and amenities that growing tourist flows demand have been debated extensively by academics, development institutions and the Lao government (Harrison 1994; Stuart-Fox 1996; Boccardi and Logan 2007). The preservation of Luang Prabang's heritage landscape has raised concern since the city was first issued World Heritage status in 1995 (Logan 2012) and, more recently, Reeves and Long (2011) have expressed trepidation over the impact of the airport, the golf course and other developments on Luang Prabang's heritage preservation.

Together these critiques share a concern that Asian investor-driven forms of development encourage modernisation, with little concern for its impact on the historic environment or the groups that live within and around them. In Luang Prabang, the development of new hotels, restaurants, golf courses, concrete factories, timber yards, fish farms and other industries has arisen quickly. While UNESCO and the local conservation office may be increasingly concerned over the region's sustainability, the growing significance of sustainability to discourses of heritage preservation and development has not been a prominent feature of growing regional FDI into the mainland of Southeast Asia's heritage landscapes. Unless UNESCO and local/national heritage sector institutions can strengthen their engagement with these new donors and investors, attempts to promote more sustainable development practices in and around Asia's historic cities are likely to be heavily compromised.

An important concern this chapter has raised in respect to the sustainable management of heritage sites is the need for development planning to more systematically incorporate the livelihoods and wellbeing of local residents. Berliner (2011), Bristol (2010) and Reeves and Long (2011) are among those noting how the development of heritage landscapes can serve to exclude and marginalise local residents. Discourses of heritage tourism too often adopt abstract representations of space that depoliticise heritage landscapes and remove local residents from development planning. Far less attention has been given, however, to how the modernisation of heritage cities beyond the buffer zones of preservation is also affecting local residents.

Unfortunately, what this chapter suggests is that the recent development of Luang Prabang as a heritage tourism landscape has focused far more on the conservation and 'authenticity' of the built environment, with far less attention given to the wellbeing of local residents. Growing tourist numbers lead to the expansion of infrastructure and amenities and, in a politically authoritarian market economy such as that found in Laos today, heritage landscapes often disproportionately benefit elites over the rights and welfare of local residents who lack the political freedom to have their own interests protected.

This is not to suggest that tourism has only been a destructive force in the livelihoods of residents. Many people, including those in the resettlement village, depend on tourism for their income and receive much higher earnings from the tourist sector than they would receive in other industries. What the upgrading of the Luang Prabang airport shows us, however, is that both heritage preservation and modernisation are conjoined processes that have myriad economic and social impacts. Too often touristscapes become spaces that exclude local residents in the name of 'accommodating' wealthy tourists. As Bunnell (2004: 10) notes, landscapes of Asian modernity are 'bound up with new geographies of exclusion' and the new connectivities and growing urbanisation that have been commonly understood as the cornerstones of the region's development have also resulted in widespread displacement, exclusion and the abjection of large segments of national populations.

Greater recognition still needs to be given to the wider social and physical impact of World Heritage listing and management. Although it is ultimately the role of the state to decide how people are treated both within and around heritage sites, the case of Luang Prabang is a stark reminder of the need for the international heritage sector to more actively engage with the complexities of modernisation and precarious development (Logan 2012). Clearly, in the arena of World Heritage governance, with all its competing, contradictory agendas, considerable work still needs to be done to ensure the cultural and economic welfare of those living in the slipstream of development features more prominently within discourses and structures of planning and change management.

Notes

1   In 2011, there were 411,759 tourist arrivals to Luang Prabang province; 115,999 came from Asia and the Pacific (48.8% of total arrivals). This is less than arrivals from Europe, at 118,084 (49.68%). However, the proportion of tourists from Asia and the Pacific rose from 41.54% in 2008 to the 2011 figure of 49.68%. Thailand had the largest percentage of visitors (18.79%), followed by France, Switzerland, the USA, Australia, China (6.82%) and Japan (5.17%). Therefore, visitor arrivals from these three countries

alone amounted to over 30% of total tourists. Visitor arrivals from all of these countries also increased in percentage from previous years. Source: Tourism Development Department, Ministry of Information, Culture and Tourism, 2011, *2011 Statistical Report on Tourism in Laos*, Government of Laos, Vientiane. See http://www.tourismlaos.org/files/files/2011%20Statistics%20Report%20(English).pdf.
2   CAMCE is a major development player in Laos and is linked to Chinese 'ODA' around the world. It has projects in Southeast, South and Central Asia as well as Africa, South America and the Caribbean (http://www.camce.com.cn/en/about/).
3   For further details see Vaenkeo (2010a).
4   To protect the identity of informants all names provided are pseudonyms.

References

Asian Development Bank (2006). *Lao People's Democratic Republic: Preparing the Greater Mekong Subregion Louangphrabang Airport Improvement Project*. Manila: ADB.

Asian Development Bank (2008). *Lao People's Democratic Republic: Greater Mekong Subregion Louangphrabang Airport Improvement Project Technical Assistance Consultant's Report, Final Report*. Manila: ADB.

Bauman, Z. (2000). *Liquid Modernity*. Cambridge and Malden: Polity Press; Blackwell.

Berliner, D. (2011). The politics of loss and nostalgia in Luang Prabang (Lao PDR). In: P. Daly and T. Winter (eds), *Routledge Handbook of Heritage in Asia*. Abingdon: Routledge, pp. 234–46.

Boccardi, G. and Logan, W. (2007). *Reactive Monitoring Mission to the Town of Luang Prabang World Heritage Property Lao People's Democratic Republic 22–28 November 2007, Mission Report*. Paris: UNESCO.

Bristol, G. (2010). Rendered invisible: urban planning, culture and human rights. In: M. Langfield, W. Logan and M. Nic Craith (eds), *Cultural Diversity, Heritage and Human Rights*. Abingdon: Routledge, pp. 117–34.

Bunnell, T. (2004). *Malaysia, Modernity and the Multimedia Super Corridor: A Critical Geography of Intelligent Landscapes*. Abingdon and New York. Routledge Curzon.

Burke, A. and Vaisutis, J. (2010). *Lonely Planet Laos*. Footscray, Oakland and London: Lonely Planet.

Evans, G. (2000). Transformation of Jinghing, Xishuangbanna, PRC. In: G. Evans, C. Hutton and K.E. Kuah (eds), *Where China Meets Southeast Asia: Social and Cultural Change in the Border Regions*. Singapore: Institute of Southeast Asian Studies, pp. 162–82.

Evrard, O. and Goudineau, Y. (2004). Planned resettlement, unexpected migrations and cultural trauma in Laos. *Development and Change*, 35(5), 937–62.

Harrison, D. (1994). Tourism, capitalism and development in less developed countries. In: L. Sklair (ed.), *Capitalism and Development*. Abingdon: Routledge, pp. 232–57.

Harvey, D. (2005). *A Brief History of Neoliberalism*. Oxford and New York: Oxford University Press.

Howe, B. and Sims, K. (2011). Human security and development in the Lao PDR: freedom from fear and freedom from want. *Asian Survey* 51(2), 333–55.

Lao National Tourism Administration (2009). *2009 Statistical Report on Tourism in Laos*. Vientiane: Government of Laos.

Laovoices (2011). *Travel Agents Uurged to Focus on Asian Market*. Available at: http://www.tourismcambodia.com/news/worldnews/4438/travel-agents-urged-to-focus-on-asian-market.htm (accessed 8 July 2015).

Logan, W. (2012). States, governance and the politics of culture: World Heritage in Asia. In: P. Daly and T. Winter (eds), *Routledge Handbook of Heritage in Asia*. Abingdon: Routledge, pp. 113–28.

Pansivongsay, M. (2010). Airport upgrade to boost Xieng Khuang transport services. *Vientiane Times*, 30 September 2010, B3.

Petit, P. (2008). Rethinking internal migrations in Lao PDR: the resettlement process under micro-analysis. *Anthropological Forum*, 18(2), 117–38.

Reeves, R. and Long, C. (2011). Unbearable pressures on paradise? Tourism and heritage management in Luang Prabang, a World Heritage site. *Critical Asian Studies*, 43(1), 3–32.

Stuart-Fox, M. (1996). *Buddhist Kingdom, Marxist State: The Making of Modern Laos*. Bangkok and Cheney: White Lotus.

United Nations (2010). *An Investment Guide to the Lao People's Democratic Republic: Opportunities and Condition*s. Available at: www.hdr.undp.org/en/statistics (accessed 7 January 2014).

Vaenkeo, S. (2010a). Luang Prabang gives land to families making way for airport. *Vinetiane Times*, 24 February 2010, p. 3.

Vaenkeo, S. (2010b). Work Begins on New Luang Prabang Airport. *Vientiane Times,* 16 February 2010, p. 1.

Voice of Asia (2008). *Korean, Lao Companies to Develop a New City in Luang Prabang*. Available at: http://lao.voanews.com/content/a-52-2008-11-09-voa1-90691919/1188086.html (accessed 10 July 2014).

Winter T. (2010). Heritage tourism: the dawn of a new era? In: C. Long and S. Labadi (eds)*, Heritage and Globalisation*. Abingdon and New York: Routledge, pp. 117–29.

Chapter 3

Conserving a World Heritage Site in Mozambique

Entanglements between politics, poverty, development and governance on the Island of Mozambique

Albino Jopela

> Twenty-one years have passed since the Island of Mozambique was declared a World Heritage Site, since then, what has changed in peoples' lives? Some say *Ilha* [the island] has a special status, what does that really mean? The urban sanitation is poor, the population is poor, unemployment is high, and the one health centre is inadequate, with just one doctor on call for the entire district of more than fifty thousand people. There are serious problems of water supply on the Island; therefore, I do not see the importance of it [the World Heritage status]. Where are the incentives that allude to support the population to conserve the World Heritage?
>
> > (Local resident of the Island of Mozambique.
> > Omar 2013: 153).

The Island of Mozambique (or *Ilha*) is a small UNESCO World Heritage island city on the East African coast. It has a rich architecture that reflects an exceptional example of an urban dichotomy resulting from cultural diversity and interaction among people from different cultures of Bantu, Swahili, Arab, Persian, Indian and European origins (ICOMOS 1991: 2). Despite these unique values, the majority of the island population has not fully embraced the declaration of outstanding universal value that had justified the inscription of the island on the World Heritage list in 1991 (Jopela and Rakotomamonjy 2012). Development agencies and heritage institutions, at both national and international levels, identify poverty as the culprit. It is blamed for the degradation and poor up-keep of the island's built heritage as witnessed in the decaying architecture and as the reason for what is seen as an impoverished awareness of the outstanding universal value of the island's heritage by the local communities (see, e.g. Mutal 1998). In fact, poverty has been singled out as the major threat to ensuring the effective conservation of heritage and the sustainable development of *Ilha*.

Since 1991, the government of Mozambique has tried, in response to the UNESCO World Heritage Committee's recommendations, to reverse the increasing degradation of the island's built heritage and to improve the living conditions of its inhabitants. Under the auspices of UNESCO and international agencies (e.g. the United Nations Development Programme – UNDP), several studies were conducted and a number of programmes implemented to assess and improve the state of conservation of the built heritage and the living conditions of the island's inhabitants. After a number of years when 'great concern' was expressed (WHC 2006a: 82), monitoring missions dispatched and, at one stage, threats made to list the property on the World Heritage List in Danger due to the State Party failure to take 'necessary actions' (WHC 2007: 79), the World Heritage Committee has recently praised the Mozambican government for the 'considerable progress made in improving the state of conservation of the property' (WHC 2012: 95). Yet the gloomy scenario described above by an ordinary local inhabitant (or *Ilhéu*) is symptomatic of the widespread opinion among *Ilhéus* that little has improved since the island was inscribed on the World Heritage list (see, e.g. Dantas e Sá and Mather 2011; Omar 2013).

In addition to poverty, both the government and international partners have also pointed to the lack of financial resources, in adequate infrastructure, poor local population awareness, no management plan (until 2010), and the weak institutional capacity for conservation and management as the 'root causes' of the conservation problems on *Ilha* (see GACIM 2010; WHC 2006b, 2014). While these factors doubtless contribute to the current state of affairs, I would argue that the often neglected aspect of governance of heritage conservation beyond regulatory frameworks (i.e. the power relations and dynamic processes involving key stakeholders who have influenced and shaped decision-making about *Ilha*) have at times undermined the implementation of the different and often well thought-out approaches and projects for effective conservation of *Ilha*. This paper discusses the complex relationship between world heritage, poverty, sustainable development and governance within the nexus of concerns related to heritage conservation and management on *Ilha*.

Between heritage conservation, sustainable development, poverty and governance: an appraisal from Mozambique

Today, the thinking about sustainable development is firmly embedded in the field of cultural heritage (see Introduction to this volume). Despite the common belief that securing sustainable development is an essential condition to guarantee the conservation of heritage (see, e.g. Galla 2012), at the practical level, there are still numerous challenges that often hamper the implementation of sustainable development approaches to the conservation of heritage; mainly the inadequate staff and resources, the lack of stakeholders' engagement and an inadequate system of governance (WHC 2010: 4). In fact, despite the widespread discourse on the benefits of World Heritage listing for local communities, with some noticeable exceptions (see, e.g. Taruvinga 2014), one still struggles to find successful examples whereby heritage is used to generate meaningful and sustainable livelihoods for communities living in and around many African sites inscribed on the World Heritage list, as I witnessed at the 2012 International Conference on 'Living with World Heritage in Africa' in Johannesburg, South Africa.

Most so-called developing countries adopted the short-term (2000–15) goals that the sustainable development agenda specifically seeks to achieve (i.e. the Millennium Development Goals, MDGs). However, there are still tensions and contradictions between the priorities of global and local actors over the shift from the 'conventional development paradigm' (a growth-based economic model) to the current 'sustainability paradigm' (focusing on sustainable and equitable economies and societies worldwide) (Rijnhout *et al.* 2014: 2). As Pascall Taruvinga (2014: 2) noticed, the World Heritage Community often refers to concepts and the relationship between '[heritage] conservation', 'outstanding universal value', and 'sustainable development', whereas government institutions and development agencies are more comfortable with terms such as 'job creation', 'economic growth' and 'poverty alleviation'. In fact, poverty and poverty alleviation have become the catchwords within development circles and are increasingly entangled with concerns regarding heritage conservation. Yet, policy makers and development experts often struggle over questions of what poverty is, how to measure it and the best ways to alleviate it (Samuels 2009: 71).

Responding to the World Bank (WB) and International Monetary Fund (IMF) conditionality policies for development assistance, Mozambique, in 2000, produced the Action Plan for the Reduction of Absolute Poverty (PARPA I). Under PARPA I, poverty levels were reduced from 70 per cent in 1997 to 54.1 per cent in 2004, leading the government, civil society and the international community to believe that the country was on track to meet the MDG 1 on poverty and hunger (Vollmer 2012: 4). Following the failure of PARPA II (2006–9) to reduce poverty to 45 per cent in 2009, in 2011, the government approved the Poverty Reduction Action Plan (PARP) 2011 to 2014 aimed at reducing the incidence of food poverty levels from the current 54.7 per cent to 42 per cent by 2014 (GdM 2011: 7). However, a Multidimensional Poverty Index (MPI) estimation, made in 2011, revealed that 70.2 per cent of the population are 'multidimensionally poor', while an additional 14.8 per cent are 'near multidimensional poverty' (UNDP 2014: 5).

Two main factors might help explain the failure of PARP(A)s to meet their goals. These are the neoliberal development models that operate within a framework of neoliberal bias and the political discourse about poverty in Mozambique. PARP(A)s are based on the assumption that both donors and the government should invest in human capital (health and education) and infrastructure and leave economic development and poverty reduction as a mainly private sector responsibility. Thus, the emphasis of government intervention has been on the MDGs 2 to 6 (education, gender and health), relinquishing the MDG 1 on poverty eradication to the private sector and foreign investment (Cunguara and Hanlon 2010: 14–15). Therefore, Mozambique does not seem to be successful in achieving the MDG 1, which is a milestone towards achieving sustainable development. Contributing to this scenario is also the political discourse about poverty in Mozambique. Since

2005, when the former President Armando Guebuza made the elimination of poverty his main policy goal, the official political discourse puts the focus of the fight against poverty on economic growth and the transformation of the mind, or culture, of the poor (i.e. people are poor because they are lazy, they lack self-esteem or they have a fear of being rich) (Chichava 2010; Brito 2010). The belief is that 'the poor are materially poor because they suffer from mental poverty' (Castel-Branco 2010: 6). This political discourse on poverty removes the responsibility from the State and foreign developmental agencies and places the failure of the fight against poverty on the poor themselves. It is against this socio-economic and political backdrop that the conservation efforts in Mozambique, especially with regard to the World Heritage Site of *Ilha*, should be understood.

Within the donor-driven neoliberal policies aimed at addressing world poverty, good governance is elevated as the most important platform for poverty alleviation (Bush 2007: 180). Instead of good governance, this study is more concerned with the notion of governance, and cultural governance most specifically, defined as 'the field for the regulation and contention of political and economic dynamics through culture, comprising a variety of procedures, technologies, organisations, knowledge, discourses and actions' (Wang 2012: 10). Thus, in a context where the development cooperation plays a major and decisive role in Mozambican politics, which often results in the asymmetrical co-production in the policymaking process (see, e.g. Macamo 2006), the notion of cultural governance is useful not only to grasp the macro trend of cultural policy, and to highlight the close interaction among culture, politics and economy, but also to scrutinise various processes that are part of the World Heritage system (see, e.g. Logan 2012) based in the specific context of *Ilha*.

Locating the setting: Island of Mozambique

The city of *Ilha de Moçambique*, from which the name of the country is derived, is a calcareous coral reef situated 4 km from the mainland coast at the entrance to the Mossuril bay of the Indian Ocean in Nampula province, northern Mozambique (Figure 3.1). *Ilha* is 3 km long and 200 to 500 meters wide, with an urban area of approximately 1 km². It forms an archipelago with the two small, uninhabited islands of Goa and Sena, and it is now connected to the mainland, at Sanculo-Lumbo, by a bridge that was built in the 1960s (GACIM 2010: 28).

Inhabited by Bantu speakers at around AD 200 and recorded in the navigation routes of the Indian Ocean since the first millennium, *Ilha* was dominated by Arabian trading between the eighth and the sixteenth centuries AD. There was Portuguese settlement in the sixteenth and seventeenth centuries AD, followed by Indian economic dominance and the slave trade in the next two centuries, and thus, the island became an intercultural melting pot (Aarhus Arkitektskolen 1985). This dramatic and rich history is expressed in the historic urban landscape of the island that is divided into two different types of dwellings and urban systems: the city of Stone and Lime in the north and the city of Macuti to the south of the island (Figure 3.2).

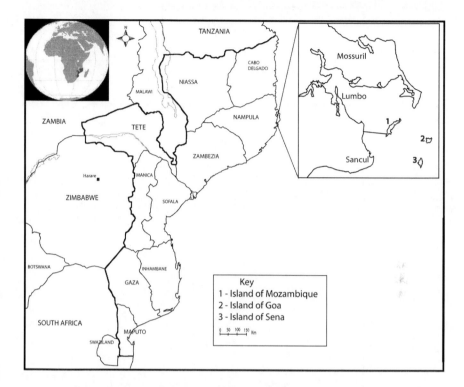

Figure 3.1 Map showing the location of the Island of Mozambique.

The city of Stone and Lime, commonly designated Stone Town, has Swahili roots but with strong Arabic and Portuguese influences. It comprises numerous administrative, commercial, religious and military buildings testifying to the first seat of the Portuguese colonial government between 1507 and 1898. Occupying approximately two-thirds of the island, Stone Town is organised in 33 city blocks with a total of 379 original buildings and it is inhabited by a relatively small part of the island population (Forjaz 2010; GACIM 2010) (Figure 3.3).

The city of Macuti, named after the original coconut palm leaf roofing (*macuti*) of local houses, is also of Swahili origin and it hosts many different variations of the vernacular type of architecture, ranging from precarious stick huts, without plaster and windows, to solid houses built of a stone, lime and sand mixture (Sollien 2013: 50) (Figure 3.4). This area of *Ilha*, also known as *Ponta da Ilha*, is organised into seven neighbourhoods (*Bairros*)[1] with 1,330 original buildings. The *Bairros* of Macuti are already predominantly built using other types of material (e.g. concrete block and the metal industrial roof sheet) and suffer from an acute water shortage, a lack of sanitation and a serious flooding danger at certain times of year (Forjaz 2010; GACIM 2010).

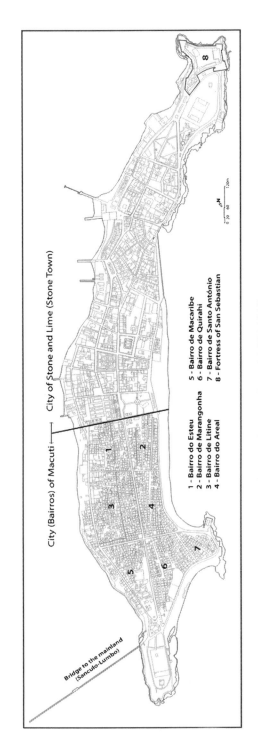

City (Bairros) of Macuti — City of Stone and Lime (Stone Town)

Bridge to the mainland
(Sanculo-Lumbo)

1 - Bairro do Esteu   5 - Bairro de Macaribe
2 - Bairro de Marangonha 6 - Bairro de Quirahi
3 - Bairro de Litine   7 - Bairro de Santo António
4 - Bairro do Areal   8 - Fortress of San Sebastian

0 20 60   120m

Figure 3.2 Map showing Stone Town and the city of Macuti (adapted from GACIM 2010).

Figure 3.3 Image showing part of Stone Town (photo: A. Jopela).

Figure 3.4 Image showing part of the city of Macuti (photo: A. Jopela).

The state of conservation of *Ilha*

The concerns regarding the conservation of *Ilha* have focused, over the years, on two major areas: the condition of life and habitation in the *Bairros* of Macuti and the general degradation of the built heritage in Stone Town. A well-known Mozambican architect, José Forjaz (2010: 57), has argued that before any elaboration on the abstract concept of 'patrimony' [heritage] can be discussed it is important to establish and accept that 'the so-called "Macuti" town is a slum'. In fact, since their inception in the nineteenth century the *Bairros* of Macuti have been perceived as a 'dangerous place to urban hygiene' (Sollien 2013: 52), given the serious problems of sanitation and drainage, especially in the current *Bairros* of Esteu and Litine. In addition, the island's population has increased from 7,760 inhabitants in 1980 to 14,889 in 1997 and 17,356 in 2007, transforming the *Bairros* of Macuti into a poorer quality construction environment, characterised by the progressive encroachment of private and public spaces for new housing, and the subdivision of existing housing and plots, resulting in the impoverishment of the quality of life in general, as well as the disruption of basic services such as water and sewerage (Forjaz 2010).

Adding to this scenario is the absolute poverty in which the majority of the population lives. In 2009, the gross per capita income in *Ilha* was US$ 0.21 daily, well below the US$ 1 per day established as the poverty threshold in Mozambique (CESO-CI 2009: 49). This is why the poverty has been considered the biggest threat to the conservation of *Ilha* as World Heritage. It is often argued that the ordinary *Ilhéus* do not participate actively in conservation because their basic needs are a constant daily concern and priority (see, e.g. Mutal 1998). Although I do not disagree with this view, I contend that given the current ritualised political discourse on poverty, the elevation of poverty as the primary cause of the degradation of the built heritage in *Ilha* also attempts to depoliticise the heritage management process by downplaying the role of politics and power relations among key stakeholders who shape the governance of heritage conservation on the island (although they actually remain instrumental in the process).

There is a record of the 'general degradation' of the built heritage in Stone Town. In fact, a recent survey revealed that the condition of the buildings in the Stone and Lime part of the island has decreased (minus 15 per cent) between 1983 and 2012 and that such 'general degradation is indeed posing a threat to these buildings of outstanding universal value' (Pereira Roders *et al*. 2012: 178). The list of the causes of degradation on the island, as discussed by the World Heritage Committee, include, amongst others: (i) the insufficient regulatory framework (including conservation and management plans and urban plans); (ii) the insufficient implementation or enforcement of a regulatory framework; and (iii) the lack of insufficient human, financial and technical resources (Damen *et al*. 2013: 84). Although this list touches on some issues concerning the governance of heritage (e.g. the lack of a regulatory framework), I suggest that there has been a predominantly technical approach to the causes of the conservation issues at *Ilha* that downplays the problem of the confrontation between the different views and interests of stakeholders at both local and national levels. For example, many reports indicate that one of the key conservation issues was the lack of a conservation and management plan, which was finalised in 2010, to be implemented until 2014. However, annual reports from GACIM between 2011 and 2013 clearly illustrate that the problems reaches beyond the 'insufficient regulatory framework' such as a management plan or the 'insufficient human, financial and technical resources' to implement the plan. Although these are factors that cannot be overlooked, the problem also lies with the way in which political, economic, administrative and ideological authority is exercised by some stakeholders on issues of heritage conservation. To put it simply: the issue lies with the way *Ilha* has been governed through heritage conservation.

Governing the conservation of heritage in *Ilha*

Colonial creation of heritage (1855–1975)

From 1855, the Portuguese colonial administration undertook efforts to clear huts (*palhotas*) out of Stone Town by moving slaves to *Ponta da Ilha*. In 1878 the colonial authorities passed a by-law prohibiting the construction of houses with *macuti* roofs in Stone Town, setting the division of the island into two towns of different building materials, urban patterns and occupants (Sollien 2012: 3–4). The Commission for Monuments and Historic Relics in Mozambique (CMRHM) was created in 1947, responsible for carrying out an investigation into the classification and conservation of the monuments in the colony. In 1955, the core urban area of *Ilha* was classified as 'buildings of public interest' and some architectural intervention guidelines were introduced (GACIM 2010: 116). During the late 1960s and early 1970s, the CMRHM carried out a number of conservation and reconstruction works including the creation of museums in Stone Town and a campaign to valorise the old traditional houses in the *Bairros* of Macuti (Hougaard 2011). The colonial authority's interest was fuelled by the growing tourist interest in the island (particularly the exotic and picturesque *macuti* houses) as well as the shift of the colonial ideology to a multiracial colonialism, in response to the growing nationalist contestation for independence (as materialised in the liberation struggle initiated by Frelimo in 1964). Although there is a widespread belief that during this period the residents of Macuti were not allowed to change their roofs, it has been suggested that such conservation guidelines were never legally formalised. Nevertheless, the fact that people had to place a written request to undertake any building work and to pay a fee to do so was itself prohibitive of change (Sollien 2012: 9).

Post-independence inheritance of colonial heritage (1976–91)

Mozambique gained its independence from Portugal in 1975 and the emphasis in terms of cultural heritage policy was placed on the creation of a new national cultural identity based on the official selective memories of the armed liberation struggle (1964–74) led by Frelimo (Barnes 1978). Seen through the lens of the Socialist Frelimo leadership, *Ilha* was the 'cradle of colonialism'. As Samora Machel, the first President of Mozambique, described it in 1977 in the daily newspaper *Notícias*, *Ilha* was a place where capitalism had installed its repressive machine and used it to plan military operations against Frelimo . . . It was also the stronghold of prostitution, luxury, obscurantism and the backward ideas of colonialism' (Rosário 2012: 309). This conception of *Ilha* has resulted, over the years, in a relationship of conflict between Frelimo and the local *Ilha* elites, seen in the political and economic marginalisation of local elites and the ambivalent position taken by central government on matters such as the conservation and management of the island and the solution to the precarious living conditions of the majority of the island's inhabitants.

A debate on how best to integrate the 'Portuguese colonial monuments' of *Ilha* into the national cultural strategy resulted, in 1975, in the creation of a National Service for Museums and Antiquities, followed in 1980 by the setting up of a Restoration Office on the island, aimed at assuring its conservation. In order to gain broader private support for the conservation of *Ilha*, the government promoted the creation of a local NGO (the Association of the Friends of the Island of Mozambique) and approached UNESCO and the Gulbenkian Foundation in Portugal for support. This resulted in two consultant visits to the island in 1981. The first UNESCO visit report by Krzysztof Pawlowski suggested that enlisting *Ilha* as a UNESCO World Heritage Site could be one way to get support for its conservation (Pawlowski 1981). The postcolonial government enthusiastically embraced the idea of World Heritage nomination as a strategy for getting external support from international donors for the conservation of *Ilha*. In fact, one of the aspects of the cultural governance of the island over the years has been that conservation is highly dependent on foreign donors' support.

Between 1982 and 1985, the Restoration Office carried out a series of conservation studies that were compiled in the *Report of the Island of Mozambique 1982–1985* (Aarhus Arkitektskolen 1985). In 1985, the work stopped due to the civil war between the Frelimo government and the Renamo (Mozambican National Resistance) guerrillas from 1977 to 1992, which made any conservation initiative in *Ilha* very difficult and contributed to its continuing degradation. In terms of cultural governance it is interesting to note that although the postcolonial government sought to reform the legacy and the *modus operandi* of the colonial bureaucracy, many ideas and practices of the colonial period were in fact carried over into the years that followed independence (Gonçalves 2012: 36). For instance, despite technical recommendations regarding intervention in Macuti (Aarhus Arkitektskolen 1985), just as the colonial authorities before them, the postcolonial State adopted a Western monumentalist approach to heritage conservation (Jopela 2011) and has been ambivalent as to how to treat the Macuti houses in a heritage conservation policy (Sollien 2012: 2). I shall return to this point below.

World Heritage listing and the quest for sustainability (1991–2006)

In 1991, *Ilha* was inscribed on the World Heritage list under criteria (iv) and (vi). A year later the Rome General Peace Accords ended 16 years of civil war and in 1994 the country hosted its first multiparty democratic elections, won by Frelimo ever since. From 1992, attention was mostly directed towards the social and economic reconstruction of the country leaving little space for concerns about historical conservation (Hougaard 2013: 39). In 1997, the Director General of UNESCO, Federico Mayor, launched an international campaign to 'safeguard the Island of Mozambique'. Under this initiative, the World Heritage Centre spearheaded a Programme for Sustainable Human Development and Integral Conservation funded by UNDP, UNESCO, the European Union and the Finnish Government. This programme resulted in the design of 50 microprojects in areas such as water and sanitation, tourism development and heritage restoration. The rehabilitation of the architectural, urban and cultural heritage component of the programme was estimated in the region of USD 11,737,000 (Mutal 1998).

This programme constituted the first application of the sustainable development approach to heritage conservation in Mozambique. As the coordinator of the programme, Silvio Mutal puts it: 'In addressing the question of conservation of the *Ilha* (World Heritage Site), the aspects of people and sustainable development and culture outweigh aspects of place, building and physical heritage *per se*' (Mutal 1998: 8). Despite presenting a forward-looking approach to heritage conservation and providing important recommendations (e.g. the need for a Special Status of *Ilha* in the form of a law which was only adopted in 2006), this programme was not implemented, at least not in its integrated format. Two main reasons have contributed to this. Firstly, the programme was based on the assumption of the availability of donor, government and private funding that did not materialise despite the fact that different donors continued to bilaterally invest in specific projects on the island. Second, as Jen Hougaard (2011) noticed, the Ministry of Culture was given the responsibility to be the direct interlocutor for the implementation of the programme, while the tools for action were in the hands of other ministries (i.e. the Ministries of Finance, Public Works and Housing, Tourism and others), making it difficult for the Ministry of Culture to impose cultural concerns as crosscutting issues in any development strategy.

In terms of institutional framework, *Ilha* is both a District and Municipality. In 1997, Law no. 10/97 of 31 May, created the City Council of the Island of Mozambique, which comprises the island and the *Posto Administrativo* of Lumbo in the mainland. In addition, the State Local Authority Act (LOLE) (Law no. 8/2003 of 19 May 2003) created the District of the Island of Mozambique (with exactly the same territorial boundaries as the City Council), which has a District Government (CESO-CI 2009: 162). Until 2006, the City Council was the main local actor in charge of the conservation and management of heritage in *Ilha*.

Conservation of Ilha under GACIM (since 2007)

In 2006, an Action Plan for the Management and Development of the Island of Mozambique World Heritage Site (2007–11) was drawn up in order to take urgent measures against the increasing degradation of the island (Hougaard 2013: 42). The following was achieved:

- The Conservation Office of the Island of Mozambique (GACIM) was created in 2006 and made operational in 2007;
- An Integrated Development Plan for the Island of Mozambique, commissioned by the Ministry of Education and Culture and funded by the African Development Bank, was finalised in May 2009;
- A Conservation and Management Plan for the Island of Mozambique was drawn up by the Ministry of Education and Culture, with support from UNESCO and the African World Heritage Fund (and finalised in October 2010).

In the same year, two Council of Ministers' Decrees approved the Special Status of the Island of Mozambique (Decree no. 27/2006 of 13 July 2006) and created GACIM, under Decree no. 28/2006 (also of 13 July). This Decree defines the protection of architectural, historical and archaeological heritage as well as the promotion of cultural tourism as the key areas of GACIM's intervention. Despite the competences of the City Council as the primary authority for the management of *Ilha* as an urban environment, under the Special Status regulations (Decree no. 27/2006), it became necessary to gain authorisation or prior approval from GACIM to: (i) implement projects concerning the conservation, restoration and protection of cultural heritage; (ii) change internal or external architectural features of the built heritage; (iii) use different/exotic materials or introduce foreign elements into the island's architecture; and (iv) construct and reconstruct buildings.

Although the Organic Statute of GACIM of 2007 creates a Technical Committee, composed of representatives from the District Government, the City Council and other institutions, as the consultation and coordination body, the inter-institutional coordination with the City Council does not always occur seamlessly and without conflicts. For instance, until the end of 2008, the main factor undermining the coordination between GACIM and the City Council was the fact that the State administration was under the ruling Frelimo Party, while the local government (i.e. City Council) was under the Renamo Party. The victory by Frelimo in the first municipal elections in 1998 was followed by five years of alleged 'bad governance' by the City Council. Consequently, Renamo won, with an absolute majority, the second municipal elections in 2003. In response, between 2004 and 2008, Frelimo mobilised all resources at its disposal to block the municipal management policies of Renamo through its administrative and financial State powers. Thus, in the context where the political governance is characterised by the political dominance of the ruling party (Frelimo), where local authorities are considered 'municipalities of poverty' due to their fragile tax-payer base and overwhelming dependency on central government budget transfers, Renamo failed to implement its initial programme (there were also internal politics that had weakened the Party) and to renew its mandate. The November 2008 elections confirmed the return of the Frelimo to the municipality with 64 per cent of the votes against 35 per cent for Renamo (Rosário 2012: 317–24).

One of the practical implications of this political scenario for the conservation of *Ilha* was the loss of institutional memory and poor capitalisation of the activities and initiatives undertaken between 1998 and 2003, when the Municipality was under Frelimo, and between 2004 and 2007, when the city was under Renamo. For instance, when Renamo took office in 2003, it found no administrative or financial records from the previous municipal government. These documents were 'captured and transferred to the local headquarters of the Frelimo Party, as if it was the end of the public administration in this municipality' (Rosário 2012: 325). A similar attitude from Renamo, after losing the municipal elections in 2008, was reported during a stakeholder meeting in *Ilha* in 2009. This contest between political forces also resulted in the greater intervention by the central government, for instance, through the creation of GACIM in 2006 and rehabilitation work on the Fortress of San Sebastian in 2007, as a response to the pressure from the World Heritage Committee, and at the same time as a means to regain and to consolidate Frelimo's authority in *Ilha*. This case clearly illustrated the inability of the existing 'regulatory framework' to ensure effective coordination mechanisms between key stakeholders in the conservation of *Ilha*, in the context of a disputed multiparty democratic dispensation.

Since 2009, all key government institutions are under Frelimo and the institutional relationship between GACIM and the City Council has improved significantly. In 2010, the City Council Code of Postures regulating the conditions to conserve and develop *Ilha* was approved (Resolução n° 22/AMCIM/2010). In principle, no new construction is allowed in *Ilha*. Exceptions can be made if there is evidence of indisputable public interest and if conservation principles are adhered to. Despite this high level of the 'limit of acceptable change' (Pereira Roders 2013: 43), it is obvious that between 1983/5 and 2012 many changes did take place in *Ilha* and the urban landscape is continuously changing (Metgod *et al.* 2012: 150). A critical issue is that the Code of Postures is not very clear in its heritage guidelines and part of the development in *Ilha* seems to be happening without the acknowledgement of GACIM or against its often 'non-mandatory' advice (Pereira Roders and Hougaard 2012: 197). In fact, there are numerous cases in which the City Council has promoted and authorised new constructions that violate the Code of Postures, against GACIM's advice, resulting in a loss of moral and legal authority of both GACIM and the City Council in the eyes of the *Ilhéus* (Forjaz 2010: 53). The fact that *Ilha* is a small and friendly community, with strong social relations among the relevant stakeholders, makes confrontations and law enforcement difficult at times. Often, 'compromises are reached, even in infringement of conservation and urban planning policies, which causes a snowball effect of subsequent cases' (Pereira Roders 2013: 44).

There are many competing development trends in *Ilha*, and therefore GACIM is just one voice amongst many (Hougaard 2013: 42). In order to adopt a shared vision in terms of development strategy and build effective coordination mechanisms, the government, with support from development partners, including UNESCO, carried out successive coordination seminars in 2006 and 2007 and produced an Integrated Development Plan for the Island of Mozambique (hereafter IDP) in 2009 and a Conservation and Management Plan for the Island of Mozambique (hereafter CMP) in 2010. With its catalogue of 25 programmes, including 112 budgeted projects, the IDP has a close resemblance to the PSHDIC presented in 1998. In fact, as with the PSHDIC, the implementation of the IDP is dependent mostly on availability of foreign donor and other private funding as well as strong political commitment from central government. Similarly, the success in the implementation of the CMP, between 2010 and 2014, was dependent on the:

- Approval of the plan by the central government in order to ensure the direct involvement of all stakeholders;
- Existence of adequate State funding to ensure public participation in conservation projects and on-going operating costs of local authorities (e.g. budget for maintenance of real estate in possession of GACIM);
- Strengthening of human and technical resources available to GACIM for the implementation of various activities as defined in the Specific Statute of *Ilha* (GACIM 2010: 109).

Despite being presented publicly, both plans were never formally approved by the Ministry of Culture or by the Council of Ministers. Although local stakeholders made it clear that the CMP had to be formally approved so that the local administration could access State funding, during the presentation of the plan to the Ministry of Culture in 2010, some top officials argued that 'we [the Ministry] cannot be seen to send everything to the Council of Ministers' and that 'the Province has money to implement these plans [IDP and CMP]'. A key reason for the need to have some sort of formalisation of the CMP is that the existing legal framework in terms of State funding allocation recognises other types of planning instruments (e.g. General Urbanisation Plans) but not Heritage Conservation and Management Plans. Thus without formal government approval, it was left to GACIM to use the CMP as a guiding tool to its activities each year, but they are limited by having to fall within the normal budget set by the Ministry of Culture, and mostly allocated to running costs. In fact, the 2013 Annual Report of GACIM indicates that in terms of the institutional relationship with central government, GACIM still awaits a response from the Ministry of Culture in relation to:

- A clear definition of the authority of GACIM in order to give it a greater degree of authority on the island;
- The rapid adoption of the proposed use of the spaces of the Fortress of San Sebastian;

- The approval and submission of the Adjustment of the Organic Statute and Professional Qualifier of GACIM to the Ministry of Public Administration (GACIM 2013: 19).

These points deserve further consideration. Between 2007 and 2009, UNESCO coordinated the first phase of the rehabilitation project of the Fort of San Sebastian, which focused on urgent structural consolidation and restoration works to prevent further deterioration and the provision of basic services and facilities. This initiative was praised for combining heritage conservation and development needs (e.g. through the employment of 100 local community members and installation of a water fountain outside the Fortress for public use) (see Eloundou and Weydt 2009). However, in my recent visit to *Ilha* and to the Fortress, in July 2014, heritage officers from GACIM were still lamenting the undefined future use of the Fortress, as the proposal for utilisation sent by GACIM to the Ministry of Culture in 2011 is still awaiting approval. In addition, eight years after its creation, GACIM still needs an 'Adjustment of the Organic Statute and Professional Qualifier'. The current organisation chart of GACIM provides for the Director's Office, two Departments with five Divisions and a General Secretary with 78 employees and a budgetary impact of about 3 million Meticais (approximately US$ 100,000) (CESO-CI 2009: 178). Of these, GACIM had only 13 employees in 2013 and a budget for the operation of about 3.24 million Meticais. Although GACIM considers itself 'a public institution with the mandate to manage and preserve the cultural and natural heritage of the Island of Mozambique' (GACIM 2013: 7), as it is, this institution does not seem to meet the institutional, organisational and financial conditions to provide the technical and political-institutional support for the promotion of the much desired sustainable development of *Ilha*.

Although I do not disagree with the multiple reasons advanced in several studies and considered by the World Heritage Committee as the 'root causes' for the current state of affairs in *Ilha*, here I have illustrated that the complexities in terms of the governance of heritage conservation have undermined the implementation and sustainability of the different conservation efforts on the island. The issue of governance will undoubtedly continue to determine the fate of the new 'sustainable development' approach to heritage conservation such as the UNESCO recommendation on the Historic Urban Landscape (HUL), adopted in 2011 by the UNESCO Member States. Like any other non-binding standard-setting instrument for heritage management at the international level, the success of the HUL approach is dependent on its adoption and domestication by national and local institutions (van Oers and Roders 2012). Even though *Ilha* benefited from a five-day workshop on the 'Application of the Historic Urban Landscapes on the Island of Mozambique' in 2011, the full implementation of the HUL approach still requires the development of some practical guidelines and tools, for instance, on how to deal with change (e.g. how to accommodate contemporary interventions and regulate the 'uncontrolled development' in both Macuti and Stone Town) (Jopela 2013: 94). Most importantly, the implementation of the HUL approach transcends the purely technical sphere to the attitudinal and calls for the political willingness of central government to move beyond the existing empty political discourses on the importance of culture and heritage for development, which finds no translation into the main development policy documents (i.e. PARP(A)s), to a meaningful devolution of decision-making powers and resources (human and financial) to local institutions such as GACIM.

Concluding remarks

Against the background of opinion among some *Ilhéus* that little has improved since *Ilha* was inscribed on the World Heritage listing in 1991, this chapter discusses the complex relationship between World Heritage, poverty, development and governance within the nexus of concerns related to heritage conservation and management on the Island of Mozambique. I have demonstrated that the government's neoliberal development polices and the political discourse about poverty in Mozambique have contributed significantly towards the country's failure to achieve some of the targets of the sustainable development agenda. It is against this socio-economic and political backdrop that the challenges of connecting heritage conservation, poverty alleviation and sustainable development in Mozambique, especially with regard to *Ilha,* should be understood.

I have argued that while factors such as widespread poverty, lack of financial resources, in adequate infrastructure, poor community awareness and weak institutional capacity for conservation and management, doubtless contribute to the current state of continuous degradation of *Ilha*, the often neglected aspect of governance of heritage conservation, specifically the power relations and dynamic processes involving key stakeholders who have influenced and shaped decision-making in *Ilha*, has been a key factor and it has undermined the implementation of the different and often well thought-out approaches and projects for the island. In fact, the conception of *Ilha* as 'the cradle of colonialism' by the Frelimo elite has, over the years, created conflicting relationships between Frelimo and local elites often manifested in the ambivalent positions and 'foot dragging' of the central government regarding issues of conservation and management of *Ilha*. Thus, the conservation strategy has been based on advocacy for international donor funding and less on domestic measures that would empower the local authorities in charge of conservation on the island.

Acknowledgements

Thanks to Lynn Meskell for the invitation and sponsorship that made possible my participation in the Conservation of Historic Urban Landscapes and Sustainable Development Conference, held at the Stanford Archaeology Center, between 7 and 8 March 2013, where I presented an earlier version of this paper. I am grateful to Sophia Labadi for conversations and valuable comments on a draft of this chapter. My work would not have been possible without the support of colleagues at the

Conservation Office of the Island of Mozambique (GACIM), especially Jano Paixão, Claudio Zonguene and Celestino Girimula, the Director of GACIM. I am also grateful to Hafiz Jamu and the communities of the Island of Mozambique for their willingness to share their time and opinions with me.

Note

1   The *Bairros* are Litine, Esteu, Marrangonha, Makaribe, Areal, Quirahi and Santo Antonio or Unidade.

Bibliography

Aarhus Arkitektskolen (1985). *Ilha de Moçambique: Relatório 1982–85*. Aarhus: Phønix A/S.

Barnes, B. (1978). Creating a national culture: an overview. *A Journal of Opinion*, 8(1), 35–8.

Brito, L. (2010). Discurso Político e Pobreza em Moçambique: análise de três discursos presidenciais. In: L. Brito, C. Castel-Branco, S. Chichava and A. Francisco (eds), *Pobreza, Desigualdade e Vulnerabilidade em Moçambique*. Maputo: IESE, pp. 49–64.

Bush, R. (2007). *Poverty and Neoliberalism: Persistence and Reproduction in the Global South*. London: Pluto Press.

Castel-Branco, C. (2010). *Pobreza, Riqueza e Dependência em Moçambique: Discussão Crítica*. Paper presented at the launch of two books of the Institute of Social and Economic Studies, Maputo, 2010.

CESO-CI (2009). *Plano de Desenvolvimento Integrado da Ilha de Moçambique*. Maputo: BAD/MEC.

Chichava, S. (2010). Por que Moçambique é Pobre? Uma Análise do Discurso de Armando Guebuza sobre a Pobreza. In: L. Brito, C. Castel-Branco, S. Chichava and A. Francisco (eds), *Pobreza, Desigualdade e Vulnerabilidade em Moçambique*. Maputo: IESE, pp. 65–82.

Cunguara, B. and Hanlon, J. (2010). *O Fracasso na Redução da Pobreza em Moçambique. Crisis States Working Papers Series, 2*. Available at: http://eprints.lse.ac.uk/28467/2/WP74.2portugues.pdf (accessed 21 September 2012).

Damen, S., Derks, R., Metgod, T., Veldpaus, L., Silva, A. and Pereira Roders, A. (2013). Relating the state of authenticity and integrity and the factors affecting World Heritage properties: Island of Mozambique as case study. *International Journal of Heritage and Sustainable Development*, 3(1), 81–90.

Dantas e Sá, V. and Mather, C. (2011). Ilha de Moçambique: conserving and managing World Heritage in the developing world. *Tourism Review International*, 14, 1–12.

Decree no. 27/2006 of 13 July 2006. *Estatuto Específico da Ilha de Moçambique*. Maputo: Assembleia da República de Moçambique.

Decree no. 28/2006 of 13 July 2006. *Gabinete de Conservação da Ilha de Moçambique e aprova o respectivo Estatuto Orgânico*. Maputo: Assembleia da República de Moçambique.

Eloundou, L. and Weydt, J. (eds) (2009). *Reabilitação da Fortaleza de São Sebastião na Ilha de Moçambique*. Paris: UNESCO-WHC.

Forjaz, J. (2010). *Island of Mozambique – Architectural Survey and Study on Local Vernacular Architecture. Reference Nr: 513MOZ4001*. Maputo: José Forjaz Arquitectos.

GACIM (2010). *Plano de Gestão e Conservação 2010–2014 Ilha de Moçambique*. Maputo: DNPC.

GACIM (2011). *Relatório Anual do Gabinete de Conservação da Ilha de Moçambique 2011*. Ilha de Moçambique: GACIM.

GACIM (2012). *Relatório Anual do Gabinete de Conservação da Ilha de Moçambique 2012*. Ilha de Moçambique: GACIM.

GACIM (2013). *Relatório Anual do Gabinete de Conservação da Ilha de Moçambique 2013*. Ilha de Moçambique: GACIM.

Galla, A. (ed.) (2012). *World Heritage – Benefits Beyond Borders*. Cambridge: Cambridge University Press.

GdM (2011). *Poverty Reduction Action Plan (PARP) 2011–2014*. Maputo: Governo de Moçambique.

Gonçalves, E. (2012). Chronopolitics: Public Events and the Temporalities of State Power in Mozambique. Unpublished PhD thesis. Johannesburg: University of the Witwatersrand.

Hougaard, J. (2011). *Enforcement of Planning Instruments for Conservation of Island of Mozambique*. Paper presented at the Historic Urban Landscape Workshop, 10–15 July 2011, Island of Mozambique.

Hougaard, J. (2013). Mozambique island development and conservation strategies and practises, with focus on the period 1943 to 2011. In: A. Seifert (ed.), *Global City-Local Identity?* Dar es Salaam: Mkuki na Nyota Publishers Ltd, pp. 36–47.

ICOMOS (1991). *Advisory Body Evaluation. Ref. 599*. Available at: http://whc.unesco.org/archive/advisory_body_evaluation/599.pdf (accessed 12 May 2012).

Institute on Governance (2000). *Governance in the New Millennium: Challenges for Canada*. Ontario: Institute on Governance.

Jopela, A. (2011). Traditional custodianship: a useful framework for heritage management in Southern Africa? *Conservation and Management of Archaeological Sites*, 13(2–3), 103–22.

Jopela, A. (2013). *The Historic Urban Landscape and the Conservation and Management of the Island of Mozambique World Heritage Site. Swahili Historic Urban Landscapes – Report on the Historic Urban Landscape Workshops and Field Activities on the Swahili Coast in East Africa 2011–2012*. Paris: UNESCO, pp. 92–5.

Jopela, A. and Rakotomamonjy, B. (2012). *How to Raise Local Awareness on the Unique Values of World Heritage? The Case of the Island of Mozambique World Heritage Site*. Paper presented at the Interregional Conference Europe–Africa 'Living with World Heritage', 13–17 May 2012, Røros, Norway.

Logan, W. (2012). States, governance and the politics of culture: World Heritage in Asia. In: P. Daly and T. Winter (eds), *Routledge Handbook of Heritage in Asia*. Abingdon: Routledge, pp. 113–28.

Macamo, E. (2006). *Political Governance in Mozambique – Final Report*. Maputo: DFID-Mozambique.

Metgod, T., Silva, A. and Pereira Roders, A. (2012). Changes. In: A. Pereira Roders, J. Aguacheiro and J. Hougaard (eds), *Island of Mozambique Historic Urban Landscape in Perspective Part 1: Stone Town – 2011/2012*. Eindhoven: Eindhoven University of Technology, pp. 127–51.

Mutal, S. (1998). *Island of Mozambique – World Heritage Site: A Programme for Sustainable Human Development and Integral Conservation*. Maputo: UNESCO/UNDP.

Omar, L. (2013). Os Desafios para Conservação Ambiental e Património Cultural na Ilha de Moçambique. Unpublished MA dissertation. São Paulo: Universidade de São Paulo.

Pawlowski, K. (1981) *Rapport Technique,* Les Problèmes de la sauvegarde de l'Ilha de Mozambique. Paris: UNESCO.

Pereira Roders, A. (2013). *Lessons from the Island of Mozambique on Limits of Acceptable Change. Swahili Historic Urban Landscapes – Report on the Historic Urban Landscape Workshops and Field Activities on the Swahili Coast in East Africa 2011–2012.* Paris: UNESCO, pp. 40–9.

Pereira Roders, A. and Hougaard, J. (2012). Conclusions and recommendations. In: A. Pereira Roders, J. Aguacheiro and J. Hougaard (eds), *Island of Mozambique Historic Urban Landscape in Perspective Part 1: Stone Town – 2011/2012.* Eindhoven: Eindhoven University of Technology, pp. 197–200.

Pereira Roders, A., Aguacheiro, J. and Hougaard, J. (eds) (2012). *Island of Mozambique Historic Urban Landscape in Perspective Part 1: Stone Town – 2011/2012.* Eindhoven: Eindhoven University of Technology.

Resolucao n° 22/AMCIM/2010 (2010). *Codigo de Posturas – Code of Postures.* Ilha de Mocambique: AMCIM.

Rijnhout, L., De Zoysa, U., Kothari, A. and Healy, H. (2014). Towards a global agenda of sustainability and equity: civil society engagement for the future we want. *Perspectives,* 12.

Rosário, D. (2012). Alternância Eleitoral do Poder Local – Os Limites da Descentralização Democrática: O Caso do Município da Ilha de Moçambique, 2003–2008. In: B. Weimer (ed.), *Moçambique: Descentralizar O Centralismo-Economia Política, Recursos E Resultados.* Maputo: IESE, pp. 300–28.

Samuels, K. (2009). Trajectories of development: international heritage management of archaeology in the Middle East and North Africa. *Archaeologies: Journal of the World Archaeological Congress,* 5(1), 68–91.

Sollien, S. (2012). The persistence of the myth of the native hut and the cradle of Portugueseness on the Indian Ocean. *Traditional Dwellings and Settlements Working Paper Series,* 253, 1–25.

Sollien. S. (2013). Approaching the Macuti House – identity and heritage conservation in Ilha de Moçambique. In: A. Seifert (ed.), *Global City-Local Identity?* Dar es Salaam: Mkuki na Nyota Publishers Ltd, pp. 48–58.

Taruvinga, P. (2014). *Africa Celebrating the 40th Anniversary of the World Heritage Convention. Proceeding of the Conference on Living with World Heritage in Africa, 26–29 September 2012, Johannesburg, South Africa.* Midrand/Pretoria: AWHF/DAC.

UNDP (2014). *Mozambique – Human Development Report 2014.* Maputo: UNDP.

van Oers, R. and Pereira Roders, A. (2012). Historic cities as model of sustainability. *Journal of Cultural Heritage Management and Sustainable Development,* 2(1): 4–14.

Vollmer, F. (2012). *'Capabilitizing' the Poverty Challenge: the case of Mozambique, paper presented in the III International Conference of IESE 'Moçambique: Acumulação e Transformação em Contexto de Crise Internacional',* 4–5 September 2012, Maputo, Mozambique.

Wang, C.H. (2012). Heritage formation and cultural governance: the production of Bopiliao Historic District, Taipei. *International Journal of Heritage Studies,* 19(7), 1–16.

WHC (2006a). *Decision 30 COM 7B.42 – Island of Mozambique (Mozambique) (C 599).* Paris: UNESCO. Available at: http://whc.unesco.org/archive/2006/whc06-30com-19e.pdf (accessed 29 November 2014).

WHC (2006b). *State of Conservation: Island of Mozambique (Mozambique).* Paris: UNESCO. Available at: http://whc.unesco.org/en/soc/1166 (accessed 6 January 2015).

WHC (2007). *Decision 31 COM 7B.48 – Island of Mozambique (Mozambique) (C 599)*. Paris: UNESCO. Available at: http://whc.unesco.org/archive/2007/whc07-31com-24e.pdf (accessed 29 November 2014).

WHC (2010). *World Heritage Convention and Sustainable Development. World Heritage Committee Thirty-Fourth Session, Brasilia, Brazil, 25 July–3 August 2010*. Paris: UNESCO.

WHC (2012). Decision 36 COM 7B.46 – Island of Mozambique (Mozambique) (C 599). In: *Decisions Adopted by the World Heritage Committee at its 36th Session (St Petersburg, 2012)*. Paris: World Heritage Centre-UNESCO, p. 95. Available at: http://whc.unesco.org/archive/2012/whc12-36com-19e.pdf (accessed 29 November 2014).

WHC (2014). *State of Conservation: Island of Mozambique (Mozambique)*. Paris: UNESCO. Available at: http://whc.unesco.org/en/soc/2863 (accessed 6 January 2015).

Chapter 4

Interrogating the 'implementation' of international policies of urban conservation in the medina of Tunis

Bianca Maria Nardella and Elisabete Cidre

> In this way, a historical perspective can sensitize us to alternative states of being and ways of acting, and thereby challenge managerialist 'one best way' type of thinking.
>
> (Lewis 2009: 43)

In 1881, the Mission de Tunisie[1] (1881–3) was charged by the French government with

> a complete study of the country, to undertake the excavation of ancient cities and in particular on the site of Carthage; scholars had to research, draw and describe all antique monuments, from prehistory to the Roman conquest, and record all inscriptions anterior to the Arab conquest.
>
> (Bacha 2006: 124)[2]

A century later, in 1999, the World Bank sponsored a feasibility study for a *Projet de gestion et de valorisation du patrimoine culturel*[3] (cultural heritage management and enhancement project), a country-wide assessment to study and record the cultural heritage sector in Tunisia.

Although separated by a century, what is common to both studies is the idea of recording and cataloguing cultural heritage 'things'; of making *order* by creating a system for their management and administration through the rule of law. As Mitchell suggests, Europeans believed that modern government, like modern science, was based on principles true in every country, the strength of which lay in their universality (Mitchell 2002: 54). Both studies refer to a realm of 'external' knowledge (*scientific* in nineteenth-century ideology and *technical* in the twentieth century), depicted as higher than the existing system (status quo), and in both studies, either the creation of *ex novo* institutions or the reform of existing ones is proposed with the implicit aim of healing cultural heritage structures and systems described as neglected, not properly exploited, and ultimately, in danger. The former study sees colonial heritage legislation represented as superior to Ottoman norms for maintaining vestiges of the past,[4] while current policies of urban heritage and development are framed as belonging to an international sphere higher than national laws.

Both narratives claim their guiding principles are universal, as opposed to the particular management systems of the built environment already in place, echoing French enlightenment thinking (Rabinow 1989). Universal values are also at the centre of the UNESCO World Heritage Convention of 1972, which remains the key normative reference for an international authorised heritage discourse (Smith 2006) in cataloguing vestiges of the past (Titchen 1996; Turtinen 2000; De Cesari 2010; Labadi 2013).

This chapter tells a story of urban heritage conservation in Tunis focusing on the articulation of imported and home-grown knowledge practices in the creation of Tunisian legislation and institutions for the *sauvegarde et mise en valeur du patrimoine culturel* (safeguarding and economic valorisation of cultural heritage). The text is based on archival research and fieldwork interviews carried out by Nardella as part of a PhD dissertation and developed as a paper with Cidre. Through narratives of colonial rule of law (Riles 1995), cultural heritage conservation, sustainable urban development (UNESCO 1996) and intellectual cooperation in the Euro-Mediterranean region (Pace 2007), we explore how, from the French colonial period (1881 to 1956) to the independent State (1956 to present), international normative frameworks intersect with political processes and local practice structures and systems. Our narrative sidelines the self-representations of bureaucratic rationality in order to uncover more about the inner workings of the development agencies (Lewis and Mosse 2006: 3). It is supported by the voices of primary actors, following the anthropology of development critique that insists on the primacy of contingent practice over the conceptual work of policy (ibid.).

What do international organisations (IOs) mean by policy categories as 'legislative reform' and 'institutional strengthening'? How do actors themselves reflect on reasons for *failure* in implementation? And how can we understand what seems a standstill in urban conservation and development policy implementation other than as governance failure?

To answer these questions we start by interrogating the genealogy of heritage law and its institutions, further recounting how regime ideologies intersect with urban conservation processes. By exploring selected development projects relating to IOs' accounts of success and failure with relevant actors' voices, this story then illustrates how international policy tends to gloss over the historical and epistemological reasons underpinning institutional conflict and legislative impasses. The narrative highlights instances where disjunctures between urban conservation planning policy and practice become evident before reflecting on what lessons can be learned from Tunis as an established laboratory for urban conservation and development.

Genealogy of institutions

> The break in history caused by the colonial occupation, by the arrival of modernity and civilization, helped to establish the universal character of law.
> (Mitchell 2002: 57)

Tunis was founded by Arab tribes who settled, around the seventh century AD, in the north coastal plains of Tunisia. The site had already a long history dating back to Punic and Roman civilisations in nearby Carthage. The capital of several influential dynasties, such as the Almohads and the Hafsids, from the twelfth to the sixteenth century, Tunis flourished as one of the most important cities in the Maghreb and the Arab world. The medina expanded progressively outside its walls to include two neighbourhoods (rabads) within a second walled tier, each punctuated by splendid palaces and religious buildings.

Under the Ottoman rule of Tunisia (1574 to 1881), the *Habous* charitable trust fulfilled a pivotal role in the maintenance of a large number of properties in Tunis and its countryside. As the Ottoman Empire weakened and gave way to French occupation, the traditional system of building maintenance was slowly undermined and replaced by imported notions of *patrimoine* and of historic preservation based on aesthetic canons. Until then, rules 'were not fixed in an abstract code of law, but were guided by legal precedents and by prescriptions developed in response to actual circumstances and events' (Mitchell 2002: 57). The *Habous* (الحبوس), known as *Waqf* (وقف) outside of the Maghreb, is an institution derived from Islamic law to regulate

> the donation of an individual property in perpetuity for the public welfare and under the possession of God . . . As the continuity of the *waqfs* had essentially depended on the survival of their assets, regular maintenance and repair of buildings was prioritised.
>
> (Sabri 2015: 513; see also Hakim 2008: 108–9)

Tunisian cultural heritage legislation today (see Figure 4.1) is still based on French norms, while the traditional *Habous* system has been erased. Institutional change started in 1884 when the Protectorate on the Tunis Regency established the *Commission de la Tunisie*[5] located in Paris. The following year, the first delegate arrived, tasked with cataloguing archaeological treasures and the creation of an administrative service to manage the historical monuments. A specific legislation for the protection of heritage assets was set up together with a museum to be located in the Beylical palace at Bardo[6] (Bacha 2006: 126–7).

The colonial *Service des Antiquités, Beaux-arts et Monuments Historiques*[7] was instituted in 1885 with a mandate to research, list, conserve and display vestiges of the past under a new 'scientific' scrutiny. Indeed, in the subsequent three decades, heritage and conservation in Tunis remained a scholarly affair under the direction of the Ministry of Education in Paris with imposed limitations to study only pre-Islamic monuments, thus fixing the supremacy of antiquities above historic cities and their monuments. There was a tacit agreement that the *Habous* would continue its work on the Islamic heritage; however, from the 1910s, its role was progressively restricted through new forms of government based on colonial legislation and city administration (Abdelkafi 1989; Bacha 2008; Matri 2008). The 1920s witnessed a major shift in the approach to urban

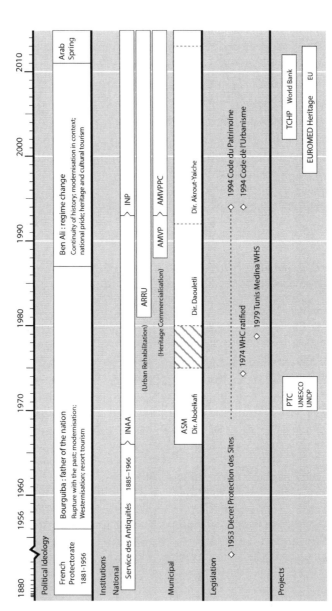

Figure 4.1 Overview of urban heritage conservation context in Tunis (1880s–2010s).

Source: author (Nardella); illustration A. Mallinson.

conservation as economic parameters gained the upper hand in deciding how to treat vestiges of the past; at the same time, political authorities started to appropriate the heritage discourse, infiltrating its governing institutions. To support tourism development as a direct source of revenue, the colonial administration promoted an orientalist, picturesque interpretation of old cities repackaged as attractions for European visitors (Figure 4.2). As such, the medina of Tunis was subject to a beautification (*embellissement*) plan, known as Plan Valensi, and legislation designed to protect archaeological sites was applied and transferred to large living sectors of it (Matri 2008).

Tunisia became independent in 1956 and in doing so embraced modernity and progress. Its champion and first president Habib Bourguiba saw the past as restrictive, oppressive and characterised by cycles of invasion, infighting between factions and tribes and opportunist colonisers. Bourguiba considered it 'absurd to extol their legacy, to worship a past in which they were "masters", to see oneself in a history written by others or, worse, to identify with a heritage built by conquerors' (Saidi 2008: 106). His modernist regime completed the dismantling of the traditional system of building 'conservation' with the abrupt abolition of the *Habous* in July 1957. Hundreds of historical buildings were left to abandonment and/or disrepair (ASM *et al.* 1974) and the medina was represented by the regime as a relic of the past. At the time, a project of the (French) presidential architect called for demolitions (*percée*) through the medina to establish a large vehicular access (Abdelkafi 1989).

In 1966, the *Service des Antiquités* was restructured as *Institut National d'Archéologie et d'Art* (INAA)[8], and still an archaeological understanding of heritage remained prevalent and prioritised Punic and Roman antiquities over the 'living heritage' of the medinas (Bacha 2008; Abdelkafi and Zaki 2011). To counterbalance the progressive decay of the old city, the mayor of Tunis[9] created,

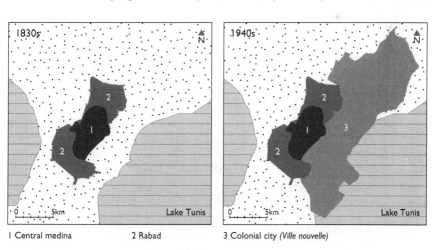

1 Central medina   2 Rabad   3 Colonial city *(Ville nouvelle)*

Figure 4.2 The medina in context and the urban form of Tunis: 1830s and 1940s.

Source: author (Nardella); illustration A. Mallinson.

in 1967, the *Association du Sauvegarde de la médina de Tunis* (ASM),[10] an advisory agency in matters of protection and enhancement, which provided decision-makers with an alternative vision to the dominant urban planning paradigm concerned with vehicular traffic and high-rise buildings. In 1968, the *ASM Atelier d'Urbanisme*[11] led by Jellal Abdelkafi, a young architect-urbanist trained in France, set up a new 'scientific' study of the medina with an interdisciplinary team of architects, geographers and historians. Thus, ASM offered an alternative to colonial representations of the medina: 'no trace of earlier ideologies of the picturesque; the medina is perceived from the point of view of its spatial organisation, as a *velum* of low courtyard buildings served by a hierarchy of streets and blind alleys' (McGuinness 1997: 41). However, ASM ideas antagonised regime views and staff were linked to the 1970s political unrest. Abdelkafi departed and a new director was formally put in place to 'normalise' the association (Chabbi 2011: 34). The ASM was dormant until 1980 when it was resuscitated as 'an institution able to measure and evaluate the urban fabric with objectivity, validity and a high degree of precision still intact' (McGuinness 1997: 42). Under the presidency of a new mayor, the leadership of architectural historian Abdelaziz Daouletli[12] brought in a more pragmatic approach, capable of attracting national and international funding for 'grand urban projects' strategically framed *within* the national political agenda of upgrading insalubrious settlements.

In the 1980s, new actors emerged to administer processes of urban and economic development, push heritage out of its scholarly niche and contribute to larger visions of growth. The INAA was flanked by new institutions. In 1981, a World Bank study sponsored the *Agence de Réhabilitation et de Rénovation Urbaine* (ARRU),[13] a new urban development agency capable of acting as contracting authority and undertaking several large-scale projects under the auspices of IOs (The World Bank 1994: 11). In 1988, the institutional framework was completed by the *Agence National de Mise en Valeur et d'Exploitation du Patrimoine Archéologique et Historique* (AMVP),[14] charged with development of cultural tourism and promotion of cultural industries linked to the national heritage for, explicitly, commercial purposes.

The following decade witnessed major reorganisation and restructuring in the cultural heritage administration. In 1992, the ASM changed leadership and its new *Directeur* Semia Akrout-Yaiche (1992 to 2012) and team (of mainly architects and urban designers) produced studies, detailed design projects and management plans. They advised national and municipal institutions while trying to preserve their unique status as a public-private entity (Mouhli *et al.* 2013). A new generation of projects moved away from social housing and urban rehabilitation schemes of the 1980s to focus on the *embellissement* of the medina at different scales. The aim was to gain greater visibility for conservation efforts, lure residents back into the historic city and, last but not least, attract cultural tourism in line with the new regime ideology that explicitly linked cultural heritage sites, national pride and economic development (see Figure 4.3). The ASM included the city of the nineteenth and twentieth century within the conservation agenda for the historic city.

Figure 4.3 Urban conservation project (*embellissement*): heritage trail in the medina of Tunis, ASM Tunis: 2008–10 (photographs: B. M. Nardella 2012).

In 1993, former ASM director Daouletli led the transformation of INAA into the *Institut National du Patrimoine* (INP):[15] 'a scientific and technical institution responsible for establishing the inventory of cultural heritage, archaeological, historical, civilizational and artistic, of its study, its backup and its development' (INP online). In the same year, the AMVP was restructured as *Agence de Mise en Valeur du Patrimoine et Promotion Culturelle* (AMVVPC).[16] While the present heritage governance is basically the same as that in the 1990s, the overlapping competences of 'old' and 'new' institutions remain a cause of frictions and conflict (see Figure 4.4).

The genealogy of the current institutions reveals their deep involvement in changing political agendas. The following section looks in more detail at the relationship between political ideologies at play in the urban conservation of the Tunis medina, namely the two regimes that governed Tunisia in the past 60 years and the promulgation of legislation for the protection of heritage assets.

Regimes ideology and legislation to protect vestiges of the past

Le jeune État tunisien qui pris les commandes du pays en 1956 hérita ainsi d'une législation pensée en premier lieu pour les vestiges de l'Antiquité par les scientifiques, mais reprise en main per le politique pour des raisons, à l'origine, essentiellement économiques. Par ailleurs, malgré la multiplication de mesures en faveur des monuments et des ensembles islamiques, l'action patrimoniale menée pendant le Protectorat, fur longtemps considérée comment une politique de justification de la colonisation. Ainsi, l'État tunisien héritait d'une législation entachée d'une forte charge idéologique impérialiste.

(Bacha 2008: 99–122)

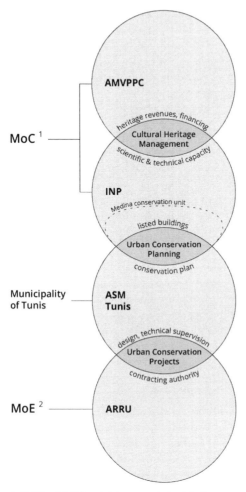

1 - Ministère de la Culture et de la sauvegarde du patrimoine
2 - Ministère de l'Equipement, l'habitat et l'aménagement du territoire

Figure 4.4 Governance structures and systems at play in the medina of Tunis, 2000s.

Source: authors; illustration A. Mallinson.

The stance of the modern Republic of Tunisia towards the past, its classification as memory or heritage, is characterised by different phases (Bacha 2008; Escher and Schepers 2008; Larguèche 2008; Matri 2008). During the 1960s, the State was largely preoccupied with matters of economic development and modernisation, leaving scholarly matters of cultural heritage in the hands of the antiquities service (inherited from the Protectorate) and later in INAA. Between the abolition of *Habous* in 1957 and 1985 there was only one entry for a listed building, no listing of sites nor reforms to the colonial heritage legislation. The consequences for the living heritage of the medinas was disastrous (Abdelkafi 2012).

It was only with the end of the Bourguibian regime and the coup of new President Zine Abidine Ben Ali (former Prime Minister) in 1987 that heritage conservation came to the forefront of the political agenda. Ben Ali portrayed himself as motor of change whilst showing continuity with the father of the nation. He renegotiated the troublesome relationship of the postcolonial state with the past and forged a new correlation between cultural heritage conservation, economic growth and the promotion of cultural tourism (reminiscent of the 1920s). This narrative

> enabled the new government to show that it is rooted in the country's history while being open to the world – particularly the West, where most tourists come from – through an advertising discourse that constantly emphasises the country's past and present position as a link between East and West, a meeting place where civilisations were forged and Other peoples and cultures are welcomed with open arms; [such slogans] directly affect Tunisians by writing the hagiography of their history and territory . . . [and convey] a political determination to make tourism a way for Tunisians to cultivate patriotism and assert national pride.
>
> (Saidi 2008: 103)

A visible result of this change was the elaboration in the 1990s of new legislation that addressed both heritage conservation (*Code du Patrimoine*[17] (CdP)) and urban development (*Code de l'Urbanisme*[18] (CU)). The transformation of the INAA into the INP, and the promulgation of the CdP, marked a distinct move towards international normative frameworks. In particular, the CdP moved heritage conceptualisation from a national to a universal value (in line with the World Heritage Convention), introducing urban conservation areas (*secteurs sauvegardés* based on the French model) and the requirement of conservation plans for historical ensembles (*Plan du Sauvegarde et Mise en Valeur*). The technical discourse of urban conservation (strengthened by the success of rehabilitation projects in the medina of Tunis) called for the 'integration of the heritage' in processes of urban and economic development (ASM 1994). Last but not least, the nuanced appropriation of the past also legitimised the listing and conservation of colonial architecture of the nineteenth to twentieth century as national heritage. As stated by McGuinness:

> [a]s so often in Tunisia, it appeared to me that it was a question of the right persons in the right posts, the right professional network reaching a position of seniority where it could actually influence the course of events. The practical consensus-experts of the 1980s had proved their worth, the time was ripe for a move towards a certain professionalism in the field of heritage. The initiative came from a nexus of professionals in their forties and early fifties, based in the ASM and the INP.
>
> (McGuinness 1997: 45)

The central professionals behind the text of the CdP and the transformation of INAA into the INP[19] were A. Daouletli (ASM, INP, ICOMOS), D. Lesage (ASM, INP and later WB) and J. Abdelkafi (ASM).

Currently, Tunisian legislation for urban heritage conservation comprises international laws (Tunisia ratified the World Heritage Convention in 1974) and national ones (CdP) in addition to specific norms for individual assets and municipal regulations specific to each medina (UNESCO 2009: 18–19). In recent years, legislative frameworks, institutional structures and management capacity have remained the main preoccupation of IOs funding urban heritage conservation and development projects in Tunisia and, while the CdP formally provides a legislative instrument long demanded by experts, in practice its implementation is still awaited:

> in two years we'll mark the twentieth anniversary of the *Code du Patrimoine*, since its publication we say it has to be revised . . . that it has to be done . . . but, until now, nothing has been done to update it or upgrade it.
>
> (Khanoussi interview 2012).

Internationally constructed projects and knowledge dissipation: bureaucratic versus the understanding of actors of 'failure' in implementation

This section introduces relevant projects of urban conservation and development carried out by Tunisian institutions in collaboration with IOs in the period from the 1970s to the 2010s. Each one contributed to the current legislative and institutional framework governing *safeguarding and valorisation* for old Tunis. We will focus on two projects and one programme chronologically illustrating the evolution and practical application of heritage discourses.

Project Tunis-Carthage (1970–4): coupling urban conservation and (economic) development

The report *Sauvegarde et mise en valeur de la médina de Tunis*[20] (1974) provided the seminal case of international intellectual cooperation with long-lasting influence on the agenda of urban conservation and development of Tunis and Tunisia. The study, carried out by the ASM and INAA, respectively as municipal and national partners, was supervised by UNESCO (with UNDP[21] funding) within the larger *Projet de protection et de sauvegarde du patrimoine monumental de la médina de Tunis et de Carthage aux fins du développement économique.*[22] Commonly known as *Projet Tunis-Carthage* (hence PTC), this aimed to link cultural heritage conservation and economic development through tourism as a way to fit the urban conservation agenda with Bourguiba modernisation ideals.

With the departure of French civil servants in the postcolonial aftermath

> Tunisia had a severe shortage of professionally qualified people, and one of the more interesting aspects of the UNESCO-funded *Projet Tunis-Carthage* was

to place a young Tunisian in training alongside each foreign expert. Unusually for the time . . . the experts were chosen by the Tunisians, not imposed from outside.

(McGuinness 1997: 39)

The multidisciplinary team guided by Georges Fradiér (UNESCO) and Jellal Abdelkafi (ASM) introduced French models of typo-morphological thinking together with sociological enquiry as new knowledge tools in the study of the medina. The research diagnostic followed the research agenda started in 1968 by the ASM-AU[23] and completed physical surveys (at scale 1: 250) of the two historic neighbourhoods (*rabad*) outside the central medina, coupled with questionnaires to understand its changing population (e.g. provenance, household structure, economic activities). UNESCO expertise was key in supporting the formulation of objectives and formalisation of an action plan, including how to use juridical tools for conservation (Abdelkafi and Zaki 2011: 56). Project recommendations were quite ambitious in scope and included technical tools (e.g. inventories, servitudes, zoning), pilot projects (adaptive reuse for the notable family mansion of *Dar Lasram* into ASM headquarters and recovering the Hafsia quarter's devastated urban fabric) and new legislative decrees and institutional actors (e.g. AMVP). For Tunis, the report suggested measures for both so-called 'passive safeguarding' (e.g. legislation, classification and inventory) and 'active safeguarding' (adaptive reuse of historic buildings and valorisation through tourism). A *Plan de Sauvegarde et Mise en Valeur* (PSMV)[24] was designed as a key conservation planning tool for the medina but it was never approved.

In the end, the foreseen agency for economic exploitation of heritage (AMVP) was instituted in 1988, while the suggested PSMV was included in the *Code du Patrimoine* in 1994 as a required planning tool for urban conservation but, after some updating at the time, it is still pending. Back then, international recognition provided heritage administrators[25] and practitioners with credible arguments to stop demolitions and it initiated a political debate about the value(s) of urban conservation that still echoes in Tunis today, thanks to the lobbying of professionals trained over the years at the ASM (Chabbi 2011). The project diagnostic is still considered by Tunisian professionals 'an accurate photography of the medina at the time',[26] and the 1968 to 1975 survey has remained foundational, becoming 'a monument in itself' in the words of ASM director Akrout-Yaiche:

that is to say the force of the ASM began with that database and thanks to it the association has become an irreplaceable partner for all institutions; thus, if the Ministry of Tourism wants to carry out a project in the medina, it cannot do it without recurring to the services of the ASM!

(Akrout-Yaiche interview 2012)

Arguably, while overall implementation of the *Projet Tunis-Carthage* failed in the short term for political reasons, it succeeded in the long term and the knowledge capital produced by the project allowed the ASM to remain central in envisioning and carrying out urban conservation activities in Tunis that resonated also internationally. For example, the pilot projects of Dar Lasram (UNESCO funding) and Hafsia quarter (State and World Bank funding) gained recognition as best-practices for actively intervening in the medina (Unit for Housing and Urbanization, Graduate School of Design, Harvard University and ASM 1999; Bigio and Licciardi 2010), whilst respecting the traditional morphology and, indeed, it repeatedly won the Aga Khan Award for Architecture (Cantacuzino 1985; Davidson and Serageldin 1995).

Tunisia Cultural Heritage Project (2002–12): cultural heritage conservation for tourism development

In the late 1990s, the World Bank, thus far an unlikely lender in the rehabilitation of historic cities, produced 'Cultural heritage and development. A framework for action in the Middle East and North Africa' (Cernea 2001) as a strategic paper to position itself in the culture and sustainable development arena and boost its credentials in linking cultural heritage conservation and economic development (Nardella and Mallinson 2014). The document generated a new line of projects, such as the Tunisia Cultural Heritage Project (TCHP), whilst supporting pilot schemes that framed 'culture' as a 'sector' for national economic growth by making heritage conservation a means to tourism development. Based on the Bank's commissioned study of the late 1990s assessing the Tunisian heritage sector (physical assets, human resources and legal framework), the TCHP was the first loan of its kind taken by Tunisia.

The official Project Development Objective (PDO) was quite ambitious, aiming 'to ensure the sustainable management of the country's cultural heritage with a view to developing cultural tourism' (The World Bank 2012: iii) and proposed actions to reform *both* institutions *and* management practices while delivering physical improvements at key heritage sites (e.g. Bardo national museum) within just five years. We will consider the Policy Development and Capacity Building component in particular. It aspired

> to assist the Government authorities responsible for cultural heritage in strengthening (i) implementation of the country's policies governing the management of cultural heritage assets and (ii) the operating capacity of AMVPPC and INP, the two key agencies in charge of the sector, including the preparation of recruitment and training programs.
>
> (The World Bank 2012: 3)

To control project implementation the Bank established the *Unité de Gestion du Projet* (UGP)[27] as an ad-hoc counterpart. While being formally attached to the AMVPPC, as the main implementing agency, the UGP, in effect, acted autonomously under the auspices of the Ministry of Culture (MoC) and it was endowed with a small team of experts operating to bypass red tape and institutional conflicts.

The capacity-building component was based on the MoC's commitment to limit the respective responsibilities of the National Heritage Institute (INP) and the Agency for the Valorisation of Heritage and its Cultural Promotion (AMVPPC), which disputed respective competences. De facto conflicts were never resolved. The INP – as the main beneficiary of the training – proved resistant to transforming its original *scientific* mandate into proactive site management and tourism valorisation, and to conceding part of its powers to the AMVPPC. By 2005; the lender had to recognise its mistake. As the UGP technical director described it: 'because the INP didn't seem to be really interested we have diminished the budget of the institutional strengthening component and channelled those funds on the sites management component' (Denis Lesage, interview 2012; see also The World Bank 2012: 4). The shift was quite significant: the initial budget of US$ 2.15 million was lowered to US$ 0.7 million with a consequent massive reduction of specialised training.

The Bank's reflection on TCHP results are written in its *Implementation Completion and Results Report*, which valued the PDO results as 'moderately unsatisfactory', stating that '[w]hile the project contributed significantly to improving the prospects for the development of culture based tourism, the lack of institutional change, . . . was essential to reaping the benefits from the project' (The World Bank 2012: 16). Over ten years, the TCHP produced many studies and some physical works but demonstrated 'major shortcomings in achieving the institutional objective' (The World Bank 2012: 17). The Tunisian government was blamed for its 'unwillingness' to undertake essential reforms and for hesitation in 'implementing the proposed coordination between AMVPPC and INP' (The World Bank 2012: 19) but, at the same time, reviewers admitted that the PDO 'institutional objective . . . was somewhat unrealistic in the containing bureaucratic environment at that time' (The World Bank 2012: 35). The report also praised the UGP for being 'highly skillful in implementing the project with efficiency under extremely difficult circumstances and in bringing it to a successful completion' (The World Bank 2012: 20), while lamenting the lack of ownership and commitment demonstrated by both the Agency and Institute (AMVPPC and INP).

Reflecting on capacity building we would like to counteract the bureaucratic narrative with comments from the Project Management Unit (UGP) Technical Director on the project hand-over and knowledge transfer:

> capitalisation of experience, alas, there is none! . . . for example our team as executing agency [UGP] has been appointed to the Heritage Agency [AMVPPC], which is positive . . . but not all the team was allocated, the specialist of promotion and communication has left, our procurement specialist preparing and supervising contracts – who had become a 'top' expert with ten years of experience – has gone somewhere else . . . that is to say that the team – the specialists of procurement, communication, and myself as interface between the technical and managerial aspects – each of us is going its own

way, but the strength resided in the teamwork rather than in individual capacities! Unfortunately it's a history repeating itself.

(Lesage, interview 2012)

Lesage added:

anyhow, it will not be possible to have a real improvement until coordination of activities between the INP and the Agency [AMVPPC] will happen in a way that has not happened yet . . . when the INP will understand that its mission is no longer a purely scientific one.

(Lesage, interview 2012)

Based on these reflections, we argue that failure in TCHP 'implementation' is significantly due to an over-optimistic project design that overestimated achievable results given both the authoritarian regime in charge and existing, long-lived, institutional conflicts. In addition, by considering heritage conservation only as a means to tourism development and thus charging the AMVPPC as main implementing agency, the Bank touched the susceptibility of INP, as the technical conservation body, which, in turn, rejected the proposed training and failed the TCHP capacity-building component.

Euromed Heritage Programme (1995–2013): dialogue and knowledge transfer

For nearly two decades, the Euromed Heritage Programme was the main European Union cultural diplomacy tool in promoting 'dialogue between cultures and exchanges at [the] human, scientific and technological level'[28] framing its neighbouring states as 'Mediterranean Partner Countries'. It was part of a larger diplomatic strategy, known as the Barcelona Process, aiming to achieve partners' 'common objectives of pursuing political, social and economic reforms towards regional stability and prosperity' (Pace 2005: 67). Cultural heritage conservation projects were funded over four programme cycles to bring together experts from the different shores. Tunisian institutions participated in several projects inventorying traditional architecture, digitally mapping heritage assets, training conservation architects and conserving colonial architecture. In particular, Euromed Heritage 4 (2008–13)[29] included assistance for legislative reforms as the key programme feature for 'strengthening the Mediterranean cultural heritage institutional and legislative frameworks' (EH4 website),[30] whilst a legal expert with a strong normative understanding of urban heritage conservation joined the programme Regional Management Support Unit (RMSU).

During the closing EH4 conference in Fes (2013), many practitioners voiced appreciation of the opportunity for exchanging experiences among Mediterranean colleagues, but also dissent from the underlying Eurocentric normative discourse on heritage. The point emphatically expressed during the debate by Jellal Abdelkafi (invited by the RSMU as senior expert) is that within international cooperation, as we have today within Euromed Heritage, we would like to see something beyond wishes expressed by the European Union on mutual understanding, dialogue, etcetera . . . we agree with all of it, but how to get there? We would like to hear from the EU something else than *normativité* [regulations].

(Abdelkafi 2013)

Our interviews with local actors reiterated this argument and offered themes such as *hope* and *despair* as an alternative to positivistic faith in regulation. Typically, such headings are not used in bureaucratic reports submitted to international donors and they deserve further attention to understand how actors make sense of their practice and how they perceive or interpret failure in 'implementation'. For instance, the RMSU manager expressed hope as the only guarantee that monitoring tools would be used after project completion: 'you just *pray* and *hope* that someone enlightened will use inventories properly'; or that training would actually modify behaviour in practice: 'you just do it and *hope* that it will change!' (Dabdoub-Nasser interview 2012). A beneficiary heritage administrator also rationalised through *hope* his ongoing engagement despite institutional fallacies: 'nevertheless I do not lose hope and continue making a personal investment [*m'investir*] in heritage protection!' (Dabdoub-Nasser interview 2012).

The counterpart to an optimistic faith is the perception of heritage conservation and development narratives as cynical and hypocritical tools of cultural diplomacy, often advantaging the donor rather than the recipient. During interviews, different actors questioned the real benefits for Southern partners of 'knowledge exchange', as Euromed brands its projects, arguing these unidirectional knowledge transfers (North to South) protract dependency on Eurocentric knowledge rather than promoting the partners' autonomy:

Europe has reached the development it has reached through knowledge, through research . . . if they really want the South to develop, they really have to allow the South to build a strong sound research-based knowledge . . . unless they want us, the South, to be always dependent on them, on the West . . . and always dance to the tune of the West . . . I'm cynical, but that is true if you really want development.

(interviewee 2012)

Likewise, interviewees also claim that development money is spent and circulates in the name and for the image return of IOs' image and cultural diplomacy rhetoric, while, benefits in Tunisia are limited to individual experts without permanent gains for the heritage governance:

lots of money has been spent and we continue to do I'm not sure what . . . because things didn't get better . . . for the Mediterranean Partner Countries, as they [EU] like to call them, but are there any real benefits for these countries and their institutions?!

Finally, another recurrent critique was the scarcity, and limited shelf-life, of project results when compared with initial investments:

> a lot of money has been dilapidated in travel expenses, hotels, etcetera, and then they say we're going to do this project and afterwards it is up to the State party to continue with its own means . . . but when European funding is terminated and the project completed we even forget that it existed! Even if in the beginning the State promised to institutionalise results and make them sustainable, to ensure continuity.
>
> (interviewee 2012)

Common threads

To conclude this section, we reflect on themes that run through the three projects and interrogate commonalities in the implementation of *training* and *capacity building*.

As illustrated by challenges in legislative reforms faced in the 1970s (PTC) and in the 1990s (*Code du Patrimoine*), the application of the law remains a political affair outside the powers of technical advisors. However, the PTC *Sauvegarde et Mise en Valeur de la médina de Tunis* introduced, for the first time, urban conservation knowledge tools that have been subsequently used to train generations on the Association for the safeguarding of the medina of Tunis (ASM) architect-urbanists. Over the years, these professionals moved on to create an expert-network across institutions and influence Tunisian heritage discourses. As Lesage stated in reflecting on his three decades of practice across the ASM (1980s), INP (1990s), and TCHP (2000s), 'the only experience of knowledge capitalisation which has lasted in time is the ASM Tunis!' (interview 2012).

We have further learned from Euromed Heritage and the TCHP results that if training is not paired with permanent hiring of specialised personnel, 'knowledge exchange' and 'capacity building' remain beneficial for individuals but do not build the knowledge capital of heritage institutions: both training efforts and funding are dissipated. The training of urban conservation architects is an example of this point. A professional figure almost absent in the National Heritage Institute (INP) until 1995 (with only three staff at the national level), urban conservation architects largely benefited in the late 1990s from the so-called *Cours de Tunis* internationally sponsored by UNESCO, ICCROM (under a Euromed Heritage project), the French Ministry of Culture and the Getty Foundation. However, as a senior INP staff member indicated:

> we have trained conservation architects and even the institution in charge of heritage administration [INP] has not found the means to hire its own graduates, the very people who have received a specialised training, and in their place hired instead young people who had just finished the school of architecture.

, further lamenting:

> as you can see there is no coherence between [capacity building] programmes,
> commitment and actual implementation.
>
> (Khanoussi, interview 2012)

The failed TCHP attempt to resume training for urban conservation architects in
the 2000s further illustrates that institutional change at the INP is a long-term
political process and not merely a technical one. According to a key practitioner
(active both at INP and the TCHP on this matter):

> as INAA was transformed into INP we added directives of enhancement, of
> museum care and museographic development, of economic valorisation of
> heritage in addition to scholarly research . . . it seemed back then that they –
> the archaeologists and historians animating INAA - didn't understood this
> change, so we added different personnel and I was in charge of a course to
> train conservation architects [*cours de Tunis*] . . . we hired some but, after the
> revolution, I am not sure of what is happening . . . there seems to be a will
> from historians and archaeologists to take back control of INP and go back to
> a scholarly (scientific) mission, which is in the opposite direction of ideas
> behind the transformation of the Institute.
>
> (Lesage, interview 2012)

In conclusion, international organisations (IOs) could learn from the case of
INP reform and reflect on practical implications of the policy category 'institutional strengthening' beyond technocratic formulations. This means recognising
the political nature of an ongoing negotiation process between actors: on the one
side, those enacting knowledge practices inherited by INAA (and the colonial
service) and, on the other, those proposing to move beyond scholarly research and
accept the role of heritage management and economic valorisation as a way to
engage with the international urban conservation and development paradigm,
being mindful of its funding agenda.

Conclusions: learning from Tunis

Our story reveals a self-referential *international* normative order that downplays
local political processes made of ideologies, politicians' personalities, long-standing
institutional conflicts, pressures for raising the inhabitants' quality of life and so
forth. We argue these processes actually underpin any rule of law and make its
implementation, or reform, possible and, by acting in a realm of abstraction, IOs
ignore crucial factors determining 'implementation'.

Therefore, what do IOs mean by 'legislative reform' and 'institutional strengthening'? As a start, the design of projects barely acknowledges the agonistic nature of
politics and of authoritarian regimes at play. Such intricacies are never confronted

as essential factors for the implementation of reform, otherwise funding might never be assigned in the first place. Further, the dissonance (Graham *et al.* 2000) underpinning how heritage is understood by different parties – institutions, inhabitants, experts, decision-makers, etc. – is not made explicit: normative universal conceptualisations are taken for shared beliefs. In this regard, we have seen the genealogy of heritage law implanted in Tunisia by French colonisers who aimed to substitute the Islamic jurisprudence that had structured the life of cities like Tunis, both in their physical manifestations (city form) and social life, for centuries. The effects of its substitution with a modern, Eurocentric understanding of law are still present (Nardella 2013).

And how do actors themselves reflect on reasons for *failure* in implementation? Interviews highlighted that scarcity of specialised human resources does not simply translate as lack of (international) knowledge. Instead, it crucially relates to budget shortages for permanently hiring personnel formed by international projects and relates to scarce institutional appropriation of project results once international funding terminates. Further, we learned there is no capitalisation of knowledge if highly qualified teams are dispersed and political nominees are the only ones to remain in place. Governance failure is then too crude a justification for standstill in policy implementation.

So, how can we understand what seems a standstill in urban conservation and development policy implementation other than as government failure? Learning from Tunis, IOs should be mindful that good theory without application remains sterile, that urban conservation is a matter of *political* conflict rather than of policy 'implementation', and legislative action comes long after experience in practice (universal following rather than preceding the particular).

First, as demonstrated by the PTC narrative, law reforms follow – do not precede – studies and projects. In Tunis, technical knowledge of urban conservation was tested in practice and gained international recognition through projects over a long time, thus allowing a network of national experts to exert a growing influence on decision-makers about values and benefits derived from protecting the ancient core of Tunis, al-medina (المدينة). Further, the storyline of the *Code du Patrimoine* illustrated how a legislative reform is *un-implementable* in practice without the political will to proceed from simply listing conservation principles to making them applicable. Second, legislative action results from long-term lobbying and the presence of architect-urbanists spreading from the ASM across other institutions mandated to conserve the medina (INP, ARRU and Ministry of Culture) and the private sector has been a crucial factor in achieving reforms (Lewis 2012). As discussed by other narratives of heritage conservation (Cidre 2010: 228), key personalities at crucial points in time lead the evolution of the conservation planning system and processes and help shape the transformation of the important institutions and changes in policy approaches. Third, without political will, legislation is a mere manifesto of intention formally responding to the expert-consensus and IO pressures. The vicissitudes of the PSMV illustrate this: foreseen in the 1970s by UNESCO-ASM, sanctioned by law in the 1994

Code du Patrimoine, commenced in the 1990s by a INP-ASM convention, it was never completed. Waiting for a PSMV that never comes, the ASM substituted, in practice, the missing jurisprudence by adapting a less conflicted planning instrument – the *Reglement d'Urbanisme pour la médina de Tunis*[31] (1980, 1987) – to guide a process of conservation and controlled change, at the same time managing to comply with UNESCO's changing requirements for the World Heritage Site medina of Tunis (listed in 1979). However, as systematically reiterated by interviewees,

> the biggest damages to the built cultural heritage are caused by the State itself . . . with its grandiose projects of infrastructures, of economic valorisation, etcetera . . . the State does not respect the same laws it has promulgated or it does not endow the administrative units in charge of enforcing the law with appropriate means.

As our account showed, while an abstract understanding of universal law might serve IOs' spending justifications in support of ideal objectives (Green 2007), actors in Tunis have seen through the looking glass of international aid (Apthorpe 2011) and demanded a different level of knowledge exchange as voiced in the Euromed Heritage debate about the future of a Mediterranean urban conservation and development agenda:

> we are within a political context that I believe has to be considered, because without this we are simply part of an international normative system, which I find respectable, but I insist on the fact that this normative system is not self-sufficient.
>
> (Abdelkafi, 2013)

In conclusion, we strongly believe that the implementation of international policy of urban conservation cannot dispense with questioning the historical and epistemological premises (genealogy) of its application and IOs should be mindful that policy categories, such as 'legislative reform' and 'institutional strengthening', do not translate in Tunis, or elsewhere, on a blank canvas.

Notes

1 Mission for Tunisia, financed by the *Division Sciences et Lettres* and the *Commission des Voyages et des Missions Scientifiques et Littèraires*.
2 Author translation. Note: all quotes are the author's translations of other scholars' work and interviews.
3 Empreinte et Communication, Dirasset, Group Huit (1999). *Projet de gestion et de valorisation du patrimoine culturel. Etude de stratégie et de faisabilité.*
4 Law could claim to be universal, and thus non-arbitrary, only by appearing as the expression of civilisation (Mitchell 2002: 56).
5 Commission for Tunisia.

6 The museum still exists today, as a national museum with a large archaeological collection, and its redevelopment in the 2000s was a primary objective of the World Bank (as a Tunisia Cultural Heritage Project).

7 Service for Antiquities, Fine Arts and Historic Mmonuments.

8 National Institute for Art and Archaeology.

9 Hasib ben Hammar, who had family ties with Bourguiba, was raised in the medina. He was concerned with its dilapidation and had his own post-independence vision of what a modern(ist) Tunis should look like.

10 Association for the Safeguarding of the medina of Tunis.

11 ASM Urbanism Studio.

12 Daouletli, in addition to an academic interest in the built heritage and political pull (Vice-President 1980–90), also had connections with international conservation institutions, notably the ICOMOS (McGuinness 1997: 43).

13 ARRU, Agency for Urban Renovation and Rehabilitation, is a public enterprise of an industrial and commercial nature set up through law No. 81–69 of August 1981. It is responsible for implementing the State's policy in urban renovation and rehabilitation under the authority of the Ministry of *Équipement, l'habitat et l'aménagement du territoire* on behalf of the State and public collectivities and mainly the communes. ARRU's intervention takes place within a contractual framework with the local public collectivities responsible for the project.

(official website)

14 National Agency for the Valorisation and Exploitation of the Archaeological and Historic Heritage.

15 National Heritage Institute.

16 Agency for the Valorisation of Heritage and its Cultural Promotion.

17 *Code du patrimoine archéologique, historique et traditionnel* (Law n° 94–35 of 24/2/1994).

18 *Code d'aménagement du territoire et de l'urbanisme* (Law n° 94–122 of 28/11/1994): includes the statute of the ASM Tunis (chapter 1).

19 Conservation architects were put together with archaeologists.

20 Safeguarding and Valorisation of the medina of Tunis, ASM, INAA, UNESCO and PNUD (February 1974). *Rapport de synthèse*, including portfolios of architectural (medina and rabads) and socio-economic surveys.

21 United Nations Development Programme.

22 Project for the Protection and Safeguarding of the Monumental Heritage of the medina of Tunis and Cartage for Economic Development.

23 Urbanism Studio at the Association for the Safeguarding of the medina.

24 Safeguarding and Valorisation Plan.

25 Such as the Tunis mayor (Ben Hammar) and State Secretary for Cultural Affairs (Klibi).

26 The metaphor of the photograph (and radiography) was mentioned on several occasions during Nardella's fieldwork to denote precision in the scientific imaging of the city.

27 Project Management Unit.

28 Barcelona Declaration, 1995, adopted at the Euro-Mediterranean Conference held on 27–8 November 1995. Available at: http://www.eeas.europa.eu/euromed/docs/bd_en.pdf (accessed 24 June 2015).

29 Euromed Heritage 4 represents a further milestone in the process of recognising 'culture' as a catalyst for mutual understanding between the people of the Mediterranean region. Today embedded in the European Neighbourhood Policy (ENP) and with a budget of 17 million euros, Euromed Heritage 4 intends to facilitate the appropriation by people of their own national and regional cultural legacy through easier access to education and knowledge on cultural heritage (Euromed Heritage 4 website).

30 'In response to requests from partner countries, the RMSU establishes specific actions for updating the laws and services to reflect the evolution of the concept of heritage' (Euromed Heritage 4 website).

31 Urbanism Code for the medina of Tunis.

References

Abdelkafi, J. (1989). *La médina de Tunis: Espace Historique*. Paris: Presses du CNRS

Abdelkafi, J. (2012). Evolving medinas. In: M. Balbo (ed.), *The medina: The Restoration and Conservation of Historic Islamic Cities*. London and New York: I. B. Tauris, pp. 55–96.

Abdelkafi, J. (2013). *Euromed Heritage 4 Final Conference, Fes, January*. Available at: http://www.euromedheritage.net/intern.cfm?menuID=16&submenuID=22&sub submenuID=34 (accessed 13 March 2013).

Abdelkafi, J. and Zaki, L. (2011). Une carrière d'urbaniste en Tunisie. In: L. Zaki (ed.), *L'Action Urbaine au Maghreb: Enjeux Professionnels et Politiques*. Paris and Tunis: Éditions Karthala and IRMC, pp. 49–76.

Apthorpe, R. (2011). Coda: with Alice in Aidland: a seriously satirical allegory. In: D. Mosse (ed.), *Adventures in Aidland. The Anthropology of Professionals in International Development*. New York and Oxford: Berghahn Books, pp. 199–220.

ASM, INAA, UNESCO and PNUD (1974). *Sauvegarde et mise en valeur de la médina de Tunis. Rapport de synthèse*. Tunis.

Association Sauvegarde de la médina de Tunis (1994). La médina de Tunis. L'intégration de l'heritage. In: S. Akrout-Yaïche, Z. Mouhli, F. Béjaoui and J. McGuinness, J. (eds), *Actes du Colloque de Tunis, Juin 1992*. Tunis: ASM de Tunis.

Bacha, M. (2006). La création des institutions patrimoniales de Tunisie: œuvre des savants de l'Académie des inscriptions et des belles-lettres et des fonctionnaires du Ministère de l'instruction publique et des beaux-arts. *Livraisons d'histoire de l'architecture*, 12(2), 123–34.

Bacha, M. (2008). La construction patrimoniale tunisienne à travers la législation et le journal officiel, 1881–2003: de la complexité des rapports entre le politique et le scientifique. *L'Année du Maghreb*, (IV), 99–122.

Bigio, A.G. and Licciardi, G. (2010). *The Urban Rehabilitation of medinas. The World Bank Experience in the Middle East and North Africa*. Washington, D.C.: The World Bank.

Cantacuzino, S. (ed.) (1985). *Architecture in Continuity*. New York: Aperture.

Cernea, M.M. (2001). *Cultural Heritage and Development. A Framework for Action in the Middle East and North Africa*. Orientations and Development Series. Washington, D.C.: The World Bank.

Chabbi, M. (2011). Role et fonctions des urbanistes dans la fabrication des villes du Sud: le cas de Tunis (1960–2009). In: L. Zaki (ed.), *L'Action Urbaine au Maghreb: Enjeux Professionnels et Politiques*. Paris and Tunis: Editions Karthala and IRMC, pp. 32–47.

Cidre, E. (2010). Planning for Public Realm Conservation: The Case of Portugal's World Heritage Cities. PhD thesis. London: University of London.

Davidson, C. and Serageldin, I. (eds) (1995). *Architecture Beyond Architecture*. London: Academy Editions.

De Cesari, C. (2010). World Heritage and mosaic universalism: a view from Palestine. *Journal of Social Archaeology*, 10(3), 299–324.

Escher, A. and Schepers, M. (2008). Revitalizing the medina of Tunis as a national symbol. *Erdkunde*, 62(2), 129–41.

Graham, B., Ashworth, G.J. and Tunbridge, J.E. (2000). *A Geography of Heritage: Power, Culture and Economy*. London: Hodder Arnold.

Green, M. (2007). Delivering discourse: some ethnographic reflections on the practice of policy making in international development. *Critical Policy Studies*, 1(2), 139–53.

Hakim, B.S. (2008). *Arabic-Islamic Cities: Building and Planning Principles*, 3rd edn. London: EmergentCity Press.

Labadi, S. (2013). *UNESCO, Cultural Heritage, and Outstanding Universal Value: Value-based Analyses of the World Heritage and Intangible Cultural Heritage Conventions*. Plymouth: AltaMira Press.

Larguèche, A. (2008). L'histoire à l'épreuve du patrimoine. *L'Année du Maghreb*, IV, 191–200.

Lewis, D. (2009). International development and the 'perpetual present': Anthropological approaches to the re-historicization of policy. *European Journal of Development Research*, 21(1), 32–46.

Lewis, D. (2012). Across the little divide? Life histories of public and third sector 'boundary crossers'. *Journal of Organizational Ethnography*, 1, 158–77.

Lewis D. and Mosse, D. (2006). Encountering order and disjuncture: contemporary anthropological perspectives on the organization of development. *Oxford Development Studies*, 34(1), 1–13.

Matri, F. (2008). *Tunis sous le Protectorat: Histoire de la Conservation du Patrimoine Architectural et Urbain de la médina*. Tunis: Centre de Publication Universitaire.

McGuinness, J. (1997). Political context and professional ideologies: French urban conservation planning transferred to the Médina of Tunis. *The Journal of North African Studies*, 2(2), 34–56.

Mitchell, T. (2002). *Rule of Experts: Egypt, Techno-Politics, Modernity*. Oakland: University of California Press.

Mouhli, Z., Béjaoui, F. and Gazzah, A. (2013). *Tunis Patrimoine Vivant. Conservation et Créativité Association Sauvegarde de la Médina (1980–2012)*. Tunis: ASM de Tunis.

Nardella, B.M. (2013). Orienting the knowledge of international urban conservation in the light of the Arab revolutions. Cities to be tamed? Standards and alternatives in the transformation of the urban South. Conference proceedings, Milan 15–17 November 2012. *Planum. The Journal of Urbanism*, 26(1).

Nardella, B.M. and Mallinson, M. (2014). 'Only foreigners can do it?' Technical assistance, advocacy and brokerage at Aksum, Ethiopia. In: P. Basu and W. Modest (eds), *Museums, Heritage and International Development*. London: Routledge.

Pace, M. (2005). EMP cultural initiatives: what political relevance? In: H.A. Fernandez and R. Youngs (eds), *The Euro-Mediterranean Partnership: Assessing the First Decade*, pp. 59–70. Madrid: Elcano Royal Institute of International and Strategic Studies.

Pace, M. (2007). *The Politics of Regional Identity: Meddling with the Mediterranean*. London: Routledge.

Rabinow, P. (1989). *French Modern: Norms and Forms of the Social Environment*. Cambridge, MA: MIT Press

Riles, A. (1995). The view from the international plane: perspective and scale in the architecture of colonial international law. *Law and Critique*, 6(1), 39–54.

Sabri, R. (2015). Transitions in the Ottoman Waqf 's traditional building upkeep and maintenance system in Cyprus during the British colonial era (1878–1960) and the emergence of selective architectural conservation practices. *International Journal of Heritage Studies*, 21(5), 512–27.

Saidi, H. (2008). When the past poses beside the present: aestheticising politics and nationalising modernity in a postcolonial time. *Journal of Tourism and Cultural Change*, 6(2), pp. 101–19.

Smith, L. (2006). *The Uses of Heritage*. London: Routledge.

Titchen, S.M. (1996). On the construction of outstanding universal value: some comments on the implementation of the 1972 UNESCO World Heritage Convention. *Conservation and Management of Archaeological Sites*, 1(4), 235–42.

Turtinen, J. (2000). *Globalising Heritage: On UNESCO and the Transnational Construction of a World Heritage*. Stockholm: Stockholm Centre for Organizational Research.

UNESCO (1996). *Our Creative Diversity. Report of the World Commission on Culture and Development: Summary Version*. Paris: UNESCO.

UNESCO (2009). *Gestion et Conservation du Patrimoine Culturel Immobilier dans les Pays du Maghreb. La Tunisie*. Rabat: UNESCO.

Unit for Housing and Urbanization, Graduate School of Design, Harvard University and Association Sauvegarde de la medina de Tunis (1999). *Case Study: Tunis, Tunisia – Rehabilitation of the Hafsia Quarter. Culture in Sustainable Development*. Washington, D.C.: The World Bank.

The World Bank (1994). *Third Urban Development Project. Project Completion Report*. Washington, D.C.: The World Bank.

The World Bank (2012). *Tunisia Cultural Heritage Project. Implementation Completion and Results Report*. Washington, D.C.: The World Bank.

Chapter 5

Challenges for implementing UNESCO's Historic Urban Landscape Recommendation in Canada

Stacey R. Jessiman

Two recent events in Canada that garnered significant media attention signal potential challenges for the implementation of UNESCO's Recommendation on the Historic Urban Landscape ('HUL Recommendation') in territories that are the subject of ongoing disputes over Aboriginal title. The first is a six-month continuous outdoor protest in 2012 by the Musqueam First Nation over the proposed construction of a condominium complex on top of their ancient midden in metropolitan Vancouver and the subsequent cancellation by the British Columbia (BC) provincial government of the private landowner's construction permits. The second is the June 2014 Supreme Court of Canada decision in *Tsilhqot'in Nation v. British Columbia* (2014 SCC 4, hereafter '*Tsilhqot'in*'), in which the court not only elucidated in accessible language the law on Aboriginal title in Canada but also confirmed the Tsilhqot'in Nation's right to over 1,750 km^2 of its traditional territory.

The aim of this chapter is to examine whether and how the HUL Recommendation, as presently worded, is situated to address sustainable development of historic urban sites in Canada, particularly in areas where unresolved land claims and other impacts of colonialism are still felt deeply in Aboriginal communities. As part of this analysis, this chapter asks certain important questions. First, does the HUL Recommendation as currently worded demonstrate adequate sensitivity to colonial harms such that it would encourage Aboriginal stakeholders in Canada to facilitate implementation of the HUL Recommendation in contested territories? Specifically, does it adequately address the problem of ongoing grievances of Indigenous peoples relating to land title and urban planning and development? Does it support the decades of work by UN Member States in developing and adopting the United Nations Declaration on the Rights of Indigenous Peoples ('UNDRIP')? Moreover, in view of the fact that the HUL Recommendation does not use the terms 'Indigenous' or 'Aboriginal' even once, does it adequately recognise Indigenous peoples' contributions and rights to historic urban landscapes and their conservation? Is it important that the HUL Recommendation specifically refers to Indigenous peoples within its text, and if so, what is it that differentiates Indigenous peoples from other peoples included in the generic references to 'local communities' and 'stakeholders'?

The Marpole Midden controversy

On 31 May 2012, traffic on the Arthur Laing Bridge – the bridge linking Vancouver International Airport in Richmond, BC, and downtown Vancouver – was blocked by a large demonstration of Musqueam First Nation peoples in full regalia protesting at the proposed construction by a private developer of a condominium complex on top of cəsna:əm, a sizeable ancient Musqueam village and burial site located beside the bridge (the 'Marpole Midden') (CBC News 2012). The site was first subject to digging in the 1880s, when road construction at the north arm of the Fraser River uncovered an extensive shell midden containing ancestral remains and cultural objects including bone and stone tools and carved objects (Roy 2006: 68). Local archaeologists removed the ancestral remains and gave them to the Natural History Museum of New Westminster (where they were destroyed in a fire 14 years later) (Musqueam Indian Band 2011). In the late 1890s, Harlan I. Smith of the American Museum of Natural History in New York City removed numerous human skeletal remains and cultural objects from the site to the museum's collections (Roy 2006: 69, 2010: 53). In the 1920s and 1930s, further extensive excavations by Charles Hill-Tout revealed over 700 human skeletal remains, which were removed to what is now the Museum of Vancouver. Some were discarded in the rubbish because of lack of space at the museum (Musqueam Indian Band 2011). That museum currently holds about 4,500 objects from the midden (Vancouver Sun 2007). Skeletal remains were also sent to the Royal College of Surgeons in London, England, where they were later destroyed in the WWII Blitz, and to other museums in North America (Musqueam Indian Band 2011).

In 1933, the Marpole Midden was declared a Canadian National Historic Site by the Historical Sites and Monuments Board of Canada. A cairn placed in a nearby park stated it was 'the site of one of the largest prehistoric middens on the Pacific Coast of Canada. It originally covered an area of about 4½ acres, with an average depth of 5 feet and a maximum depth of 15 feet' (Musqueam Indian Band 2011). The midden was therefore recognised to be significant evidence of Musqueam presence and culture over thousands of years.

In early 2011, the Musqueam Indian Band learned about plans to construct a 108-unit residential condominium complex on the land without consultation with the Band. The Band met with the provincial archaeology branch in an effort to prevent issuance of permits under the BC Heritage Conservation Act for investigation and alteration of the site (Musqueam Indian Band 2011). In December 2011, permits were issued despite the Band's protests. In early 2012, preliminary construction on the site unearthed an intact burial of an adult ancestor. In an effort to stave off any further digging or construction, Musqueam people protested at the site, resulting in a month-long suspension of digging. After digging recommenced, two infant burials were discovered, which the developer indicated he intended to remove (Musqueam Indian Band 2011). The Musqueam attempted to negotiate a land swap with the private developers of the proposed condominium complex, Gary and Fran Hackett, who claimed 50 years' title to the land. By protesting on the Arthur Liang Bridge in May of that year, the Musqueam were trying to force the provincial government to prevent further digging and give its formal agreement to the swap. To increase public awareness of their distress over the proposed desecration of their ancestral burial grounds, they also demonstrated in front of a nearby public cemetery, pretending to be a construction company that was going to build on top of the gravestones (Zeschky 2012).

On 10 August 2012, the one-hundredth day of the Musqueam First Nation's vigil was marked in front of the Marpole Midden. By that point, their efforts had resulted in considerable public support for their position, including from many unions and popular Vancouver Mayor Gregor Robertson, who rode his bicycle to the midden site to drum with the Musqueam (Luk 2012).

The public discord created by the Musqueam peoples' protests may have gone unnoticed by visitors to the province, who arrive at the Vancouver airport and pass through an impressive display of Aboriginal art in a setting of tranquil nature sounds seemingly intended to lull visitors into believing in harmonious cultural diversity in the province. But ultimately, no doubt due in part to considerable media attention, the protests did not go unnoticed by the British Columbia government. On 28 September 2012, the BC government decided to block the condominium development by allowing the permits that it had previously issued to expire, and ordering Mr and Mrs Hackett to return the land to its original condition (Clark 2012). The decision received enormous media attention and it provoked considerable concern among private landowners in British Columbia about the implications of the decision for their own property development plans (The Province 2012; Zeschky 2012).

Similar controversies erupted in BC in 2014 – over the building of a luxury home on a sacred burial site on Grace Islet and over proposed construction of a farm equipment dealership in Abbotsford. In the former case, the BC government purchased the land for $5.45 million and tore down the partially built home. In the latter case, the city of Abbotsford refused to issue construction permits because the property contains a mass grave site of the Sumas First Nation. Developer John Glazema, who bought the property at an auction in 2011 but failed to carry out archaeological assessments, commented: 'I feel betrayed because there shouldn't be these types of encumbrances against private properties without having it highlighted on land title' (McCue 2014).

Thinking critically about what happened at a historic urban landscape in metropolitan Vancouver in 2012, and subsequent events, should lead one to be concerned about potential complications in implementing the HUL Recommendation in BC. Indeed, the long, very public protest by the Musqueam peoples, and the government's subsequent well-publicised ruling, serve as reminders that a good part of British Columbia, including the entire Vancouver metropolitan area, is land which was never formally ceded to the British Crown or the succeeding Canadian government through negotiated treaty. In certain other parts of Canada, the federal government took pains to respect the provisions of the British Crown's Royal Proclamation of 1763 by entering into 11 numbered treaties between the 1870s and

1920s. Most of British Columbia, however, and other parts of Canada, including the land on which the federal parliament buildings stand, are subject to outstanding land claims by Aboriginal peoples.

In order to lay the groundwork for my analysis of whether and how the HUL Recommendation, as presently worded, is situated to address sustainable development of historic urban sites in complicated Aboriginal title situations, I first provide a brief history of the Aboriginal title issue in Canada, and then analyse its meaning for implementation of the HUL Recommendation.

Aboriginal title and the 'game changing' *Tsilhqot'in* Supreme Court of Canada decision

In 1763, at the end of the Seven Years War, King George III of Britain signed a Royal Proclamation declaring that it was in the Crown's interest that the various 'Indian Nations' 'should not be molested or disturbed in the Possession of such Parts of Our Dominions and Territories as, *not having been ceded to or purchased by Us, are reserved to them*, or any of them, as their Hunting Grounds'.[1] At the same time, the British Crown gave itself a monopoly on all future purchases of unceded land and decreed that all such purchases would form part of a formal negotiation at 'a public Meeting or Assembly of the said Indians' and would be recorded in writing. The Royal Proclamation formed the basis for future treaty negotiations between the British Crown and Aboriginal peoples in Canada and for modern-day land claims covering unceded territories in Canada.

In the 150 years that followed the Royal Proclamation, as increasing numbers of missionaries and European settlers arrived on the North American continent, certain Aboriginal nations entered into numbered treaties with the Crown as a means of securing for themselves at least part of their traditional territories and concessions and payments that would allow them and their cultures to survive. However, in much of British Columbia, treaties were not negotiated between the government and Aboriginal nations. The sole exceptions are the portion of Treaty 8 covering the northeast of the province, and the 'Douglas Treaties' negotiated between 1850 and 1854, which cover only 358 square miles of land on Vancouver Island. Otherwise, the colonial government in British Columbia, even after it joined confederation in 1871, behaved as if the land was *terra nullius*, confining First Nations to small reserves, declaring that it owned all of the natural resources of British Columbia and that First Nations had no right to any of the decision-making about those resources, nor any right to any revenues arising out of those resources.

The government's appropriation of Aboriginal peoples' unceded traditional lands has been a significant source of unrest in British Columbia and other parts of Canada, as have its harmful assimilation policies, most notoriously the Indian Residential School system, which operated for over a century across Canada and has been described by British Columbia Supreme Court Justice Douglas Hogarth as 'nothing more than institutionalized pedophilia' (Fournier and Crey 1997: 72).

Such harms are an integral part of the Marpole Midden protest as well as the Idle No More Indigenous rights movement, which saw Aboriginal and non-Aboriginal peoples nationwide and internationally protesting against the Canadian government's violations of constitutionally protected Aboriginal rights and title (McKibben 2013).

The existence and nature of Aboriginal title in Canada has been the subject of numerous Supreme Court of Canada decisions beginning in the 1970s and culminating most recently in the *Tsilhqot'in* decision in June 2014. Before discussing the meaning of that decision for the HUL Recommendation, however, I will briefly discuss how land claims issues have been dealt with by the provincial and federal governments, in order to provide context for my argument as to the complexities of implementing the HUL Recommendation in Canada.

In response to land claims litigation in the 1970s, the federal government developed a comprehensive claims process for dealing with Aboriginal claims to land not covered by historical treaties – a process aimed at extinguishing Aboriginal title in exchange for rights and benefits outlined in the settlement (McMillan and Yellowhorn 2004: 326). The BC government, however, did not initially cooperate with the federal government's land claims process (Tennant 1990; Foster 2002). During the 1980s and 1990s, a number of British Columbia First Nations set up roadblocks in attempts to force the government to recognise their right to jurisdiction over their territories. The protests, which reached their height in the summer of 1990, disrupted daily operations within the natural resource sector and discouraged businesses from investing in BC (Blomley 1996).

Meanwhile, by the late-1980s, many BC First Nations had filed land claims in the courts with respect to their traditional territories. In 1993, the provincial government created the BC Treaty Process in 1993 in order to reach agreements with First Nations over title to unceded land.

The BC Treaty Process has been controversial, however, and not overly successful (Canadian Press 2014). Approximately 60 First Nations have participated in the process, but only a handful of claims have resulted in treaties (BC Treaty Commission 2014). About 40 per cent of First Nations in BC are not involved in the treaty process at all. Many First Nations groups have refused to participate based on their belief that the process will be held to extinguish Aboriginal title in favour of government and big business interests and allow development of lands at the expense of Aboriginal peoples, territories and cultures.

The four treaties that have been ratified through the BC Treaty Process since the programme's inception are with the Maa-Nulth First Nation in 2006, the Tsawwassen First Nation in 2009, the Yale First Nation in 2013, and the Tla'amin First Nation in 2014. In several cases, ignored overlapping land claims are a source of ongoing controversy. For example, the Tsawwassen treaty more than doubles the size of the Tsawwassen reserve by 400 hectares and reserves a portion of the Fraser River salmon catch to the Tsawwassen. Four First Nations from the nearby cities of Victoria and White Rock allege that their rights were abrogated by the BC Treaty Process. An 1852 Douglas Treaty had granted those four First

Nations land and harvesting rights in Boundary Bay and Pender, Mayne and Saturna Islands – areas now included in the Tsawwassen treaty.

Many First Nations have opted to pursue their title and rights grievances in the courts rather than through a treaty process. Indeed, the question of Aboriginal title to unceded lands has been repeatedly litigated in the Supreme Court of Canada since the 1970s. The *Tsilhqot'in* decision in June 2014 is, however, considered a 'game changer' by many. In confirming the *Tsilhqot'in* Nation's title to a 1,750 km^2 region of its traditional territory, the court sent a clear message to the public that Aboriginal title is not a theoretical concept, but instead has important, concrete implications. As barrister Christopher Devlin summarised: 'the Supreme Court of Canada's decision overturns the Court of Appeal's narrow view of Aboriginal title being limited to instances of intensive, site-specific occupation and restores the trial judge's view that Aboriginal title exists on a territorial basis' (Devlin 2014). According to the court, Aboriginal title involves 'the right to use and manage land, enjoy it, occupy it, possess it, and profit from its economic development' (Devlin 2014; see also *Tsilhqot'in*, paras 70, 73, 75). Moreover, the court ruled that the Crown can only encroach on such lands in specific circumstances and only if it has met its duty to consult and accommodate (*Tsilhqot'in*: para 78) and if such encroachment is justified and consistent with the Crown's fiduciary duty (*Tsilhqot'in*: paras 77, 90) 'such that the future generations of the Aboriginal groups are not substantially deprived of the benefits of the land' (*Tsilhqot'in*: para 86).

University of Saskatchewan professors Ken Coates and Dwight Newman write of the *Tsilhqot'in* decision:

> There is no question that the Supreme Court judgment has altered the relationship between First Nations and provincial, territorial and federal governments . . . The decision will not have much impact on areas such as the Prairie West, Ontario and large parts of the North, where aboriginal communities have surrendered their lands through historic or modern treaties. In unceded areas, including most of British Columbia and other significant parts of the country, however, the ruling carries considerable weight. Recognizing aboriginal title, a major legal achievement for the Tsilhqot'in, conveys real and substantial authority over specific lands.
>
> (Coates and Newman 2014)

The *Tsilhqot'in* decision is also noteworthy because of its recognition that the *Tsilhqot'in* Nation hold title to almost 40 per cent of the traditional territory cited in its original land claim. Under the BC Treaty Process, in contrast, negotiating Nations have had as little as 5 per cent of their claimed land recognised by the government during the negotiations.

One other BC land claims-related agreement worth mentioning, in view of its importance to understanding the challenges involved in implementing the HUL Recommendation on non-treatied lands in Canada, is the 2000 Nisga'a Final

Agreement, a comprehensive agreement outside the BC Treaty Process between the Nisga'a Nation and the federal and provincial governments covering a variety of Aboriginal rights, including land and return of cultural heritage. That agreement took almost 27 years to accomplish.

Analysing the HUL Recommendation

What do the Marpole Midden and *Tsilhqot'in* decisions mean for implementing the HUL Recommendation in Canada? First, the international community should be on notice that there remains legal uncertainty about who rightfully holds title to considerable tracts of land in BC, including most of the urban centres, and in certain other parts of Canada not covered by treaty. Until the question of title to those tracts of land has been resolved through a treaty process (which considering the settlement track record seems unlikely to happen any time soon) or by the courts, whether and how best to implement the HUL Recommendation raises some important questions. Even before the *Tsilhqot'in* decision, the BC provincial government clearly demonstrated in the Marpole Midden dispute that it had serious concerns about the rights of private landholders to make development decisions that negatively impact Aboriginal rights and title.

In view of these factors, the important question becomes, 'is the HUL Recommendation, as currently worded, sensitive enough to outstanding Aboriginal title issues that it would encourage Aboriginal stakeholders to facilitate implementation of the Recommendation in British Columbia?'

Unfortunately, the very first sentence of the HUL Recommendation seems problematic from a 'decision-maker alienation' standpoint. It says: 'Considering that historic urban areas are among the most abundant and diverse manifestations of our common cultural heritage . . .' The Marpole Midden protest by the Musqueam was not about protecting a heritage that is common to all Canadians. For the Musqueam, the protest was about protecting their ancestors, who had inhabited the Fraser River region for thousands of years prior to the arrival of White settlers, and about asserting not only Aboriginal title to land that had been taken from them without their consent, but also their personal and individual right to determine the nature and meaning of their own heritage. The ruling by the provincial government seems to have confirmed their interpretation of the heritage value of that site.

Another problem for implementing the HUL Recommendation in Canada is that the final paragraphs of the Preamble ask Member States to 'adopt the appropriate legislative institutional framework and measures, with a view to applying the principles and norms set out in this Recommendation in the territories under their jurisdiction'. That paragraph is an example of the inadequate recognition in the HUL Recommendation of ongoing conflict within the political landscape of Member States with colonial histories with respect to land title and urban planning and development. Indeed, such implementing legislation would be complicated to achieve in BC and other territories subject to land claims. First Nations across the country have made it clear through numerous public Idle No More protests that they object to the federal government passing legislation that has an impact on their traditional territories. Meanwhile, Canada – as the Member State of UNESCO – may not have an interest in highlighting its internal political unrest to the rest of the Member States. Indeed, Prime Minister Harper declared at the G20 Pittsburgh Summit in 2009, a year after his public apology to survivors of the Indian Residential School system, that 'there are very few countries that can say for nearly 150 years they've had the same political system without any social breakdown, political upheaval or invasion. We are unique in that regard. We also have no history of colonialism' (Henderson and Wakeham, 2009: 1).

Despite the fact that the international community recognised, in negotiating and adopting the UNDRIP, colonial forces' violations of Indigenous peoples' rights with respect to their traditional territories, the HUL Recommendation does not adequately take into consideration that Indigenous peoples may not accept the authority of Member States' federal and provincial/state governments to take decisions over their lands. For example, the sixth paragraph of the Preamble says that 'emphasis needs to be put on the integration of historic urban area conservation, management and planning strategies into local development processes and urban planning', but it does not simultaneously recognise that such local development processes and urban planning depend on clarity about who the decision-makers are or consensus among the stakeholders when such clarity does not exist.

Moreover, as previously noted, considering Indigenous peoples' contributions to the creation and development of historic urban landscapes, it is striking that the HUL Recommendation does not mention the words 'Indigenous' or 'Aboriginal' *once* in the text. Paragraph 6 of the Introduction to the Recommendation summarises the stakeholders as 'local, national, regional, international, public and private actors'. Similarly, the Tools section of the HUL Recommendation simply refers to a 'cross-section of stakeholders'. This is disappointing when one takes into consideration the long-term efforts of the United Nations to achieve recognition of Indigenous peoples and their particular rights with respect to their traditional territories and cultural heritage, as enshrined in Articles 25 to 29 and 32 of UNDRIP, and the international community's indication of its support for that document.

For example, Article 26 of UNDRIP specifically recognises that 'Indigenous peoples have the right to own, use, develop and control the lands, territories and resources that they possess by reason of traditional ownership or other traditional ownership or use'. Article 25 confirms their right 'to maintain and strengthen their distinctive spiritual relationship with their traditionally owned or otherwise occupied and used lands, territories, waters and coastal seas and other resources and to uphold their responsibilities to future generations in this regard'. Then, Article 29 emphasises that they have rights to 'conservation and protection of the environment and the productive capacity of their lands or territories and resources'. Perhaps, most importantly for my analysis, Article 32 emphasises their 'right to determine and develop priorities and strategies for the development or use of their lands or territories and other resources'. And, in the Preamble to that document, the Member States confirm they are

> convinced that control by indigenous peoples over developments affecting them and their lands, territories and resources will enable them to maintain and strengthen their institutions, cultures and traditions, and to promote their development in accordance with their aspirations and needs.

One hundred and forty-four UN Member States voted to adopt that document in 2007. Canada, however, was one of four settler colonial nations (along with Australia, New Zealand and the United States) that voted against its adoption. Eventually, under pressure from the Assembly of First Nations to resign its membership on the United Nations Human Rights Council, Canada officially endorsed UNDRIP in November 2010. The Conservative government's Statement of Support making Canada's endorsement official clarifies, however, that the government sees UNDRIP as a 'non-legally binding document that does not reflect customary international law nor change Canadian laws' and that

> at the time of the vote during the United Nations General Assembly, and since, Canada placed on record its concerns with various provisions of the Declaration, including *provisions dealing with lands, territories and resources*; free, prior and informed consent when used as a veto; self-government without recognition of the importance of negotiations; intellectual property; military issues; and the need to achieve an appropriate balance between the rights and obligations of Indigenous peoples, States and third parties. These concerns are well known and remain.[2]

> (Emphasis added)

It went on to insist that Canada would 'interpret the principles expressed in the Declaration in a manner that is consistent with our Constitution and legal framework'. In reality, however, the way the federal government has interpreted the principles expressed in UNDRIP is at odds with Section 35(1) of Canada's Constitution Act, 1982, which provides that 'the existing aboriginal and treaty rights of the aboriginal peoples of Canada are hereby recognized and affirmed',[3] and with a series of Supreme Court cases culminating with the *Tsilhqot'in* decision that also confirmed the existence of Aboriginal rights and title.

One example is Canada's behaviour within the process of the HUL Recommendation's development. In 2011, Canada's Ambassador to UNESCO, André Bachand, submitted comments to Francesco Bandarin, then Director of UNESCO's World Heritage Centre, on the draft Recommendation. His first comment, relating to footnote 1 of the Draft Recommendation, recommended removing the reference to the 2003 UNESCO *Convention for the Safeguarding of Intangible Cultural Heritage* from the list of UNESCO standard-setting documents on the conservation of historic areas, because, Canada said, it 'cannot be considered a tool for managing historic areas' (Bachand 2011). From the standpoint of the goals of the HUL Recommendation, his allegation makes little sense. Indeed, paragraph 9 of the HUL Recommendation defines Historic Urban Landscape as including '*social and cultural practices and values*, economic processes and the *intangible dimensions of heritage as related to diversity and identity*' (emphasis added). Clearly then, the HUL Recommendation recognises the importance of intangible heritage to historic urban landscapes.

Moreover, in their recent book, *The Historic Urban Landscape*, Bandarin and van Oers (2012: xvii) state that the objective of the Historic Urban Landscape approach is 'to ensure urban conservation models that respect the values, traditions and environments of different cultural contexts'. They go on to say that the 2003 UNESCO Convention 'facilitates the recognition of the role of multiple layers of identity and other associated intangible aspects in cultural landscapes and historic urban landscapes. . .' (Bandarin and van Oers 2012: 50).

In addition, the proposition that historic urban landscapes incorporate intangible elements is also supported in ICOMOS' 2008 *Quebec Declaration on the Spirit of the Place*, which recognised that intangible elements, such as memories, narratives, written documents, festivals, commemorations, rituals, traditional knowledge, etc., all contribute to making a place and giving it spirit and that intangible cultural heritage must be taken into account in all conservation projects for landscapes. Indeed, Aboriginal communities have survived for thousands of years in what we now know as Canada – including on the land where cities such as Vancouver were constructed – through the oral transmission of rights and knowledge about history, culture and traditions. Since time immemorial, intangible cultural heritage has been an *essential* part of managing the historic urban landscape in Canada.

One questions therefore why Ambassador Bachand would advocate the removal of the reference to a convention whose very purpose is to safeguard intangible heritage, on the basis it would not be a very useful 'tool for managing historic areas'. Was the point of doing so exclude Aboriginal people from key decision-making processes relating to their traditional territories?

I note that there is, however, some scope in the HUL Recommendation for engaging with Aboriginal stakeholders in Canada over proper implementation of the Recommendation. The last paragraph of the Preamble advises Member States to bring the Recommendation to the attention of 'institutions, services or *bodies* and associations concerned with the safeguarding, conservation and management of historic urban areas and their wider geographical setting' (emphasis added). This could be interpreted as encouraging Member States to recognise that Aboriginal peoples have valid and vested interests in conservation of the land they have occupied since time immemorial. Nevertheless, the HUL Recommendation could profit from being more explicit that those bodies include Aboriginal communities. In a post-UNDRIP, post-*Tsilhqot'in* era, such an action seems both a moral and political imperative.

Indeed, especially in parts of Canada not covered by treaty, Indigenous peoples' long-term presence on, and careful stewardship of, lands that are now considered historic urban landscapes, and UNDRIP's recognition of the need to redress harmful colonial takings of those lands without consent, are two good reasons why the HUL Recommendation should include a specific reference to Indigenous peoples when it states in Article 13 that 'the historic urban landscape approach learns from the traditions and perceptions of local communities, while respecting the values of the national and international communities'. Not doing so is an abrogation of Indigenous peoples' rights enshrined in UNDRIP to control and sustainably develop their traditional territories. It also could very well alienate the people who, as the Marpole Midden controversy and the *Tsilhqot'in* decision make clear, may be key decision-makers in the sustainable development of historic urban landscapes in Canada.

Conclusion

As Armin Grunwald (2011: 19) points out, conflict forms a natural part of any discussion on sustainable development. The HUL Recommendation cannot be expected to be an exception to that rule. However, the Marpole Midden protest and ruling and the *Tsilhqot'in* decision highlight a more fundamental problem for implementing the HUL Recommendation in areas of Canada with unresolved land claims than simply figuring out optimal methods of managing conflict.

The real possibility of controversy over who holds title to historic urban sites on suh lands and the consequent lack of clarity as to who holds decision-making power with respect to those sites, renders any negotiation and decision-making processes over sustainable development of those sites highly challenging.

This lack of clarity complicates the formation of a 'balanced and sustainable relationship', which the HUL Recommendation recognises as the foundation for its historic urban landscape approach. Moreover, the Recommendation does not yet incorporate enough key language and elements showing respect for Indigenous peoples that would bring those important stakeholders to the table. In failing to refer specifically to Indigenous peoples within its text, the HUL Recommendation subtly, yet seriously, undermines recent UN efforts such as UNDRIP aimed at recognising and redressing harms done to Indigenous peoples. It fails to uphold Indigenous peoples' rights to control and sustainably develop their traditional territories, as enshrined in UNDRIP. Indeed, as currently worded, the HUL Recommendation could alienate rather than convene people who, as the Marpole Midden controversy and *Tsilhqot'in* decision make clear, may be key to implementing the HUL Recommendation in Canada.

Notes

1   The Royal Proclamation of 7 October 1763. Available at: http://www.bloorstreet.com/200block/rp1763.htm (accessed 24 June 2015).
2   Available at: http://www.aadnc-aandc.gc.ca/eng/1309374239861/1309374546142 (accessed 14 July 2013).
3   Constitution Act 1982, Schedule B, Part II.

References

Bachand, A. (2011). Ambassador of the Permanent Delegation of Canada to UNESCO, letter to Francesco Bandarin, Director of UNESCO's World Heritage Centre, 21 January 2011, regarding 'Canada's response to the consultation on the Draft Recommendation on the Historic Urban Landscape'.

Bandarin, F. and van Oers, R. (2012). *The Historic Urban Landscape: Managing Heritage in an Urban Century*. Chichester: Wiley-Blackwell.

BC Treaty Commission (2014). Tla'amin becomes eighth First Nation to reach a modern treaty in the BC Treaty negotiations process. Available at: http://www.bctreaty.net/documents/NewsReleaseJune202014Tlaaminfinalagreement_000.pdf (accessed 20 November 2014).

Blomley, N. (1996). 'SHUT THE PROVINCE DOWN': First Nations blockades in British Columbia, 1984–1995. *BC Studies*, 3.

The Canadian Press (2014). First Nations alliance launches court challenge of BC Treaty process. Available at: http://www.cbc.ca/news/aboriginal/first-nations-alliance-launches-court-challenge-of-b-c-treaty-process-1.2734282 (accessed 30 October 2014).

CBC News (2012). Musqueam wins fight over Marpole Midden. Available at http://www.cbc.ca/news/canada/british-columbia/musqueam-wins-fight-over-marpole-midden-1.1191445 (accessed 24 October 2014).

Clark, B. (2012). Final decision made on Marpole Midden permits. Ministry of Forests, Lands and National Resource Operations. Available at: http://www.newsroom.gov.bc.ca/2012/09/final-decision-made-on-marpole-midden-permits.html (accessed 24 October 2014).

Coates, K. and Newman, D. (2014). Tsilhqot'in ruling brings Canada to the table. Available at: http://www.theglobeandmail.com/globe-debate/tsilhqotin-brings-canada-to-the-table/article20521526/ (accessed 30 October 2014).

Devlin, C. (2014). Case Brief – *Tsilhqot'in Nation v. British Columbia*, 2014 SCC 44. Devlin Gailus Westaway Law Corporation, unpublished.

Foster, H. (2002). Litigation and the BC Treaty Process. Notes for speech at BC Treaty Process Conference 'Speaking Truth to Power III: Self Government: Options and Opportunities', 14–15 March 2002. Available at: http://www.bctreaty.net/files/pdf_documents/hamar_foster_speech.pdf (accessed 1 November 2014).

Fournier, S. and Crey, E. (1997). *Stolen from our Embrace: The Abduction of First Nations Children and the Restoration of Aboriginal Communities*. Vancouver: Douglas and McIntyre.

Grunwald, A. (2011). Conflict-resolution in the context of sustainable development. In: O. Parodi, I. Ayestaran and G. Banse (eds), *Sustainable Development Relationships to Culture, Knowledge and Ethics*. Karlsruhe: KIT Scientific Publishing.

Henderson, J. and Wakeham, P. (2009). Colonial reckoning, national reconciliation? Aboriginal peoples and the culture of redress in Canada. *English Studies in Canada*, 35, 1–26.

Luk, V. (2012). Musqueam plan protest at Marpole Midden to mark 100 days vigil at ancient Vancouver site. Available at: http://www.vancouversun.com/news/Musqueam+plan+protest+Marpole+Midden+mark+days+vigil+ancient+Vancouver+site/7067805/story.html (accessed 1 November 2014).

McCue, D. (2014). Aboriginal gravesites halt $40M development plan in Abbotsford. Available at: http://www.cbc.ca/news/aboriginal/aboriginal-gravesites-halt-40m-development-plan-in-abbotsford-1.2852924 (accessed 3 November 2014).

McKibben, B. (2013). Idle No More rises to defend ancestral lands – and the planet. Available at: http://www.yesmagazine.org/people-power/idle-no-more-rises-to-defend-ancestral-lands-and-fight-climate-change-bill-mckibben (accessed 3 November 2014).

McMillan, A. and Yellowhorn E. (2004). *First Peoples in Canada*. Vancouver: Douglas and McIntyre.

Musqueam Indian Band (2011). *c̓əsnaʔəm*. Available at: http://www.musqueam.bc.ca/c%CC%93%C9%99sna%CA%94%C9%99m (accessed 24 June 2015).

The Province (2012). BC government cancels Marpole development protested by Musqueam band. Published 29 September 2012, not available online.

Roy, S. (2006). Who were these mysterious people? c̓əsna:m, the Marpole Midden, and the dispossession of Aboriginal lands in British Columbia', *BC Studies*, 152.

Roy, S. (2010). *These Mysterious People: Shaping History and Archaeology in a Northwest Coast Community*. Montreal and Kingston: McGill-Queen's University Press.

Tennant, P. (1990). *Aboriginal Peoples and Politics: The Indian Land Question in British Columbia, 1849–1989*. Vancouver: UBC Press.

The Vancouver Sun (2007). Treasure beneath our feet. Available at: http://www.canada.com/vancouversun/news/westcoastnews/story.html?id=95c25371-1314-4c14-84d2-9d8a7f7162ec (accessed 24 October 2014).

Zeschky, J. (2012). Marpole developer says cancellation will cost 'millions'. Available at: http://www2.canada.com/theprovince/news/story.html?id=de07c71c-5e67-4a49-9b46-7330fa309c38 (accessed 30 October 2014).

Chapter 6

Using the Historic Urban Landscape to re-imagine Ballarat

The local context

Kristal Buckley, Steven Cooke and Susan Fayad

Urban environments and their complex economic, social, cultural and physical settings have proved to be a challenging context for heritage work and for ideas of sustainability. These environments must be dynamic to prosper and they are intensive locations for flows of people, ideas, capital, physical resources and environmental services (Castells 1989; Evans 2002; Logan 2002; Dovey 2005). Cities and regional settlements are engaged in local, regional and international competitive relationships that favour a myriad of orientations and characteristics, including local definitions of cultural heritage.

Globally, the major debates and advances in developing and applying social and political processes of cultural heritage conservation find their greatest challenges and innovations in cities and towns. More than a quarter of the World Heritage List is composed of areas, precincts or significant parts of cities; and many of the most contested heritage cases concern the limits of acceptable change in the fabric of these places. Advocates of design professions, such as architecture, urban design and planning, often position 'heritage' as an obstacle to the betterment of their cities, blocking the creativity and dynamism that characterise attractive, socially nurturing and economically powerful cities and towns.

As the seminal work of Delores Hayden (1995) argued, urban renewal can cause significant dislocation for local communities as familiar landmarks and landscapes undergo change. Communities can struggle to find the right mix in safeguarding the tangible expressions of their identity and history alongside the need to advance the well-being of residents, citizens and visitors. The Historic Urban Landscape (HUL) approach has been developed as a way of rethinking the relationship between heritage and development and managing change in sustainable ways. Adopted by UNESCO's General Conference in 2011 following several years of exploration of the ideas in different geo-cultural contexts, the *Recommendation on the Historic Urban Landscape* sets out a broad agenda for re-thinking approaches to urban heritage conservation.

Work on the HUL was a response to escalating tensions, particularly in visible and politically charged World Heritage contexts that polarised processes of heritage conservation and development. While the potential heritage significance of larger areas and urban systems was easily recognised, and some landscape concepts had been borrowed from cultural geography by heritage discourses in the 1980s, heritage conservation tools are not especially effective in addressing processes of change in urban settlements. As Bandarin (2012: 220) argues, a 'review of the main international conservation tools shows the fragility of a conceptual and policy guidance system that has to deal with an evolving [urban] heritage'. Conventional heritage approaches, essentially 'Eurocentric' in their underlying philosophical bases and oriented to the authentic fabric of individual monuments and sites selected for their static historical and aesthetic values, were failing to effectively address the pressures evident in the late twentieth century onwards. Rapid processes of change arising from globalisation, technological advances in materials and infrastructure, population and demographic changes and socio-economic inequalities have produced a vast casebook of urban conservation 'crises'.

The HUL Recommendation (UNESCO 2011) specifically attempts to address these challenges by providing a platform for managing change in complex local urban environments. Importantly, it is a new approach for UNESCO, building upon past recommendations and conventions, but without intending to be prescriptive. The HUL has been designed to be an enabler of practices that are holistic, strategic and integrated. It consists of a set of high-level principles in the form of a framework and it is reliant on all levels of government, public and private stakeholders, international organisations and NGOs to adapt locally and develop innovative approaches in order to deliver the proposed outcomes. It applies a cultural landscape lens, broadening the definition of urban heritage and the scope of management approaches and processes.

The HUL framework (UNESCO 2011) consists of four tools and a six-point action plan. Recommended tools to be developed include civic engagement tools, knowledge and planning tools, regulatory systems and financial tools using collaborative and participatory approaches that can be responsive to dynamic local settings. The six-point action plan outlines a framework for implementing HUL (see Figure 6.1).

UNESCO's World Heritage Centre had supported the development of the HUL through its World Heritage Cities programme and it began to disseminate the HUL, supported by academic institutions and others such as ICOMOS, the Organization of World Heritage Cities, League of Historic Cities and the Getty Conservation Institute. An existing UNESCO Category 2 Centre in the field of World Heritage, the World Heritage Institute of Training and Research for Asia and the Pacific (WHITR-AP) began to promote the application of the HUL in an exploratory pilot programme of experience sharing that will be reported to UNESCO's Executive Board and General Conference. This pilot is exploring various ways of implementing the HUL in a number of cities around the world. Each pilot city exhibits different dominant forms of cultural heritage, has distinct challenges, varying levels of existing conservation approaches and different key stakeholders (WHITR-AP 2014; City of Ballarat 2013a).

Much of the development versus conservation debate facing historic cities is played out at the local government level, with a focus on the management of

- Undertaking comprehensive surveys and mapping of the city's natural, cultural and community resources.
- Reaching a reasonable degree of consensus, through the use of participatory planning and stakeholder consultations, regarding what cultural heritage values to protect for inspiration and enjoyment of present generations as well as transmission to future ones, and determining the attributes that carry these values.
- Assessing the vulnerability of these attributes to socio-economic pressures and impacts of climate change.
- Integrating urban heritage values and their vulnerability status into a wider framework of city development, which shall provide indications of areas of heritage sensitivity that require careful attention to planning, design and implementation of development projects.
- Prioritising policies and actions for conservation and development.
- Establishing the appropriate partnerships and local management frameworks for each of the identified projects for conservation and development, as well as to develop mechanisms for the coordination of the various activities between different actors, public, private and civic.

Figure 6.1 The Six-Point Action Plan adopted by UNESCO with the 'Recommendation on the Historic Urban Landscape'.

Source: UNESCO (2011). See also http://www.historicurbanlandscape.com/index.php?classid=5354& id=22&t=show (accessed 7 July 2015).

cultural heritage, particularly through the mechanisms of land-use planning and development approvals. At the same time, new theoretical and methodological questions are being asked in the academic literature on the relationship between theory and practice for cultural landscapes, broadening the concept to include the role of emotion in our understanding of the connections between people and place. Given the perceived disconnection between academics and practitioners in some recent work on heritage (Smith 2006) and illustrated by the Association of Critical Heritage Studies Manifesto (Witcomb and Buckley 2013), a particular challenge is to develop the mechanisms to incorporate these new ways of understanding the relationship between heritage, places and community in the management of urban change. How can the HUL, with its flexible, holistic approach to heritage conservation, be a potential mechanism through which new theoretical insights can be brought into heritage practice? While much of the scholarly and applied literature has focused on the globalisation of cultural heritage practice, particularly the promulgation of Western (or 'Eurocentric') ideas and inter- and intra-regional sharing of urban heritage tool kits, we focus in this chapter on the centrality and agency of local government. The local level, especially in the planning, development and community services functions of municipal and city governments, is where these tensions are most acutely experienced and addressed. As a result, local government officials and politicians, as well as community-based activists, are seeking to identify alternative models for considering change.

We explore the experiences of one local council, the City of Ballarat in central Victoria, Australia, in its efforts to consider, embrace and use the HUL and take

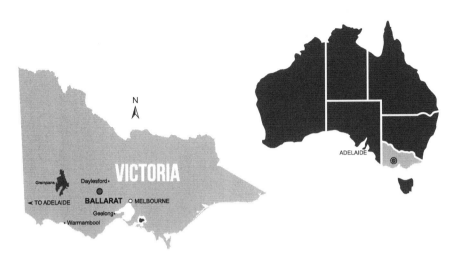

Figure 6.2 The location of Ballarat in the southern Australian State of Victoria.
Source: City of Ballarat.

part in WHITR-AP's pilot programme (see Figure 6.2). Through this example, we examine the interplay between heritage theory and practice in the implementation of the HUL, charting how the local council has attempted to deal with the 'intricacies' of the city (Amin and Thrift 2002: 1) in its strategic planning using an intuitive form of action research. We contend that the perspective of local government is a specific space for innovation and that local institutions and governance are critical to advancing new concepts and approaches to urban heritage conservation. Without the direct engagement and 'take-up' by local government, it is doubtful that this particular product of international heritage doctrine can meet the kinds of 'paradigm-shifting' aspirations that UNESCO has set for it.

While in its early stages of implementation, the HUL process in Ballarat has created opportunities for the city planners and communities to explore more community-centred and values-based approaches to the management of change. We conclude by offering our observations on the challenges encountered in using the HUL and the questions it poses for future work in this area, including the interface with current heritage legislation and planning frameworks that are inescapable realities for those working within local government.

The HUL approach in an Australian context

Bandarin and van Oers (2012: 23) chart a number of trajectories in understanding the historic urban landscape in an attempt to recover from the 'fracture of modernism'. Key elements include the shift from sites to landscapes, and the idea of the landscape as a 'palimpsest' where the '[l]ayering of significance makes it possible to identify the conservation policies and trade-offs between conservation and development facing communities and decision-makers' (Bandarin and van Oers 2012: 69). Building on the Vienna Memorandum (UNESCO 2005), this approach 'stresses the link between physical forms and social evolution, defining historic cities as a system integrating natural and man-made [*sic*] elements, in an historical continuum, representing a layering of expressions throughout history' (Bandarin and van Oers 2012: 72).

Advocates of the HUL argue for a more flexible and integrated approach to urban conservation that recognises change and provides relevant and effective tools. Nevertheless, this view of the urban landscape as part of a continuum is open to critique as part of a modernist discourse of linear development (DeSilvey 2012). However, the HUL does provide a framework to think about the ways in which a number of key theoretical developments in heritage studies can be brought into contemporary heritage practice.

One advantage of the HUL approach is the shift from a focus on specific sites to seeing how heritage is expressed and represented across larger areas, an approach that has also been developed within cultural geography (Atkinson 2007, 2008). This is particularly important in relation to 'ordinary' or everyday landscapes that would not necessarily meet the thresholds of significance in heritage schemes, but are nonetheless important locations through which a sense of place and local identity is made and re-made (Tuan 1977), an approach implicit in the broad definition of cultural heritage contained in the Faro Convention on the Value of Cultural Heritage for Society (Council of Europe 2005). Within heritage practice, this has also been explored through the development of the European Landscape Convention, whereas Peter Howard argues, it is these 'ordinary' landscapes that are most in need of protecting (Howard 2012).

Despite the critique of the cultural determinism in the work of Carl Sauer (Mathewson 2000; Wylie 2007), much of the thinking about cultural heritage landscapes remains focused on the material and the visual, with less attention given to the way that representations of landscapes are an important component in how they are understood. The idea of landscape as a set of representations has in turn been challenged by approaches which stress that the landscape is 'more than representational' (Lorimer 2005): 'an acknowledgment that our understandings of the world are lived, embodied and tangled up with how we *do* things, our doings and our enactments in the moment' (Waterton 2011: 66). This approach draws attention to the need to think about multi-sensuous landscapes. This is not either/or, rather an '*and*', where representational and non-representational approaches are examined. As Wattchow (2011: 87) argues, we need to explore the inter-relationships between the 'material nature we inhabit and the ideal nature we carry in our heads'. Rather than another 'type' or 'category' of cultural landscape, the HUL is a way of applying a cultural landscape *approach* to managing urban environments and their broader settings. Such an approach foregrounds the way in which 'historical landscape character is a function of perception and understanding' as well as interaction (Bandarin and van Oers 2012: 66).

The development of the HUL approach has begun to stimulate a refreshed dialogue about urban conservation, oriented around what it might mean to think and treat cities as landscapes. However, global progress in direct implementation of the HUL has been gradual and relatively modest (hence the usefulness of the HUL pilot programme). In Australia, it is our perception that there was not much engagement with the HUL initially. The text of the HUL Recommendation does not have an inspirational tone, and many of its 'new' ideas, such as the need to recognise social values and contemporary meanings and to employ community-centred methods of assessment and decision-making, seemed to be 'business-as-usual' due to the widespread use and evolution of the Australia ICOMOS Burra Charter (Australia ICOMOS 2013a).[1] Although there are a number of Australian sites and landscapes on the World Heritage List, none of them are focused on urban themes[2] and government agencies and practitioners are just beginning to engage in the development of the HUL.

Despite its status as a continent nation with a relatively modest population size and density, Australia's population is highly concentrated in urban settlements that include a mix of capital cities in coastal locations and rural/regional cities across a vast span of ecosystems and climatic zones. Established as a nation via a federation of States in 1901, the Australian Constitution allocates most powers relevant to urban planning, land use and development to the States, rather than to the national (or Commonwealth) sphere. Local governments are established through State legislation, although the steady process of decentralisation in decision-making over recent decades has resulted in a substantial suite of responsibilities being carried in practice by Australia's 562 local government councils (ALGA 2010).

Although there are national and State government laws directed at the identification and protection of Australia's most significant heritage places, the largest share of heritage places in Australia is identified through local government planning mechanisms that operationalise heritage concerns through the lens of land use and development controls (Productivity Commission 2006). In practice, this means that decisions about change are made on a site-by-site basis and heritage is positioned as a problem to be solved, rather than an economic and social resource and a key component of individual and collective identities. Heritage values often enter approvals processes at relatively late stages, after much human, financial and social capital has already been invested in specific proposals. Heritage 'battles' are then posed as anti-change and are either won or lost as local councils attempt to 'balance' competing values. It is within this context that the City of Ballarat has used the HUL to reframe debates about conservation, change and the city's future strategic directions.

Finding the HUL in Ballarat

Located within the country of the Wadawurrung and Dja Dja Wurrung Traditional Owners (Indigenous communities), the City of Ballarat, in Victoria's Central Highlands region, is the State's third largest urban area and one of several significant gold-rush era boomtowns. The natural landscape of Ballarat began developing

500 million years ago and it was through a series of massive changes caused by tectonic forces, erosion, volcanic activity, climate change and subsequent water flows that Ballarat's alluvial and deep lead gold deposits were formed.

Beginning over 30,000 years ago, two Aboriginal language groups, the Dja Dja Wurrung to the north and the Wadawurrung to the south, inhabited and developed a deep connection to the land (country), which has great sacred and symbolic significance to both past and current Aboriginal peoples. It was the gold rush in particular that signalled the beginning of Ballarat's current urban form. Beginning in 1851, Ballarat's extensive gold resources resulted in a population explosion and an unprecedented era of rapid growth and development. The importance of Ballarat as a major generator of wealth for the then Colony of Victoria is evidenced today by its grand public spaces, urban form, features and cultural traditions that hark back to this earlier period. Noted for the city's conserved nineteenth-century urban fabric, Ballarat is a major regional tourism destination, selling itself through this heritage of 'elegant architecture, broad tree-lined streetscapes and cultivated gardens' (City of Ballarat 2014c) (see Figure 6.3). With a population of over 98,000 people (State of Victoria 2014) and an area covering some 740 square kilometres, Ballarat's major employment has moved from mining to health care and social assistance, retail and manufacturing. As an industry sector, tourism is considered to be Ballarat's sixth largest employer (City of Ballarat 2014b).

For a regional city that has built its image and economy at least in part on the character and importance of its nineteenth-century post-contact settlement history, there have been many positive outcomes of heritage planning in Ballarat. Heritage protection has been in place and changed incrementally since the 1970s through the mechanisms available in the planning system, resulting in strong planning controls covering large urban areas, many individual buildings and other struc-tures, street trees and archaeological sites that illustrate the tangible expressions of Ballarat's history. Today, there are over 10,000 places in protected historic areas, creating a substantial workload for Council officers and advisors who process

Figure 6.3 Two images of Ballarat's urban landscape: Lydiard Street verandas, part of the nineteenth-century historic fabric of the city (left); Lake Wendouree parklands (right).

Source: City of Ballarat.

applications for permission to enable changes to these places and the government officials who may be required to endorse or reject planning decisions.[3]

However, like many local government authorities, the City of Ballarat faces ongoing challenges of balancing conservation with change and to build community consensus on what change should occur. 'Conventional' heritage planning practices have not been accompanied by an application of the concept of cultural heritage in its broadest sense, including the intangible dimensions. Heritage planning decisions are often made through adversarial processes that require all parties to become familiar with the intricacies of the planning schemes and to adopt defensive positions, enhancing the expectations of conflict for Council and many communities.

With population growth projections of up to 50 per cent over the next 15 to 25 years (City of Ballarat 2014a), Ballarat is amongst Australia's fastest-growing regional cities. As a result, pressures on the existing urban form (including the historic city centre) and significant social and demographic changes are anticipated. The challenges for future urban heritage conservation can only increase in intensity and complexity. The City of Ballarat began investigating ways to manage change in Ballarat more proactively and it has opted to adopt the language, concepts and directions established by the HUL to guide the city's strategic planning processes.

The ability to reflect on the initial stages of implementation of a HUL process in Ballarat provides an opportunity to chart the ways in which heritage has been understood as a framework or process through which the re-imagining of the city's sustainable future can occur. In 2006, the City of Ballarat hosted the tenth Conference of the League of Historical Cities, a time when furthering the Council's role in heritage met with some reluctance to impose further restrictive controls on private property and some frustration with existing heritage controls within both the community and the local government. Ballarat Council officers began a slow process of developing a more collaborative and empathetic approach to implementing the Council's heritage responsibilities, and in 2012, at the League of Historical Cities' thirteenth World Conference in Hue, Vietnam, they recognised that many other historic cities around the world face similar challenges in managing change. In 2012, it was agreed to explore the application of UNESCO's *Recommendation on the Historic Urban Landscape* in Ballarat.

Globally, Ballarat became the first known local government authority to begin implementing HUL within its strategic processes in the comprehensive way that was envisaged by UNESCO. In order to mainstream the approach, the HUL process has included the entire area of the municipality and its broader regional setting, not just the historic city centre. Given the lack of an existing implementation strategy provided by UNESCO, and very little literature about practical applications of these directions, the City of Ballarat was invited and agreed to join WHITR-AP's pilot programme to implement UNESCO's HUL (Fayad 2013).

Ballarat's exploratory approach to operationalising the HUL posed a number of early and continuing challenges. The first task was to better understand the consequences of looking at the municipality from a landscape perspective (Mayrinck de

Oliveira Melo 2012), whilst at the same time implementing both new and renewed processes for city planning. Being part of WHITR-AP's pilot programme meant that Ballarat's Council officers have had access to international experts, networks and interpretation of the HUL (WHITR-AP 2013; City of Ballarat 2013a). However, specific knowledge about the practical application of HUL in a local government setting, particularly in Australia, was not available and needed to be charted by the City of Ballarat through the implementation process itself. In many ways, it was unclear what practical application and localisation of HUL meant due to its broad statements and aspirational orientation.

The HUL Action Plan became the stimulus for innovation in Ballarat, but it required new techniques and local approaches to be developed. Stage 1 began with an overview study *Mapping Ballarat's Historic Urban Landscape* (Context Pty Ltd 2013), which aimed to explore what HUL could mean in practice and in this specific locality. Undertaken collaboratively with Council officers and consultants,[4] the study also relied on the establishment of an advisory group comprising academics from Deakin University's Cultural Heritage Centre for Asia and the Pacific (CHCAP) and Federation University Australia, Council officers and the consultant team. This collaboration made it possible to move forward with the large task of mapping, documentary research, data collection, and community engagement necessary for the first attempt at a synthesis; and to build a broader consensus while also keeping alive the conceptual and theoretical debates. Pushing the boundaries of usual practices, to unsettle taken-for-granted assumptions, became a prerequisite.[5]

The Stage 1 study developed an indicative landscape characterisation framework (Clark *et al.* 2004) including urban areas and created a map titled 'a visual analysis of the municipal area' (see Figure 6.4). This simple map, in particular, highlighted a number of key visual elements and view lines that are not typically considered in the system of planning scheme overlays, historic precincts and planning zones that create a complex set of bounded parcels out of the urban landscape. While this landscape characterisation is predominantly visual, and is preliminary and imperfect, it has been a useful first step in stimulating discussions and encouraging a broad range of stakeholders to see Ballarat in a new light.

The study also began to explore some new community-based cultural mapping methods. This is a key feature of the HUL approach identified by Bandarin and van Oers (2012: 155) where 'cognitive mapping by participant groups, anthropology and cultural geography insights, and documentation by locals of oral traditions and customs' are central to the process. The advisory group worked with some of the members of a community advocacy group, the Ballarat East Network. Walking and driving through Ballarat East together highlighted the importance of the 'rural feel' and the importance placed on individual expressions and uses of space. It identified some special views, informal walking routes and quirky features that are often overlooked in local/municipal heritage studies and planning processes. While this was only a first effort to understand Ballarat East in this experiential way, the outcomes for the longer-term Ballarat HUL processes have been significant, underscoring the need to augment the usual studies with other inquiries as

MT BECKWORTH

MT BOLTON

LEARMONTH VOLCANIC CONES

FORESTED RIDGE

FORESTED RIDGE

MT
WARRENHEIP

MT
BUNINYONG

0 1 2 3 5km

Figure 6.4 Map showing the outcomes of the landscape characterisation analysis conducted by Context Pty Ltd in Stage 1 of the HUL process.

Source: Context Pty Ltd 2013: 53; City of Ballarat.

there are risks in managing change when the values of some elements have not been recognised by the existing heritage and planning arrangements.

Building on these first steps, work in several new areas commenced (loosely termed together as 'Stage 2'). These were focused on providing new tools that an ongoing commitment to a 'HUL-approach' will need and enabling the development of sustainable approaches to often costly and lengthy community engagement programmes, as well as some stocktaking to ensure that previous data collection work by the Council could inform continuing efforts. Briefly, these included:

- A preliminary review of current planning and regulatory policy, including recommendations on how to embed HUL in the Ballarat Planning Scheme (Planisphere, Forest and City of Ballarat 2014);
- Scoping the development of interactive mapping tools, including potential 3D and 4D technologies and other online engagement tools (CeRDI 2014; Omnilink 2014);
- A Cultural Mapping Audit to better recognise and utilise the knowledge and data collected in existing community-initiated programmes that relate to community values (Tsilemanis 2014).

The City of Ballarat began developing the new long-term land-use strategy *Today, Tomorrow, Together – The Ballarat Strategy* in 2013 (City of Ballarat 2014a). A step in the strategy's development was *Ballarat Imagine*, the largest community conversation ever held in Ballarat (City of Ballarat 2013b), which used a values-based approach, inspired by the HUL. With over 6,500 responses, the *Ballarat Imagine* community engagement programme assisted by enabling a better understanding of what different communities value most in Ballarat, what they imagine for their future and what they do not want to lose. By setting the engagement programme firmly in the context of future change, *Ballarat Imagine* was able to begin to address the question of the 'limits of acceptable change', albeit at a very broad and preliminary level. Three open-ended questions elicited the themes of heritage, history, natural beauty and a great lifestyle as the most strongly valued characteristics; with Ballarat's historic streetscapes, places and features rated the most highly. The timing of *Ballarat Imagine* allowed its findings to be incorporated into the HUL studies, as well as establishing the vision for the Ballarat Strategy and achieving high-level commitment to the HUL approach. The outcomes have helped to ensure that the needed political support for the HUL process can continue and they have underpinned the agreement to place 'heritage' in a central place in the planning for the future, rather than as a separate – albeit important – sector of activity.

Pausing to reflect

Points for review and reflection are important built-in parts of the process. The completion of Stage 1 of the HUL programme was marked by an international symposium on the Historic Urban Landscape in Ballarat in September 2013, and while the tools developed in Stage 2 are continuing to be refined, the public launch of an interactive 'HUL Ballarat' website and 'Visualising Ballarat' mapping tool[6] designed to facilitate inclusive engagement and participation coincided with a second international symposium in February 2015 (titled 'Participate, Imagine, Innovate: Revitalising Historic Cities').

An important and influential outcome has been to shift established mindsets inside the Council offices and in the communities, allowing an emerging understanding of the urban landscape in the context of management and change. Without acceptance of the need to see Ballarat's urban landscape differently and to change practices accordingly, the HUL programme could not have attained the needed level of formal support from the elected Councillors and Council senior managers. As noted above, one symbolic measure of this was the decision by Ballarat City Council to enter into a strategic cooperation agreement to operationalise HUL as part of the pilot programme with WHITR-AP. Linking Ballarat's strategic processes to an international programme and finding an approach that had the potential to integrate conservation with socio-economic development goals were elements contributing to the appeal this arrangement had for the Council (Figure 6.5). On the side of WHITR-AP, it was clear that finding a partnership with a municipal authority was highly valued in its efforts to more deeply explore and implement the HUL framework.

At this stage, the implications for the future application for the HUL approach seem very positive, but of course, there are some tensions and vulnerabilities too.

- The process is highly dependent on continuing political support from the Councillors and Council's senior management and experience shows that this can change quickly. Some of the work that has been undertaken – particularly in relation to the existing planning mechanisms (Planisphere, Forest and City of Ballarat 2014) – has been consciously oriented at ensuring there are some early and useable outcomes for the existing strategic planning and development approvals processes that can allow the thinking about innovation to continue.
- So far, the HUL process has been developed alongside the existing heritage identification and management arrangements. Making changes to well-established processes and frameworks might meet significant resistance, especially given that many are established at the State level (and so not easily amended at the local level).
- One of the most powerful components of the HUL is the idea that the 'limits of acceptable change' can be determined, allowing change to occur without losing the most valued and distinctive characteristics. In Ballarat, this has only begun to be understood and operationalised, although creating a more collaborative and inclusive dialogue and breaking down the visual and the fabric orientations of conventional heritage practices have assisted this part of the process.

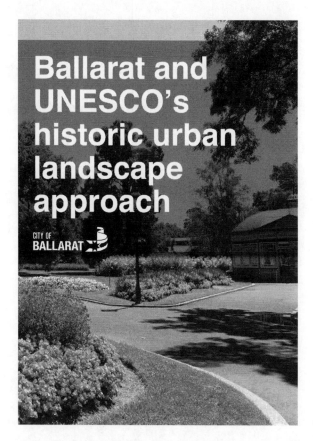

Figure 6.5 Promoting Ballarat's HUL experience internationally has been an element in maintaining political and community support for the programme.

Source: City of Ballarat.

Collaboration between consultants, planners, academics, community organisations and across Council, along with a willingness to accept the need for change, have been the essential ingredients in the progress made in Ballarat to date. Other important enabling factors have been the ability to stimulate a new dialogue about urban conservation through the platform of UNESCO's HUL approach, sidestepping the existing urban conservation paradigm – or at least the ways in which it is typically received and applied by local governments. As discussed in the final part of this chapter, we have begun to identify the ways in which heritage practice can be changed through the adoption of the HUL approach (see Figure 6.6).

The process to date has raised an awareness of the potential of adopting the HUL approach, resulting in the HUL being embedded into the high-level Ballarat

The Burra Charter says …	Conventional heritage practice	New 'HUL' practice
… for places of cultural significance Cultural significance is embodied in the place itself, its fabric, setting, use, associations, meanings, records, related places and related objects [Article 1.2]	'Heritage' is focused on spatially located 'places' Values are tangibly expressed and embedded in place	More than places Values embodied in people
Policy for managing a place must be based on an understanding of its cultural significance [Article 1.1]	Statements of Significance are adopted and applied through formal processes and are fixed for long periods	Significance as fluid, contestable
Place may have tangible and intangible dimensions [Article 1.1] – comprising fabric, associations and meanings	Focus on fabric, especially the exterior fabric and appearance of historic buildings	People carry values which are attributed to tangible and intangible elements More than visual Depending on values, fabric could be just one way of transmitting meanings
Cultural significance means aesthetic, historic, scientific, social or spiritual value for past, present or future generations [Article 1.2]	Victorian State legislation refers to aesthetic, archaeological, architectural, cultural, historical, scientific or social significance In practice, aesthetic, architectural and historical significance are used more frequently than the others	Cultural significance is localised – defined by the distinctiveness of the place and values held by people
Use can be part of significance [Article 7.1] Compatible use respects the cultural significance of a place [Article 1.11]	Adaptive re-use is common Uses are generally not included in statutory requirements	Values guide the approach to the management of change. For example people may value use above fabric in particular instances
Conservation of a place should identify all aspects of cultural and natural significance … [Article 5.1]	Natural values are considered through separate systems of decision making Indigenous cultural heritage values are considered through separate systems of decision making	Practice needs to reflect cultural perspectives that do not separate nature and culture (including Indigenous cultures)
The setting of a place can be significant [Article 8]	Heritage places are strictly bounded Precincts/areas are a focus for contestation and patchy outcomes	Landscapes are permeable and experiential
Oriented at people who provide advice, make decisions or undertake works [Preamble]	Methods are expert-led	Methods are community-centred and locally focused
Conservation should make use of all the knowledge, skills and disciplines which can contribute to the study and care of the place. [Article 4]	Methods are focused on physical recording and historical documents	New visual and spatial methods, cultural mapping and localised approaches
Cultural Significance is defined very broadly [Australia ICOMOS 2013b]	Aboriginal heritage is often equated with pre-contact archaeological sites	Aboriginal and settler communities associate their heritage with landscapes comprised of diverse elements and periods of history, including contemporary associations

Figure 6.6 Emerging HUL practice in Ballarat and its links with Australian practice.[7]

Strategy – a useful determinant of how new development and new growth will occur sustainably in the municipality over the next 30 years. The momentum that continues to build around Ballarat's HUL pilot programme is enabling opportunities to explore complex issues such as vulnerability, resilience and virtuous economic futures with a growing set of stakeholders, helping to make Ballarat's approach to the management of change more sophisticated than had previously been the case. The staged exploratory approach to implementing HUL in Ballarat has enabled a feeling of ownership of the change management process and has opened up a dialogue with a different set of people – including the local communities. By embarking on this together, the process has enabled the approach to seem more powerful.

Conclusions: learning from – and for – Ballarat

Seeing urban settlements as landscapes has had more profound impacts on the rethinking of approaches and methods than was anticipated at the start of the project for the City of Ballarat.

The experience of the Ballarat HUL programme has led us to tentatively conclude that incremental change to the existing systems has possibly gone as far as it can, and that working 'off the grid' for a while is necessary, even though maintaining sufficient local political support will require some attention to a series of shorter-term outcomes at regular intervals.

The commitment to concepts and methods that are more genuinely community-centred rather than practitioner-driven will take us beyond the current capacity and scope of Australian standards such as the Burra Charter (Australia ICOMOS 2013a), which works best when applied to individual 'places' of cultural significance, but struggles with large and diverse areas and is not oriented to non-place components of culture, memory and identity. Embedding values-based thinking and processes has been the particular gift of the Burra Charter to the ongoing dialogue in Australia (and elsewhere) and it has allowed us to begin to appreciate an entirely different dimension of heritage work. However, as Figure 6.6 demonstrates, its ideas are not always fully implemented, especially in local heritage planning contexts. It seems that the idea of values-based heritage work – if expanded in this way – could be the way to go, but the transformations foreshadowed in Figure 6.6 could be very significant for the heritage practices of the future.

Because heritage controls often function to limit or prevent demolition of existing building fabric, ideas of 'heritage' have been distorted – and sometimes appropriated to unrelated causes and reactions against change. Perhaps one of the opportunities that the HUL presents communities with is the chance to take back and re-appropriate ideas of 'heritage' to those that are more inclusive, diverse and community-centred.

The previous approaches to heritage identification and assessment typically used in Ballarat had focused primarily on individual buildings or groups of buildings in certain streetscapes. This has been essential work, supported by the community, but the HUL approach has begun to shift to a broader understanding of heritage conservation at the local level. Increased attention to the processes of community engagement has therefore been a central feature of this work, one that demonstrates how such an approach can 'recover the significance of everyday landscapes' of the past (Finch 2011: 14), as well as providing a new context for those conventionally designated as 'significant'.

Surveys such as *Ballarat Imagine*, walking with the local community and the development of new community engagement tools are only first steps in what could lead to greater changes in approaches. Experiences in Ballarat highlight the importance of having the political support and space to try new things, and for some of them to work (and others not).

The early progress in this work has strengthened the capacity of the Council and its partners to continue. Future work will employ cultural mapping and visual methods to examine in more detail the interaction between people and place, the 'embodied politics present in the everyday material world' (Rose and Tolia-Kelly 2012: 1). The implementation of such methods and their incorporation into the HUL approach could have substantial impacts on local heritage practice. For example, we can foresee the need for more malleable statements of significance that are structured around the experiences of place and landscape. The discussions and decision-making processes might allow emerging concepts such as 'tolerance for change' and 'resilience' to be more commonly used as the authentic fabric might not be the sole or primary carrier of value in all cases (see Araoz 2011).[8]

Despite the pessimism of Smith and Waterton (2012) about the continued resilience of the 'authorized heritage discourse', the advisory group was able to support the sustained quality of being unsettled, while also recognising that there are many emotional dimensions to contemplating major changes. We have encountered the difficulty of letting go of the way things are, even when they are not working well enough. The community heritage advocates seem understandably wary about what could be lost if we loosen the strongly regulated and adversarial character of decision-making. Government officials are also cautious about loosening the tightly scripted parameters in which heritage decisions are taken, fearing an escalation of contestation and the loss of the consistency and predictability of outcomes that involve investment and risk. Practitioners might resist sharing more of their control of the processes and risk becoming marginalised or even irrelevant in their own fields of passionate commitment. However, for all these actors there can also be appeal in finding a way to work differently. There is value in finding new forms of language that can allow us to begin anew, freed from the contested, expensive and ineffective characteristics of the status quo.

The emerging HUL approach has also had the beneficial effect of breaking down some of the traditional boundaries between the different areas of council activities. This has enabled the HUL work to move to the centre of the city's strategic planning, rather than the usual positioning for 'heritage' as a separate concern on the edge of these major planning processes.

Given this initial analysis, it should be evident that local government operates as a pivot point between these different actors – and between the duality of 'bottom-up' and 'top-down' influences. More importantly, local governments are potentially more nimble, able to innovate without relying on an alignment with other spheres of government. The fact that the City of Ballarat has been able to forge a working relationship with the WHITR-AP and participate directly in the activities of UNESCO without the involvement of the national government demonstrates this ability.

The HUL programme in Ballarat has challenged practitioners and council officers, and engaged researchers from a broad range of disciplines to critically reflect on current urban heritage and planning practices and conceptual assumptions. This has started to suggest methods that can delve more deeply into the way change is considered. By being open to this process, it has also enabled existing practices to be validated or strengthened and new ones to be designed and implemented. Overwhelmingly, however, by stepping back as experts, the experience has been instructive, and it has fuelled the conviction that it is possible to embrace new approaches on how to manage change in historic areas.

Our progress in Ballarat is tentative and exploratory and will need to progress much further before we can claim a paradigm shift and a new way to work. We are also taking many of these lessons into research and practice contexts in other urban settings in Asia to discover other enabling factors and sticking points. However, the most fundamental shift that underpins all this is the one that sees heritage values as embedded in place (as explained in the Burra Charter Article 1.2) to one that acknowledges that it is also embedded in the memories and experiences of people and their communities. These findings have underscored the importance of continually moving between theorisation, experimentation and applied learning – even in such constrained and pragmatic processes as local city planning and development.

Acknowledgements

This chapter arises from ongoing cooperative work supported by the City of Ballarat in part fulfilment of commitments made in its Memorandum of Understanding with the World Heritage Institute for Training and Research in Asia and the Pacific (WHITR-AP). Our thinking has been assisted by the work of a range of consultants and partners working on aspects of the HUL in Ballarat (as cited in the text) and the participants of two international symposia held in Ballarat in September 2013 and February 2015, particularly the late Dr Ron van Oers. We are also grateful for the feedback provided by William Logan and Sophia Labadi, which assisted us in sharpening our discussion.

Notes

1   First adopted by Australia ICOMOS in 1979 as a local adaptation of the Venice Charter, the *Australia ICOMOS Charter for Places of Cultural Significance (Burra Charter)* has been revised a number of times and the current version is dated 2013. The substantial 1999 revisions particularly moved the Charter to balance the focus on fabric with intangible associations and meanings and emphasised the importance of community-based processes.

2   Several of Australia's World Heritage properties inscribed in the past decade are individual buildings/sites located in urban settings – Royal Exhibition Building and Carlton

Gardens (2004), Sydney Opera House (2007) and components of the Australian Convict Sites (2010). The natural World Heritage property of the Greater Blue Mountains is located adjacent to the Sydney metropolis (2001).

3   For Aboriginal cultural heritage, conventional practice has focused on the identification of archaeological resources and the regulation of their disturbance. However, recent State legislation creates an important intersect between planning processes and the decision-making roles of the organisations that represent the two Traditional Owner groups. The modes of collaboration are still being found but the recognition of the municipality as a number of landscapes with multiple Indigenous and 'settler' values and associations is consistent with the emerging HUL approaches.

4   The consultant's Project Manager relocated to City of Ballarat offices for the duration of the study in order to work collaboratively with Council officers. This collaborative process has now been adopted as a core requirement for any consultants working on HUL studies in Ballarat.

5   This is a subject that has been well covered in management disciplines (see for example Shugan 2004) but less so in the humanities and social sciences.

6   The 'Historic Urban Landscape Ballarat' website was launched on 21 February 2015. It has various materials useful for visualising the city, accessing resources, and 'talking' about the HUL – see http://www.hulballarat.org.au/ (accessed 23 February 2015).

7   Work by Planisphere, Forest and City of Ballarat (2014) has also looked at these transformations of practice.

8   Linking research with practice is a core focus of the City of Ballarat's work. For example, PhD work to develop a new phenomenological methodology for practitioners to enable identification of dynamic social and historical values has been financially supported.

Bibliography

Amin, A. and Thrift, N. (2002). *Cities: Reimagining the Urban*. Cambridge: Polity.

Araoz, G.F. (2008). World Heritage Historic Urban Landscapes: defining and protecting authenticity. *APT Bulletin*, 39(2/3), 33–7.

Araoz, G.F. (2011). Preserving heritage places under a new paradigm. *Journal of Cultural Heritage Management and Sustainable Development*, 1(1), 55–60.

Atkinson, D. (2007). Kitsch geographies and the everyday spaces of social memory. *Environment and Planning A*, 39, 521–40.

Atkinson, D. (2008). The heritage of mundane places. In: B.J. Graham and P. Howard (eds), *The Ashgate Research Companion to Heritage and Identity*. Aldershot: Ashgate.

Australia ICOMOS (2013a). *The Burra Charter: The Australia ICOMOS Charter for Places of Cultural Significance*. Burwood: Australia ICOMOS.

Australia ICOMOS (2013b). *Practice Note: The Burra Charter and Indigenous Cultural Heritage Management*, version 1, November 2013. Burwood: Australia ICOMOS.

Australian Local Government Association (ALGA) (2010). *Facts and Figures on Local Governments in Australia*. Available at: http://alga.asn.au/?ID=59 (accessed 14 October 2014).

Bandarin, F. (2012). From paradox to paradigm? Historic Urban Landscape as an urban conservation approach. In: K. Taylor and J. Lennon (eds), *Managing Cultural Landscapes*. London: Routledge.

Bandarin, F. and van Oers, R. (2012). *The Historic Urban Landscape: Managing Heritage in an Urban Century*. Chichester: Wiley-Blackwell.

Biosis Research Pty Ltd (2007). *Lake Wendouree, Ballarat, Victoria: Cultural Heritage Management Plan*. Port Melbourne: City of Ballarat.

Byrne, D., Brayshaw, H. and Ireland, T. (2001). *Social Significance: A Discussion Paper.* Sydney: New South Wales National Parks and Wildlife Service.

Cameron, C. (2006). *Proceedings: Heritage and the Conservation of Historic Urban Landscapes. Round Table organized by the Canada Research Chair on Built Heritage, University of Montreal.* Montreal: University of Montreal.

Castells, M. (1989). *The Informational City: Information Technology, Economic Restructuring, and the Urban-Regional Process.* Oxford: Blackwell.

Clark, J., Darlington, J. and Fairclough, G. (2004). *Using Landscape Characterisation.* London: English Heritage.

Centre for eResearch and Digital Innovation (CeRDI) (2014). Visualising Ballarat – past, present, future. A collaborative research proposal to develop online tools to support Ballarat's Historic Urban Landscape program. Unpublished report to the City of Ballarat. Ballarat, Australia.

City of Ballarat (2013a). *Ballarat and UNESCO's Historic Urban Landscape Approach* (brochure). Ballarat: City of Ballarat.

City of Ballarat (2013b). *Ballarat Imagine.* Available at: http://www.ballarat.vic.gov.au/haveyoursay/2013/ballaratimagine.aspx (accessed 12 October 2014).

City of Ballarat (2014a). *Ballarat Strategy.* Available at: http://www.ballarat.vic.gov.au/pbs/city-strategy/ballarat-strategy.aspx (accessed 12 October 2014).

City of Ballarat (2014b). *Economic Profile.* Available at: http://www.economicprofile.com.au/ballarat/ (accessed 12 October 2014).

City of Ballarat (2014c). *Visiting.* Available at: http:// www.ballarat.vic.gov.au/vs (accessed 12 October 2014).

Context Pty Ltd (2013). Mapping Ballarat's Historic Urban Landscape. Stage 1 Final Report. Unpublished report to the City of Ballarat. Brunswick, Australia: Context.

Council of Europe (2000). *European Landscape Convention.* Available at: http://www.coe.int/t/dg4/cultureheritage/heritage/Landscape/default_en.asp (accessed 5 February 2015).

Council of Europe (2005). *Framework Convention on the Value of Cultural Heritage for Society* (the 'Faro Convention', Faro, Council of Europe). Available at: http://www.coe.int/t/dg4/cultureheritage/heritage/Identities/default_en.asp (accessed 5 February 2015).

D'Auvergne, P. (2009). *Deep Lead Mines of Ballarat.* Available at: http://education.sovereignhill.com.au/media/uploads/audio/LeadsandDeepLeads.pdf (accessed 25 June 2015).

DeSilvey, C. (2012). Making sense of transience: an anticipatory history. *Cultural Geographies*, 19(1), 31–54.

Dovey, K. (2005). *Fluid City. Transforming Melbourne's Urban Waterfront.* Sydney: University of New South Wales Press.

Evans, G. (2002). Living in a World Heritage City: stakeholders in the dialectic of the universal and particular. *International Journal of Heritage Studies*, 8(2), 117–35.

Fayad, S. (2013). 11.4 League of Historical Cities – UNESCO's Historic Urban Landscapes Pilot Program and LHC Board Meeting. In: *Ordinary Council Meeting 10 April 2013, Council Chamber, Town Hall, Sturt Street, Ballarat. Agenda. Public Copy*, pp. 26–30. Available at: http://www.ballarat.vic.gov.au/media/1467111/10_april_public_agenda.pdf (accessed 10 October 2014).

Finch, J. (2011). Historic landscapes. In: P. Howard, I. Thompson and E. Waterton (eds), *The Routledge Companion to Landscape Studies*. London: Routledge.

Gabrielli, B. (2010). Urban planning challenged by Historic Urban Landscape. *World Heritage Papers*, 27. Paris: UNESCO.

Hawke, S.K. (2012). Heritage and sense of place: amplifying local voice and co-constructing meaning. In: I. Convery, G. Corsane and P. David (eds), *Making Sense of Place: Multi-disciplinary Perspectives*. Woodbridge: Boydell Press.

Hayden, D. (1995). *The Power of Place: Urban Landscapes as Public History*. Cambridge, MA and London: MIT Press.

Howard, P. (2012). *An Introduction to Landscape*. Farnham: Ashgate.

Jokilehto, J. (2010). Notes on the definition and safeguarding of HUL. *City & Time*, 4(3), 41–51.

The League of Historical Cities (website). Available at: http://www.city.kyoto.jp/somu/kokusai/lhcs/ (accessed 25 February 2015).

Lennon, J.L. and Taylor, K. (2011). Prospects and challenges for cultural landscape management. In: K. Taylor and J. Lennon (eds), *Managing Cultural Landscapes*. London: Routledge.

Logan, W. (2002). Introduction. In: W. Logan (ed.), *Disappearing Asian City: Protecting Asia's Urban Heritage in a Globalizing World*. Hong Kong: Oxford University Press.

Lorimer, H. (2005). Cultural geography: the busyness of being 'more than representational'. *Progress in Human Geography*, 29(1), 83–94.

McGinniss, D. (2014). Social value, historic value and urban change in Ballarat. Unpublished PhD confirmation paper. Victoria: Federation University Australia.

Mathewson, K. (2000). Carl Sauer and his critics. In: W.M. Denervan and K. Mathewson (eds), *Carl Sauer on Culture and Landscape: Readings and Commentaries*. Baton Rouge: Louisiana State University Press.

Mayrinck de Oliveira Melo, V.L. and Cadena de Melo Filho, D. (2012). Significance and cultural landscape: a new approach to heritage management. In: S. M. Zancheti and K. Similä (eds), *Measuring Heritage Conservation Performance. Proceedings, 6th International Seminar on Urban Conservation*. Olinda: CECI (Centro de Estudos Avançados da Conservação Integrada) and Rome: ICCROM.

Omnilink (2014). 3D Mapping System – Scoping Study. Unpublished report prepared by Omnilink for the City of Ballarat Historic Urban Landscape Pilot Program – Stage 2.2.

Planisphere, Forest and City of Ballarat (2014). Ballarat's Historic Urban Landscape Program – Stage 2.1 – Results-based investigation of the Ballarat's Planning System for potential Historic Urban Landscape program implementation (draft). Unpublished report to the City of Ballarat.

Productivity Commission (Australia) (2006). *Conservation of Australia's Historic Heritage Places*. Productivity Commission Inquiry Report No. 37, Canberra.

Rodwell, D. (2012). Rethinking heritage. *Context*, 127, 29–31.

Rose, G. and Tolia-Kelly, D.P. (2012). Visuality/materiality: introducing a manifesto for practice. In: G. Rose and D.P. Tolia-Kelly (eds), *Visuality/Materiality: Images, Objects and Practices*. Aldershot: Ashgate.

Ruggles, D.F. (2012). Introduction: the social and urban scale of heritage. In: D.F. Ruggles (ed.), *On Location: Heritage Cities and Sites*. New York: Springer.

Shugan, S.M. (2004). Editorial: consulting, research, and consulting research. *Marketing Science*, 23(2), 173–9.

Smith, J. (2010). Marrying the old with the new in Historic Urban Landscapes. *World Heritage Papers* 27. Paris: UNESCO.

Smith, L. (2006) *Uses of Heritage*. London: Routledge.

Smith, L. and Waterton, E. (2012). Constrained by commonsense: the authorized heritage discourse in contemporary debates. In: R. Skeates, C. McDavid and J. Carman (eds), *The*

Oxford Handbook of Public Archaeology. New York: Oxford University Press. Available at: http://www.oxfordhandbooks.com/view/10.1093/oxfordhb/9780199237821.001.0001/oxfordhb-9780199237821-e-9 (accessed 6 October 2014).

State of Victoria (2014). *Victorian Population Bulletin 2014.* Available at: http://www.dtpli.vic.gov.au/__data/assets/pdf_file/0008/222974/2014-Victorian-Population-Bulletin.pdf (accessed 5 October 2014).

Tsilemanis, A. (2014). Ballarat Research. Unpublished report to City of Ballarat, Australia.

Tuan, Y. (1977). *Space and Place: The Perspective of Experience.* London: Edward Arnold.

Turner, M. (2013). UNESCO Recommendation on the Historic Urban Landscape. In: M.T. Albert, R. Bernecker and B. Rudolff (eds), *Understanding Heritage: Perspectives in Heritage Studies.* Berlin: De Gruyter.

UNESCO (2005). *Vienna Memorandum on 'World Heritage and Contemporary Architecture – Managing the Historic Urban Landscape'.* Paris: UNESCO.

UNESCO (2011). *Recommendation on the Historic Urban Landscape.* Adopted by the 36th session of the UNESCO General Conference, Paris.

UNESCO (2013). *Summary of the Reflection Meeting on the Implementation of the Recommendation on the Historic Urban Landscape Two Years after its Adoption (HUL+2).* Paris: UNESCO.

van Oers, R. (2007). Towards new international guidelines for the conservation of Historic Urban Landscapes (HUL). *City & Time,* 3, pp. 43–51.

Waterton, E. (2011). Landscape and non-representational theories. In: P. Howard, I. Thompson and E. Waterton (eds), *The Routledge Companion to Landscape Studies.* London: Routledge, pp. 66–75.

Wattchow, B. (2011). *Pedagogy of Place: Outdoor Education for a Changing World.* Melbourne: Monash University Publishing.

Witcomb, A. and Buckley, K. (2013). Engaging with the future of 'critical heritage studies': looking back in order to look forward. *International Journal of Heritage Studies,* 19(6), 562–78.

World Heritage Institute of Training and Research in Asia and the Pacific (WHITR-AP) (2013). Agreement on Strategic Cooperation Concerning the Implementation of UNESCO's Recommendation on the Historic Urban Landscape between the City of Ballarat and WHITR-AP. Unpublished document, Shanghai and Ballarat.

World Heritage Institute of Training and Research in Asia and the Pacific (WHITR-AP) (2014). *The Historic Urban Landscape Website.* Available at: http://historicurbanlandscape.com/index.php?classid=5351 (accessed 28 September 2014).

Wylie, J. (2007). *Landscape.* London: Routledge.

Chapter 7

Safeguarding intangible cultural heritage in the urban environment

Some experiences gained from implementing UNESCO's 2003 convention

Janet Blake

The question of urban heritage or heritage within urban spaces has, of course, been well considered over many years with regard, particularly, to the urban fabric of historic towns and cities and World Heritage Sites that are located in urban contexts (Worthing and Bond 2008; Bandarin and van Oers 2012). However, the question of how 'living' cultural heritage traditions and practices and their associated know-how and material elements are affected by being introduced into an urban context, and, even, how they may themselves impact upon the social and physical fabric of the urban setting, is less well considered.[1]

A recent evaluation report by UNESCO has asserted that:

> the concept of intangible cultural heritage (hereafter ICH) itself is quite new and its use has largely been credited to the 2003 Convention. As recently as ten years ago the term ICH was almost unknown and was only used by a small group of experts.[2]

Although this is not wholly accurate, as academic programmes in cultural heritage management and related areas had already been employing this term and it had been currency in UNESCO debates since at least the 1980s, it is true that it was virtually unknown in international law circles until the discussions on this Convention were initiated in the early 2000s. By addressing the specific question of safeguarding intangible cultural heritage (ICH) within the urban environment, illustrated by some experiences gained from implementing UNESCO's Convention on Safeguarding Intangible Cultural Heritage (2003), this chapter is intended to contribute towards debate on this issue. The UNESCO Convention has been in force since 2006 and it had secured nearly 160 ratifications by April 2014.[3] It can be regarded, therefore, as providing a rich source of information as to what is being identified and celebrated as 'intangible cultural heritage' within the urban setting, how this is being incorporated into broader cultural and other policies and what impact this process is having on the urban fabric, the local heritage community and the ICH itself. It should be borne in mind, however, that the examples seen thus far tend to reflect a state-driven view and they are not necessarily what urban inhabitants themselves would regard as their important cultural traditions.[4]

The long-term trend globally is towards increased urbanisation[5] and, given the general tendency towards urbanisation of many societies, this is an important issue for societies seeking to safeguard this heritage and set cultural and other policies (including, for example, local government frameworks) that will affect its condition. In countries around the world and on all continents, ICH elements have disappeared as a consequence of a shift towards urban living, although some have been transferred to the urban context. Here the living tradition may continue in modified contexts and forms (e.g. through concerts, festivals, publishing, etc.), but it remains open to question whether this is a positive or a negative evolution. Rural-to-urban migration obviously has a growing impact on ICH and its transmission within the associated cultural communities and it is necessary to develop new and creative approaches towards ICH safeguarding that minimise negative impacts of urbanisation while tapping into its potential to contribute to social relations. Moreover, as a result of economic development and the concomitant industrialisation and urbanisation of societies, traditional modes of transmission are becoming devalued within the communities that have traditionally maintained them, with young people favouring gaining a formal certificate or degree.

On the credit side, the living traditions, know-how and cultural practices that make up ICH are understood more and more to have the potential for helping urban communities, especially those who have migrated from other often rural locations, to strengthen their sense of identity and social cohesion as well as providing a bridge with other communities (UNESCO 2012j).[6] In this way, ICH can play a key role in equipping people with tools that help them to live better in urban settings and to overcome a sense of social and cultural dislocation. Given that the process of identifying, giving significance to and safeguarding ICH under the Convention remains a primarily state-driven process, it is important to consider whether the urban ICH currently being recognised represents the full extent of this heritage or should be expanded to include, for example, more popular and contemporary forms of heritage. This is despite the prominent role accorded to communities and groups in the Convention text, especially in Article 15 that calls upon Parties to ensure 'the widest possible participation of communities, groups and, in some cases, individuals that create, maintain and transmit such heritage, and to involve them actively in its management'.

The interplay between the physical fabric of the urban setting and related ICH is frequently a central consideration, and there are many examples of where the safeguarding of cultural spaces and places for the performance of ICH in urban contexts is a question of major importance. For example, these include the routes of processions as well as city squares and other public spaces of performance and less public places of ritual; at times, the loss or change of these may impact directly on the ICH and its content.[7] In addition, processions and other elements that attract large numbers of spectators are now facing the challenge of how to provide public access, and the necessary infrastructural and security arrangements, while preserving the physical urban environment and the core character of the ICH element itself.

Municipal authorities, often operating through local museums, libraries and cultural centres, clearly have a key role to play in providing infrastructural, administrative and financial support for the practice and enactment of ICH. This support may be in the form of providing spaces for rehearsals, performances, training and other ICH-related activities, travel expenses, informal and further education and folk costumes, musical instruments and technical equipment (as well as storage space for these). This help is also often given in the form of collaboration with NGOs, experts and the private sector; the last is of interest as the role of the private sector in ICH safeguarding remains an under-explored question that has great potential as well as posing dangers of distortion, appropriation, etc. This is probably a more pressing issue in the urban setting than the rural one and deserves further research.

A further consideration that has recently been given attention at the international level is that of the gender dynamics of ICH practice and its safeguarding (Blake 2014). In relation to this question, heritage can be understood as a process in which identity (including gender identity) and social and cultural meaning are mediated, evaluated and worked out. What is at issue here, then, is how far there is any difference in these terms when the ICH is an urban heritage: are the gender dynamics at play in any sense transformed by the urban setting?

Defining urban ICH

Here, I wish to address the question as to whether the ICH currently being recognised (primarily, under the 2003 Convention) represents the totality of this heritage or should be expanded to include, for example, more popular and contemporary forms of heritage. This is an issue that is perhaps more germane to urban forms of ICH than rural ones. The definition of intangible cultural heritage for the purposes of the 2003 Convention is generally accepted as the currently applicable understanding of the content of this form of heritage.[8] There are, of course, a number of elements in this definition that respond equally well to urban as to non-urban forms of ICH, and some important aspects of this definition include the following. First, it clearly characterises this as a *living culture* that evolves as it is transmitted from one generation to another. Second, the cultural community is seen as the real bearer of ICH and it is in terms of the community that this heritage is defined. Five main (but not exclusive) domains of ICH are set out in paragraph 2 of Article 2 and these are: oral traditions and expressions, including language as a vehicle of the intangible cultural heritage; the performing arts; social practices, rituals and festive events; knowledge and practices concerning nature and the universe; and traditional craftsmanship. Of these it is clear that, with the possible exception of 'knowledge and practices concerning nature and the universe', they all respond to forms of heritage that can be found in urban settings and, in some cases (e.g. performing arts), their presence in the urban context may be more prominent than in a non-urban one.

However, there remains a range of 'living heritages' that could, perhaps, be added to the definition and/or domains of ICH and that are not at present explicitly recognised by the Convention's definition as part of 'intangible cultural heritage'. In particular, with reference to urban heritage, one might wish to add some popular forms of cultural expression that are not currently included. For example, could graffiti ever be considered as a form of urban ICH and, if so, how would we distinguish it from state-sponsored wall art or that of political groups? Would we rule out the images of the martyrs of the imposed Iran–Iraq War on the walls of Tehran but include the IRA- and UDR-inspired wall 'art' of Northern Ireland? Some cities have begun to address this question as a policy issue, although not yet specifically as a form of ICH. The City of Melbourne, for example, has acknowledged its importance in contributing to a vibrant urban culture and, as a consequence, has implemented a Graffiti Management Plan developed on the basis of research and community consultation (www.melbourne.vic.gov.au; accessed 26 June 2015). There is no doubt that applying the notion of ICH to the urban setting introduces a new set of challenges that may not yet have been fully acknowledged or appreciated by the government bodies and others involved in its safeguarding. This is especially true of counter-cultural forms of expression that tend to be more common in the freer and less convention-bound urban societies where a wide variety of social groups flourish, some of which may be regarded as posing a serious challenge to mainstream society.

An example of ICH where the social constraints that frame people's normal lives are temporarily loosened is that of the Aalst carnival in Belgium. This festival overturns for a few days the normally prevailing relationship between the authorities and local inhabitants, and the former are subjected to subversive and anarchic approaches from the latter. In addition, there is a fairly broad range of ICH that challenges accepted gender roles and that may be deeply subversive as a consequence; it is fair to argue that many such elements may flourish more freely in urban than non-urban environments, including theatrical performances, festivals and processions of various kinds. Indeed, the aforementioned question of the gender dynamics of ICH brings this question sharply into focus as there is a fairly broad range of ICH that challenges accepted gender roles and that may be deeply subversive as a consequence. Formal recognition of such forms of ICH would clearly pose a challenge to many governments. It is still open to question whether India (whose Supreme Court has recently held that a third gender of transsexuals should be officially recognised) (Reuters 2014) would seek to nominate the ICH of the trans-gender *hijaira* community on an international list or Germany or the UK to celebrate the vibrant cross-dressing culture of their annual Gay Pride Festivals. Certain 'counter-culture' forms, however, have now been officially recognised at the national and/or international levels. For example, Vietnam has recently nominated for inscription on the Representative List the *Hát chầu văn* that is performed during the mediumship rite of *Hầu đồng*. Traversing gender is integral to this ritual: when they are possessed by male spirits, female mediums take on male roles and vice versa, cross-dressing and adopting the gender characteristics of the other sex (Norton 2009; Endres and Lauser 2012). Also, some internationally recognised ICH represents a form of social commentary that may be socially subversive, such as the Karagöz shadow puppets of Turkey that present a bottom-up critique of authority and political corruption. In some cases, this represents a transformation of the original element as with a sacred ritual from West Africa that has been re-contextualised and transformed into a burlesque performance involving inversion of gender roles (de Jong 2007).

Some examples of ICH already given formal recognition through inscription on the Convention's Representative List (RL) suggest that this is already happening. For example, the tango in Argentina and Uruguay, inscribed as an ICH element in 2009, is not only a purely urban form, but also represents the heritage of very specific social groups, being judged as fulfilling inscription criterion R.1 as it is 'considered one of the main manifestations of identity for the inhabitants of the Río de la Plata region'. It was created by the urban lower classes in Buenos Aires and Montevideo who comprised a mix of European immigrants, descendants of African slaves and the local indigenous population, representing a fusion of a wide range of customs, beliefs and rituals that became transformed into a distinctive cultural identity. As for Fado from Portugal, it has been inscribed on the RL explicitly as an 'urban popular song' and is described as:

> [A] genre widely practised by various communities in Lisbon, represented by numerous neighbourhood associations and other grass-root groups as well as by individual agents such as artists (singers and musicians), authors (composers and poets), instrument makers, book and record publishers and other leading exponents of the genre's practice. It is practised professionally both in the concert circuit and in a network of small 'Fado houses' with resident artistic staff, but it is also sung by amateurs in numerous grass-root associations located throughout all older neighbourhoods of Lisbon.
>
> (UNESCO 2011)[9]

This description clearly demonstrates the different social groups and associations involved in this urban form of ICH. Another urban ICH element anchored firmly in the local, urban community is the Fiesta of the Patios in Cordova (Spain) that takes place during 12 days at the beginning of May. The patio houses are communal, family or multi-family dwellings or sets of individual houses with a shared patio in the historical quarter of Cordova and, during this fiesta, people visit each other's patios and share food and drink. This contributes to local harmony and conviviality as well as demonstrating ancestral practices of sustainable communal coexistence.[10]

In its reaffirmation of international human rights instruments, the Convention's definition of ICH respects also the special status rights of women, children, migrant workers and minorities, all of whose lives may be more or less affected by living in an urban environment or moving to it. At an early meeting on ICH and gender held in Paris in 2003, Adraina Gonzalez gave the example of female Mexican migrants to New York. They face extremely difficult living conditions, with their men-folk abused and exploited outside the home and, as a consequence, becoming increasingly abusive towards them inside it (UNESCO 2003: 4–5). As migrants, these women have a typically ambivalent attitude towards their heritage and traditions, wishing to safeguard them, on the one hand, and to escape them, on the other. They are also creating a new 'fusion' culture which mixes their cultural traditions with elements of the culture of New York – is the latter simply an 'American' culture or is it really representative of a modern, urban culture? In other words, is this experience one of foreign migrant (women) or one common to migrants from rural to urban settings? Moreover, does it suggest that the gender dynamics at play are, in some sense, transformed by the urban setting? In either case, this points to several important issues. ICH has an important survival value for migrants as an identity marker but it may also become the vehicle for expressing tensions faced by migrant families. Hence, efforts should be made to preserve and enhance those aspects of this heritage that support the cohesion of the community and the agency of the migrants while seeking to mitigate any negative aspects and impacts. It can also evolve and fuse with 'local' and/or globalised urban cultural forms and this points to an essential characteristic of all ICH, which is its dynamic and continually evolving nature.

Another issue related to the ICH of urban migrants is: how should we respond if a group creates a new 'tradition' that it believes is 'authentic'[11] that researchers and other local communities regard as a fabrication? Such examples can typically be found in the transmission of ICH within urban migrant communities: here, the transmission is not strictly speaking inter-generational and the ICH created is largely adapted to the new environment of the migrants' life. As inter-generational transmission is a fundamental definitional requirement for heritage to be considered as ICH under the 2003 Convention, such heritage would not fall within the scope of that Convention (unless it has been handed down over several generations of immigrants). Despite this, it can still function as a powerful statement of cultural identity and 'can be richly invested with meanings for those involved, and can be part of communicating and establishing gender-balances' (UNESCO 2003: 8). The transformation of Nôgaku (a traditional, male-dominated Japanese performing art) when transposed to an urban context and re-interpreted in such a way that roles traditionally played by men are played by women is a further example of this process (Yuko Toyoshima in UNESCO 2003). An even more intriguing set of transformations has occurred with the art of Kabuki which, at the beginning of the seventeenth century, was a mixed-sex form dominated by women. Over time, however, women were prohibited from performance on the public stage on moral grounds as public theatrical performance was traditionally associated with prostitution at that time and young boys quickly took over all the traditionally female roles (UNESCO 2012b).[12] This change would appear to reflect notions of morality developed in response to the requirements of urban living where the greater population numbers led to strangers living alongside each other. Nowadays, in response to newer forms of urban morality, some theatre groups have begun to perform Kabuki with women playing the female roles.

ICH transmission in urbanised societies

The shift in many, if not most, societies towards urbanisation seems to be a continuing and permanent trend and is one that poses a serious policy challenge for
many Parties to the 2003 Convention. A central challenge posed by social shifts
occurring as a result of urbanisation, itself often a response to environmental and
other factors, is how to ensure the continued transmission of ICH in these changed
social circumstances. Mali, for example, is experiencing a weakening of traditional modes of transmission (due to pressures of globalisation, urbanisation and
the demands of modern life) and the education in cultural heritage to young school
pupils has become an important means for them of acquiring knowledge and
understanding of the past, safeguarding of ICH and strengthening of cultural
identity. Hence, the African School of Heritage, a national network in Mali, was
created to advocate for integrating heritage elements in teaching programmes and
teacher training and to prepare an educational guide for this. In these new contexts
and in response to different opportunities and pressures, the communities that
have maintained traditional modes of transmission are losing them and young
people prefer to achieve a formal certificate or degree to validate their new skills.
As noted above in relation to migrants' ICH, the shift from non-urban to urban
living can often affect and even cut the traditional modes of transmission. A notable
contrast to that general trend is found in Peru where even the children of migrant
Chanka communities in big cities show great interest in performing the Scissors
Dance (UNESCO 2012a). Nevertheless, that seems to be exceptional and it is
therefore important to understand how this occurs and to identify new ways in
which inter-generational transmission can be ensured in this novel context. In
order to understand the nature of ICH transmission, we need to ask the following
questions: Who transmits what and how? Within which social networks, forms of
organisation and ideologies has such heritage been handed down? Are these
processes gendered or related to specific age or other social groups, and how?
What are the sites and the generational contexts in which they take place (Berliner
2013: 75)? It is also important to realise that through implementing safeguarding
measures, we effectively transform transmission. This is a process that Berliner
calls 'UNESCOization' (Berliner 2012). In addition to this, what is getting produced
draws on the past, but also (re)produces it as something new.

Many of the Parties reporting to the ICH Intergovernmental Committee have
noted impacts on ICH transmission that relate directly or indirectly to social evo-
lutions related to urbanisation. Lithuania, for example, has observed for some
time a general decline in traditional culture, due to the transformation of agricultural technologies and working methods, demographic changes, the urbanisation
of society and, more generally, the processes of globalisation. As a consequence,
many ICH elements have disappeared while others have been transferred to the
urban context and continue in the frame of modified contexts and forms: through
organised concerts, festivals, stage activities, etc. rather than more informal and
impromptu forms of performance. It is left open to question whether this is a

positive or a negative evolution and it is a question that deserves further research. The Periodic Report submitted by Lithuania to the ICH Committee in 2012 (UNESCO 2012c) notes that it is essential to find a balance between more traditional features of the element and contemporary ideas, sensibilities and artistic language.

Rural–urban migration has for some time been a central feature of Mongolian society as a result of economic development, environmental challenges and increasing industrialisation. It is notable, for example, that four of the Mongolian elements inscribed on the Representative List relate to the country's traditional nomadic culture. This suggests that national cultural identity leans heavily towards the traditional nomadic lifestyle and, at the same time, that there is a sense of the need to celebrate and defend this in the face of modern living. Indeed, in its Periodic Report to the Intergovernmental Committee under the 2003 Convention, Mongolia notes the strong influence of increasing urbanisation of the country's population as a potentially damaging factor for the continuance of many cultural traditions (UNESCO 2012k). Traditionally, non-formal means of transmission of ICH have been strong in Mongolia and the main mode has been through home tutoring and apprenticeship training; the latter is based on techniques of performance and lead-training that require genuine effort and creativity from the apprentices. Unfortunately, this is no longer sufficiently well recognised within cultural communities and, as a result, most people active in the field of culture prefer to gain a formal certificate or degree. In response to this, the Mongolian government is seeking to support community elders who are trainers in ICH skills and know-how by providing them with allowances, and local authorities also attempt to support and promote such non-formal training. Another means of non-formal transmission is through training conducted at local Cultural Centres, schools, kindergartens and other public or private organisations. Hence, the home-based and apprenticeship-based transmission has been transformed into training offered through largely urban institutional forms.

Although inter-generational transmission (often in families) is still viable in many societies, transmission through formal schooling is becoming increasingly necessary too, especially in the urban context. Moreover, in some cases, only the knowledge taught at schools is considered to be 'official', greatly reducing the roles of the elders in the families and society (UNESCO 2012c, 2012d). In Vietnam, traditional forms of ICH transmission within families and guilds remain valid but, in addition, capacity-building activities for safeguarding ICH are organised within communities by the local branches of the Department of Culture, Sports and Tourism, such as a training workshop on management skills for heads of Gong clubs of Đắk Nông Province. ICH classes are also regularly held for young people by different bodies, including the Hue Monument Conservation Centre, while teacher training is given to increase the necessary knowledge and skills for teaching ICH elements, such as Gongs (in the Central Highlands) and Quan ho Bắc Ninh folk songs (in Bắc Ninh and Bắc Giang Provinces). Public presentations and performances in museums, heritage sites, trade or cultural tourism fairs, etc. provide other forms of non-formal transmission and are supported by the government though a number of incentive policies such as providing spaces, tax exemptions or reductions, etc. (UNESCO 2012d). Another example can be found in the Republic of Korea where a dual-track approach of formal education and non-formal methods of transmission is consciously applied (UNESCO 2012d, 2012e). Mali is also experiencing a weakening of traditional modes of transmission due to the twin pressures of globalisation and the demands of modern urban-based life. In response, education in cultural heritage to young school pupils has become an important means for them of acquiring knowledge and understanding of the past (UNESCO 2012f).

The Ohgi Festival (Japan) presents an interesting case where a new institutional space for its enactment was created that opened it up to the wider involvement of community members, both male and female, as well as of teenagers (Arantes 2007).[13] As a result of this there has been a strengthening of public support and interest in Noh as an art and larger audiences for public performances: making the rules of participation more flexible and appropriate to contemporary social reality was vital to safeguarding the practice of Noh in its local and traditional setting. This case provides a strong illustration that historical circumstances may produce changes in the social basis of ICH transmission and/or production. Arantes asserts that, in such cases, the safeguarding challenge is to strike an appropriate balance between continuity and change and to realise that, in real situations, these forces are not as conflicting as they might appear to be in abstract. In fact, it is unrealistic to expect genres of cultural performance and their transmission to remain unchanged throughout decades, or even centuries, of reproduction through inter-generational transmission and in response to changed realities. The capacity to evolve is, after all, an integral characteristic of ICH.

Interplay between the physical fabric of the urban setting and its related ICH

The importance of spaces and places for the performance, enactment and practice of some forms of ICH is recognised by the inclusion of such spaces in the international lists of the Convention (many having previously been proclaimed as cultural spaces under the Masterpieces of Oral and Intangible Heritage programme of UNESCO and, later, incorporated automatically into the RL). Here, the concept of 'cultural spaces' is understood to encompass both physical and temporal spaces that owe their existence to cultural activities that have traditionally taken place there. The temporal spaces are generally characterised by periodicity that is cyclical, seasonal, tied to the calendar, etc. Places are more specifically understood to be the locations in which ICH is practised and performed. Probably the most prominent example of such is the cultural space of the Jemaa el-Fna Square in Marrakesh (Morocco) in which a unique concentration of popular Moroccan cultural traditions is performed through musical, religious and artistic expressions, while also acting as a commercial centre, a meeting point for the local population and visitors and the provision of a variety of services (including dental care, traditional medicine, fortune-telling, preaching and henna tattooing).[14]

Urban environments offer a variety of spaces that can host ICH and related transmission and training activities such as cultural centres, museums, libraries and theatres. Conversely, the move from a rural to an urban environment may also make it difficult to find appropriate performance and other spaces for the enactment of ICH. For example, a decline of the area around the station where carnival bands for the Carnival of Binche (Belgium) traditionally practise in cafés, as well as the impact of the recent economic crisis, has led to a decline in participants in the carnival banquets and fewer Gilles attending the Sunday processions of other groups. An interesting counter-example (also found in Belgium) is the way in which the inscription of the Procession of the Holy Blood has encouraged the citizens of Bruges, itself inscribed as a World Heritage Site, to value not only the physical fabric of the historic city but also its intangible heritage (UNESCO 2013a).

Municipal authorities, often operating through local museums, libraries and cultural centres, clearly have a key role to play in providing infrastructural, administrative and financial support for the practice and enactment of ICH. In response to the loss of traditional spaces for performance and/or enactment of ICH, both local and governmental authorities may step in to rehabilitate these or provide new ones. In Syria, for example, the physical spaces necessary to the continued enactment and performance of ICH were being renovated up to the time of writing the country's report during 2011, with the Ministry of Tourism, for example, rehabilitating traditional bathhouses (e.g. the Hammam Yalbuga Al-Nasiri in Aleppo) and their associated customs. The Ministry of Waqf (Islamic Charitable Foundations) also contributes to the rehabilitation of places whose existence is necessary for expressing ICH, especially traditional *souqs*, where the traditional practice of storytelling is directly linked with the space in which it is enacted (UNESCO 2012m).

In Turkey, increased urbanisation (and the lack of suitable spaces available in modern apartments) has led to the need for new places for performing the Traditional Sohbet Meetings, gatherings of which the main element is 'talking' (sohbet), but that also include folk music, folk dances, indoor plays, village spectacle plays and dining. Support from both the private sector and public authorities has been necessary to ensure the continuity of this element in urban areas, demonstrating the range of actors involved in this process. The Ministry of Culture and Tourism (MOCT) has provided financial support for organising these meetings and Çankırı Municipality and the Governor's Office of Çankırı have provided support for the restoration of a historical house known as a venue for the tradition. The Semah Alevi-Bektaşı ritual in Turkey, which takes place in a number of different places (such as houses, buildings, complexes, social and cultural associations), and the Regulation on the Mevlevi Order and the Sema Ceremony (2008) have been adopted with the aim of preventing the risks of degeneration/distortion of the performing spaces as well as of its music and spiritual elements. It is questionable, however, how effective this legislation can be as the performance of the Mevlevi Sema Ceremony of Turkey (which includes the dance of the whirling dervish) has been commercialised by the tourist industry and this has resulted in the performance of more compressed and less complex ceremonies (UNESCO 2008; Pietrobruno 2009).

For the Āşıklık tradition of minstrels in Turkey, a performing space has been created through establishing a 'Culture House' in the town of Kars. Similarly, the Kırkpınar House in Edirne has been established as a documentation and information centre (UNESCO 2013b).

Local authorities also play an important role in providing such spaces in Bulgaria where care for significant physical spaces is undertaken by the local community along with local mayors, museums and community cultural centres. In addition, the Ministry of Culture works with such bodies and may grant funds for the purchase of equipment and for repairing buildings and their surroundings, including the places where local traditions are practised. An example is the specific activities undertaken to safeguard the Nestinarstvo or 'messages from the past' element which is a ritual complex for Saints Constantine and Helena held in the village of Bulgari Nestinarstvo on the general village feast and temple festival to its patron Saints Constantine and Helena. The ritual includes ceremonial actions, music, dancing, food, objects and clothes; the culminating moment is walking on burning embers. These actions include establishing an Information Centre in the Mayor's Office of Bulgari, providing a space for discussions, lectures, films, etc. and equipment, developing a local tourist marketing strategy and creating information materials, and the maintenance of the ritual places related to the Panagyr (UNESCO 2013c). After 1945, Vietnam's Nha Nhac element lost its traditional performing space when the royal musicians left the Imperial Palace to make a living through playing folk music in ceremonies in temples, pagodas, village festivals and ancestor worshipping ceremonies. In response, the Hue local government has restored a Nha Nhac performing space for selected royal ceremonies (UNESCO 2012d).

The Houtem Jaarmarkt (Belgium) represents a related but rather specific challenge as regulations governing markets and mass gatherings are making it increasingly difficult to hold such markets (UNESCO 2013a). In such cases, it may be necessary to create some 'cultural exception' to the governing regulations. In Peru, the main square at Mito is the place where the Huaconada Dance is performed and the local city council has enacted a decree regulating trade in the vicinity, the upkeep and hygiene of the urban space, as well as safety measures for spectators and dancers. With the Carnival of Binche (Belgium), the practical aspects of holding the carnival have been carefully considered and security measures taken to ensure safety (such as erecting crowd barriers and appointing local Commissaries to administer it). In addition, transport links have been provided and access for disabled people ensured (UNESCO 2013a). This illustrates the great importance of ensuring that such carnivals, festivals and processions that often take place within a historic urban environment do not pose a threat to the physical historic fabric and remain safe for the performers and the spectators. This is particularly important in view of the great touristic appeal of such events.

The Busó festivities in Hungary also illustrate this point well: in 2002, this Sunday procession lasted hardly an hour while, in 2012, it took two hours due to its increased popularity and the great number of participants. Hungary's Periodic Report goes further to suggest that these greatly increased numbers are directly impacting on the content of the festivities as the traditional primitive role-playing and mischief is seen as contrary to the public profile now enjoyed by the event; this has resulted in some limitation in the wilder aspects of this role-playing, as deemed necessary during the procession (UNESCO 2013d). In addition, this 'success' from the point of view of tourism threatens the fabric of the small, historic town of Mohacs whose narrow lanes cannot cope with numbers of visitors beyond a certain level. In response, the municipality and festival organisers have prepared plans over the past few years for the Busó festivities to be able to welcome greater visitor numbers. They have identified two additional locations outside the central square (Szechenyi ter) into which the activities can spread. Procession of the Holy Blood in Bruges (Belgium) element shows the interesting mutuality in the relationship between historic towns and their ICH. Its inscription has also shown inhabitants of Bruges (already a World Heritage Site) that their heritage is not restricted to the physical but includes also the intangible elements (UNESCO 2013a).

The role of different actors

First and foremost, it is necessary to address the key but not easily resolved question as to who are the 'communities' and 'groups' of the 2003 Convention who are seen as having a legitimate stake and a role to play in safeguarding 'their own' ICH. As the bearer community is viewed as the actor with the most important responsibility for safeguarding its own ICH (as well as the closest relationship with it in terms of cultural rights), a new set of relationships between states and local communities has started to develop. A useful discussion of the different levels of relationship and rights of various actors (cultural community, local community, national community, etc.) is presented in the report on cultural heritage and human rights by Farida Shaheed, UN Special Rapporteur on Cultural Rights (Human Rights Council 2011). A UNESCO expert meeting (UNESCO 2006) addressed the question of 'Who are the "communities, groups and . . . individuals" referred to in the Convention text?' The expert meeting produced the following definition of 'groups' that is worth revisiting here, especially in view of the fact that the notion of 'group' has not been greatly developed in subsequent work on the Convention.[15]

> *Groups* comprise people within or across communities who share characteristics such as skills, experience and special knowledge, and thus perform specific roles in the present and future practice, re-creation and/or transmission of their intangible cultural heritage as, for example, cultural custodians, practitioners or apprentices.

What is important for the purposes of this chapter is that this definition of 'groups' hangs on 'shared characteristics' which, although further qualified here as 'such as skills, experience and special knowledge', are not limited to those specific characteristics. This leaves open the possibility of including other social groups based

on the shared characteristics of sexual orientation, for example, or a shared interest in a particular urban style of dress, hair or body art. Would the wearing of
tattoos among urban youth qualify them to be a group for the purposes of the
Convention? If not, would the same approach be applied to the body art of Maoris
in New Zealand?

From this, we see that there is a lot of room for development in the understanding we have of the full range of ICH and its associated groups and communities
and research on urban ICH will surely contribute in an important way to this.
Further important issues that will need to be addressed concern the approaches
that can be taken for ensuring effective and appropriate community participation
in ICH safeguarding as envisaged in the Convention. The specific measures
involved in this, according to Article 2(3) of the 2003 Convention, include 'the
identification, documentation, research, preservation, protection, promotion,
enhancement, transmission, particularly through formal and non-formal education, as well as the revitalization of the various aspects of such heritage'. This is
not just a question of importance for ICH safeguarding, but is also significant for
protecting the physical heritage as seen in the example of preserving the World
Heritage Site of Timbuktu through using a participatory management approach,
initiated by the Timbuktu Cultural Mission. Some of the challenges in expanding
the involvement of local communities have been demonstrated in a case study and
the conclusion is drawn that the local community has a duty to participate in the
maintenance of the mosques, while the ability to continue this tradition represents
an essential aspect of their cultural rights (Ould Sidi 2012).

Chapter III of the Operational Directives to the 2003 Convention addresses this
question of how the participation of communities and groups, as well as of individuals (where applicable), experts, centres of expertise and research institutes in
the implementation of the Convention is to be ensured (UNESCO 2010: paras
79–89). Measures that Parties are encouraged to undertake to this end include
sensitising communities (groups and individuals) about the significance of their
ICH, making results of research available to them, sharing documentation with them
and other Parties and supporting the development of regional and sub-regional
networks. In addition, in the nomination files for inscription on the Representative
and Urgent Safeguarding Lists established under the Convention, Parties are
required to demonstrate that the ICH element in question has been nominated
'following the widest possible participation of the community, group or, if applicable, individuals concerned and with their free, prior and informed consent'. When
filling in Section C of their Periodic Reports on the legislative, regulatory and other
measures taken for the implementation of the Convention (on the current status of
inscribed elements) they 'shall endeavour to ensure the widest possible participation of the communities, groups and, where applicable, individuals concerned
during the process of preparation of such reports' (UNESCO 2010: para 157).
This is a well-intentioned attempt to ensure that Parties fulfil the, admittedly very
soft law, requirement to ensure community participation in ICH safeguarding but
its implementation is rather patchy. For example, in the case of the Periodic
Reports community participation in drafting the reports on ICH elements often

appears to be a rubber stamp, based on a very limited and top-down consultation with the communities, although there are also some good examples where cultural associations and bearer communities have themselves contributed directly to the report writing.

The general picture that comes across from the Periodic Reports submitted for the 2012 reporting cycle is that the local museum or other local representative of the central cultural authority (e.g. the Ministry of Culture) makes contact with the relevant associations or other organisations representing the practitioners and/or performers of the elements and then prepares the report for each element on the basis of information supplied by them. In some cases meetings are organised for this purpose with the various stakeholders. Typically, a questionnaire is sent to all communities concerned with the element in question and the final report reflects generalised information based on their replies as well as interviews and consultations (Lithuania). In some cases, consultations are held in different regions of the country with local cultural leaders, active members of communities, municipality representatives, cultural centres, NGOs, etc. What is much less clear is how far the communities have an opportunity to vet the report once it is written and how far their opinions can be taken into account at this stage. The overall impression is more of a passive than a proactive role on the part of communities in the actual drafting of the reports and this experience would suggest that requiring Parties to submit a form showing community consent in these activities is not sufficient in itself to ensure a truly participatory process.

As the previous section clearly demonstrates, a range of different actors – from municipal authorities, museums, local libraries, cultural centres to the private sector, NGOs and civil society groups (such as practitioner associations) – all play important roles in safeguarding urban ICH. In some countries, on-the-ground safeguarding activities and even policy-making are decentralised to a lower administrative authority (to provincial, regional and/or local levels). Belarus, for example, has six regional Cultural Resource Centres that work alongside community representatives and local authorities for safeguarding ICH and coordinate the work of over 70 'Houses' and Centres of Folklore and more than 90 Houses of Crafts (UNESCO 2012g). An important part of ICH safeguarding in Latvia is undertaken by the 119 city and municipal authorities, mainly though providing rehearsal spaces, travel expenses, further education, folk costumes, musical instruments, technical equipment, etc. The Intangible Cultural Heritage of Liepna Parish Project (2006 to 2008) is an interesting initiative as one of its objectives was to ascertain how effective cooperation was among state, local government authorities, research institutions, the private sector and the local community in the determination, identification and promotion of ICH (UNESCO 2012g). Municipal authorities in Turkey have done a lot of work in developing ICH training, including through a public–private initiative with a leading insurance company through which vocational courses are given by masters and successful students receive certificates and they are offered the opportunity of micro-credit facilities upon demand.[16] In its Municipal Vocational Courses (Belmek), Ankara Metropolitan Municipality trains women in new skills, many of which include traditional arts and crafts, thus preparing them for work to strengthen the financial condition of the families (UNESCO 2013b). For the Busó festivities mentioned above, a detailed programme is put together based on prior consultation with a wide range of local stakeholders who include municipal organisers, NGO representatives and leaders of the performing groups. A twice-yearly consensus forum is also organised, led by the Mayor, that consists of representatives of the regional and municipal security, health and transport/traffic authorities, museum experts and the representatives of NGOs, as well as the leaders of the Busó groups (UNESCO 2013d). Similarly, for the Procession of the Holy Blood in Bruges (Belgium) an auditing committee has been set up for its organisation, composed of members of the communal administration, the Bishopric of Bruges, the Bruges heritage cell and the procession committee.

The level of engagement of NGOs and civil society organisations (such as cultural associations) in ICH safeguarding varies greatly between countries, as does the relationship between these bodies and the central government. In the Republic of Korea, Peru and Croatia, for example, almost all listed ICH elements have professional associations related to them that are active in identifying, inventorying, documenting, performing, researching, teaching and promoting ICH (UNESCO 2012a, 2012e, 2012j). In contrast, interestingly, there are few NGOs related to ICH in Mali; this may reflect the fact that other forms of traditional community structures exist to fulfil this role, including village elders and councils as the traditional authorities, socio-professional groups such as *griots* (masters of words) and religious leaders (UNESCO 2012f). The Programme of Support to the Municipal and Communitarian Cultures (PACMYC) (2007 to 2011) in Mexico views people and social groups as direct agents for the development of culture and provides economic support to initiatives and projects presented by NGOs and popular and indigenous creators. For example, by 2012 it had supported 79 projects related or linked directly with the Festivity of the Dead operating in 23 states of Mexico.

Conclusion

This chapter suggests that now, over ten years since the adoption of the UNESCO Convention on Intangible Cultural Heritage in 2003, it is timely to consider how ICH safeguarding is being and can be incorporated into the everyday life of the urban fabric and the local heritage community. Addressing these questions within an urban environment introduces a new set of challenges that may not yet have been fully acknowledged or even appreciated by all those involved in this endeavour. As we have seen, the five main domains of ICH set out in UNESCO's 2003 Convention all respond to forms of heritage that may be found in urban settings and which, in some cases such as the performing arts, may be more prominent in urban than rural contexts. In addition, there is a range of 'living heritages' and popular forms of urban cultural expression not at present explicitly recognised by the Convention that could, perhaps, be added to the aforementioned domains of ICH.

In an urban context, ICH frequently has a close interaction with the physical fabric of the city or town in which it is performed, practised and enacted, and there are many examples of where safeguarding cultural spaces and places for the performance of ICH has become a question of major importance. These include, for example, the routes of processions and city squares, theatres and other public spaces of performance as well as less public places of ritual; at times, the loss or change of these may impact directly on the ICH and its content. Related challenges include how urban areas can respond to the pressures of increasing numbers of cultural tourists related to ICH attractions. In setting policies and managing urban ICH, we have seen that a number of stakeholders and actors have their own roles to play and these include not only the bearer communities themselves and their associations, but also municipal authorities, museums, libraries, cultural centres and the private sector.

With a long-term global trend towards increased urbanisation, it is vital that we examine ways in which urban ICH can be harnessed for helping people to live better lives. Rural-to-urban migration obviously has a growing impact on ICH and on its transmission within the associated cultural communities and it is necessary to develop new and creative approaches towards ICH safeguarding in response to this. The living traditions, know-how and cultural practices that make up ICH are understood more and more to have the potential for helping urban communities, especially those who have migrated from other often rural locations, to strengthen their sense of identity and social cohesion as well as providing a bridge with other communities. In this way, ICH can play a key role in equipping people with tools that help them to live better in urban settings and to overcome any potential sense of social and cultural dislocation.

Notes

1 This may be slowly changing. For example, the Korean international NGO Inter-city Cultural Network for ICH concentrates on ICH in an urban context. The Maharana of Mewar Charitable Foundation and UNESCO New Delhi held the Second International Conference on Living Heritage from 13 to 16 March 2014 in City Palace, Udaipur, Rajasthan, and chose as its main theme various approaches towards the promotion of living heritage and its integration in urban space and structures. The conference programme is available online at: http://www.eternalmewar.in/WLHF/Index.shtml (accessed 25 June 2015).

2 Barbara Torggler and Ekaterina Sediakina-Rivière (2013). *Evaluation of UNESCO's Standard-setting Work of the Culture Sector. Part I – 2003 Convention for the Safeguarding of the Intangible Cultural Heritage – FINAL REPORT* (October 2013) (consultant: Janet Blake) UNESCO Doc. IOS/EVS/PI/129 REV. at para. 36.

3 There were 158 States Parties to the Convention with the ratification by Comoros on 20 November 2013. Information available at: http://www.unesco.org/eri/la/convention.asp?KO=17116&language=E (accessed 25 April 2014).

4 This reflects the debate that has existed since the 1990s as to how this aspect of heritage should be named, with suggestions ranging from 'popular culture' to 'traditional culture' and 'folklore'. The terminology 'intangible cultural heritage' is one that strongly reflects an artificial dichotomy created through UNESCO's law-making in this area and many commentators would prefer a term such as 'living cultural traditions' that emphasises the essential human element in this form of heritage.

5 According to UNFPA, it is estimated that 5 billion of the world's population (today estimated at a total population size of *c*.7 billion) will be living in cities by 2030. For more information, see: UNFPA (2007). *Urbanization: A Majority in Cities*. Available at: http://www.unfpa.org/pds/urbanization.htm (accessed 25 April 2014).

6 As noted by Croatia in its Periodic Report no.00787/Croatia adopted by the Intergovernmental Committee for the Safeguarding of the Intangible Cultural Heritage at its seventh session held in Paris, France, December 2012.

7 The concept of 'cultural spaces' encompasses both physical and temporal spaces that owe their existence to cultural activities that have traditionally taken place there. The temporal spaces are generally characterised by periodicity that is cyclical, seasonal, tied to the calendar, etc. Places are more specifically understood to be the locations in which ICH is practised and performed.

8 Art. 2(1) of the Convention reads:

> The 'intangible cultural heritage' means the practices, representations, expressions, knowledge, skills – as well as the instruments, objects, artefacts and cultural spaces associated therewith – that communities, groups and, in some cases, individuals recognize as part of their cultural heritage. This intangible cultural heritage, transmitted from generation to generation, is constantly recreated by communities and groups in response to their environment, their interaction with nature and their history, and provides them with a sense of identity and continuity, thus promoting respect for cultural diversity and human creativity. For the purposes of this Convention, consideration will be given solely to such intangible cultural heritage as is compatible with existing international human rights instruments, as well as with the requirements of mutual respect among communities, groups and individuals, and of sustainable development.

9 The nomination file also mentions that Fado is

> a practice deeply ingrained in the daily life of the local communities in the older neighbourhoods of Lisbon, such as Alcântara, Alfama, Bairro Alto, Bica, Madragoa, Mouraria and others. It was also carried into other cities of Portugal as well as into the Portuguese migrant communities abroad.

10 Information available at: http://www.unesco.org/culture/ich/index.php?lg=en&pg=00011&RL=00258 (accessed 25 April 2014).

11 The concept of authenticity, used as a central notion with regard to inscribing sites on the World Heritage List of the 1972 Convention of UNESCO, is a problematic term when applied to ICH and it was not deemed appropriate as a measure of ICH significance. As a consequence, inter-generational transmission is used as a listing criterion instead.

12 As occurred in Shakespeare's time in Elizabethan England.

13 An Executive Committee was set up to improve the *Rosoku-Noh* (literally 'candle-lit Noh') as a special feature of this annual festival.

14 The cultural space of Jemaa el-Fna Square was originally proclaimed as a Masterpiece of the Oral and Intangible Heritage of Humanity in 2001 and subsequently inscribed on the RL in 2008. For more information, refer to the UNESCO website available at: http://www.unesco.org/culture/ich/index.php?lg=en&pg=00011&RL=00014 (accessed 25 April 2014).

15 It is notable, for example, that the *Operational Directives for the Implementation of the Convention for the Safeguarding of the Intangible Cultural Heritage* as adopted by the General Assembly of the States Parties to the Convention at its second ordinary session (Paris, France, 16 to 19 June 2008) and amended at its third session (Paris, France,

22 to 24 June 2010) refer in several places to 'communities' and 'groups' without defining the terms.
16 This is called the '1000 Masters Project' co-funded by the Anadolu Sigorta insurance company.

Bibliography

Arantes, A. (2007). A place for intangible cultural heritage in our common future. In: *ACCU, Workshop for Youth Participation for Safeguarding the Intangible Cultural Heritage and Community Development – Final Report.* Tokyo: ACCU.

Bandarin, F. and van Oers, R. (2012). *The Historic Urban Landscape: Managing Heritage in an Urban Century.* London: John Wiley.

Berliner, D. (2012). Multiple nostalgias: the fabric of heritage in Luang Prabang (Lao PDR). *Journal of the Royal Anthropological Institute,* 18, 769–86.

Berliner, D. (2013). New directions in the study of cultural transmission. In: L. Arizpe and C. Amescua (eds), *Anthropological Perspectives on Intangible Cultural Heritage. SpringerBriefs in Environment, Security, Development and Peace,* 6, 71–8.

Blake, J. (2014). Gender and intangible cultural heritage. In: UNESCO *Gender Equality – Heritage and Creativity.* Paris: UNESCO, pp. 49–59.

de Jong, F. (2007). A masterpiece of masquerading: contradictions of conservation in intangible heritage. In: F. de Jong and M. Rowlands (eds), *Reclaiming Heritage: Alternative Imageries of Memory in West Africa.* Walnut Creek: Left Coast Press.

Endres, K.W. and Lauser, A. (eds) (2012). *Engaging the Spirit World: Popular Beliefs and Practices in Modern Southeast Asia.* New York and Oxford: Berghahn Books.

Human Rights Council (2011). *Report of the Independent Expert in the Field of Cultural Rights, Farida Shaheed.* Human Rights Council Seventeenth Session Agenda Item 3, 21 March 2011 (UN Doc. A/HR/C/17/38). Available at: http://www.unesco.org/new/fileadmin/MULTIMEDIA/HQ/CLT/images/Report%20of%20Farida%20Shaheed.pdf (accessed 30 June 2015).

Norton, B. (2009). Engendering mediumship. In: B. Norton (ed.), *Songs for the Spirits – Music and Mediums in Modern Vietnam.* Champaign: University of Illinois Press, pp. 155–89.

Ould Sidi, A. (2012). Maintaining Timbuktu's unique tangible and intangible heritage. *International Journal of Heritage Studies,* 18(3), 324–31.

Pietrobruno, S. (2009). Cultural research and intangible heritage. *Culture Unbound,* 1, 227–47.

Reuters (2014). Supreme Court recognises transgenders as third gender in landmark ruling, Tuesday 15 April 2014. Available at: http://in.reuters.com/article/2014/04/15/india-transgenders-idINKBN0D10A 320140415 (accessed 17 August 2014).

Taylor, P. (2007). *Modernity and Re-enchantment: Religion in Post-revolutionary Vietnam.* Available at: http://www.tienghatquehuong.com/FolkSongs/ChauVan.htm (accessed 26 June 2015).

UNESCO (2003). *Final Report of the Expert Meeting on Gender and Intangible Heritage, Paris, 8–10 December 2003.* Intangible Heritage Section, UNESCO.

UNESCO (2006). *Final Report of the Expert Meeting on Community Involvement in Safeguarding Intangible Cultural Heritage, Tokyo, Japan, 13–15 March 2006.* Paris: UNESCO.

UNESCO (2008). *The Mevlevi Sema Ceremony*. Available at: http://www.unesco.org/culture/ intangible-heritage/39eur_uk.htm (accessed 26 June 2015).

UNESCO (2010). *Operational Directives for the Implementation of the Convention for the Safeguarding of the Intangible Cultural Heritage.* Adopted by the General Assembly of the States Parties to the Convention at its second ordinary session (Paris, France, 16 to 19 June 2008) and amended at its third session (Paris, France, 22 to 24 June 2010). Paris: UNESCO.

UNESCO (2011). *Nomination file no. 00563 for Inscription on the Representative List of the Intangible Cultural Heritage of Humanity in 2011 adopted by the Intergovernmental Committee for the Safeguarding of the Intangible Cultural Heritage at its sixth session held in Bali, Indonesia, November 2011.* Paris: UNESCO.

UNESCO (2012a). *Periodic Report no. 00793/Peru adopted by the Intergovernmental Committee for the Safeguarding of the Intangible Cultural Heritage at its seventh session held in Paris, France, December 2012.* Paris: UNESCO.

UNESCO (2012b). *Nomination file no. 00846 for Inscription on the Representative List of the Intangible Cultural Heritage of Humanity in 2012 adopted by the Intergovernmental Committee for the Safeguarding of the Intangible Cultural Heritage at its seventh session held in Paris, December 2012.* Paris: UNESCO.

UNESCO (2012c). *Periodic Report no. 00779/Lithuania adopted by the Intergovernmental Committee for the Safeguarding of the Intangible Cultural Heritage at its seventh session held in Paris, France, December 2012.* Paris: UNESCO.

UNESCO (2012d). *Periodic Report no. 00792/Viet Nam adopted by the Intergovernmental Committee for the Safeguarding of the Intangible Cultural Heritage at its seventh session held in Paris, France, December 2012.* Paris: UNESCO.

UNESCO (2012e). *Periodic Report no. 00781/Republic of Korea adopted by the Intergovernmental Committee for the Safeguarding of the Intangible Cultural Heritage at its seventh session held in Paris, France, December 2012.* Paris: UNESCO.

UNESCO (2012f). *Periodic Report no. 00785/Mali adopted by the Intergovernmental Committee for the Safeguarding of the Intangible Cultural Heritage at its seventh session held in Paris, France, December 2012.* Paris: UNESCO.

UNESCO (2012g). *Periodic Report no. 00780/Belarus adopted by the Intergovernmental Committee for the Safeguarding of the Intangible Cultural Heritage at its seventh session held in Paris, France, December 2012.* Paris: UNESCO.

UNESCO (2012h). *Periodic Report no. 00778/Latvia adopted by the Intergovernmental Committee for the Safeguarding of the Intangible Cultural Heritage at its seventh session held in Paris, France, December 2012.* Paris: UNESCO.

UNESCO (2012i). *Periodic Report no. 00798/Mexico adopted by the Intergovernmental Committee for the Safeguarding of the Intangible Cultural Heritage at its seventh session held in Paris, France, December 2012.* Paris: UNESCO.

UNESCO (2012j). *Periodic Report no. 00787/Croatia adopted by the Intergovernmental Committee for the Safeguarding of the Intangible Cultural Heritage at its seventh session held in Paris, France, December 2012.* Paris: UNESCO.

UNESCO (2012k). *Periodic Report no. 00786/Mongolia adopted by the Intergovernmental Committee for the Safeguarding of the Intangible Cultural Heritage at its sixth session held in Bali, Indonesia, November 2011.* Paris: UNESCO.

UNESCO (2012m). *Periodic Report no. 00783/Syrian Arab Republic adopted by the Intergovernmental Committee for the Safeguarding of the Intangible Cultural Heritage at its seventh session held in Paris, France, December 2012.* Paris: UNESCO.

UNESCO (2013a). *Periodic Report no.00812/Belgium adopted by the Intergovernmental Committee for the Safeguarding of the Intangible Cultural Heritage at its eighth session held in Baku, Azerbaijan, December 2013*. Paris: UNESCO.

UNESCO (2013b). *Periodic Report no. 00815/Turkey adopted by the Intergovernmental Committee for the Safeguarding of the Intangible Cultural Heritage at its eighth session held in Baku, Azerbaijan, December 2013*. Paris: UNESCO.

UNESCO (2013c). *Periodic Report no.00808/Bulgaria adopted by the Intergovernmental Committee for the Safeguarding of the Intangible Cultural Heritage at its eighth session held in Baku, Azerbaijan, December 2013*. Paris: UNESCO.

UNESCO (2013d) *Periodic Report no. 00809/Hungary adopted by the Intergovernmental Committee for the Safeguarding of the Intangible Cultural Heritage at its eighth session held in Baku, Azerbaijan, December 2013*. Paris: UNESCO.

Worthing, D. and Bond, S. (2008). *Managing Built Heritage*. London: John Wiley.

Websites

City of Melbourne. *Street Art*. http://www.melbourne.vic.gov.au/ForResidents/StreetCleaning andGraffiti/GraffitiStreetArt/Pages/Whatisstreetart.aspx (accessed on 11 December 2014).

Periodic Reports are available on the UNESCO website at: http://www.unesco.org/culture/ ich/index.php?lg=en&pg=00460.

Part II

Reconciling urban heritage conservation and development?

Chapter 8

The impacts of culture and heritage-led development programmes

The cases of Liverpool (UK) and Lille (France)

Sophia Labadi

In the past 20 years, derelict cities, often characterised by a significant industrial past, have attempted to transform themselves through comprehensive culture- and heritage-led regeneration programmes. Regeneration has been defined as thorough and integrated actions that aim to 'bring about a lasting improvement in the economic, physical, social and environmental conditions of an area' (Roberts and Sykes 2000: 296). In this chapter, culture- and heritage-led regeneration programmes are considered as leading – *a priori* – to models of virtuous and sustainable development. Indeed, as clearly stressed by the quote by Roberts and Sykes, these programmes should aim to protect heritage, bring about lasting economic improvements and jobs opportunities and foster positive social impacts.

The aim of this chapter is to analyse critically whether culture- and heritage-led regeneration programmes in the derelict and former industrial cities of Liverpool and Lille are truly models of sustainable development. In order to do so, this chapter will focus, after a small presentation of the case studies, on image building and branding through title accumulation. The second section will analyse the economic impacts of these strategies and programmes of title accumulation and branding. This chapter will then analyse critically the social impact of these strategies and programmes.

History of the case studies: from grandeur to dereliction

This chapter focuses on two case studies: Lille in France and Liverpool in the United Kingdom. Lille, in northern France, close to the border with Belgium, is the fourth largest metropolitan area of France, behind Paris, Lyon and Marseille. From the beginning of the nineteenth century to the Second World War, Lille, and its wider region, was one of the richest economic territories in France, thanks to its mining and textile industries. After the Second World War, Lille's industries declined rapidly. Over 40 years (1946 to 1986), the Nord-Pas de Calais region lost 400,000 jobs in a process of deindustrialisation that continues through to today. Faced with poor job opportunities, people have left not only the city but also the region. The fabric of the city has suffered, with increasingly derelict private, public and commercial buildings. Since the turn of the millennium, local authorities and businesses have developed clear strategies for the regeneration of Lille and its region, based on its culture, heritage and history.

The city of Liverpool is situated in northwestern England. In the eighteenth century, Liverpool became the most important centre in the world for the organisation of the slave trade and took part in the triangular trade of cotton, manufactured goods and black slaves between Africa, the West Indies, America and Europe. In the nineteenth century, it became Britain's Atlantic gateway and the emigration port for much of Western Europe. The prosperity of the city in the nineteenth century was also generated by shipping and trade of goods for Britain's burgeoning industries. This prosperity was reflected in the construction of prestigious public and private buildings. After the Second World War, Liverpool's docks and traditional manufacturing industries went into sharp decline. The advent of containerisation meant that Liverpool's docks became obsolete. As a result of this economic decline, jobs have been massively cut and the city has lost nearly half of its inhabitants (from 850,000 in 1930 to 450,000 today), which has had a major negative impact on the fabric of the city centre. Similar to Lille, since the turn of the century, strategies have been developed for the regeneration of Liverpool, based on its culture, heritage and history.

Image transformation, title accumulation and performative branding

Heritage-led development varies significantly from city to city. This chapter focuses on Liverpool and Lille. For these two cities, the key aim of the heritage-led development strategies is to transform their image, from derelict cities to creative, confident and dynamic post-industrial territories (Bell 1974). This change of image is almost impossible to quantify, but it is the catalyst for social and economic transformations and impacts, detailed in the following sections. Thus, this change of image is only the first step in the economic and social development of a city, based on its heritage. Yet, this first step is essential as this change of image will attract investments that will help to switch the main focuses of economic activities from the extraction of raw materials and manufactures to an economy based on culture and services.

This change of image or reinvention, at the heart of heritage-led regeneration, has been based on raising the international profile of Liverpool, Lille and their wider regions (Palmer-Rae Associates 2004a). International and regional title accumulations have clearly been the strategy used by these two cities. The cases of Lille and Liverpool demonstrate that one international title does not seem to be enough to transform the image of derelict territories; hence this phenomenon of title accumulation. The strategy related to title accumulation has, however, differed between Liverpool and Lille. For Liverpool, this title accumulation has concentrated on the historic centre, included on the World Heritage site. In 2004, Liverpool-Maritime Mercantile City was inscribed on the World Heritage List under criteria (ii), (iii) and (iv), as witness to the development of one of the world's major trading centres in the eighteenth and nineteenth centuries. In addition, it was European Capital of Culture in 2008.

Title accumulation for Lille has followed a different strategy, as it focuses on the surrounding Nord-Pas de Calais region as well, for in-depth transformation of the wider region. Lille was European Capital of Culture in 2004. The belfries of Flanders, Artois, Hainaut and Picardy, located in Nord-Pas de Calais and Picardy, were inscribed as a UNESCO World Heritage site in 2005 as an extension to the Flemish belfries World Heritage site (nominated in 1998 and inscribed in 1999). In addition, Arras, another city from the Nord-Pas de Calais region, saw its fortifications, designed by Vauban, inscribed on the World Heritage List as part of the serial nomination 'Fortifications of Vauban' in 2008. In 2005, the processional giants from Douai and Cassel were proclaimed – as part of a wider nomination of giants and dragons from Belgium and France – Masterpieces of the Oral and Intangible Heritage of Humanity by UNESCO. The last piece in this title accumulation scaffolding was the inscription of the Nord-Pas de Calais mining basin on the World Heritage List in 2012 (Labadi 2011). This focus on the whole territory, rather than on the historic part of a city, aims to distribute more equitably the benefits of heritage-led regeneration. This more equitable strategy might be considered as a sustainable approach to territorial development. In theory, it should lead to wider distribution of the benefits of regeneration to the whole region, with fewer disparities between the different parts of this territory compared with a strategy of only focusing on the city.

Place branding is at the heart of this title accumulation strategy, which comes in addition to raising the international profile of these cities. Place branding focuses on creating a positive reputation for the city. This is done through reinventing and reimagining the city and/or its region and highlighting its uniqueness, distinctiveness and outstanding character, based on its heritage and history (Ashworth and Kavaratzis 2009; Boland 2013). Brands act as positive images, reputations and symbols that audiences associate almost instinctively with the city or territory. Branding is a 'mental processes of cognition' (Kavaratzis and Ashworth 2005: 507) and relates to people's emotional reaction to a city. Branding based on title accumulation has been fundamental in giving a new identity to Lille and Liverpool. It has helped audiences to associate these cities with confidence, creativity, innovation or style (Hannigan 2003: 354). As further detailed below, this place branding as uniqueness and distinctiveness has been built on the conservation and restoration of the heritage of Lille and Liverpool and on raising confidence and pride in their industrial history.

I have just explained that branding is associated with title accumulation, as exemplified by Liverpool but most clearly by Lille. Branding is also associated with overstating the positive benefits of the impact of these international accolades, primarily of the European Capital of Culture. Therefore, there is a performative element in the use of these brands for reimagining the city. I define performative branding as those situations where describing a situation creates a new reality; in other words, it is performative utterance (Austin 1962). Performative branding aims to create a reality of successful economic and social regeneration through the acquisition of titles. This is clearly exemplified in the very positive official reports of the impacts of the European Capital of Culture commissioned by the city councils of both Lille (Werquin 2005) and Liverpool (Garcia *et al.* 2011). Summaries of these reports with quantified social and economic impacts of the regeneration of these two cities are easily accessible online,[1] to give credibility to a narrative of success. This has been accompanied by intense communication of these results in local, regional, national and international media. Most importantly, these overtly positive results are performance branding because they aim to create a reality that does not necessarily exist. As explained in the next sections on economic and social impacts, the regeneration of both Lille and Liverpool is not as successful as claimed in these official documents and narratives.

This strategy of title accumulation and performative branding certainly reflects the attempts by local authorities to change durably the reputation, images and symbols associated with Lille and Liverpool (Landry and Bianchini 1995: 12). It might also reflect the intense competition between cities, also called 'place wars' (Haider 1992), to market themselves as investment locations and places of creativity and uniqueness. The successive accumulation of titles as well as this performative branding based on intense communication might also reflect the fear of 'brand decay' (Tallon 2010: 254), characterised by an area losing its reputation and distinctive image within the national and international spheres. To maintain visitor appeal distinction requires regular investment in new cultural facilities and clever marketing. This is reflected in this phenomenon of accumulation of titles, as well as the opening of regional antennae of iconic and heavily branded museums. One example is the opening of Louvre Lens in the Nord-Pas de Calais region in 2012.

These phenomena of re-imaging and branding of Liverpool and Lille have been based on and anchored in the conservation, restoration or re-use of their heritage, mainly for creative or cultural activities, services and accommodations. These two phenomena have also been based on public space management and beautification, through landscaping and new signage of public spaces. The wealth of heritage that has been conserved or restored has further highlighted the unique, distinctive and creative nature of the two cities. The scale of conservation, restoration and re-use of heritage and the landscaping of public space as part of Lille 2004 European Capital of Culture have been such that local authorities called it 'a metamorphosis' of the urban landscape (Palmer-Rae Associates 2004b: 346). The use of this term 'metamorphosis' strengthens the idea of in-depth transformation of Lille.

The title of European Capital of Culture for Lille has thus led to the extensive and prompt renovation of monuments of high historic and architectural significance, such as Lille Opera, the Palais des Beaux-Arts in Lille or the Musée de l'Hôtel Sandelin in Saint-Omer. Derelict industrial structures were also rehabilitated and turned into cultural centres, including the transformation of 12 derelict industrial buildings (former factories, mills, breweries and so on) spread across the region into 'Maisons Folie'. These 'Maisons Folie' were deemed to contain important architecture, worth conserving with the aim of transforming them into performance areas and workshops for local artists. As industrial structures, they embody the spirit of the northern region as well as the social, economic and cultural history of their local neighbourhoods, in which they historically played a large part (Labadi, 2011).

These programmes of restoration of historic monuments and re-use of former industrial buildings, accompanied by the beautification of urban spaces, have been criticised as focusing on the aesthetic and architectural values of the urban landscapes. The intangible values associated with these places by local communities have not been taken into account. This can lead to cities becoming bland and sanitised places for the gaze of tourists through the erasure of more negative aspects of the city, including its poverty or diversity (Dreyfuss *et al.* 2013: 3897–8). This also results in changing these old urban landscapes of production into new landscapes of consumption, with heritage sites being transformed into trendy bars, restaurants or luxury flats. These landscapes of consumption tend, as detailed in the next sections, to lead to gentrification with the arrival of wealthier residents.

This first section has explained that the first step in heritage-led regeneration is the change in the narratives associated with former and derelict industrial cities. In the case of Liverpool and Lille, the strategies have focused on title accumulation (World Heritage site and European Capital of Culture mainly), performative branding through overstating the positive impacts of these titles, as well as grounding this new image in the extensive renovation of the historic environment and re-use of its (derelict) industrial heritage. Nevertheless, what have been the economic impacts of these regeneration programmes and how has this branding affected these impacts? This is the focus of the next section.

Economic impact, job opportunities and sustainability

Economic impacts have often been identified as the main outcome of heritage-led regeneration programmes (Evans and Shaw 2004: 20; Bowitz and Ibenholt 2009), as is also clearly the case for Lille and Liverpool (Werquin 2006; Garcia *et al.* 2011). However, no information is available on the impact of all the titles and schemes from which Lille or Liverpool benefited. Impacts are integrated within the reporting cycle of one specific title. In other words, there exists no comprehensive and holistic assessment of all the different impacts related to all the titles won by Liverpool and Lille over the past decade. With regards to Lille and Liverpool, impacts have been clearly identified for the European Capital of Culture programme, which has an effective system of monitoring (Werquin 2005; Garcia *et al.* 2011). This is also the case for national schemes, including the Townscape Heritage Initiative (THI), funded by the Heritage Lottery Fund in England, awarded to Liverpool Rope Walks conservation area. Conversely, there is no systematic data collection on the socio-economic impacts of the inscription of sites on the World Heritage List (Labadi 2013). Besides, all the official evaluation reports refer only to the title being assessed; they do not adopt a horizontal and encompassing approach. For instance, the official evaluation of the impact of Liverpool, European Capital of Culture, refers neither to the World Heritage status of Liverpool nor to the multi-million pound rehabilitation of Liverpool Rope Walks conservation area through the THI programme (Garcia *et al.* 2011). As a result, any analysis of the impacts of regeneration programmes and title accumulations will provide fragmented information of the changes on the urban landscape, preventing a full understanding of the situation.

Despite this lack of a global approach and analysis, a diversity of indicators have been released on the economic impact of the culture- and heritage-led regeneration of Lille and Liverpool. Most official reports identify employment as a key impact (Werquin 2005; Garcia *et al.* 2011). These official documents, for both Lille and Liverpool, emphatically highlight the extremely positive impacts of the European Capital of Culture in terms of job creation. The evaluation for Lille, European Capital of Culture, for instance, reports a 7 per cent increase in jobs created in Lille in the hotel, restoration and culture sectors combined between 2003 and 2004, a figure much higher than for the regional level (+1.5 per cent) or national level (+1.1 per cent) (Werquin 2005). These figures have been widely reported in the press and they have been identified as important impacts for the local economy. They have helped the local authorities in justifying the continuation of a programme of public and private investment in heritage preservation and cultural manifestations entitled 'Lille 3000'. These positive impacts have been extensively communicated in the press and they have helped to sustain the re-imagination and branding of the city, analysed in the previous section.

Despite these positive claims, the economic impacts of Lille as the European Capital of Culture presents a number of shortcomings. The previous section detailed the local authorities' attempts to spread the benefits of this title to the whole region. Yet, it was mainly Lille that benefited from this scheme: 22 per cent of the new jobs created in the culture sector were based in Lille itself. The figures were less impressive for the wider region, as this sector only increased by 4 per cent at regional level. The clear strategy of more equitable distribution of the benefits across the whole region therefore did not work. One explanation is that foreign tourists tended to stay in Lille (Liefooghe 2010). This situation created some frustration, in particular on the part of some business owners from the Nord-Pas de Calais region (Werquin 2006: 218). In addition, the jobs created were short-term (Labadi 2011) and no thorough analysis exists of a long-term evolution of the employment in the tourism and culture sectors.

The example of Liverpool further demonstrates the difficulty of associating heritage-led regeneration with job creation for local inhabitants, which is often a key aim of these programmes. As indicated earlier, one conservation area of the Liverpool World Heritage site, commonly called Rope Walks, benefited from the Heritage Lottery funding for a five-year (2000 to 2005) Townscape Heritage initiative scheme to conserve, restore and re-use its historic buildings. One of the aims of this regeneration project was to increase local training opportunities in heritage skills (Labadi 2011). The ten-year evaluation report of this scheme conducted by

Oxford Brookes University concluded that employment rose for the Rope Walks, to such an extent that unemployment levels were less than in the city as a whole, in an area that used to be highly deprived (Oxford Brookes University 2013: 84). Yet, figures on unemployment have changed between the beginning and end of this regeneration scheme because of the gentrification of this quarter, with the arrival of new residents to this area who are younger and better off than the original population. This is not because the THI scheme created new employment opportunities for the original population of this quarter. This is implied by the ten-year review report (Oxford Brookes University 2013). Oxford Brookes sent 500 questionnaires to the inhabitants of the area – only 36 questionnaires were returned (Oxford Brookes University 2013: 83). Therefore, the original residents of the Rope Walks seem to be disinterested in the scheme because they were not involved in it.

This example of Liverpool demonstrates the difficulty of using data on employment without contextualisation, as this might not reflect employment opportunities obtained by the targeted population of the heritage-led regeneration programme. Worse, the regeneration of Liverpool has created pockets of unequal geographies, with wealth concentrated in the city centre. This has been clearly acknowledged by Liverpool City Council: 'while evidence points to significant GVA growth in the city, it is apparent that not all of Liverpool's residents are benefiting from this' (Liverpool City Council 2010: 5). There are, indeed, major spatial disparities, with deprivation levels being high in the north of Liverpool compared with low levels of deprivation for the city centre (Boland 2013: 266).

Despite the creation of wealth in the city centre and the attraction of new, more creative and affluent creative classes, Liverpool has remained the most deprived local authority in England for at least seven years, according to the latest official reports on Indices of Deprivation (2007 and 2010).[2] Data reflect this situation: as of May 2014, Liverpool's employment rate was 61.0 per cent, compared with 71.5 per cent for the whole of Great Britain. At that date, the level of job seekers' allowance claimants was 5.1 per cent whilst claimants were 2.9 per cent for the whole of Great Britain, and total worklessness (which includes those who are unemployed, economically inactive or claiming particular benefits) reached 18.9 per cent for Liverpool but 10.9 per cent for Great Britain (Liverpool City Council 2014). These data clearly demonstrate the limits of the culture- or heritage-led regeneration approaches. They also clearly show the discrepancy between the impacts of these approaches as presented in official reports and the reality.

These data also illustrate the need for Liverpool to move to a new model of development that uses heritage as a catalyst to attract bigger investments (Ashworth, 2014: 15). This new model has taken the form of Liverpool Waters, a major redevelopment scheme of the historic docklands north of the city centre, part of both the boundaries of Liverpool World Heritage site and its buffer zone. Over a 30-year period and an investment of £5.5 billion, this project will have 1,278,000 m² of mixed-used development with residential, offices, restaurants, cafés, shops and community services, in addition to 413,000 m² of underground parking (Rodwell 2015: 39). The scale and density of this proposed development directly threatens the outstanding universal value of the Liverpool World Heritage site because of two clusters of high-rise buildings, including the 192 m high 'Shanghai Tower'. As indicated by the state of conservation report

> the introduction of a cluster of high-rise buildings, with towers three times the height of the Three Graces, would destroy the more or less symmetrical city profile which is expressed as a three-tiered urban structure including the waterfront, the massing and height of the Three Graces, and the shoulders of the Anglican Cathedral on the ridge overlooking the city, with the historic docklands to the north to complement those to the south, putting the Three Graces centre-stage.
>
> (UNESCO 2012b: 183)

In 2012, the World Heritage Committee inscribed Liverpool Maritime Mercantile City on the World Heritage List in Danger, based on the threats caused by this authorised development to its outstanding universal value.

The example of Liverpool demonstrates clearly the limits of a model of economic regeneration based solely on culture or heritage. Heritage can only be the first step or catalyst for more in-depth and larger-scale territorial transformation. This example also questions the notion of sustainability, understood differently by the key stakeholders. Indeed, on the one hand, English Heritage and the World Heritage Committee have concluded from available reports and impact assessments that the Liverpool Waters proposal would have major negative impacts on the values of the site. They were of the opinion that a Historic Urban Landscape approach should be adopted, taking the Three Graces as the referential point for any future development and building a connection between the historic environment and the social and economic development of the city (UNESCO 2012a).

On the other hand, the impact assessment conducted by both the developer of Liverpool Waters, Peel Holdings, and Liverpool City Council concluded that 'there would be considerably more positive heritage impacts arising from the proposed development than negative impacts' (UNESCO 2012a). This view demonstrates a shift in the city council's approach to development. Fearing maybe a 'brand decay', the city council seems to be counting more on high-rise buildings to maintain the association of Liverpool with creativity, innovation and investment than on heritage and culture, even if some of the genius loci and heritage views used to create this brand in the first place will be destroyed. This example of Liverpool might demonstrate the difficulty in implementing a Historic Urban Landscape approach for cities wanting to compete internationally and to reinvent and rebrand themselves constantly as innovative and creative places. This example also demonstrates issues with the notion of sustainability. A heritage-based approach to development might not lead to the creation of sufficient employment for local residents and economic growth. Whilst the council could have tried to negotiate revised heights for Liverpool Waters, they did not want to impose too many constraints on the developer (Garcia, pers. com.). The case of Liverpool shows how difficult it is for the city council to balance heritage preservation and economic impacts and job creation for local residents.

This section has explained, first, the lack of comprehensive analyses of the impacts of culture- and heritage-led regeneration schemes. These schemes do create employment opportunities, but these tend to be short-term, as demonstrated by the case of Lille. The case of Liverpool has illustrated that heritage-led regeneration is the first step and the catalyst for larger projects tackling wide-scale unemployment and deprivation. Unfortunately, this large-scale development programme, in the case of Liverpool, has threatened the outstanding universal value of the waterfront. This demonstrates the conflict between the preservation of heritage and large-scale projects with major employment opportunities for local residents. The last section of this chapter focuses on deeper analyses of the social impacts of culture- and heritage-led regeneration programmes.

Social impacts, gentrification and participation

Derelict territories often suffer from a deficit of social cohesion, as their decline exacerbates communal fragmentation (Hall and Robertson 2001: 10). Culture- and heritage-led regeneration programmes in these territories are often claimed to result in major social impacts. These include strengthened social inclusion and cohesion, increased social capital and trust between people and empowered communities as well as the improved ability for residents to act as citizens (Landry *et al.* 1993; Dodd and Sandell, 2001; Murzyn-Kupisz and Dzialek 2013). Regeneration can also build or strengthen a sense of community through stronger links to a common identity, history and heritage (Swales 1992: 63).

Public participation is fundamental to ensure that regeneration programmes lead to the achievement of this long list of social benefits. Such public participation was an expected outcome of Liverpool Rope Walks THI. However, as explained in the previous section, the low return of the questionnaires sent by Oxford Brookes University as part of its evaluation of this scheme seems to indicate a lack of involvement of local residents. Worse, this ten-year evaluation points towards the gentrification of this quarter. Indeed, this scheme has facilitated the restoration of Georgian (eighteenth- and early nineteenth-century) houses and old private warehouses and their re-use as luxury flats, bars and restaurants. As a result of these transformations, a more affluent population has arrived in this area. Whilst gentrification has been heavily criticised in academic literature, this seems an obvious consequence of regeneration schemes. Indeed, one of the key aims of these schemes is to change the image and branding of the city. This metamorphosis of the city must be associated with a change in its original residents with the arrival of more affluent, dynamic and creative ones. Yet, gentrification does not necessarily mean the departure of all the original residents. Before being regenerated, the Rope Walk area was a highly derelict area and it could have been expected that its residents were living in properties owned by the city council. There is no indication whether these properties have remained within the local authorities' responsibilities or been sold to private owners, or whether the rents have been controlled to ensure that the original local residents could stay in this area (Robbins 2002). Without precise information on these aspects, the association between heritage regeneration and positive social impacts cannot be substantiated (see Belfiore 2006; Pollock and Sharp 2012). The example of Liverpool Rope Walk reflects the fact that any meaningful social impacts cannot be obtained without carefully defined programmes involving local residents. Essential mechanisms, such as rent controls, should also be put in place to ensure that the gentrification of regenerated quarters does not lead to the departure of the original residents.

The example of Liverpool Rope Walks seems to point towards a lack of public participation in regeneration programmes and of social benefits for local residents. Conversely, the example of Lille, European Capital of Culture points towards wide-scale public participation. The official report on the impact of this European programme clearly details the successful participation of local communities and of 17,000 artists, half of whom came from the Nord-Pas de Calais region (Werquin 2005). Yet, such participation does not necessarily lead to the social benefits mentioned in the opening paragraph to this section. Asymmetrical power relations between the different stakeholders participating in the regeneration programme can create frictions. In addition, different groups do not necessarily share the goals of the regeneration programme. For instance, some local artists had some of their artworks censored, as part of an exhibition on consumption and gratuitousness organised at the Tri Postal, a historic building previously used as a mail sorting plant, in the centre of Lille. Some of the censored artworks were on shoplifting and did not correspond to the message that the main commercial sponsor, a supermarket chain, wanted to spread (Labadi 2011: 98). Because of their censored artworks, these artists did not take part in this exhibition. This example shows that local communities' possibilities for participation are controlled by, and have to be aligned with, the local authorities' and commercial sponsors' objectives and vision for regeneration (see Morrison 2000; Taylor 2007; Dicks 2013).

The previous sections of this chapter have clarified the objectives and visions for culture- and re-heritage-led regeneration: to create a new dynamism based on re-imagining and re-branding the territory and attracting private investments and enterprises in order to encourage economic growth and the development of employment opportunities. However, there seems to be a disconnect between these top-down goals and approaches and the more bottom-up narratives on local participation. The two cases of Liverpool and Lille demonstrate the difficulty in building social cohesion and inclusion, as well as empowering residents, when these residents have not been given the opportunities to make meaningful decisions about, and take responsibilities for, the future of their locality. In other words, positive social impacts cannot be obtained when residents are not given the opportunity to take part in the governance, planning and implementation of heritage-led regeneration programmes (Kearns 1992; Raco 2000; Hickey and Mohan 2004).

Conclusions

The aim of this chapter, as detailed in the introduction, was to analyse critically whether culture- and heritage-led regeneration programmes implemented in the derelict and former industrial cities of Liverpool and Lille are truly models of sustainable development. The preceding paragraphs have highlighted a number of issues with these programmes. The first issue relates to the importance of creating a positive brand associated with these former derelict territories. This branding, built around positive narratives, does not necessarily reflect the reality of the social and economic impacts of regeneration, as highlighted in the preceding paragraphs. The second issue relates to the economic impacts of culture- and heritage-led regeneration. This chapter has demonstrated that culture and heritage were the first step and the catalyst to attract bigger investments for deeper economic regeneration. Yet, these bigger and second-stage investments can lead to the destruction of the historic and heritage values of the city, as argued by English Heritage and UNESCO, with the case of the major development scheme of Liverpool Waters. Hence, these second-stage investments can destroy the heritage and culture that led to securing these investments in the first place. Finally, this chapter has demonstrated that gentrification may be intrinsically embedded within regeneration programmes. Indeed, one of the key aims of these programmes is to promote a positive image of the city through branding. This metamorphosis of the city must be associated with a change in its original residents with the arrival of more affluent, dynamic and creative residents. The example of Lille has also demonstrated the top-down and very controlled approaches to heritage-led regeneration, which have excluded dissident voices and approaches to regeneration.

Notes

1 *Indicateurs de Lille 2004*. Available at: http://lille2004lille.free.fr/indicateurs_bilan.pdf (accessed 26 June 2015).
2 The indices of deprivations are available at: http://webarchive.nationalarchives.gov. uk/20120601152500/ and http://www.communities.gov.uk/communities/research/ indicesdeprivation/deprivation10/ (accessed 26 June 2015).

Bibliography

Ashworth, G.J. (2014). Heritage and economic development: selling the unsellable. *Heritage and Society*, 7(1), 3–17.

Ashworth, G.J. and Kavaratzis, M. (2009). Beyond the logo: brand management for cities. *Journal of Brand Management*, 16(8), 520–31.

Austin, J.L. (1962). *How to Do Things with Words*. Oxford: Clarendon Press.

Belfiore, E. (2006). The social impact of the arts: myth or reality? In: M. Miraz (ed.), *Culture Vultures: Is UK Arts Policy Damaging the Arts?* London: Policy Exchange.

Bell, D. (1974). *The Coming of Post-Industrial Society.* New York: Harper Colophon Books.

Boland, P. (2013). Sexing up the city in the international beauty context: the performative nature of spatial planning and the fictive spectacle of place branding. *TPR: Town Planning Review*, 84(2), 251–74.

Bowitz, E. and Ibenholt, K. (2009). Economic impacts of cultural heritage: research and perspectives. *Journal of Cultural Heritage*, 10, 1–8.

Dicks, B. (2013). Participatory community regeneration: a discussion of risks, accountability and crisis in devolved Wales. *Urban Studies*, 51(5), 959–77.

Dodd, J. and Sandell R. (2001). *Including Museums: Perspectives on Museums, Galleries and Social Inclusion.* Leicester: Research Centre for Museums and Galleries. Available at: https://www2.le.ac.uk/departments/museumstudies/rcmg/projects/small-museums-and-social-inclusion/Including%20museums.pdf (accessed 26 June 2015).

Dreyfuss, G., Mifsud, M. and Van Malderen, T. (2013). The architectural practice of regeneration. *Sustainability*, 5, 3895–905.

Evans, G. and Shaw, P. (2004). *The Contribution of Culture to Regeneration in the UK: A Review of Evidence. A Report to the Department for Culture, Media and Sport.* London: London Metropolitan University.

Garcia, B., Melville, R. and Coz, T. (2011). *Creating an Impact: Liverpool's Experience as European Capital of Culture.* Liverpool, European Capital of Culture Research Programme: University of Liverpool and Liverpool City Council.

Haider, D. (1992). Place wars: new realities of the 1990s. *Economic Development Quarterly*, 6, 127–34.

Hall, T. and Robertson, I. (2001). Public art and urban regeneration: advocacy, claims and critical debates. *Landscape Research*, 26(1), 5–26.

Hannigan, J. (2003). Symposium on branding, the entertainment economy and urban place building: introduction. *International Journal of Urban and Regional Research*, 27(2), 352–60.

Hickey, S. and Mohan, G. (eds) (2004). *Exploring New Approaches to Participation in Development.* London: Zed Books.

Kavaratzis, M. and Ashworth, G.J. (2005). City branding: an effective assertion of identity or a transitory marketing trick? *Tijdschrift voor Economische en Sociale Geografie*, 96(5), 506–14.

Kearns, A. (1992). Active citizenship and urban governance. *Transactions of the Institute of British Geographers*, 17, 20–34.

Labadi, S. (2011). *Evaluating the Socio-Economic Impact s of Selected Regenerated Heritage Sites in Europe.* Amsterdam: European Cultural Foundation.

Labadi, S. (2013). *UNESCO, Cultural Heritage and Outstanding Universal Value.* Plymouth: AltaMira.

Landry, C. and Bianchini, F. (1995). *The Creative City.* London: Demos in association with Comedia.

Landry, C., Bianchini, F., Maguire, M., and Worpole, K. (1993). *The Social Impact of the Arts: A Discussion Document.* Bournes Green, Stroud: Comedia.

Liefooghe, C. (2010). Lille 2004, capitale européenne de la culture ou la quête d'un nouveau modèle de développement. *Méditerranée*, 1(114). Available at: http://mediterranee.revues.org/4249 (accessed 30 November 2014).

Liverpool City Council (2010). *Liverpool Economic Briefing*. Liverpool: Liverpool City Council.

Liverpool City Council (2014). *Key Statistics Bulletin*, Issue 18. Available at: http://liverpool. gov.uk/media/820333/2014-05-may-key-statistics-bulletin-issue-18-update.pdf (accessed 30 November 2014).

Mellor, R. (2002). Hypocritical city, cycles of urban exclusion. In: J. Peck and K. Ward (eds), *City of Revolution: Restructuring*. Manchester: Manchester University.

Miles, S. and Paddison, R. (2006). Introduction: the rise and rise of culture-led urban regeneration. In: R. Paddison and S. Miles (eds), *Culture-led Urban Regeneration*. London: Routledge.

Morrison, J. (2000). The government–voluntary sector compacts: governance, governmentality and civil society. *Journal of Law and Society*, 27(1), 98–132.

Murzyn-Kupisz, M. and Dzialek, J. (2013). Cultural heritage in building and enhancing social capital. *Journal of Cultural Heritage Management and Sustainable Development*, 3(1), 35–54.

Oxford Brookes University (2013). *Townscape Heritage Initiative Schemes Evaluation. Ten Year Review Report. Final Report*. Oxford: Oxford Brookes University.

Palmer-Rae Associates (2004a). *European Cities and Capitals of Culture. Part I. Study Prepared for the European Commission*. Brussels: Palmer-Rae Associates. Available at: http://ec.europa.eu/culture/tools/actions/documents/ecoc/cap-part1_en.pdf (accessed 30 November 2014).

Palmer-Rae Associates (2004b). *European Cities and Capitals of Culture – City Reports. Part II. Study Prepared for the European Commission*. Brussels: Palmer-Rae Associates. Available at: http://ec.europa.eu/programmes/creative-europe/actions/documents/ecoc/cap-part2_en.pdf (accessed 26 June 2015).

Pollock, V. L. and Sharp, J. (2012). Real participation or the tyranny of participatory practice? Public art and community involvement in the regeneration of the Raploch, Scotland. *Urban Studies*, 49(14), 3063–79.

Raco, M. (2000). Assessing community participation in local economic development: lessons for the new urban policy. *Political Geography*, 19, 573–99.

Robbins, G. (2002). Taking stock – regeneration programs and social housing. *Local Economy*, 17(4), 266–77.

Roberts, P. and Sykes, H. (2000). Current challenges and future prospects. In: P. Roberts and H. Sykes (eds), *Urban Regeneration: A Handbook*. London: Sage Publications.

Rodwell, D. (2015). Liverpool: heritage and development – bridging the gap? In: H. Oevermann and H. Mieg (eds), *Industrial Heritage Sites in Transformation. Clash of Discourses*. London: Routledge.

Swales, P. (1992) 'Approaches', in S. Jones (ed.), *Art in Public: What, Why and How?*, Sunderland: AN Publications.

Tallon, A. (2010). *Urban Regeneration in the UK*, 2nd edn. London: Routledge.

Taylor, M. (2007). Community participation in the real world: opportunities and pitfalls in new governance spaces. *Urban Studies*, 44(2), 297–317.

UNESCO (2012a). *Item 7 of the Provisional Agenda: State of Conservation of Properties on the World Heritage List and/or on the List of World Heritage in Danger. Mission Report: Liverpool – Maritime Mercantile City (United Kingdom of Great Britain and Northern Ireland)*. Available at: whc.unesco.org/document/116981 (accessed 30 November 2014).

UNESCO (2012b). *Item 7B of the Provisional Agenda: State of Conservation of World Heritage Properties Inscribed in the World Heritage List.* World Heritage Committee, 36th session: WHC-12/36.COM/7B.Add. Available at: http://whc.unesco.org/archive/2012/whc12-36com-7BAdd-en.pdf (accessed 30 November 2014).

Werquin, T. (2005). *Indicateurs de Lille 2004.* Available at: http://lille2004lille.free.fr/indicateurs_bilan.pdf (accessed 30 November 2014).

Werquin, T. (2006). Impact de l'infrastructure culturelle sur le développement économique local. Thèse pour le Doctorat en Sciences Economiques. Lille: University of Lille.

Chapter 9

Management strategies for historic towns in Europe

Rob Pickard

In a recent position paper developed by the Organisation of World Heritage Cities Regional Secretariat for Northwest Europe (OWHC 2013), it has been indicated that literature on UNESCO World Heritage Sites makes very little reference to local administrative actions or to integrated urban development. Whilst the UNESCO Recommendation on Historic Urban Landscapes (UNESCO 2011), which builds on the UNESCO Recommendation Concerning the Safeguarding and Contemporary Role of Historic Areas (UNESCO 1976) and the ICOMOS International Charter for the Conservation of Historic Towns and Urban Areas (ICOMOS 1987), promotes the idea of integrated site management, there are few case studies to review practice across Europe.

A number of specific country examples can be cited (Pickard 2010). In Germany, the *Städtbaulicher Denkmalschutz* programme linking urban development, planning and conservation has operated since 1991, with initiatives for revitalisation in 296 cities (Bundestransferstelle Städtebaulicher Denkmalschutz 2014). In the UK, character appraisals and management plans and associated funding mechanisms for regenerating historic places in social and economic decline, such as the Townscape Heritage Initiative, which has supported over 170 towns and cities since 1998 (Reeve and Shipley 2013), can be combined to make effective strategies and actions. In France, the system of *Secteurs Sauvegardés* designated in 103 towns and cities since 1962, and *Zones de Protection du Patrimoine Architectural, Urbain et Paysager* (ZPPAUP) ('architectural, urban and landscape protection zones') established in over 600 urban areas, and currently being transferred into *Aires de Mise en Valeur de l'Architecture et du Patrimoine* (AVAP) ('architectural and heritage enhancement areas'), are integrated into plan mechanisms with sustainable development objectives to enable the protection and management of the urban heritage (Association Nationale 2014). Whilst these management systems can provide evidence of good management practice, they are dependent on national mechanisms and legal procedures, which makes their transferability less certain. However, one study in which a broader examination of issues, taken from practice in several cities in different countries, can be cited is the INHERIT report produced by the European Association of Historic Towns and Regions (now known as HERITAGE EUROPE) (EAHTR 2007), although this is limited in that it focuses on six case study cities and mainly concerns heritage-led regeneration strategies, rather than wider management issues.

Since the INHERIT study, a broader approach to balancing the safeguarding of heritage resources and development in cities through an integrated and multi-level approach was initiated through URBACT, which is a European Union exchange and learning programme to promote sustainable urban development and enable cities to work together to develop solutions to major urban challenges. The 2008 to 2011 URBACT II Project HerO (Heritage as Opportunity) was designed as a city network to facilitate the exchange of ideas between heritage cities about common challenges and opportunities (URBACT 2014).

In referring to the requirement of UNESCO that all World Heritage Sites should have a management plan, the OHRC position paper refers to the idea that integrated cultural heritage management plans in all historic towns can be effective instruments for pursuing cultural heritage-based development, citing the HerO initiative as a method that has been tried and tested (Stadt Regensburg 2011). The network of HerO was based on a partnership of ten cities in the European Union and it was aimed at developing integrated and innovative management of historic urban landscapes, balancing preservation of the built heritage with the sustainable socio-economic development of historic towns. The HerO network cooperated closely with Heritage Europe, which was formed as 'The European Association of Historic Towns and Regions' by the Council of Europe in October 1999 as part of the initiative 'Europe – A Common Heritage'. It is an alliance of over 1,000 historic and heritage towns, cities and regions in 30 European countries; its principal objective is to promote the interests of historic towns and cities across Europe through international cooperation, sharing experience and good practice and promoting vitality, viability and sustainable management of historic towns, cities and regions.

However, it should be remembered that the concept of 'integrated conservation', in the context of the architectural heritage, has been promulgated through various Council of Europe reference texts since the 1970s (Pickard 2010). Moreover, the notion of integrated mechanisms relating to the architectural heritage (Council of Europe 1985) was extended in relation to the archaeological heritage (Council of Europe 1992) and landscape (Council of Europe 2000) (including urban, peri-urban landscapes and even industrial landscapes). By recognising the value of heritage for society (Council of Europe 2005a), the integrated approach to cultural heritage management should be taken to mean integration between different levels of public authorities (local, regional and national), including between different policy sectors and domains and by encouraging the public to become involved in the development process through setting priorities for the sustainable use of heritage resources.

The 1976 resolution (Council of Europe 1976) concerning the adaptation of laws and regulations to the requirements of integrated conservation of the architectural heritage defined two main objectives for the integrated conservation of the architectural heritage:

- The conservation of monuments, groups of buildings and sites through measures to safeguard them, steps to ensure the physical preservation of their constituent parts and operations aimed at their restoration and enhancement;

- The integration of these assets into the physical environment of present day society through revitalisation and rehabilitation programmes including by the adaptation of buildings for a social purpose and to the needs of modern life, compatible with their dignity, preserving features of cultural interest and in keeping with the character of their setting.

These objectives are still relevant today. Moreover, whilst the concept of sustainable development was not defined in 1976, the objectives underline that approach. Article 5 of the *Faro Convention* on the value of cultural heritage for society (Council of Europe 2005a) promotes cultural heritage protection as a 'central factor in the mutually supporting objectives of sustainable development, cultural diversity and contemporary creativity'. Council of Europe guidance has further emphasised that the conservation of heritage can no longer be considered on its own as a (cultural) objective in itself but rather that it should be regarded as an essential tool for making concrete the global objective of sustainable development at the economic, social and environmental level: 'this new approach of integrated conservation of cultural heritage within the sustainable development concept is a highly important evolution. It implies a new behaviour in the drafting and practical applications of laws and policies' (Council of Europe 2011a).

This guidance further identifies the use of specific management plans for historic districts, towns and cities, taking into account the character of the place, local interests and identifying particular issues to take into account (for example, views, new functions and scale of development, environmental enhancement of the area, traffic management, rehabilitation strategies, funding and monitoring change). Moreover, the Council of Europe's Guidance on Urban Rehabilitation provides further advice on the use of management plans to assist in the facilitation of sustainable local development strategies in which different sectors concerned may work in an integrated manner (Council of Europe 2005b). This guidance emphasises the importance of involving the local population and community groups to ensure democratic participation in the decision-making process of the rehabilitation project. It also refers to the need for a technical and multidisciplinary management team or bureau to coordinate activities and for both financial resources and legal measures to ensure there is proper coordination, issues that are further considered in guidance on funding mechanisms (Pickard 2009).

In addition, through the recent Kyiv Initiative Regional Programme: Black Sea and South Caucasus, Council of Europe experts have developed the concept of a Town Reference Plan (TRP) through the Pilot Project on the Rehabilitation of Cultural Heritage in Historic Towns (Council of Europe 2011b) (jointly implemented by the Council of Europe and the European Commission), which is a heritage-led approach to urban development, examining ways of reinvesting in the urbanity by identifying targeted interventions on the historic heritage in degraded areas. The terms of reference of the TRP introduce the concept of 'Rehabilitation of Cultural Heritage in Historic Towns' to be adopted locally, defining an ensemble of strategic interventions, and act as a guide for public and private investment.

In Phase 1 of this pilot project, which commenced in the autumn of 2009 and lasted for two years, 45 Priority Intervention Towns where initially identified in five countries (Azerbaijan, Armenia, Georgia, Moldova and Ukraine) and Preliminary Technical Files have since been published for 23 of these towns (Council of Europe 2011c). The TRP concept is still in the process of development. Its next stage has commenced by the agreement to launch 'Community-led Urban Strategies in Historic Towns' (COMUS) at the beginning of 2015 in the six countries (adding Belarus to the original list) taking part in the European Union's Eastern Partnership programme that aims to deepen and strengthen relations between the European Union and its six Eastern neighbours (European Commission 2014).

The TRP has been directed to 'revitalisation in small and medium-sized towns and their surrounding environments'. As such, it provides a useful contrast to the Integrated Cultural Heritage Management Plan developed through the HerO initiative, which has been directed specifically at 'cities' and 'the protection of World Heritage Sites for present and future generations', particularly as it identifies a basis for local administrative actions for integrated urban development in historic towns. The HerO approach, based on an exchange of experiences through network partners in nine cities in individual countries, aims at being applicable and transferable to all historic towns across Europe and beyond (Stadt Regensburg 2011: 11).

Similarly, the TRP also aims to be transferable for historic towns facing similar development challenges as initially examined through 23 towns in five countries. However, it can be differentiated as it has been directed towards countries-in-transition. This stems from the fact that social and economic development initiatives no longer lie exclusively with central government in these countries, but now also lie with the private sector and local players, who have had little experience in this field, highlighting the difficulty in maintaining a balance between the preservation of the heritage and the requirements for sustainable growth. It should be noted that for many counties in the Balkans, Black Sea and South Caucasus regions of Europe, urban and spatial planning systems are not well developed. Despite the existence of legal systems to introduce new types of planning systems, their implementation is often difficult (due to a lack of financial resources and professional experience, amongst other matters). Moreover, there has been some consideration for utilising the Town Reference Plan methodology as a way of introducing local planning systems until other systems can be introduced. Thus, this chapter is directed at examining the merits of the two systems and the possibilities for learning from them to develop systems of assessment and management that are truly transferable to historic towns in Europe that could be used elsewhere.

Aims of the two systems

Town Reference Plan

The TRP terms of reference are currently contained in an unpublished document, which introduces the concept of 'Rehabilitation of Cultural Heritage in Historic

Towns' to be adopted locally, defining an ensemble of strategic interventions, and it acts as a guide for public and private investment. The context of the project has also been set out in a general brochure entitled 'Heritage for a new urbanity: think differently; live differently' and through more extensive national brochures for each of the five countries (Council of Europe, European Commission and Ministère de la Culture et de la Communication 2011).

Its main aim is 'to assist national, regional and local authorities in implementing strategic revitalisation in small and medium-sized historic towns and surrounding environments to contribute to social and economic sustainable development', using the built heritage as an economic and social factor, going beyond simple conservation and restoration, to encourage and facilitate rehabilitation to create new opportunities for use by the local population. Additional aims are to increase awareness about heritage, initiate reflection and debate on priorities, enable a transversal process to take place (involving multiple public and private partners), create synergies for a set of actions between separate ongoing initiatives and encourage a wide debate with the inhabitants and elected representatives.

Integrated Cultural Heritage Management Plan

The key document for the HerO initiative is the guidebook entitled *The Road to Success*. This provides a description of the objective and purpose of the Integrated Cultural Heritage Management Plan (ICHMP) in Section 3.2 of the *HerO Guidebook*, which introduces the concept as a new management approach with the fundamental purpose being 'to safeguard cultural heritage for the benefit of local stakeholders'.

Its aims are to determine and establish the appropriate strategy, objectives, actions and management structure to safeguard the cultural heritage and to balance the different demands while using historic urban areas and their cultural heritage as a significant development asset. Its guiding principle is the pursuance of sustainable development of a city and linking and balancing the safeguarding and development of historic urban areas and their cultural heritage 'with the intention to have attractive, competitive and multifunctional places'.

Development of methodology

Town Reference Plan

The TRP methodology was developed by a number of international experts from the collection of experiences and European best practices. It has also included new ways of collecting information, including through questionnaires and correspondence between international and local experts (a heritage assessment of the legal and institutional capacity in the countries) (Council of Europe 2010a, 2010b, 2010c, 2010d, 2010e); practical workshops and field study including testing mechanisms for developing various thematic maps with local specialists in a test town – Ivano-Frankivsk (see Figure 9.1); training workshops for preparing preliminary

Figure 9.1 Central Square and former town hall in the centre of Ivano-Frankivsk, Ukraine © R. Pickard 2010.

technical files (PTFs) demonstrated in five demonstration towns – Gyumri (Armenia), Zagatala (Azerbaijan), Gori (Georgia), Soroca (Moldova) and Lutsk (Ukraine) – one in each country, involving local representatives from several identified 'priority intervention towns' (and resulting in the publication of 23 PTFs); and training workshops for analysing the information gathered in PTFs (again demonstrated in five demonstration towns); as well as meetings of international experts following the training workshops to refine the methodology.

In addition, in relation to the second part of the operational phase of the TRP (see Phases section below), the methodology concerns the implementation of Heritage Rehabilitation Projects that draws on experience developed through the Council of Europe's Regional Programme on Cultural and Natural Heritage in South East Europe (RPSEE), jointly funded by the European Commission since 2003, in particular the Ljubljana Process I and II, 2008–2014, concerning funding and rehabilitation action (Council of Europe 2014a; Rikalović and Mikić 2014).

This methodology is well tested as it has allowed work on approximately 200 monuments and sites, benefiting from funds generated including from the European Union's pre-accession programmes, combined with public and private investment. This has been through specific actions for the implementation of rehabilitation projects including preliminary technical assessments for buildings and sites, feasibility studies/business plans, project promotion, fund-raising and project management and implementation.

Integrated Cultural Heritage Management Plan

The HerO approach is based on 'exchange of experience through a series of seminars and two expert workshops and case studies of the network partners'. The thematic network was developed through the EU programme URBACT II in cooperation with Heritage Europe. The network is based on ten cities in countries that are member states of the European Union (not wider Europe). The network cities are all significant places that are mainly World Heritage Sites or include inscribed sites: Regensburg (Germany), Liverpool (UK), Graz (Austria), Naples (Italy), Valletta (Malta), Sighisoara (Romania), Vilnius (Lithuania), Poitiers (France) – which includes the church of Saint-Hilaire-le-Grand, one of 77 other sites linked to the Routes of Santiago de Compostela in France World Heritage inscription – and Valencia (Spain), which includes the World Heritage Site of La Lonja de la Seda de Valencia, with Lublin (Poland) having the European Heritage Label rather than a World Heritage inscription.

The HerO approach is explained in the *HerO Guidebook*, and the *HerO Good-Practice-Compilation* gives interested parties a first overview about good practices and experiences derived from the HerO network cities. It uses 18 'good-practice' examples to explore particular issues based around two main HerO topics of pro-tecting visual integrity and integrated revitalisation approaches to balance differ-ent needs.

The HerO assessment is therefore based on examples from particular cities and it does not particularly reflect on policies adopted by national authorities in relation to urban rehabilitation/regeneration. It does not correspond directly to the situation in countries-in-transition, as it does not undertake a pre-assessment of capacities. As such, it relies on examples but does not test a whole (strategic) approach and it does not have specific methodologies. However, the examples are well defined through various HerO network publications including HerO Thematic Reports, *HerO Good-Practice-Compilation*, HerO Local Action Plans and websites includ-ing HerO Results (URBACT 2011).

Stakeholder involvement/local support groups

Town Reference Plan

The terms of reference for the TRP identify the need to involve partners and create debate amongst inhabitants and elected representatives, etc. and other local stake-holders. It states a number of aims of the TRP process in this context, including increasing awareness about the value of the architectural and urban heritage, initi-ating reflection and debate on priorities, enabling a transversal process to take place, involving multiple partners (state institutions, local authorities, private actors) in the global action plan and encouraging wide debate with the inhabitants about the future of their living environment.

However, in practice, the stakeholder involvement at the beginning of the process was largely limited to the involvement of local technical teams (sometimes other local officials and elected representatives in demonstration workshops). This was largely due to the fact that the priority intervention towns generally did not have any significant form of integrated process or planning documents (as distinct from the major historic centres in EU countries considered amongst the HerO network) and needed a much greater and detailed technical analysis (although it can be argued that this should be done for all historic town/city management plans). So wider stakeholder involvement has not generally been considered at the start and it is less well developed as compared with the approach used via HerO. However, the need to involve partners and seek opinions throughout the process is clearly addressed in the terms of reference and in the diagnosis stage (see below 'Assessment of issues' for the TRP: analysis of heritage and urban resources: Appendix C), which has not yet been completed.

Integrated Cultural Heritage Management Plan

Section 4.1.1 of the *HerO Guidebook* (Stadt Regensburg 2011: 27–31) refers to a need for 'building up a local support group' (LSG) in order clarify the general framework of the ICHMP and to ensure that the needs of the historic urban area and its users are taken into account (i.e. the coordination of different stakeholders to give a sense of ownership). It gives the example of Liverpool where a stake-holder analysis was first carried out (other examples are given for Regensburg and Lublin).

This analysis was used to identify persons and representatives of institutions concerned with the place that are highly concerned (i.e. have an interest in the area) and in a strong position to support or block the safeguarding of the cultural heritage and the development of the heritage area (i.e. have power/ influence) and from this analysis to identify who should be kept informed (from a power perspective), the level of civic participation interest/action (from an interest per-spective), and, from this, who should be 'involved' in the LSG.

Typical stakeholder groups were identified as:

*   Local Council, Mayor's Office;
*   Municipal departments responsible for building conservation, urban plan-ning and development, economic development, culture, social affairs and the environment;
*   Tourism office, monuments preservation authorities and city manager/city marketing associations;
*   House owners' associations, real estate development associations, chamber of industry and commerce, entrepreneurs, cultural institutions, universities, citizens (associations), regional authorities (e.g. managing authorities of the EU ERDF and ESF operational programmes) and other professionals/experts.

The HerO partners identified the bringing together of people from different (professional) backgrounds in an interdisciplinary team as an important factor for the successful work of the LSG. Moreover, they found it to be very effective in explaining the very beginning of the benefits of being part of and participating in the LSG to the potential participants (by personal talks, letters and informa-tional meetings).

Phases

Both approaches are developed through a series of phases/stages.

Town Reference Plan

The TRP approach has been developed in relation to a *preliminary phase* and an *operational phase* (the latter being in two parts). Prior to developing the methodology for the TRP, the preliminary phase involving *national authorities* in five developing/in-transition countries was initiated. This phase has included:

1   *Development of coordination and management structures.* This includes the signing of Memoranda of Understanding between the Council of Europe and the national authorities to confirm their support and expectations in terms of impact of the action, the establishment of terms of reference, steering committees, programme and project coordinators, project managers and local technical teams and an agreement to conduct coordination and expert meetings.
2   *Heritage Assessment Reports for each country.* These reports assess the legal and institutional framework for cultural heritage, how it is managed in practice, the extent of integration with urban and spatial planning and other systems and assesses where there are shortfalls in policy, legal procedures and management structures.
3   *Identification of Priority Intervention Towns.* The original 45 towns identified by the five countries were photographically illustrated in the general brochure 'Heritage for a new urbanity: think differently; live differently' (Council of Europe 2011b), with each country additionally producing national brochures with more extensive illustration of the towns chosen for intervention action.

The first part of the operational phase involves a number of stages including:

1   *Diagnosis Stage* – to be completed through a diagnostic report comprising three elements:

   • PTF (which have been completed for 23 out of 45 towns);
   • Analysis of heritage resources and urban situation (commenced but not completed);
   • Synthesis: identification of the main issues at stage (not started).

2   *Strategic Stage* – to be completed through a strategy report comprising the identification of strategic actions and challenges for a town, or part of it, in an operational document.
3   *Planning Stage* – to be completed through a planning report (for designing operational rehabilitation projects and prioritising and phasing the implementation of actions).

In addition, *other actions* have been anticipated including maintaining/consolidating heritage assets, awareness-raising and education, consideration of visitors/tourists and the involvement of the civil society.

The second part of the operational phase concerns the implementation of heritage rehabilitation projects (including preliminary technical assessments, feasibility studies/business plans, project promotion, fund-raising, project management and project implementation).

Integrated Cultural Heritage Management Plan

The HerO approach has three phases: a *preparatory phase*, a *development phase* and an *implementation phase*:

The *preparatory phase* aims to ensure that that an ICHMP will have both a 'solid basis and real legitimacy, both among inhabitants and users' and identifies four elements as being key ingredients in the successful application of this approach. These are to make cultural heritage a top policy priority (to attract funding from different sources); to develop an integrated approach (based on a strong support coming from the municipality and other stakeholders around a shared project); to engage with stakeholders (involving inhabitants and users and taking their expectations into account); and to focus on action and delivery (i.e. policy and managerial support, cooperation with managing authorities to secure funding and setting up a coordinated structure with procedures for evaluation and monitoring). A key aspect is the focus on 'building a local support group' (i.e. bringing all the stakeholders to the table: local public and private along with the managing authority).

A second part of the *preparatory phase*, which aims to analyse the current situation in a historic city and identify the challenges, expectations and directions for making progress, leads to the development of a detailed road map. These actions are directed at enabling the formulation of an initial plan (for securing political support from the municipality to continue the project and funding for the *development phase*).

The *development phase* includes consultation and coordination with representatives of the municipality in charge of writing the final plan, working closely with the local support group. Public debates are seen as a way to create a 'shared vision' of the future of the neighbourhood by consensus. There are also actions to secure funding for the action phases including the definition of a framework and procedure for implementation including development of local action plans.

The *implementation phase* includes prior actions to identify progress *indicators*, then on-going monitoring (to ensure the successful implementation of the ICHMP) to enable proactive revising of certain aspects of the initial plan.

Assessment of issues

Town Reference Plan

The TRP uses a specifically devised method involving three diagnostic stages by means of a PTF and the Analysis of Heritage Resources and Urban Issues, followed by a *synthesis* of findings.

The PTF is a detailed form of assessment and information base, which was tested in Ivano-Frankivsk and refined after some other towns were assessed, and includes three component parts: a *reference file*, a series of *thematic maps* and *historic maps* (reflecting each of the important stages of the evolution of the town) if they are available. Detailed and extensive information has been gathered through the files for 23 historic towns, which can be viewed on a designated web site (Council of Europe 2012).

The *reference file* gathers general and detailed information about the town in 15 topics. The issues covered include the geographic, climatic and/or other physical factors that have influenced morphology and structure of the town; historical events that have shaped the town and its identity; the socio-economic situation; the capacity of the local administration/municipal authority to action (expertise, resources, etc.); the demand and supply for space in property; the state of the public services; the legal and institutional situation, the main features and value of the cultural heritage resource and an assessment of the contribution that the heritage assets can make to the quality of life and to the social and economic prosperity of the town; challenges and opportunities (using a SWOT analysis); and the main stakeholders and potential partners and details of any participation in international cooperation projects (including technical support to projects, type of donors, project partners, etc.).

At least 9 (and sometimes up to 15) *thematic maps* are developed for each town from local records or through small teams making rapid surveys around the town, using a number of scale-based maps (see Figure 9.2). These cover a wide range of issues that are explained by guidance on content, scales (for maps), purpose and with the provision of templates for maps and inventory files. The main topics of these plans are:

- Location of the town in the context of the country or the region (including transport infrastructure by road, rail, air, sea and physical features of the region);
- Traffic circulation, transport and access to the town;
- The main activities/functions in buildings;
- New buildings/development/interventions in the historic centre;
- Time periods/epochs of buildings;
- Cultural heritage – protected and unprotected heritage buildings of architectural interest and other heritage assets;
- Occupation status (and ownership) of buildings and undeveloped sites;
- Physical state of condition of buildings;
- Physical state of condition of roads, pavement surfaces and public areas.

Additional maps can be drawn up, allowing each town to provide further information to explain the context in the town, for example, major projects under consideration that could damage the heritage, particular architectural features and floors in buildings including the provision of cellars, etc.

The Analysis of Heritage Resources and Urban Issues is designed to cross-reference the issues from the PTF (mainly the thematic maps and reference files) to measure and assess issues of relevance for the rehabilitation of the town.

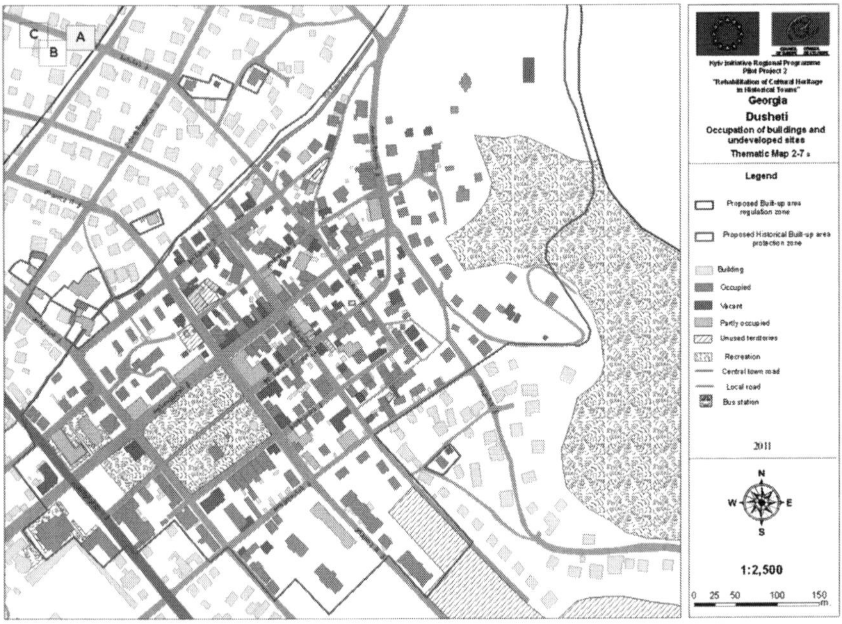

Figure 9.2 An example of a thematic map representing the occupation of buildings and sites (occupied, partly occupied, vacant and undeveloped sites) in the historic centre of the town of Dusheti, Georgia (reproduced with kind permission of the National Agency of Cultural Heritage of Georgia).

The analysis covers 13 topics. For example, one of the analysis themes concerns the assessment of land use patterns, the functional development of the town and current functions, which structure and characterise the town or historic centre and the service provision. This involves identifying the concentration of different elements that define the centre/place, for example, if the main activities are in one centre or not. It assesses any apparent zoning of activities or mixing of activities and whether there are any conflicts between land uses or activities. It examines whether the town or any part of the town/centre is presently functioning efficiently in economic and social terms and actively supports the inhabitants or if the place is more a tourist/cultural centre or a 'museum town' that does not benefit local inhabitants (lack of housing, services and business provision, etc. in the centre).

It also considers the extent to which the provision of services and institutions (for example, education, health, employment and business advice, cultural and leisure facilities) makes the town economically and culturally self-sufficient (sufficient for the inhabitants) or whether improvements (investment) will be necessary and whether the municipality has the capacity to make improvements or new investment that support new activities, functions and services. It addresses problems associated with accessibility (comfort, ease of access, clarity) to the urban functions and public services and enables an assessment of the risk of displacing certain functions that are located in the town or historic centre, which would lead to the loss of attractiveness of this area. This analysis theme also considers the epochs of buildings to assess how the evolution relates to the historical evolution of the place and identifies the opportunities that the heritage resource provides for activities and functions.

Another analysis theme assesses the risk and opportunities associated with the occupation, ownership and condition of buildings and sites reflecting the general physical situation of the area, the character of the area, opportunities for bringing underused protected historic buildings into use or rehabilitation action to meet the demand for and supply of accommodation for different users, problems associated with ownership, the potential of the municipality to assist maintenance and renovation work and the potential of vacant or underused sites for new development. It also reflects on the effectiveness of legal and institutional management systems for the safeguarding of the heritage, making particular note of examples where inadequate provisions exist for maintaining the condition of protected heritage assets.

Other analysis issues include, for example, the level of influence of the town (local, regional, national) according to the physical situation of the town, and in relation to other towns and transport infrastructure, the efficiency and quality of access by different users, the role of public and private transport and public spaces and the potential working partners and donors and investors in rehabilitation actions (including any existing partners).

The *synthesis* of findings is centred on the determination of a 'balance sheet assessment of positive and negative issues', recording and prioritising problems and assessing challenges, in particular, to assess how heritage assets can be used to improve the general prosperity and well-being of citizens.

Integrated Cultural Heritage Management Plan

The HerO approach to assessment of issues is through two stages: entitled 'Identifying issues: understanding the historic urban area and the cultural heritage and appraisal'.

The *HerO Guidebook* lists these as follows:

The first stage, 'Identifying issues: understanding the historic urban area and the cultural heritage', provides a description of the status quo of the historic urban area and the cultural heritage. This includes a description of the area (kind of cultural heritage, state of preservation, etc.); a statement of significance and identification of individual values, authenticity and integrity; identification of challenges, threats and opportunities for the cultural heritage; instruments for safeguarding the cultural heritage; and policies, concepts, plans that are of relevance to the historic urban area and the cultural heritage.

The second stage is an *appraisal* of the vision, principles, objectives, actions and management system (institutions involved and procedures) for the development of the historic urban area and the safeguarding of the cultural heritage.

In addition, the *HerO Guidebook* refers briefly to other issues. For example, in addressing what the needs and challenges for the cultural heritage of a particular place are, it refers to the kind of cultural heritage in the historic urban area (description of the cultural heritage in general as well as visually significant buildings, important views, etc.), the condition of its preservation (i.e. grade of deterioration and disuse of historic buildings), the significance and value of the cultural heritage site (what has to be safeguarded) and its needs and challenges with regard to safeguarding and development. It also looks briefly at the demands of the users of cultural heritage sites. (By contrast, the PTF and analysis of the TRP explain these types of issues in considerable detail.)

It also gives the *table of contents* (but not the detail) of the Liverpool World Heritage Site Management Plan of 2003 as an example of an approved management plan covering a historic urban area which was submitted with the nomination application for the Liverpool Maritime Mercantile City World Heritage Site (subsequently inscribed in 2004). This is divided into six sections: (i) introduction; (ii) description of the site (including legal issues relating to ownership, protection and responsibilities); (iii) statement of significance (including UNESCO nomination criteria); (iv) opportunities, threats and management issues (including management, new development, cultural heritage, natural environment, education and interpretation, tourism and regeneration); (v) the future for the World Heritage Site and management objective; and (vi) implementation and monitoring. In citing this example, it is still just a list, but further guidance on particular issues for assessment is given through the *HerO Good-Practice-Compilation* publication (URBACT 2009).

This publication covers a number of issues by reference to case examples. The proper safeguarding of historic urban areas and integration of new architecture and development projects is examined through the theme of 'protecting visual integrity' in Vilnius and the role of a coordination office and plan in Graz. Instruments for the proper rehabilitation of private historic buildings are examined through the provision of funds for the restoration of buildings and the appearance of the town (provided by the city and provincial authorities) in Graz and the role of community engagement in Vilnius. The improvement of mobility and accessibility is considered through the improvement of accessibility for disabled people in Poitiers and through the example of a congestion pricing scheme implemented in Valletta. Support for, and attraction of, economic and cultural activities is considered by reference to retail shopping provision in Regensburg, planning-led regeneration initiatives for Liverpool, cultural stimulation for historic town centre vitality in Lublin, economic redevelopment of deprived parts of the historic centre in Naples and a 'Streets Alive' awareness-raising event in Valletta. The securing of multi-functionality and balancing of different needs is viewed through the 'Pact for the Old Town' in Regensburg (a strategic alliance comprising the municipality, board of trade, retailers, property owners, associations and further initiatives set up to develop an action plan to promote the town), the provision of social housing and efforts to ensure a social balance in Poitiers and by the 2008 to 2013 strategy for economic and social development of the city of Sighisoara. The final issue examined is community, which is viewed through initiatives to improve neglected areas in Lublin and through the Local Agenda 21 project (or sustainable development plan) for Sighisoara.

In contrast to the TRP *synthesis*, the *HerO Guidebook* identifies the need to develop a *roadmap* to clarify the issues and objectives to be addressed in the ICHMP. It usefully addresses five questions for the elaboration of a roadmap concerning the purpose and concrete objective of the management plan, the issues to be addressed in it, the process of elaborating the plan involving the stakeholders, the responsible body for the elaboration process and the identification of 'rights and duties' of stakeholders involved in its production.

The *Guidebook* also has a section on 'Developing a vision, objectives and actions', addressing the questions that proved useful for the HerO partners in the process. These relate to the identification of the aspired future for the cultural heritage site to which the municipality and the relevant stakeholders would want to contribute, the necessary principles and objectives to support the achievement of the vision and well-balanced development of the place and the actions that must be implemented in order to achieve the defined objectives.

This then leads to the development of a *Local Action Plan* to summarise all identified key actions.

Implementation and monitoring

Town Reference Plan

The operational phase of the TRP as proposed through a first part (*strategic and planning stages*) and the second part (*implementation of projects*), as described above, has not yet been sufficiently developed to make true comparisons with the HerO system and awaits the implementation of the next phase through the COMUS project, which commenced on 1 January 2015. Monitoring will be a key part of this project.

Integrated Cultural Heritage Management Plan

The *HerO Guidebook* provides useful and clear information to describe the *implementation process* by defining the need for local action plans, coordination structures and procedures, implementation procedures and monitoring.

Examples of local action plans are provided through separate HerO publications for eight of the nine network cities (Valletta is not included). They describe the cities' main challenges with regard to safeguarding of the built cultural heritage and the sustainable development of the historic urban area, and outline their approaches to the elaboration of an ICHMP (including the measures to be implemented). Linked to this, the network partners' most important projects to be implemented have been published at http://urbact.eu/fileadmin/Projects/HERO/projects_media/HerO_Flagship_Projects_April_2011.pdf in a *list of flagship projects* (referring to responsibilities, financial resources, funding/funding programmes, financial resources secured, time schedules and links to other projects via related actions) (URBACT 2012).

The need to develop coordination structures and procedures is specified through a number of issues. These include the early identification of new challenges, threats and conflicts (including monitoring condition and approval of permits), the coordination of demands and projects (including cross-sectorial coordination of policies, concepts, plans and actions, and finding solutions to conflicts) and procedures for the implementation, compliance and review of the management plan (including compatibility check of policies, plans, etc., monitoring the objectives of the plan, controlling the implementation of actions and reviewing and adapting the management plan as a continuous process).

Implementation procedures relate to the implement on of actions, structures and procedures with particular reference to defined key actions in the management plan, defined institutions responsible for implementing each action and ensuring sufficient workers and the securing of funds for the implementation of key actions (or actions in progress to secure those funds).

The monitoring process for the cultural heritage and the implementation of the ICHMP involves the definition of objectives for monitoring (e.g. surveillance of the condition of heritage sites, assessing community satisfaction of the needs of the users of the historic urban area, etc.), reviewing the performance of the management plan, identification of which indicators help monitor what was defined to be monitored (e.g. in relation to sustainable use of the heritage, condition or vacancy of buildings, etc.), and also any requirements for adapting the ICHMP following the monitoring and review process.

The *HerO Guidebook* also offers an *example of a monitoring indicator system* and *recommendations for selecting monitoring indicators* but this is a rather basic and simple description of monitoring/indicator techniques not specifically applied to urban heritage issues.

Conclusions, comparisons and new developments

In their aims, the two systems are similar as they both focus on sustainable development, using the heritage as a resource for socio-economic development. The *Town Reference Plan* has been directed towards 'revitalisation in small and medium-sized towns and their surrounding environments', particularly for historic towns in countries-in-transition where modern systems of management are not fully established.

The ICHMP has been directed specifically at 'cities' and 'the protection of World Heritage Sites for present and future generations'. The discussion in the *HerO Guidebook* relates also to 'historic urban landscapes' (bearing in mind that the guidebook was produced before the 2011 UNESCO Recommendation on Historic Urban Landscapes was finalised). Its main focus is more directed at/ associated with World Heritage Sites or places worthy of that form of designation. The examples of the network cities are all from EU countries and largely in well-developed Western countries, where institutional capacity is much stronger and planning and conservation measures are generally well developed and more likely to be coordinated.

However, it may be argued that the *Town Reference Plan* has greater potential than the ICHMP as it has a detailed and extensive methodology of diagnosis and assessment, which is crucial in circumstances where accepted procedures (such as 'integrated conservation') are not evident and where institutional capacity is insufficient, such as is the situation in developing/in-transition countries in central and eastern Europe. In addition, the fact that there was a Heritage Assessment Report on institutional and procedural capacities for each country involved provided an insight into the types of problems encountered at the level of town administration including the inadequacy of the urban planning mechanisms and the lack of integration of different management spheres.

It is not possible to explain the full detail for the 23 towns in this chapter, but some brief illustrations can be provided in this context. In particular, in many of the towns taking part in the *Kyiv Initiative* pilot project, urban plans have not been revised since Soviet times and the work developed for the *Town Reference Plan* has created the means for an interim basis for managing the urban environment. For example, the development of the thematic maps in city of Starokostiantyniv (Ukraine) has helped to launch a project on protected zones. This allows urban development to be monitored and the cultural heritage to be safeguarded where previously the general plan for development had failed to take account of the heritage, resulting in both city officials and local entrepreneurs developing some parts of the city with detrimental consequences. Similarly, in Lutsk (Ukraine), the identification of development opportunities using vacant lots ascertained through the thematic maps, instead of destroying historic buildings in poor condition and redevelopment of the sites, as well as the instigation of effective enforcement procedures, has improved local capacity to manage the urban environment. Concerning the town of Gori (Georgia), the analysis identified problems in relation to the difficulty of access to the historic centre on foot and by car and associated parking problems, as well as noise, a frequent accumulation of domestic waste caused by the proximity to the agrarian market and the railway station and poor drainage of rainwater. Therefore, it identified the need to make improvements by the preparation of an area development plan. Moreover, apart from integration of urban planning and heritage, the need for a more integrated transport system can be illustrated by the example of Melitopol (Ukraine), where the city transportation system has been largely serviced by private carriers. The analysis identified that the lack of municipal transport has made it more difficult for people on low income to have easy access to the historic district.

While some parts of the *Town Reference Plan* methodology have not yet been developed and tested, particularly in relation to the strategic and planning stages of the first part of the operational phase, they await new actions through the COMUS project. However, through the testing of methodology and subsequent refinement, the approach should be applicable in any situation – rather than drawing on particular issues and examples from particular cities as in the HerO network, which may not necessarily be applicable elsewhere.

Indeed, it could also be argued that the HerO initiative relies too much on supposed 'good practice' by reference to particular town examples, relating to single issues through the *HerO Good-Practice-Compilation* (URBACT 2012) and other HerO publications (e.g. securing social housing and creating a preservation fund), in association with their inscription on the UNESCO World Heritage List. Moreover, the *HerO Guidebook* acknowledges that the composition of fields of actions will differ from partner to partner depending on their local situation. The broad assessment approach used by the *Town Reference Plan* will aim to ensure all relevant issues in a local situation are covered. Moreover, such 'good practice' may not be relevant to small and medium-sized historic towns due to legal constraints (e.g. for funding mechanisms, tax incentives, etc.).

Furthermore, while the example of Liverpool was cited as a good-practice model of a management plan (established in 2003), its credentials as such have been reduced as Liverpool is now the only cultural heritage site in western Europe on the World Heritage List in Danger (since 26 June 2012) due to the failure of the planning system to control the proposed construction of Liverpool Waters (Figure 9.3). This involves a massive redevelopment of the historic docklands north of the city centre,

Figure 9.3 Liverpool Maritime Mercantile City World Heritage Site in the United Kingdom, one of only four sites in Europe on the List of World Heritage in Danger. Factors listed in the state of conservation reports have included the lack of overall management of new developments, a lack of analysis and description of the townscape characteristics relevant to the Outstanding Universal Value of the property and important views related to the property and its buffer zone. There is a lack of clearly established maximum heights for new developments, for the backdrops of the World Heritage areas as well as along the waterfront, and also a lack of awareness among developers, building professionals and the wider public about the World Heritage property, its Outstanding Universal Value and requirements under the World Heritage Convention. However, it was the proposed development of 'Liverpool Waters' that was the final reason for the site being inscribed on the List of World Heritage in Danger. Photo © R. Pickard 2014.

including what has been termed 'a cloud-bursting central Shanghai Tower' (Carter 2011; Smith 2013). This is despite the fact that the World Heritage Committee had requested stricter planning guidance in 2007 (Hinchcliffe 2008), which led to the adoption of the Liverpool Maritime Mercantile City World Heritage Site Supplementary Planning Document in 2009, subsequently awarded Best Planning Document and the Royal Town Planning Institute NW and Institute of Historic Building Conservation NW Award for Conservation (Stadt Regensburg 2011: 57; RTPI 2014). Thus, whilst this addressed relevant local planning issues, met national statutory requirements and was consistent with international advice on good management of cultural heritage assets within dynamic cities, the decision-making process failed because of the Minister's general approach not to interfere with the jurisdiction of local planning authorities.

This then endorses the importance of assessing the laws and procedures and institutional capacity at the national level and the need for fully functional and integrated systems as advocated by international conventions and recommendations, before examining issues at the local level of the town.

The two approaches have emphasised the importance of local stakeholder involvement, particularly to gain local political and community support at the beginning (to ensure objectives and actions are supported by the inhabitants and users of the historic urban areas and designed to address their needs) and also the need for indicators and monitoring procedures over the time period of action. In respect to these two issues, the Town Reference Plan concept is less developed. The engagement and development of a Local Support Group has been seen as an important aspect in the successful implementation of the ICHMP in the HerO initiative, and this should be introduced into the COMUS project (from 1 January 2015 onwards for a first phase of 30 months). Similarly, the detailed information contained in the *thematic maps*, which reflect many issues of assessment, lend themselves to the possibility of monitoring and updating (e.g. in relation to condition/state of repair of buildings, roads and public spaces and function/occupation/vacancy of buildings, etc.) through to the updating of the Heritage Assessment Reports relating to institutional and procedural capacities as has been undertaken in the case of the Ljubljana Process initiative for the rehabilitation of monuments and sites in the Balkans (Council of Europe 2014a; Rikalović and Mikić 2014).

Both systems should be transferable to other places, but with one system perhaps more relevant to developed countries and major cities, as has been the case in the world heritage locations examined through the HerO network, and the other more applicable in situations where institutional and procedural capacities are less developed and where pilot projects may be more relevant. However, the importance of the two approaches has been cited by the Parliamentary Assembly of the Council of Europe in 2014 through an initiative on Europe's 'endangered heritage', which has advocated the need for greater coherency of action between the Council of Europe, the European Union and UNESCO at the European level (Council of Europe 2014b, 2014c, 2014d). In this respect, the COMUS initiative, to be tested in two pilot towns in each of the six countries, aims to combine elements of the two systems.

The methodology for COMUS is to be based on the existing conceptual guidelines inherited from the previous phase of the Kyiv Initiative Pilot Project on the Rehabilitation of Cultural Heritage in Historic Towns and from other projects related to heritage implemented by the Council of Europe or other European Partners including the Ljubljana Process and HerO. International expertise will be provided by 'partner towns' to be selected from the 141 European cities that are members of the Organisation of World Heritage Cities (OWHC) (and will include some of the experts involved in the HerO network and the pilot project). It will be developed over a 30-month period initially (to the middle of 2017) involving four phases:

> the preliminary phase (4 months) for the setting and organisation of political and technical conditions; the planning phase (8 months) to produce the urban strategy (identification of priority objectives and sites for intervention); the project phase (11 months) to produce the operational programming of rehabilitation projects (detailed technical feasibility planning); and the consolidation phase (7 months) to assess the results and institutionalise the methodology by demonstrating the benefits of including an urban regeneration and heritage-led approach in development and economic policies and national priorities.

COMUS is essentially an urban integrated process embracing all aspects related to the management and development of towns. In this sense, it will focus on a number of key issues:

> *Raising the importance of heritage* as a potential resource for reinvestment and economic activity through identification and interpretation of the towns' distinctive features. *Fostering an integrated approach* by setting up synergies between all levels of authorities in order to combine their capacities in implementing common heritage-led urban projects but also encouraging them to include heritage as a factor of development in national and local sectorial policies. *Managing existing urban constraints and pressures* through identification of problems and priorities for rehabilitation strategies including improving social relations and living in harmony. *Introducing public debate and direct participation of inhabitants in the decision-making process* through sharing of responsibilities between inhabitants, elected representatives and technicians. *Making the best of the existing urban fabric to foster a new kind of modernity* through the adaptation and recycling of old buildings with sustainable solutions in order to halt degradation of the historic environment.

Thus, the aim will be to apply a cross-sector approach to operational management (sharing responsibilities among national and local authorities and experts), as a new way of implementing and managing projects, making institutions more efficient, and by the mobilisation of all stakeholders and partners (including civil society) in debate, workshops, action and training. The structure of management will include a steering committee (made up of one national coordinator for each of the six countries, plus one representative each from the OWHC, EU and Council of Europe); a project leader (one for each town); a project manager (one by country); national experts from local or national institutions; local stakeholder groups (15 local key stakeholders by town); the OWHC (for networking the Partner Towns, including in association with the OWHC's 'City2City' programme (OWHC 2014), provision of a pool of international experts, monitoring, compilation of case studies, development of policy guidelines and dissemination of results); and the Council of Europe Secretariat for overall administration management.

The expected impacts from this initiative are three-fold. On local policies, the aim will be for pilot towns to be equipped with practical documents usable for immediate urban action responding to their problems; for municipalities' autonomy and capacity to develop initiatives to be strengthened; and for encouragement to use the same methodology to elaborate heritage-led projects that can attract investments elsewhere through debates and discussions in other historic towns facing similar development challenges. On national policies, the aim will to enhance the relevant ministry of culture's institutional role in development processes; to increase inter-ministerial cooperation; to stimulate innovative partnerships and new ways to collaborate with municipalities; to provide recommendations for developing new programmes to support local development; and to identify capacity needs for legal and institutional improvements. It is also hoped that future cooperation initiatives will be developed through regular exchanges of information and of expertise between historic towns through a consolidated network, with bilateral cooperation between historic towns encouraged and possible investors and funders, including national or international potential funding programmes, identified.

The COMUS initiative seeks to marry the ideas from the two main initiatives discussed in this chapter in order to develop methodology and procedures to provide those responsible for urban management and sustaining cultural heritage of historic towns with the tools to facilitate actions focused on the best possible solutions according to local potentials. However, there are many potential hurdles that have to be crossed in the coming years, including the need for political support for the proposed project, particularly bearing in mind the current crisis in eastern Europe, as well as the need to motivate key local stakeholders bearing in mind the long-term nature of the work being conducted.

Bibliography

Association Nationale (2014). *Outils de protection et valorisation du patrimoine, L'Association Nationale des Villes et Pays d'art et d'histoire et des Villes à secteurs sauvegardés et protégés*. Available at: http://www.an-patrimoine.org/-Outils-de-protection-et,75- (accessed 16 October 2014).

Bundestransferstelle Städtebaulicher Denkmalschutz (2014). *Programmstädte*. Available at: http://www.staedtebaulicher-denkmalschutz.de/programm/programmstaedte/ (accessed 16 October 2014).

Carter H. (2011). Liverpool's world heritage status threatened by dockside development. *The Guardian*, 23 November 2011. Available at: http://www.theguardian.com/uk/2011/nov/23/liverpool-world-heritage-status (accessed 20 May 2014).

Council of Europe (1975). *European Charter of the Architectural Heritage.* (Adopted by the Committee of Ministers in 26 September 1975.) Available at: http://www.icomos.org/en/charters-and-texts/179-articles-en-francais/ressources/charters-and-standards/170-european-charter-of-the-architectural-heritage (accessed 10 September 2014).

Council of Europe (1976). *Resolution (76) 28 concerning the adaptation of laws and regulations to the requirements of integrated conservation of the architectural heritage.* (Adopted by the Committee of Ministers on 14 April 1976 at the 256th meeting of the Ministers' Deputies.) Available at: https://wcd.coe.int/ViewDoc.jsp?id=664497 (accessed 14 September 2014).

Council of Europe (1985). *Convention for the Protection of the Architectural Heritage of Europe, Council of Europe Treaty Series, No.121 (Granada, 1985).* Available at: http://conventions.coe.int/Treaty/Commun/QueVoulezVous.asp?NT=121&CM=8&CL=ENG (accessed 14 September 2014).

Council of Europe (1992). *European Convention on the Protection of the Archaeological Heritage (revised), Council of Europe Treaty Series, No.143 (Valletta, 1992).* Available at: http://conventions.coe.int/Treaty/Commun/QueVoulezVous.asp?NT=143&CM=8&CL=ENG (accessed 14 September 2014).

Council of Europe (2000). *European Landscape Convention, Council of Europe Treaty Series, No.176 (Florence, 2000).* Available at: http://conventions.coe.int/Treaty/Commun/QueVoulezVous.asp?NT=176&CM=8&CL=ENG (accessed 14 September 2014).

Council of Europe (2005a). *Framework Convention on the Value of Cultural Heritage for Society, Council of Europe Treaty Series, No. 199 (Faro, 2005).* Available at: http://conventions.coe.int/Treaty/Commun/QueVoulezVous.asp?NT=199&CM=8&CL=ENG (accessed 14 September 2014).

Council of Europe (2005b). *Guidance on Urban Rehabilitation.* Strasbourg: Council of Europe Publications.

Council of Europe (2010a). *Kyiv Initiative Regional Programme: Pilot Project 2: 'Rehabilitation of Cultural Heritage in Historic Towns' (PP2): Heritage Assessment Report: ARMENIA, Strasbourg, 2 December 2010, KI (2010) 065.* Available at: http://www.coe.int/t/dg4/cultureheritage/cooperation/Kyiv/PP2/KI_2010_065-PP2ArmeniaHAR.pdf (accessed 20 May 2014).

Council of Europe (2010b). *Kyiv Initiative Regional Programme: Pilot Project 2: 'Rehabilitation of Cultural Heritage in Historic Towns' (PP2): Heritage Assessment Report: AZERBAIJAN, Strasbourg, 2 December 2010, KI (2010) 066.* Available at: http://www.coe.int/t/dg4/cultureheritage/cooperation/Kyiv/PP2/KI_2010_066-PP2AzerbaijanHAR.pdf (accessed 20 May 2014).

Council of Europe (2010c). *Kyiv Initiative Regional Programme: Pilot Project 2: 'Rehabilitation of Cultural Heritage in Historic Towns' (PP2): Heritage Assessment Report: GEORGIA, Strasbourg, 2 December 2010, KI (2010) 039rev2.* Available at: http://www.coe.int/t/dg4/cultureheritage/cooperation/Kyiv/PP2/KI_2010_039rev2PP2GeorgiaHAR.pdf (accessed 20 May 2014).

Council of Europe (2010d). *Kyiv Initiative Regional Programme: Pilot Project 2: 'Rehabilitation of Cultural Heritage in Historic Towns' (PP2): Heritage Assessment Report: MOLDOVA, Strasbourg, 2 December 2010, KI (2010) 064.* Available at: http://www.coe.int/t/dg4/cultureheritage/cooperation/Kyiv/PP2/KI_2010_064-PP2MoldovaHAR.pdf (accessed 20 May 2014).

Council of Europe (2010e). *Kyiv Initiative Regional Programme: Pilot Project 2: 'Rehabilitation of Cultural Heritage in Historic Towns' (PP2): Heritage Assessment Report: GEORGIA, Strasbourg, 2 December 2010, KI (2010) 049.* Available at: http://www.coe.int/t/dg4/culture heritage/cooperation/Kyiv/PP2/KI_2010_049-PP2UkraineHAR.pdf (accessed 20 May 2014).

Council of Europe (2011a). *Guidance on the Development of Legislation and Administration Systems in the Field of Cultural Heritage*, 2nd edn. Strasbourg: Council of Europe Publications, p. 107.

Council of Europe (2011b). *Kyiv Initiative: Pilot Project on the Rehabilitation of Cultural Heritage in Historic Towns: Heritage for a New Urbanity: Think Differently, Live Differently.* Available at: http://www.coe.int/t/dg4/cultureheritage/cooperation/Kyiv/urbanrehab_en.asp (accessed 14 April 2014).

Council of Europe (2011c). *Kyiv Initiative Regional Programme Pilot Project for the Rehabilitation of Cultural Heritage in Historic Towns: Activity Report 2009–2011.* Available at: http://www.coe.int/t/dg4/cultureheritage/cooperation/Kyiv/PP2/KI_2012_015-PP2_Activity_Report_2009-2011_en.pdf (accessed 14 April 2014).

Council of Europe (2012). *Kyiv Initiative: Preliminary Technical File (PTF).* Available at: http://www.coe.int/t/dg4/cultureheritage/cooperation/Kyiv/PTF/default_en.asp (accessed 20 May 2014).

Council of Europe (2014a). *IRPP/SAAH – Ljubljana Process: Benefits.* Available at: http://www.coe.int/t/dg4/cultureheritage/cooperation/SEE/IRPPSAAH/benefits_en.asp (accessed 1 December 2014).

Council of Europe (2014b). *Europe's Endangered Heritage, Doc. 13428, 18 February 2014, Report: Committee on Culture, Science, Education and Media, Rapporteur: Ms Vesna MARJANOVIĆ, Serbia, Socialist Group.* Available at: http://assembly.coe.int/nw/xml/XRef/Xref-DocDetails-EN.asp?FileID=20524&lang=EN (accessed 1 December 2014).

Council of Europe (2014c). *Resolution 1981 (2014) Europe's Endangered Heritage, Text Adopted by the Standing Committee, acting on behalf of the Assembly, on 7 March 2014.* Available at: http://assembly.coe.int/nw/xml/XRef/Xref-DocDetails-EN.asp?FileID=20548&lang=EN (accessed 1 December 2014).

Council of Europe (2014d). *Recommendation 2038 (2014): Europe's Endangered Heritage, Text adopted by the Standing Committee, acting on behalf of the Parliamentary Assembly, on 7 March 2014.* Available at: http://assembly.coe.int/nw/xml/XRef/Xref-DocDetails-en.asp?FileID=20549&lang=en (accessed 1 December 2014).

Council of Europe, European Commission and Ministère de la Culture et de la Communication (2011). *Heritage for a new urbanity: think differently; live differently, Kyiv Initiative Regional Programme: Pilot Project on the Rehabilitation of Cultural Heritage in Historic Towns: A Joint Action of the European Commission and the Council of Europe.* Available at: http://www.coe.int/t/dg4/cultureheritage/cooperation/Kyiv/PP2/Brochure.pdf (accessed 14 April 2014).

EAHTR (2007). *INHERIT – Investing in Heritage: A Guide to Successful Urban Regeneration, European Association of Historic Towns and Regions (now known as HERITAGE EUROPE).* Available at: http://www.historictownsforum.org/node/300 (accessed 14 April 2014).

European Commission (2014). *Development and Cooperation – EUROPEAID: EU Neighbourhood and Russia – Eastern Partnership, European Commission.* Available at: http://ec.europa.eu/europeaid/regions/eu-neighbourhood-region-and-russia/introduction-0_en (accessed 29 June 215).

Hinchcliffe, J. (2008). *The Conservation of Port Heritage: Lessons from Liverpool, On the Waterfront: Culture, Heritage and Regeneration of Port Cities, English Heritage.* Available at: https://www.english-heritage.org.uk/images-books/publications/on-the-waterfront/waterfront-part5.pdf (accessed 29 June 2015).

ICOMOS (1987). *International Charter for the Conservation of Historic Towns and Urban Areas (Washington Charter 1987), International Council on Monuments and Sites*. Available at: http://www.international.icomos.org/charters/towns_e.pdf (accessed 14 April 2014).

OWHC (2013). *Safeguarding and Further Developing World Heritage Cities, Organization of World Heritage Cities*. Available at: http://www.ovpm.org/en/regional_secretariats/news/position_paper_world_heritage_cities_region_north_west_europe_published (accessed on 14 April 2014).

OWHC (2014). *City2City, Organization of World Heritage Cities*. Available at: http://www.ovpm.org/en/city2city (accessed 2 December 2014).

Pickard, R. (2009). *Funding the Architectural Heritage: A Guide to Policies and Examples*. Strasbourg: Council of Europe Publications.

Pickard, R. (2010). European heritage laws and planning regulations: integration, regeneration and sustainable development. In: M. Guštin and T. Nypan (eds), *Cultural Heritage and Legal Aspects in Europe*. Koper: Institute of Mediterranean Heritage, Institute for Corporation and Public Law, Science and Research Centre, University of Primorska, pp. 56–98.

Reeve, A. and Shipley, R. (2013). *Townscape Heritage Initiative Schemes: Evaluation, Ten Year Review Report, Final Report, Heritage Lottery Fund*. Available at: http://www.hlf.org.uk/townscape-heritage-initiative-evaluation (accessed 8 July 2015).

Rikalović, G. and Mikić, H. (eds) (2014). *Heritage for Development in South-East Europe: New Visions and Perceptions of Heritage through the Ljubljana Process, September 2014*. Strasbourg: Council of Europe Publishing.

RTPI (2014). *100 Years of Professional Planning: Past Awards* [Online]. Available at: http://www.rtpi.org.uk/the-rtpi-near-you/rtpi-north-west/awards/past-awards/ (accessed 15 November 2014).

Smith, M. (2013). Liverpool Waters redevelopment gets the government green light. *The Guardian*, 5 March 2013. Available at: http://www.theguardian.com/uk/2013/mar/05/liverpool-waters-redevelopment-green-light (accessed 20 May 2014).

Stadt Regensburg (ed.) (2011). *HerO – Heritage as Opportunity. The Road to Success: Integrated Management of Historic Towns (Guidebook)*. City of Regensburg/URBACT. Available at: http://urbact.eu/sites/default/files/hero_guidebook_final_01.pdf (accessed 29 June 2015).

UNESCO (1976). *Recommendation Concerning the Safeguarding and Contemporary Role of Historic Areas, United Nations Educational Scientific and Cultural Organization*. Available at: http://portal.unesco.org/en/ev.php-URL_ID=13133&URL_DO=DO_TOPIC&URL_SECTION=201.html (accessed 14 April 2014).

UNESCO (2011). *Recommendation on the Historic Urban Landscape, United Nations Educational Scientific and Cultural Organization*. Available at: http://portal.unesco.org/en/ev.php-URL_ID=48857&URL_DO=DO_TOPIC&URL_SECTION=201.html (accessed 14 April 2014).

URBACT (2009). *HerO: Heritage as Opportunity: Sustainable Management Strategies for Vital Historic Urban Landscapes: Good-Practice Compilation, URBACT*. Available at: http://urbact.eu/sites/default/files/import/Projects/HERO/outputs_media/HerO_-_Good_Practice_Compilation.pdf (accessed 29 June 2015).

URBACT (2011). *HerO Results: 'Heritage as Opportunity', URBACT II Project*. Available at: http://urbact.eu/heritage-opportunity-hero-results (accessed 29 June 2015).

URBACT (2012). *HerO Results: Our Outputs, URBACT*. Saint Denis: URBACT.

URBACT (2014). *HerO – Heritage as Opportunity (Project completed)*. Available at: http://urbact.eu/hero (accessed 29 June 2015).

Chapter 10

Corporate visual impact on urban heritage

The corporate social responsibility framework

Celia Martínez Yáñez

Urban chaos is a global and pressing issue for the international heritage community, in which multinational corporations—amongst other causes and economic and politic sectors—play a central role. This chapter focuses on one of the several dimensions of this problem, the visual impact created by corporate brand design, which is a topic scarcely analyzed by current debates on cultural heritage and historic urban landscape, although it affects all countries around the world.

In spite of several international and national rules regulating the integration of new architecture in urban and heritage contexts, cultural properties are too frequently hidden by overlapping posters, advertising and facilities that devalue, distort and annihilate their environmental, historic and aesthetic values and, as a consequence, their entire setting. This problem affects both rural and urban areas, but is especially evident in cities, where all these evils come together and appear more crudely to reduce the quality of life and the environment.

Almost no multinational corporation has included visual impact on heritage within its corporate social responsibility strategy, although most companies report on issues concerning sustainability, environmental responsibility and commitment with local communities. This indicates that corporations do not consider heritage when dealing with these topics, although heritage conservation is widely regarded today as a key component of sustainable and fair development.

The lack of specific analysis on this topic and the absence of scientific research on the links between corporations' difficult relationship with heritage, uncontrolled urbanization and visual pollution, provides a strong reason to develop a body of research and launch public scientific debate on this global threat to heritage and urban landscape.

This chapter will therefore draw on existing scientific research, international recommendations and examples of the impact of multinational corporations on heritage protection and urban planning to offer an approach to this subject. To do so, first, it will briefly describe how the economic crisis and the increasing power of the private sector are influencing cultural heritage and urban landscape public policies, as the general framework of our analysis. Second, it will focus on the multifaceted aspects of corporations' visual impact on heritage sites and cities, going beyond corporate brand design itself to include questions such as the resulting loss of authenticity and local and cultural identity. Finally, it will analyze corporate social responsibility as an emerging framework to address these issues, as well as its strength and weaknesses. Our goal is to stimulate larger, international and coordinated studies able to assess critical negative impact, increase awareness about this issue and disseminate the urgent need to establish principles that foster a more visually compatible and ethically responsible attitude towards cultural heritage and historic urban landscape by concerned companies.

Corporate visual impact on heritage sites and urban landscape: an unexplored topic

It is not only global and brand corporations that do not properly consider their visual impact on heritage sites and urban landscape. Although urban heritage conservation is an important sector of public policy worldwide, corporations' impact on public spaces and heritage sites is a topic almost unexplored so far at all levels of cultural heritage doctrine (see Fleming 2002; Araujo Portella 2006; Porter and Kramer 2006; ICOMOS 2010b; Starr 2010; Martínez Yáñez 2012). Questions such as sustainable and unsustainable urban development, the renovation of historic areas, visual contamination, skyscraper sprawl, visual impact on skylines and special/scenic views, and heritage impact assessments are increasingly being addressed (The Landscape Institute and the Institute of Environmental Management and Assessment 2002; English Heritage 2008; Université de Montréal 2008; ICOMOS 2010a), but there is a general lack of analysis linking these problems with multinational corporations and the private sector's role in urban development.

Public authorities and international organizations responsible for heritage protection and urban planning have not specifically focused on this topic, and, in fact, ICOMOS and UNESCO themselves have not addressed it sufficiently in their recent recommendations and meetings regarding environmental questions, historic urban landscape, and threats to heritage properties.

Such an instance, the 2011 UNESCO Recommendation on the Historic Urban Landscape (HUL), the most recent international document dealing with current threats to urban heritage and historic cities, provides a very useful framework to go deeper on this subject. Nevertheless, it addresses it without pointing out the need to promote a more ethical attitude towards public values and heritage properties amongst concerned corporations. Likewise, the vast majority of the problems due to human actions and urban and economic development pressures reported in the ICOMOS Heritage at Risk (H@R) series deal with the construction of skyscrapers, buildings out of scale, shopping malls, and massive renovations in historic centers. However, they rarely mention questions relating to the role played by specific companies in this regard or the impact of corporate brands design near or within heritage sites and historic urban landscapes. Together with the difficulty of blaming specific corporations, in our opinion, the absence of programmatic visibility of this aspect of corporations' impact on cultural heritage and urban landscape might explain the scarce attention paid to this issue up to now.

ICOMOS has conducted several attempts—in which the author has been involved and which are the basis of this chapter—to include this topic in its programmes. The Corporate Visual Responsibility and Heritage Sites Initiative was first issued by the ICOMOS Scientific Council at its meeting in Valletta, Malta in October 2009, on the proposal of the ICOMOS International Scientific Committee on Cultural Landscapes (ADCOM SC 2009/10 Recommendation n°3). Subsequent recommendations were made by the Advisory Committee at its meeting in Dublin, Ireland in October 2010 (Recommendation ADCOM 2010/10 9-1-5) and in the related decisions of the Executive Committee in 2010 (Decisions EXCOM 2010/03 6-3 and EXCOM 2010/10 8-2-9). This initiative was further discussed at the meetings of the Advisory and Executive Committee in November 2011, in agreement with the Townscape Institute, which first launched the need to address this subject within the ICOMOS framework. As we will discuss below, these attempts focused on two main actions that should be implemented, namely to conduct a survey or environmental audit on corporate brands impact on heritage sites and to explore ways in which ICOMOS could encourage corporate policy change "in a world where there is increased concern about sustainability and where every major corporation has a company social responsibility element in its strategic plan with increased pressure to meet higher standards" (ICOMOS 2010b).

General framework: globalization, economic crisis, and the increasing power of the private sector

In our globalized world, and in the middle of its global economic crisis, economic forces are influencing decision-making at all levels of government (if not directly substituting them) and acquiring an unprecedented degree of power. While many countries have been able in past decades to develop adequate legislation and regulations for the protection of urban historic areas, the current effectiveness of these efforts towards conservation are being diminished owing to the scarce and dwindling public resources available for cultural investments (UNESCO n.d.).

Besides, the economic global crisis and the consequent decrease in public funds allocated to heritage conservation have driven some governments to relinquish their obligations towards heritage sites and look for private sector financial support (Starr 2010: 147). In addition, as Jokilehto (2010: 62) has acutely noted, the physical condition of vast built areas makes it economically difficult, if not impossible, for a public authority to intervene, so the initiative tends to remain in the hands of the private sector. This includes multinational companies, which often have the financial means and can justify any intervention on economic grounds without much attention to the overall impact of the projects.

On the one hand, in previous decades, we have seen how the policies that protect the historic built environment are sometimes rendered unenforceable by the power of corporations and some public authorities that are neither able nor interested in confronting their negative impact on many cities and heritage properties. Indeed, in the worst or most difficult to control cases, public authorities have even favored corporations' massive ill investments in historic cities, changing legislation in force or through land use conversion. In this regard, it is worth quoting the case of Istanbul, where the Ministry of Culture and Tourism was allowed to transfer the responsibility for the safeguarding of the World Heritage area to private and commercial users and owners, as was done in the case of a Four Seasons Hotel, whose extension would have affected the archaeological remains of the Great Palace of the Roman and Byzantine empires, one of the core areas of the World Heritage nomination. Fortunately, and partly thanks to civil society awareness about neo-liberal urban transformations causing cultural destruction and social gentrification, the permission which had been given by the local government was suspended by a court decision in 2009 (Debold-Kritter 2010: 179).

On the other hand, there is also a lack of coherence and many gaps between local, regional, national and international regulations, planning authorities, and the private sector regarding the appearance of the city and its future development. Amongst the reasons that explain this distortion, Pičíková (2008: 139) quotes the following:

> economic pressure to capitalize on valuable land; possibilities to realize large investments; desire to increase the social status; architects and investors who regard themselves as beyond the law; pressure to change the place's use and character; and changes of life style and production technologies leading to loss of details.

This situation is astonishing bearing in mind that the expertise needed to avoid it exists in many countries as the result of almost a century of urban planning and international legislation for protection of cultural heritage and historic centers, neither of which seem important when large profits are at stake. The Preliminary Report on the Proposed UNESCO Recommendation on the Historic Urban Landscape (UNESCO, n.d.) claims that this apparatus is often weak and powerless in the face of the forces of change that dominate the world and its urban scenes today and in the foreseeable future. In fact, in most urban protected areas, the key issue is not inadequate legislation, but its ineffectual application as a result of the great pressure exerted by profit-oriented property developers. As Beelen (2007) and Jokilehto (2010) observe, the growing market-oriented strategies have favored the private sector at the expense of a central public authority and state-induced planning, which have increasingly come under stress through liberal reforms compounding with the forces of capital and globalization—forces that it seeks to benefit from as well as compensate for.

Summing up, cities have become a battlefield where very different and powerful forces struggle to achieve benefits for themselves alone, usually under the astonished eyes of communities and citizens, whose values and needs are rarely taken into account. As the production of the physical urban space increasingly takes shape through an interplay—or a direct confrontation—of many actors and agents, urban planning is increasingly having to face up to this challenge.

The several faces of corporate brand impact on heritage and urban landscape

As Saskia Sassen observed (1999: 162), ranging from traffic and tourism pressures to high-rise constructions and inner-city functional changes, the issues negatively impacting on the cultural-historic significance of urban landscapes are numerous, often interrelated and increasing in complexity.

The Preliminary Report on the Proposed UNESCO Recommendation on the Historic Urban Landscape (HUL) (UNESCO n.d.) further stresses that many of the most important urban historic areas existing in Europe, Asia, and Latin America have lost their traditional functions or character. In addition, they are under pressure form tourism and other transformation agents, which tend towards globalization and making uniform all cities around the world. Multinational corporations are, of course, among these forces, given their growing influence on decision-making in all social and economic spheres and ubiquitous—and not always positive—visual and programmatic presence around the world.

The visual impact of corporate brands on heritage sites and the urban landscape is multifaceted and difficult to condense, especially taking into account the absence of global analysis on this subject and the many scales, heritage properties and urban areas affected. A summarized approach includes, amongst others, the following closely interrelated aspects.

Visual impact of corporate brand design

Corporate franchises (petrol stations, fast food outlets, drugstores, etc.) are increasingly affecting our world—especially the very places that are most obviously unique, such as World Heritage sites and conservation and historic districts or areas—with blatant colors, over-sized signage, and awkward shapes that are not compatible with existing historic townscapes and cultural properties.

Thus, the visual impact provoked by uncontrolled corporate brand design must be analyzed in the wider framework of visual pollution, which includes everything that affects or disrupts the display of a site or impoverishes the aesthetics of an area or landscape. This concept also refers to the abuse of certain elements that not only alter the aesthetics and image of the landscape, but also generate a visual overstimulation that is aggressive, invasive, and simultaneous, which can even affect the health of individuals. In fact, among all the threats that loom over heritage, the most common is this perceptual or visual pollution, usually provoked by the disrespectful design of commercial premises and outlets, many of which belong to corporate brands and multinational companies.

The absence of programmatic visibility of this facet of corporations' impact on cultural heritage and urban landscape is a major problem to analyze and solve. Although there are many examples of outlets and advertisements with negative visual impacts on heritage sites and their significance, their scale may be small or they occur in places that are rarely known or visited (although there are also

Figure 10.1 A Pizza Hut restaurant near the Pyramids of Giza (Egypt) © Atsutoms at Flickr https://www.flickr.com/photos/atsutoms/2541234398/. Creative Commons Licence https://creativecommons.org/licenses/by/2.0/.

glaring cases, such as the Pizza Hut restaurant near the Pyramids of Giza (see Figure 10.1) and the McDonald's franchise in Luxor).

In comparison with huge investments in skyscrapers, large shopping centers, etc., these examples might be negligible, but as a whole, they illustrate a high threat to the heritage values of cities and landscapes. It is by adding all impacts on all scales, when we deal with a major global damage, that critical negative impact will be assessed.

A wild consumer society permanently changing and a market-oriented economy, which usually underestimates environmental and public sense conscience, reinforce the multiplication of this kind of pollution. Facades are destroyed or hidden by overlapping posters as well as advertising and facilities disrespectful to their environment that devalue and miniaturize architecture and dilute, distort, and annihilate the environmental, urban, historical, and aesthetic values of the urban landscape. A city or a heritage site affected by this and other types of visual pollution denotes deficient or nonexistent regulation of public and private space, or, at least, poor policy implementation. Cities thus become the stage for millions of individual decisions and commercial spots that do not heed the environment, forming a living chaos, which are difficult to assimilate by the human eye.

Fast food restaurants are especially illustrative of corporate brand visual impact. According to Hoover's online business network,[1] there were 29,000 McDonald's franchises, 11,400 Burger King franchises, and 11,300 KFC franchises worldwide in 2001. As their demand for growth, profitability and new markets continues, these franchises increasingly move into historic centers, areas of small population and neighborhoods where they previously would not have entered. The negative visual effect on these places, which have usually a distinct character, is huge when these brands do not implement visual policies aimed at adapting corporate design to their scale, materials, site configuration, and heritage values. To give an overview of the global impact in this regard, it might be useful to focus on McDonald's, which is the leader of the fast food sector, and therefore a potential trendsetter,[2] and one of the most aggressive marketers in the world. This corporation invests hundreds of millions of dollars in advertising and promoting its brand image, mainly through two major marketing strategies, namely the development of a single identity and co-branding with other companies, such as petrol stations or supermarkets, to develop facilities where customers can easily go from one business to the other.[3] Its so-called "Youthful Spirit" color scheme involves painting its eligible franchises and publicity in bright red, yellow, and white (lately also in green and yellow), usually regardless of heritage values or local design aesthetics (see Figure 10.2).

This homogeneous look is supported by both the corporation and its local franchisees worldwide, which usually prefer the prototype design and colors to tie themselves to the national and international marketing campaigns rather than any local, cultural, or heritage considerations. As Barnard (1999) comments, unfortunately neither the company nor the franchisers accept that McDonald's golden arches are enough to identify the brand, so they continue using garish signs and publicity "opposed to sensitive and contextually relevant arches." This prevents them from realizing the potential value of individualizing this standard icon as a

Figure 10.2 McDonald's' garish red and yellow colors in the historic centre of Vigan World Heritage City (The Philippines) diminish its heritage values, even if the pseudo-historicism of the building roughly imitates the urban environment © Celia Martínez Yáñez.

means of stressing heritage and community values, and results in increasingly homogenized cities and heritage sites around the world (especially taking into account that most of the international chains have developed the same aggressive marketing approach).

As Fleming (2002) has shown, the irony of this situation is that corporate brands can minimize their significant contribution to visual pollution with more respectful design at limited cost, which has been proven to increase corporates' reputations and profits. In this regard, he explains the case of a franchise opened in 2000 in South Phoenix, Arizona, which was specifically designed to pay tribute to the Latin American culture and to reflect the fact that most of the population was Hispanic. Although this marketing strategy was obviously business and commercially oriented, certainly the visual impact of this outlet is less severe than most of McDonald's franchises. In fact, this "neo-Aztec style" might be questioned, but it was reasonably well designed, even from the landscape perspective, and it included a quality relief from the Mexican artist Enrique Avilez. The usual negative visual presence of this corporation was therefore minimized in this case, which helped the franchisee to gain community acceptance, showing the positive outcomes that might be attained through a sensible visual approach.

Standardization and loss of community and intangible values

Visual pollution provoked by the uncontrolled design and sprawl of corporate brands not only undermines the beauty of urban landscapes, but it also hinders their reading by citizens, eroding community values and identity and heritage ability to provide local people with a much needed feeling of belonging to a specific place. In other words, the standardization and environmental uniformity provoked by the excessive presence of the same commercial franchises, fast food chains, and overlapping publicity anywhere in the world is destroying the spirit of place, and especially of the most valuable places. In fact, in our commercialized world, the only resource that helps to differentiate one place from another is the uniqueness of cultural and natural heritage, whose potential in this regard dramatically diminishes when corporate brands erupt in heritage areas and cities, filling them with identical franchises, signs, and corporate images that make them appear identical to visitors and citizens. The situation is worse in low-income communities whose residents may feel they have no leverage in influencing franchise design and they may not have the planning or design resources to help them document the historic values of their neighborhood and community. The cases of Moscow, Lahore and Barcelona are illustrative of this problem.

Besides, as Recommendation SC 2009/10 3 by the ICOMOS International Scientific Committee on Cultural Landscapes regarding Corporate Visual Responsibility and ICOMOS Policy Leverage (ICOMOS 2010b) noted, the visual impact of corporate franchises, particularly those retailing gasoline and fast food,

> is poignant adjacent or within some of the most fragile and important world heritage sites. Many franchises are drawn to these areas because of the tourism

and so an anomaly of corporate homogeneity is nourished by the very specialness of the site. Visitors often have to run a gamut of the most banal and garish universal marketing images before they find the particular beauty of the locale they have come so many miles to see. Huge plastic shelters of gasoline stations juxtaposed against temple ruins and city fortifications come to mind. This condition is particularly arresting in some developing countries where there are often few planning constraints and where franchises are seen as economic progress.

A highly representative example of this depressing description is the Terracotta Warriors International Shopping Mall (Xi'an, China) that visitors had to traverse when visiting this World Heritage site. This shopping mall was the subject of an SOC Report in 2002, which documented that priority had been given to uncontrolled tourism development over conservation needs.

This kind of standardization also causes the loss of traditional knowledge, building skills and crafts, which are not regarded or utilized by corporate brand design, building techniques and architectural forms. In fact, according to these companies' marketing goals, they tend to be identical "to promote the security of sameness by replicating a standardized brand image, often in garish colours and shapes" aimed to stress their visual presence and catch the eye of consumers, regardless of the values and characteristics of the context (Fleming 2002: 1).

In this regard, Van Oers (2010: 13) has noted the difficult role of local and national authorities dealing with powerful companies and their much desired investments. International capital and companies have little knowledge of, or care for, local significance and values, so the ensuing balancing act that municipal authorities have to perform to interest international investors and at the same time safeguard local values "is often a mission impossible." New international accepted guidelines should be implemented to allow cities to combat this unfair negotiation, demanding concessions as regards the overall planning scheme or architectural solution chosen for the urban project to mitigate impacts on the historic environment.

Heritage and historic districts: banalization, commercialization, and gentrification

Narrowly linked with the standardization and loss of community and intangible values discussed above is the private sector's and multinational companies' tendency to negatively impact on the once diverse economic functions of historic districts, turning them into places exclusively commercially, economically, or business-oriented and tourist icons. Amongst others, the following stand out as self-explanatory glaring cases.

Wilkinson (2009: 127–9) has brilliantly reported how, in Moscow, all new development in the historic center is exclusively oriented to the rich and how "some of the most charming areas have become super-gentrified ghettos for the exclusive use of Gucci-bagged oligarchs' wives." This has provoked the loss of authenticity, identity, and social and cultural values of the historic center and the expulsion of the vast majority of the population, who cannot afford to shop in these areas, where uncontrolled advertising has covered the entire facades of numerous buildings. Although many local and national rules have adopted restrictions on large-scale advertising in protected spaces, usually these only apply to a closely defined buffer zone in the immediate vicinity of the area inscribed on the World Heritage List, leaving buildings outside them under threat. That such alterations are easily reversible does not lessen the detriment they cause to the historic cityscape:

> The devil is in details. The rough treatment of these buildings is akin to dressing a fashion model in sackcloth and putting a paper bag over her head. It diminishes the value of historic surroundings even when no actual fabric has been lost.
>
> (Wilkinson 2009: 127–9)

According to Naz and Anjum (2007), this is also the case of Lahore, once famous for its gardens, but currently characterized by the expansion of multinational companies, banks, telecommunication companies, and international food chains that has resulted in a mushrooming of shopping plazas, traffic congestion, and a loss of open spaces. Liberty Market, named after the Liberty Cinema in its vicinity, has become a hub of the fashion industry, a visit to which is considered a matter of pride across the country, and the McDonald's opening ceremony in 1998 "was like a big festival and became a trend setter for the others to follow" (Naz and Anjum 2007: 49). A large list of rules have been ignored or changed by local authority to transform the city into a niche of corporate brands and tall buildings—a question that Noman Ahmad (2007: 57) has denounced, asking the city government to assess the impacts of land use conversion and commercialization, and for professionals and architects to devise good design practices in commercial space.

Finally, it is also worth noting the complexity of these issues in Barcelona, which adds to the previous problems with a struggle led by its citizens against the impact of tourism and its main companies on city life. The market-oriented economy of the city has privileged mass tourism since the city held the 1992 Olympic Games and systematically ignores its huge negative effects on heritage as well as the sense of place and tranquillity of its inhabitants. One of the worst results of this policy is that the heritage sites and remarkable seascapes of Barcelona have literally been stolen from the citizens and offered to big tourist corporations—such as luxury hotel brands—contributing to the gentrification and commercialization of the whole city centre. The W Hotel in La Barceloneta is a good example of this trend. This huge skyscraper has not only an evident visual impact on the traditional and architectural values of this maritime district and on the city as a whole, but it has also turned a once residential and leisure area, beloved by citizens, into a privatized place they cannot enjoy anymore (Figure 10.3).[4]

Figure 10.3 Hotel W in La Barceloneta (Barcelona, Spain) © Felix König at Wikimedia Commons http://commons.wikimedia.org/wiki/File:W_Barcelona_2013. jpg. Creative Commons Attribution 3.0 Unported license.

This situation has obviously not been acknowledged by the hotel, which claims to be a "green choice" in order to sooth its customers:

> The W Barcelona is an eco-friendly hotel, where it's cool to be green. At W Barcelona, you can indulge without checking your conscience at the door. Don't worry, all of our eco-friendly hotel efforts take place behind the scenes. At the W Barcelona you can feel good about your impact on the environment

without sacrificing style or comfort. While keeping a Green Choice, we have a continued our Whatever/Whenever service promise to providing luxurious, lifestyle experiences for our guests. Make W Barcelona your luxury green hotel in Barcelona, and stay green, glamorous and global![5]

Limits of acceptability on corporate brands and citizen reactions

The many scales, facets, and effects of corporate brand visual impacts on heritage sites and historic urban landscapes, detailed above, show the need for guidelines, in order to assess the limits of acceptability on brands. Unfortunately, there are no specific analyses of these limits or projects to compare the situation in different cities and countries. The existing studies that could serve as a basis to launch research on this matter (Nasar 1988; D'Astous and Bitz 1995; Nasar and Hong 1999; Araujo Portella 2006, 2007; English Heritage 2008; ICOMOS 2010a) focus on very general—although related—questions, such as visual pollution, effects of commercial signs on consumers, and heritage views, as well as heritage and environment impact assessment. However, they do not delve into how to measure the limits of acceptability of these impacts, and particularly, of the increasing corporate brand presence in all kinds of human environments. Indeed, the results and aims of these studies (and especially of specific heritage and environment impact assessments due to public works or private investments) vary depending on who has conducted them and why, making it difficult to obtain accurate and relevant conclusions on actual impacts and damages.

It is my opinion that a comprehensive analysis of the limits of acceptability on brands should include not only the topics addressed by the above mentioned studies and assessments, but also clear statements on how corporate brand designs meet all policy levels of heritage legislation. These include urban planning management schedules and statutory regulations that state the main principles and criteria regarding the visual appearance of urban landscape. This kind of global approach should also develop surveys on heritage experts' and organizations', citizens' and communities' perception and acceptation of corporate brand design.

Citizens' acceptance of corporate brands is probably the least analyzed of these topics, although the increase of social movements against global companies' unethical, un-smart and unsustainable premises and decisions that affect heritage should be seriously taken into account by both corporations and public authorities (Castillo and Martínez Yáñez 2011). The success of citizens' opposition to the Four Seasons Hotel extension in Istanbul (quoted in the second section of this chapter) is a good example of this, but there are other cases, such as the infamous Cajasol Tower in the Cartuja Island in Seville, where the strong citizens' reaction against both the bank and its huge skyscraper's visual impact has not prevented its planned 178 meters from continuing to rise.

Although it is located outside of the core area of Seville World Heritage site, the Cajasol Tower has been subject to numerous citizens' claims, discussions at the

Figure 10.4 The visual impact of the Caja Sol Tower in Seville's urban landscape (Spain) ©Victor Fernández Salinas, with written permission.

World Heritage Committee sessions and UNESCO and ICOMOS missions to assess its huge visual impact on the whole of the historic urban landscape. The ICOMOS Report published in November 2008 stated categorically that this tower threatens the landscape values of Seville and its World Heritage area (the Cathedral, Alcazar, and Archivo de Indias) and recommended a major revision of the project (see Figure 10.4).

Encouraged by this report, the 2009 Citizen Platform against Cajasol Tower "Tumbala!"[6] brought together 20 social organizations, heritage experts, ecologists, university teachers, and neighborhood associations against it. One of the reasons that explained their refusal was the perception of the tower as a symbol of economic speculation and excess—contrary to the sustainable model of the Mediterranean city—the unjustifiable investment of public financial resources in a project that goes against the collective interest of Seville citizens, and the tower's negative impact on the landscape and heritage of the city. Although the tower continues its rise today, the actions of the Platform Túmbalá! ensured that UNESCO mentioned for four years, between 2008 and 2012, the possibility of including Seville on the World Heritage in Danger List. In 2012, UNESCO noted again the inappropriateness of such a tower in this place and decried the lack of consultation and debate and the policy of "fait accompli" perpetrated by both the bank promoters and the public authorities.

The subsequent huge discredit to the city and the State Party and the international diffusion of the campaign by Túmbala! should encourage other citizens to take action on this matter, by denouncing problems and threats which are either not sufficiently taken care of or not recognized early enough by public authorities. The momentum for this type of action is growing as communities become more conscious of their assets and of the mechanisms that can protect or degrade them. In the case of Spain, the many citizens' actions against the negative visual and ethical impact of corporate brands in heritage sites and on communities' culture and identity have been documented by the Observatory of the Spanish Historic Heritage, which provides a useful database to deepen the limits of acceptability on brands.[7] Likewise, Fleming (2002) has documented the cases of the new towns of Columbia, Lee, Palm Springs, and Berkeley in the USA, where communities have been able to organize strong opposition to the stereotyped architecture of fast food franchises and chains that refuse to comply with local design standards and they have been barred from the townscape.

Finally, the Historic Urban Landscape (HUL) shift from an emphasis on architectural monuments primarily towards a broader recognition of the importance of the social, cultural, and economic processes in the conservation of urban values should also be taken into account when defining the acceptability of brands. This can be explained because corporate visual impact is not restricted to major monuments or historic centers, but rather expanded through many city areas, which may have important heritage and social values for citizens, even if they are not nationally designated as major cultural properties. Besides, corporate brand outlets and premises (such as the Cajasol Tower) are located outside the preservation areas' boundaries, whose regulation is less strict despite the enormous impact that new buildings' visual scale or design—covering volumes, shapes and materials, etc.—might have on heritage properties and their setting. This distorts the harmonious relation with the immediate and distant environment, the city and landscape views, the preservation of the atmosphere, and the skyline, etc.

Corporate social responsibility: an emerging tool to confront corporate brand impact on urban landscapes and heritage sites

Corporate social responsibility (CSR) can be defined as a strategic decision whereby an organization undertakes an obligation to society, for example, in the form of sponsorship, commitment to local communities, attention to environmental issues, and responsible advertising (Ness 1992). Likewise, according to Porter and Kramer (2002, 2006), CSR is the main framework for major companies to align their main goals with their need to gain social legitimacy and added value, and to improve competitive advantage by addressing social, cultural, and environmental concerns. This issue has moved up the economic and political agenda internationally, through concern over corporate power linked to globalization and its impact on culture, society, environment, and international marketing practices.

Cultural heritage is not a high priority in CSR initiatives. The private sector's interest in heritage depends on its potential to increase corporations' visibility and impact and act as a factor of social legitimacy. However, heritage is starting to be included in these kind of strategies due to its ability to create shared value, to address the sustainable development agenda, and to provide corporate benefits such as reputation enhancement (Starr 2010: 15; 2013).

Although most of the major companies are not completely aware of this potential, CSR for heritage may help to reach these goals through allowing companies to achieve good publicity, to enhance their reputation through aligning themselves with cultural heritage prestige and values, and to show their commitment to cultural promotion and sustainable development.

According to O'Hagan and Harvey (2000) and D'Astous and Bitz (1995), the free access to media coverage provided by the private sector's positive presence in heritage sites has been shown to have even greater credibility than commercial publicity. As also noted by Starr (2010, 2013), in addition to reputation enhancement, conservation of cultural heritage might facilitate competitive positioning, allowing companies to consolidate relationships and exposure within existing markets and to engage with emerging markets. These benefits are even greater if the close relationship between cultural heritage and the international and powerful tourism market is taken into account, which can enhance corporations' visibility worldwide.

CSR for heritage could also provide tangible proof that a company is committed to the livelihoods of local communities. However, not all this credit can be achieved if companies do not confront two important weaknesses regarding CSR.

The first of them is that CSR for heritage is being heavily criticized as a purely commercial ploy; it raises many ethical issues and reactions amongst civil society and the heritage community that companies are not addressing sufficiently. On the one hand, private companies usually benefit from associations with heritage sites without returning any revenue to the local population or to site preservation. This is often the case with the multinational hotel and restaurant chains located at the heart of heritage properties. On the other hand, some companies try to improve their public image and reputation through investing in heritage conservation whilst at the same time engaging in commercial activities that are unethical or damaging to people and the environment. As a result, and as Starr has demonstrated in her outstanding research on CSR for heritage (2010, 2013), the involvement of the private sector in the heritage sector is perceived by the profession in many different ways, ranging from welcoming to cynical, to complete outrage at the commercial use of cultural properties. This is not surprising, if the many cases of negative corporate impact on heritage significance mentioned by Starr are considered, as well as the cases specifically dealing with corporations' negative visual impact quoted in this chapter. Corporations' attitudes towards heritage are equally diverse, ranging from supportive efforts, to ignorance of cultural heritage values, and/or simple lack of interest. A good practice standing out is the American Express financial support to the World Monument Fund and Global Heritage Fund activities, as well as many corporate investments in heritage restoration. As far as Spain is concerned, it its worth quoting the Program on Cultural Heritage of Caja Madrid,[8] which has financed the restoration of many Spanish cultural properties, or the involvement of Caixa Bank in the surveys of visitors and the economic impacts of the Alhambra that led to the establishment of this monument's carrying capacity and the publication of the scientific results of both analyses (Villafranca Jiménez and Chamorro 2007a, 2007b).

The second weakness, specifically related to our subject of study, is the unbridgeable gap and serious contradiction between corporations' growing investments in heritage conservation and restoration on the one hand, and the negative impact of their premises and franchises near heritage sites and within urban landscapes on the other. Together with the need for companies to behave more ethically when dealing with cultural heritage, as discussed in this chapter, companies themselves should address this contradiction if they expect to achieve positive outcomes through CSR for heritage. Indeed, according to Sen and Batthacharya (2001) and Starr (2013), CSR initiatives can even decrease consumers' intentions to buy a company's products, depending on the consumer's perception of the congruence between companies' actual activities and their CSR philosophy.

In this regard, it is important to note that the comparative analysis of sites that illustrate negative visual impacts and sites where corporate brand design and advertising have been able to respect heritage and community values shows that many concerned companies can be associated with both positive and negative examples. This condition not only indicates that almost no corporation has developed a specific approach to design outlets and facilities near heritage sites or valuable urban landscapes, a kind of corporate visual responsibility, but also that some of them may be encouraged to reconsider their visual impact in specific cases, if they are properly motivated to do so.

To align corporate design with heritage values, it is necessary to show how responsibility for heritage, and especially responsibility regarding the visual presence of companies in heritage areas, addresses CSR objectives. First, corporations should bear in mind that visually responsible design recognizes community character and utilizes design and landscaping treatments to protect and enhance its distinct cultural heritage. Second, corporations that build upon innovation and provide a service should be aware that they do a disservice to communities when they contract homogeneous franchise outlets that destroy a particular sense of place. Third, corporations should learn from experience and recognize that the protection of the built environment benefits not only heritage values and the people who live and work there but also corporations themselves. Indeed, by respecting public values, corporations become "a good neighbour," which is an indispensable marketing tool. And finally, they should consider that the creation of premises and facades that suit the streetscape not only results in a more humanized environment, but this also connects the customer to the particular services provided by the corporation as well as to the cultural heritage of that place (Nasar 1988; Nasar and Hong 1999; Fleming 2002; Araujo Portella 2006, 2007).

Searching for guidelines to improve corporate visual design near heritage sites

Following those very simple principles might be helpful in improving the current situation, bearing in mind that some of the above-mentioned examples have shown how responsible design may improve citizen opinion of corporations, providing them with another reason to behave ethically when dealing with heritage sites.

The "Vienna Memorandum" (adopted at the Fifteenth General Assembly of the States Parties to the World Heritage Convention in October 2005) could be effective guidance in this regard, as it is one of the few international documents that provides detailed criteria for introducing new architecture within historic urban landscapes. Although not directly addressed to corporate brands' visual impact, some of its principles demanding ethical standards and high-quality design and execution should be compulsory for the designing of brand franchises and outlets near heritage sites and within historic urban landscapes. Article 24 stresses that particular attention is to be paid to functionality, scale, materials, lighting, street furniture, advertising, and vegetation, to name a few. Article 26 indicates that as a general principle, proportion and design must fit into the particular type of historic pattern and architecture. Article 29 emphasizes that cultural or visual impact assessment studies should accompany proposals for contemporary interventions (World Heritage Centre 2005).

Bearing in mind these requests, the World Heritage Convention and Buffer Zones Symposium of the ICOMOS International Scientific Committee on Legal, Administrative and Financial Issues (Hiroshima, Japan, 29 November to 1 December 2006) drafted a Recommendation concerning buffer zones that called upon ICOMOS to

> conduct activities that emphasize the belief that corporate goals should include the continuing and genuine commitment by the business sector to behave responsibly and ethically and exercise an important duty of care to all of its stakeholders including the community at large.
>
> (Petzet and Ziesemer 2008: 185)

The ICOMOS Draft Project on Corporate Visual Responsibility and Heritage Sites, in, as yet, unaccomplished implementation of which the author has been involved in the past two years (Martínez Yáñez 2012), aimed to reach the goal of offering some practical guidelines to enhance a more ethical corporate attitude towards heritage. Amongst these, this project focused on advocacy, proposing to put corporations formally on notice for the first time that the international preservation community is concerned about the impact of advertising and corporate franchise design in heritage sites and especially in and near areas of World Heritage designation or areas eligible for such designation. This advocacy action should be based on an inventory and survey of information about sites that illustrate negative visual impacts on heritage and urban landscape due to advertising and corporate brand design and on sites where corporate brand design and advertising have been able to respect heritage and urban values and community character, showing the tangible results that can be attained at limited cost with a responsible policy. This inventory involved data collection from ICOMOS National Committees, other planning and preservation experts, and corporations themselves, which would work with corporations highly representative of the global negative visual impact on heritage to persuade them to find elegant solutions for outlets, advertisements, and other elements under their responsibility that may have a visual impact on heritage sites and urban landscapes. To ensure protocols of corporate visual behavior that increase corporate and advertising visual accountability, the project also designed some criteria to document and disseminate those changes that occur as a result of these protocols, so that other corporations and advertisers could understand the costs and benefits of making changes.

Finally, one of the project's main initiatives was to celebrate the enhanced value achieved by responsible corporate and advertising behavior, which can secure benefits for the corporations that they would find difficult to confer upon themselves, spreading good practice and examples in this field. The main aim of this step was obviously to promote and maintain a positive corporate attitude towards heritage and urban landscape and to find partners to address targeted companies and persuade them to have a more positive, ethical, and responsible attitude in this regard.

Conclusions

The cases mentioned in this chapter are just a few examples of the difficulties and concerns raised by the growing presence of corporate brands in heritage sites, showing the need for a better understanding of heritage and its values by these corporations.

In this regard, it is very important to note that the increasing international awareness on this subject and recommendations that try to mitigate negative impacts of urban sprawl will be of scarce significance and effectiveness if they are not followed by much greater efforts to disseminate, amongst targeted companies, the importance of heritage values and the international principles, recommendations, and rules dealing with their protection and the benefits that respecting these principles can provide to companies' credibility.

Specific criteria and guidelines for the introduction of new facilities in urban landscape and heritage sites are urgently needed, as existing charters and recommendations are not sufficient to help local authorities and communities to address and persuade major corporations of the need to improve their visual impact. Minimum requirements and updated design criteria for local communities, decision-makers, and targeted companies are also needed to assess and prevent potential impacts on site significance and integrity in a systematic and objective manner. As this is a widespread and international problem, it should be addressed beyond theory and through international coordinated instruments involving a variety of stakeholders—including local, national, regional, international, public, and private actors in the urban development process—and practical actions essential in assessing the global situation.

Moreover, as heritage preservation is, and will be, strongly needed for private initiatives that not only benefit from the prestige and international visibility of cultural properties but which also significantly contributes to its conservation, the so-called corporate social responsibility could be an appropriate framework of collaboration that should be further explored in the future.

Notes

1 Hoovers. Available at: www.hoovers.com (accessed 12 November 2014).
2 According to Schlosser (2001: 4), at the beginning of this century, McDonald's was the largest owner of retail property in the world and spent more money on advertising and marketing than any other brand, replacing Coca-Cola as the world's most famous brand. In fact, a survey of American schoolchildren quoted by Schlosser (McDonald's Corporation, Customer Satisfaction Department 1999: 1) found that 96 percent could identify Ronald McDonald and that the only fictional character with a higher degree of popularity was Santa Claus. This fact led him to conclude that this corporation's "golden arches are now more widely recognized than the Christian cross" (Schlosser 2001: 4).
3 McDonald's Corporation. Available at: http://www.mcdonalds.com (accessed 29 June 2015).
4 Citizens' reactions against this particular hotel can be consulted in the excellent documentary "Bye Bye Barcelona" which focuses on the darker aspects of mass tourism within this iconic city. Available at: http://www.byebyebarcelona.com/ (accessed 29 June 2015).
5 W Barcelona. Available at: http://www.w-barcelona.com/en/make-a-green-choice (accessed 29 June 2015).
6 "Tumbala!" Available at: http://ciudadaniacontralatorrepelli.blogspot.fr/ (accessed 20 July 2014).
7 Observatory of the Spanish Historic Heritage. Available at: http://www.ugr.es/~ophe/004 INICIATIVAS/004index.htm (accessed 20 July 2014).
8 They are available at: www.fundacioncajamadrid.es (accessed 29 June 2015).

Bibliography

Ahmad, N. (2007). Architecture of shopping malls. *ARCHI TIMES*, 22, 6.
Araujo Portella, A. (2006). Visual pollution in historic city centres: how to analyse this issue (Electronic version). In: *II Congress of ABEP-RU, Association of Brazilian Post-Graduate Students and Researchers in Great Britain*. London: Embassy of Brazil.
Araujo Portella, A. (2007). The effects of commercial signs on user's sense of visual quality in historic city centres of different urban contexts. *Journal of Research in Architecture and Planning*, 6, 1–14.
Barnard, M. (1999). Despite including the world's most recognized brand, the lucrative fast-food industry is reassessing its image. *Design Week*, 11 June 1999.
Beelen, K. (2007). Amsterdam's Diemer Territtory: mapping co-productions. *Journal of Research in Architecture and Planning*, 6, 33–48.
Bronovitskaya, A. (2009). Intrusions to the cityscape. In: E. Harris, A. Bronovitskaya and C. Cecil (eds), *Moscow Heritage at Crisis Point*. Moscow: SAVE Europe Heritage, DoCoMoMo International, Institut Minos, Project Russia Magazine and Archnadzor, pp. 131–43.
Castillo Ruiz, J. and Martínez Yáñez, C. (2011). La importancia del Publico en la Conservación: la movilización ciudadana a favor de la defensa del Patrimonio en España. *América Patrimonio* 1, 14–27.
D'Astous, A. and Bitz, P. (1995). Consumer evaluations of sponsorship programmes. *Journal of Marketing Research*, 29, 6–22.
Debold-Kritter A. (2010). Threats to the World Heritage in the changing metropolitan areas of Istanbul. In: C. Machat, M. Petzet and J. Ziesemer (eds), *Heritage at Risk. ICOMOS World Report 2008–2010 on Monuments and Sites in Danger*. Berlin: Hendrik Bäßler Verlag, pp. 174–9.

English Heritage (2008). *Seeing the History in the View. A Method for Assessing Heritage Significance within Views. Draft for Consultation, April 2008.* London: English Heritage.

Fleming, R.L. (2002). *Saving Face: How Corporate Franchise Design can Respect Community Character.* Chicago: American Planning Association and The Townscape Institute.

ICOMOS (2010a). *ICOMOS Guidance on Heritage Impact Assessments for Cultural World Heritage Properties.* Draft, May 2010. Available http://openarchive.icomos.org/266/ (accessed 13 July 2012).

ICOMOS (2010b). *Recommendation SC 2009/10 3 by the ICOMOS International Scientific Committee on Cultural Landscapes regarding Corporate Visual Responsibility and ICOMOS Policy Leverage.* Charenton-le-Pont: ICOMOS.

Jokilehto, J. (2010). Reflection on historic urban landscapes as a tool for conservation. In: R. Van Oers, S. Haraguchi and UNESCO World Heritage Centre (eds), *Managing Historic Cities.* World Heritage Papers 27. Paris: World Heritage Centre, pp. 53–65.

The Landscape Institute and the Institute of Environmental Management and Assessment (2002). *Guidelines for Landscape and Visual Impact Assessment,* 2nd edn, London: Spon Press.

Martínez Yáñez, C. (2012). Visual impact on heritage sites: encouraging corporate responsibility. *ICOMOS News,* 19(1), 19–21.

Nagy, G. (2008). The improper paths of urban and real estate development in Hungary. In: M. Petzet and J. Ziesemer (eds), *Heritage at Risk. ICOMOS World Report 2006–2007 on Monuments and Sites in Danger.* Altenburg: E. Reinhold Verlag, pp. 80–4.

Nasar, J. (1988). Visual preferences in urban streets scenes: a cross-cultural comparison between Japan and the United States. In: J. Nasar (ed.), *Environmental Aesthetic: Theory, Research, and Applications.* Cambridge: Cambridge University Press, pp. 260–74.

Nasar, J. and Hong, X. (1999). Visual preferences in urban signscapes. *Environment and Behavior,* 31, 671–91.

Naz, N. and Anjum, G.A. (2007). Transformation of Main Boulevard, Gulberg, Lahore: from residential to commercial. *Journal of Research in Architecture and Planning,* 6, 49–61.

Ness, M.R. (1992). Corporate social responsibility. *British Food Journal,* 94(7), 38–44.

Nishimura, Y. (2007). Integrity of Historic Urban Landscape. In: ICOMOS (ed.), *2007 ICOMOS Asia and the Pacific Regional Meeting: Heritage and Metropolis in Asia and the Pacific.* Seoul: ICOMOS-Korea.

O'Hagan, J. and Harvey, D. (2000). Why do companies sponsor arts events? Some evidence of a proposed classification. *Journal of Cultural Economics,* 24, 205–24.

Petzet, M. and Ziesemer J. (eds) (2008). *Heritage at Risk. ICOMOS World Report 2006–2007 on Monuments and Sites in Danger.* Altenburg: E. Reinhold Verlag.

Pičíková, L. (2008). Risk from development: threats to monuments caused by ignoring valid legislation. In: M. Petzet and J. Ziesemer (eds), *Heritage at Risk. ICOMOS World Report 2006–2007 on Monuments and Sites in Danger.* Altenburg: E. Reinhold Verlag, pp. 139–40.

Porter, M. and Kramer, M.R. (2002). The competitive advantage of corporate philanthropy. *Harvard Business Review,* 80, 56–68.

Porter, M. and Kramer, M.R. (2006). Strategy and society: the link between competitive advantage and corporate social responsibility. *Harvard Business Review,* 84, 78–92.

Rössler, M. (2009). New challenges: world heritage in the urban context. In: *Earth, Wind, Water, Fire: Environmental Challenges to Urban World Heritage.* Regensbourg: City of Regensbourg Planning and Building Division, pp. 36–9.

Sassen, S. (1999). Whose city is it? In: *Sustainable Cities into the 21st Century*. Singapore: NUS Press.

Schlosser, E. (2001). *Fast Food Nation: The Dark Side of the All American Meal*. New York: Houghton Mifflin.

Sen, S. and Batthacharya C.B. (2001). Does doing good always lead to doing better? Consumer reactions to corporate social responsibility. *Journal of Marketing Research*, 38(2), 225–43.

Starr, F. (2010). The business of heritage and the private sector. In: S. Labaldi and C. Long (eds), *Heritage and Globalization*. New York: Routledge, pp. 147–69.

Starr, F. (2013). *Corporate Responsibility for Cultural Heritage: Conservation, Sustainable Development and Corporate Reputation*. New York: Routledge.

UNESCO (n.d.). *New International Instrument: The Proposed UNESCO Recommendation on the Historic Urban Landscape (HUL)*. Available at: http://whc.unesco.org/uploads/activities/documents/activity-706-10.pdf (accessed 12 September 2014).

UNESCO (2011). *Recommendation on the Historic Urban Landscape, Including a Glossary of Definitions*. Available at: http://portal.unesco.org/en/ev.php-URL_ID=48857&URL_DO=DO_TOPIC&URL_SECTION=201.html (accessed 21 July 2012).

Université de Montréal (2008). *Proceedings, World Heritage: Defining and Protecting "Important Views."* Proceedings of the Round Table organized by the Canada Research Chair on Built Heritage, Faculty of Environmental Design, Université de Montreal, 18–20 March 2008.

Van Oers, R. (2010). Managing cities and the Historic Urban Landscape initiative – an introduction. In: R. Van Oers, S. Haraguchi and UNESCO World Heritage Centre (eds), *Managing Historic Cities*. World Heritage Papers 27. Paris: World Heritage Centre, pp. 7–17.

Villafranca Jiménez, M. and Chamorro Martínez, V.E. (2007a). *Estudio de impacto económico del conjunto monumental de la Alhambra y Generalife en la ciudad de Granada*. Granada: Comares.

Villafranca Jiménez, M. and Chamorro Martínez, V.E. (2007b). *Acogida de visitantes en monumentos y sitios del Patrimonio Mundial*. Granada: Patronato de la Alhambra and Generalife; Tf Editores.

Wilkinson, A. (2009). Ten threats to historic Moscow. In: E. Harris, A. Bronovitskaya and C. Cecil (eds), *Moscow Heritage at Crisis Point*. Moscow: SAVE Europe Heritage, DoCoMoMo International, Minos Institute, Project Russia Magazine and Archnadzor, pp. 119–30.

World Heritage Centre (2005). *Vienna Memorandum on "World Heritage and Contemporary Architecture – Managing the Historic Urban Landscape."* Available at: http://whc.unesco.org/document/5965 (accessed 27 April 2013).

Chapter 11

From zero sum game to arranged marriage

The struggle between built heritage conservation and urban development in post-colonial Hong Kong

Lee Ho Yin and Lynne D. DiStefano

The shrinking of the British Empire in the twentieth century was akin to the proverbial Chinese curse – an 'interesting' time wrought with political upheaval and social unrest. While the return of British Hong Kong's sovereignty to China in 1997 – called the 'Handover' with a strong dose of irony – was a relatively benign event, political and social difficulties have been part of the decolonisation experience. Interestingly, the fiercest struggles in the first post-colonial decade, from 1997 to 2007, took place in the least expected of arenas. The challenge was between built heritage conservation and urban redevelopment. The former was championed by the public, who reacted with increasing furore against an over-developed environment, and the latter by property developers, who guarded their political clout and financial gains made throughout the boom times – the last three decades of colonial Hong Kong. Caught in between was the ill-prepared post-colonial government, which managed to temper the angry public with a surprise announcement of a heritage conservation policy in 2007, much to the astonishment and chagrin of developers. Seven years on, in 2014, the staggering differences between conservation and development interests have narrowed from a zero sum game to an arranged marriage. Drawing on the authors' personal experience, this chapter examines the transformation process that has brought the two polarised interests to an uncomfortable relationship based on compromise.

Last chance for a quick buck: the rise of urban redevelopment in pre-1997 Hong Kong

Hong Kong has always been a city of two tales. It was created in the mid-nineteenth century within the context of two polarised civilisations: the expanding British Empire and a dying Chinese dynasty. In the latter part of the twentieth century, as the Cold War simmered, it benefited from the clash between two polarised ideologies, serving as a foothold for Britain and its Cold War allies at the doorstep of an emerging Communist China. With Hong Kong's cessation as a British colony in 1997, it became a Special Administrative Region (SAR) under the People's Republic of China. This new status is based on an agreement between Britain and China – the 1984 Sino-British Joint Declaration,[1] which guarantees status quo for

Hong Kong for 50 years, starting from 1997 under the 'One Country, Two Systems' policy, in which Hong Kong would maintain the administration, financial and legal systems established by the British.

Under the colonial authorities in the nineteenth century, Hong Kong developed into a striking port city for the entrepôt trade. The range of building styles and types included Victorian styles for Westerners (trading houses, public buildings, churches and houses) and Qing-dynasty Southern-Chinese architecture for local Chinese (primarily shophouses and temples) (Figure 11.1). The disposition of buildings was largely according to ethnicity, which in turn reflected the preference (by Westerners) for central locations near the harbour (for work) or for higher, cooler elevations (for living). In the first half of the twentieth century, buildings for Westerners were gradually replaced by those in the more fashionable Edwardian styles and later by those reflecting ideas associated with the Modern Movement. Chinese buildings in the urban areas were gradually redeveloped as well, and the new urban Chinese buildings, particularly the shophouses, began to acquire local characteristics with the introduction of Hong Kong's first building ordinance in 1903. The ordinance targeted the design of shophouses as a result of a major outbreak of bubonic plague in 1894, which occurred in the colony's biggest and most concentrated Chinese enclave, 'District No. 3 Taipingshan' (see Pryor 1975).

The major wave of redevelopment happened shortly after World War II, when Hong Kong's population boomed as thousands of people escaped from the newly established Communist regime in China. The influx of Chinese refugees from the 1950s to the 1970s created an unprecedented demand for housing and employment, and the solutions were found in new social and economic programmes that led to the development of new buildings for public housing and industrial estates. These new developments largely took place at the fringes of traditional urban areas, which were located on the northern coast of Hong Kong Island and on the Kowloon Peninsula, as well as, starting in the 1970s, in the rural areas of the New Territories. The urban core of Hong Kong was still largely intact and relatively undisturbed.

Figure 11.1 Urban Hong Kong during the Victorian period, c. 1860s or 1870s (courtesy of the National Archives, UK).

Figure 11.2 Urban Hong Kong after the Handover, 2009.
Source: Lee Ho Yin.

However, urban redevelopment came with a vengeance in the 1980s, when property development took off as a mainstay of the economy. During this time, almost all of the Western and Chinese urban buildings developed during the Victorian and Edwardian periods were rapidly demolished and replaced by larger and taller buildings of contemporary design (Figure 11.2). Arguably, the catalyst for this redevelopment tsunami was the 1984 Sino-British Joint Declaration, which marked the beginning of the end of Hong Kong as a British colony. With Hong Kong now living on borrowed time, the colonial government implemented a high land-price policy to boost the property market as an exit strategy for the economy. The policy was possible as 40 per cent of the territory's land is statutorily protected as country parks and nature reserves (mostly on difficult-to-develop hilly or mountainous terrain). In addition, as almost 100 per cent of the land is leasehold, the government was able to aggravate the land shortage condition and exploit its monopoly on land supply to maintain high prices for land grants.[2] To date (January 2015), less than 25 per cent of the land in Hong Kong has been developed, meaning that development has been confined to relatively small areas of original land as well as new land created by reclamation.

The pre- and post-1980s generations: generational shift in cultural identity and values in pre- and post-1997 Hong Kong

Towards the end of the colonial period, cultural identity in Hong Kong increasingly became a topic of discussion, debate and, at times, concern. The vast majority of the Hong Kong population, while of Chinese ethnicity, were legally and technically British subjects. However, a significant portion of Hongkongers after World War II were Chinese emigrants who had escaped from the economic, political and social turmoil that plagued the People's Republic of China during the reign of Chairman Mao. The most notable impetus for emigration was the disastrous Cultural Revolution from 1966 to 1976, which resulted in thousands of refugees crossing the border into Hong Kong.[3] These resettled Hongkongers were caught in an awkward position as they were unwilling to consider themselves British subjects but, at the same time, reluctant to consider themselves as Chinese nationals, thereby avoiding affiliation with the Communist regime from which they had fled. The immigrant nature of Hong Kong's population is a well-documented fact and can be seen in Table 11.1, which shows a drastic and sustained population increase after World War II.

The identity of Hongkongers was made even more complex with the enactment of the Hong Kong Act 1985, which essentially prevents Hong Kong Chinese becoming full-fledged British citizens.[4] The history curriculum taught in local government secondary schools since the 1950s and until recently reflected this complexity with its obvious avoidance of politically sensitive subjects. This was achieved by dividing the curriculum into a 'world' history that focused on past historic events and a truncated 'Chinese' history of China that stopped short at the end of the Qing dynasty in 1911 (Kan and Vickers 2002). Local history was completely neglected at the pre-tertiary level and it was not introduced until the post-1997 educational reform, which, rather belatedly, was only implemented in 2009.

The official definition of built heritage in pre-1997 Hong Kong reflected the neglect of local history by confining such heritage to 'antiquities and monuments', as is clearly reflected in the title of Hong Kong's only law on heritage protection, the Antiquities and Monuments Ordinance (Chapter 53 of the Laws of Hong Kong).[5] Enacted in 1976 and remaining virtually unchanged to this day, the ordinance was

Table 11.1 Hong Kong's population increase in the twentieth century

Year	Approximate population	Increment from previous figure
1901	0.30 million	–
1911	0.46 million	0.16 million
1921	0.63 million	0.17 million
1931	0.84 million	0.21 million
1941	1.64 million	0.80 million
Japanese occupation of Hong Kong (1941–5)		
1946	1.55 million	−0.09 million
1956	2.61 million	1.06 million
1966	3.71 million	1.10 million
1976	4.40 million	0.69 million
1989	5.40 million	1.00 million
1996	6.21 million	0.81 million

Source: Lo (1992: Table 2.1) and Fan (1974: 2).

based closely on the 1972 UNESCO Convention Concerning the Protection of the World Cultural and Natural Heritage, which focuses on antiquities and monuments by defining cultural heritage as monuments, groups of buildings and sites.[6] Conveniently, the widely accepted and rather narrow definition of built heritage fitted in well with the high land-price government policy that fostered the property development business in Hong Kong. Antiquities could be relocated to museums and monuments could be limited to government properties with no commercial development potential or private properties located away from developable urban areas. All of these factors contributed to older generations of Hongkongers maintaining a refugee or expatriate's mentality of viewing Hong Kong as a 'borrowed place living on borrowed time', to use the phrase coined by Richard Hughes (1968), and regarding urban development as a priority and urban conservation as an irrelevancy, if not an inconvenience.

After the historic return of Hong Kong to Chinese sovereignty in 1997, policies were put in place to foster a sense of belonging and identity, and one of the ways to achieve this, as it turned out, was through the promotion of Hong Kong's built heritage.[7] Coincidentally, the political agenda aligned with a rising awareness of built heritage conservation in the urban context, especially among the younger generations of Hongkongers. The first cohort of the younger generations – labelled the 'post-80s generation' by the Hong Kong press – was either growing up or entering adulthood during the first decade of post-colonial Hong Kong. Members of this cohort were mostly locally born and educated, whereas their parents and grandparents were more likely to have been born and educated in Mainland China (Wu 2010: 1–2, 10–12). In addition, many of this cohort grew up in anonymous urban neighbourhoods and public housing estates that affected how they viewed and valued built heritage: attachment was more to ordinary places associated with the community rather than officially recognised monuments and buildings associated with the elite.

This shift from an elitist to a populist point of view can be seen in the results of a 2004 public event organised by the government's broadcasting agency, Radio Television Hong Kong (RTHK): '10 iconic designs that most represent Hong Kong'. This internet event, which is likely to have attracted more respondents from the post-1980s generation,[8] asked members of the public to choose 10 designs from a list of 50 shortlisted items, ranging from ordinary objects and everyday places to public transportation and well-known monuments.[9] When the results were announced in late September 2004, the top choice was the *cha chaan teng* (literally 'tea and meal room'), the ubiquitous local diner found in many older urban neighbourhood communities. In the second and third places were two of Hong Kong's oldest means of public transportation, frequented primarily by ordinary people – the electric tramway that covers the territory's oldest urban areas on Hong Kong Island and the cross-harbour ferry service that runs between the old urban cores of Hong Kong Island and Kowloon Peninsula. Also included on the list were a distinctive local kind of bread (the 'pineapple bun', so called for its appearance, not its ingredients) and an equally distinctive local form of beverage (the 'yin-yeung', literally 'Mandarin duck', a mixture of tea and coffee), both iconic items on the *cha chaan teng* menu and popular among Hongkongers. The remaining items on the list were the urban graffiti of an old protester, which is seen as artwork by local communities, and a popular comic book character, whose antics are appreciatively identified by Hong Kong's ordinary urbanites.

It is notable that only one monument is included on the list of '10 iconic designs that most represent Hong Kong', namely the 1915 Tsim Sha Tsui Clock Tower, a statutorily protected historic monument (declared in 1990). As the sole remnant of the original southern terminus of the Kowloon–Canton Railway, it is devoid of historic context, but holds considerable importance as an orientation landmark for the Tsim Sha Tsui Promenade, a waterfront urban public space that is popular with a broad cross-section of Hong Kong people. This is most likely the reason for it being chosen as part of the list. The only other structure included is not a historic monument, but a modern suspension bridge, the Tsing Ma Bridge. It is likely that this impressive piece of engineering was chosen because many Hong Kong people consider it a memorial to the Handover, which occurred in 1997, the year of the bridge's completion.

A zero sum game: the struggle between urban conservation and urban development in post-1997 Hong Kong

During the 1980s and the 1990s, as in many cities with a booming economy, Hong Kong redeveloped its urban areas at breakneck speed (Figure 11.3). Such development came in the form of large-scale, high-investment urban projects that ranged from

Figure 11.3 A redevelopment site, which is the size of a city block, in Wanchai District, one of the older urban districts on Hong Kong Island, 2009.

Source: Lee Ho Yin.

multi-floored shopping malls, functional office towers and high-rise hotels to clusters of soaring apartment towers. To achieve the sought-after scale, the demolition of entire blocks of historical building stock in old urban districts was the norm.

In post-1997 Hong Kong, however, younger generations had started to challenge the *modus operandi* of property developers. No longer did they believe the economic benefit of redevelopment justified the demolition of familiar landmarks and the wholesale destruction of older urban communities. A belief in the importance of built heritage conservation began to build up among the younger generations of Hongkongers, and this was spearheaded by the post-80s generation, which was skilful in employing social media in organising protest campaigns.

The post-80s generation became prominent as instigators of a new wave of protest movements in post-1997 Hong Kong, including, most recently, the historic 'Umbrella Movement' (September to December 2014), which attracted the sustained attention of the international media. Previous urban conservation protests, such as those in response to the demolition of Lee Tung Street and the removal of Queen's Pier, may not have attracted the same amount of international attention, but stand out as pivotal events locally that drove the Hong Kong Government to place built heritage conservation on its 2007 to 2008 policy agenda (Cheng 2014: 22).

Chronologically, the first major demonstration of the generational struggle for urban conservation between the older decision-makers and the younger protesters was played out against an urban renewal plan to redevelop Lee Tung Street in the old Wan Chai urban district (Figure 11.4). This was a traditional neighbourhood of

Figure 11.4 Protest banners against the impending demolition of buildings along Lee Tung Street in 2007.

Source: Lee Ho Yin.

lower-income residents and wedding card design and printing shops, hence its popular name 'Wedding Card Street'. Although the buildings along the street were not considered of architectural and historical importance, there was considerable collective attachment to them and the street because of the associated product – wedding cards, a treasured part of local marriage ceremonies. Under a plan by the Urban Renewal Authority, all of the 1950s six-storey buildings that lined both sides of the street were to make way for a high-end shopping mall and three luxurious apartment towers ranging from 28 to 33 storeys. The protest began almost as soon as the plan, designated 'H15', was revealed in 2002, and local residents with the support of members of the post-80s generation formed the 'H15 Concern Group'. This led to a protracted and sometimes ferocious protest campaign that involved a hunger strike and the intervention of the police to prevent a near-physical attack on the Chairman of the Urban Renewal Authority.[10] The campaign stopped at the end of 2007 with the impending demolition of the buildings along the street. Despite the failure to save Lee Tung Street, the implications of the campaign were summed up by Kilian Tung, a local university student, who was 21 years old at the time: '[We] planted seeds of awareness. Conservation awareness is starting to grow' (Tsui 2007).

In 2007, the second major generational struggle for urban conservation took place. This occurred when the Hong Kong people collectively woke up to the call to protect their built urban heritage and staged mass protests over the demolition of the Star Ferry Pier and its associated Clock Tower as well as Queen's Pier. The spontaneous outburst caught the government and the legislature by surprise, as there had never been anything like this before. Hongkongers had gone on mass protest over political issues in the past, but no one had anticipated that the demolition of three structures that arguably had little significant historic or architectural value would caused such a furore (Lee and DiStefano, 2007b).

The mass protest against the demolition of Queen's Pier has been described as an 'incident', a term usually reserved for events of significant social magnitude. Indeed, the scale of the protest and the societal impact were so great that books (see Chan 2008), newspaper articles and dissertations (see Chai 2009; Leung 2010) were written about it. This event actually involved not only the 1961 Queen's Pier, but also the adjacent 1957 Star Ferry Pier. These were functional structures designed according to the principles of the mid-twentieth-century Modern Movement and had been much used by the public. As in the case of Lee Tung Street, the latent collective attachment by – and nostalgic sentiments among – ordinary citizens had been overlooked.

To condense a long and complicated story, the dramatic public protest for the conservation of the two piers spanned almost eight months, beginning on 12 December 2006, when protesters occupied the Star Ferry Pier worksite, and ending on 1 August 2007, when riot police forcibly evicted protesters who had relocated to the Queen's Pier worksite, one of whom chained himself to the pier (Lai 2006; Leung and Wu 2007). It is important to note that the demolition plan was not arbitrary; it made way for the construction of a new highway, which had in fact been approved in 2002 by Hong Kong's legislature body, the Legislative Council (LegCo).[11] What the government and the legislature had not foreseen were the changing societal aspirations and expectations for conserving Hong Kong's built environment in the post-1997 period. The public reaction to the demolition of the pier structures, roused by protest instigators from the post-1980s generation, marked the climactic point of accumulative public objections to the lack of consideration for urban built heritage in infrastructural planning, urban renewal and private redevelopment projects. As in the case of Lee Tung Street, the protest to save the two piers did not succeed, but it is significant for its far-reaching implications. As summarised by one of the protest organisers and participants, Wong Ho-yin, a 23-year-old university student, 'from the Star Ferry pier [and Queen's Pier] battles, I think we made a small change to society. Citizens in Hong Kong started to pay more attention to our city's development.'

A political convenience for a political inconvenience: urban conservation policy in post-1997 Hong Kong

In what could be considered a happy ending to the above two events, particularly the latter – the case of the Queen's and Star Ferry Piers – was the surprise announcement of a comprehensive and coherent urban conservation policy in October 2007. This was made by the Chief Executive of the Hong Kong Special Administrative Region, Donald Tsang, in his annual policy address: 'in the next five years, I will press ahead with our work on heritage conservation' (Office of the Chief Executive 2007a: paragraph 49).[12] The urban nature of this heritage conservation policy is clearly expressed in the introductory statement to the policy:

> Cultural life is a key component of a quality city life. A progressive city treasures its own culture and history along with a living experience unique to the city. In recent years, Hong Kong people have expressed our passion for our culture and lifestyle. This is something we should cherish.
>
> (Office of the Chief Executive 2007a: paragraph 49)

There is a telling backstory to the announcement. What actually happened was that in 2007, Chief Executive Tsang was on his way to assume the second term of his office, but was inconveniently confronted by the Queen's Pier incident, the biggest mass protest during his first term of office. To defuse the situation, Tsang revived a pre-existing Built Heritage Conservation Policy prepared by the Home Affairs Bureau, the public consultation document for which was released in February 2004 (Home Affairs Bureau 2004). However, 2004 was the worst timing for a conservation policy, as Hong Kong was facing an outbreak of severe acute respiratory syndrome (SARS) and its troubling impact on the economy. The document was largely ignored by the general public, most of whom were preoccupied by the very real threat to personal health and employment, and it was quietly shelved. It took a political crisis some three years later for the policy to see daylight in an updated form.

To Tsang's credit, the revived policy has been effective because it addresses the issue of urban conservation directly by moving it from the Home Affairs Bureau to a newly established Development Bureau. Such a move is extremely significant for Hong Kong's urban conservation, as the former bureau considered built heritage a part of its 'antiquities and monuments' responsibilities, including its responsibilities for Declared Monuments and Graded Historic Buildings, whereas the latter bureau tackles built heritage as part of the urban development agenda. Also significant is the composition of the new bureau, because it brought together ten departments previously scattered under various bureaux, including those crucial for built heritage conservation, such as architectural services, buildings, lands, land registry and planning. The new bureau was led by the Secretary for Development, Carrie Lam, who also assumed the responsibility for heritage conservation, a portfolio that carries the title of 'Antiquities Authority' that was formerly held by the Secretary of Home Affairs.[13]

During her term as bureau chief (2007 to 2012), Lam actively promoted the government's conservation policy through the mass media and educational institutions. As Lam explained to the present authors, because of the uncertainty of the survival of the policy into the next administration, her strategy for the implementation of Hong Kong's urban conservation policy was to complete as many short-term initiatives as possible during her term. By doing so, she hoped to reach a critical mass of successful projects, thereby winning sufficient hearts and minds among the general public and making a reversal of the policy socially and politically unacceptable. With this resolve, Lam was instrumental in the implementation of three key initiatives: the 'Revitalising Scheme', 'Conserving Central' and the 'Financial Scheme'. The first two stand out as particularly strategic and successful formulas and they are explored in depth in the following section. The third scheme provided government funding for the maintenance of privately owned Graded Historic Buildings.

The 'Revitalising Scheme' and 'Conserving Central' initiative: means of implementing the urban conservation policy

Arguably, the most significant of the conservation initiatives is the cumbersomely titled 'Revitalising Historic Buildings Through Partnership Scheme', which, unsurprisingly, has been unofficially and popularly referred to as the 'Revitalisation Scheme' ('revitalisation' spelt with an 's' in the British manner). It is in fact the main vehicle for the implementation of the urban conservation policy announced by Chief Executive Tsang in his *2007–08 Policy Address*, where he expressed his view that 'revitalisation, rather than preservation alone, should be pursued to maximise the economic and social benefits of historic buildings'. (Office of the Chief Executive 2007b: paragraph 51)

Under this on-going scheme, 16 government-owned heritage properties have been (or are to be) adapted for new uses proposed, implemented and operated by social enterprises that are non-profit-making and non-governmental organisations. Qualified organisations are invited to submit proposals and selected operators are charged a nominal rent and provided with grants to cover the construction work and the start-up costs, as well as any operating deficits during the first two years of operation. The selection of operators is based on four abilities: (i) to express the significance of the building through conservation; (ii) to carry out the conservation of the building; (iii) to ensure a financially sustainable operation; and, most importantly, (iv) to demonstrate how the community will benefit from the new use (Legislative Council Secretariat 2009: 3). In other words, instead of the previous dogmatic approach of preserving heritage buildings as monuments or museums, the approach has shifted to the identification of appropriate new uses relevant to the needs of the community and the identification of a non-governmental operator able to carry out adaptive reuse within the context of international best practice in conservation.

The Revitalisation Scheme ushered in the 'official' recognition of a conservation approach relatively unknown in the field of built heritage conservation in Hong Kong. It had been an uphill task to promote new ideas that had not yet gained widespread professional and public acceptance. Fortunately, with the completion of six projects under the Revitalisation Scheme (as of 2014), two of which have received UNESCO Asia and Pacific Awards for Cultural Heritage Conservation, the public has begun to understand and appreciate this more sustainable approach to conservation.

The two UNESCO award-winning projects are worth mentioning in greater detail. The first project (Honourable Mention in the 2011 awards) is the revitalisation of a 1960 courthouse, the former North Kowloon Magistracy, as the Hong Kong branch of a US-based tertiary educational institute, the Savannah College of Art and Design (SCAD). Opened in 2010, it was the first completed project under the Revitalisation Scheme and forms part of the hardware for advancing Hong Kong's creative industries. The second project (Award of Merit in the 2013 awards) is the revitalisation of the 1902 Tai O Police Station as the Tai O Heritage Hotel. Opened in 2012, this project is significant for being the first conservation project involving a property developer. However, the involvement is indirect, through a non-profit NGO set up by the developer, which functions as the hotel operator. The project has benefited the fishing community of Tai O through its catalytic effect in enabling a successful transformation of the local economy from one based on the fading trades of commercial fishing and dried seafood to one based on cultural tourism.

As a result of the successful Revitalisation Scheme, and especially with its clear focus on adaptive reuse, the public readily supported the second most important initiative – Conserving Central (Development Bureau 2010). Announced by Chief Executive Tsang in his 2009 to 2010 Policy Address (Office of the Chief Executive 2009: paragraphs 53–7), the initiative involves seven heritage sites in Central District, the very heart of urban Hong Kong: six government-owned heritage sites and one owned by Hong Kong's Chinese Anglican Church. Similar to the Revitalisation Scheme, the buildings on these sites have been or are to be adapted for new uses, but not necessarily operated by social enterprises (non-profit-making NGOs). The core projects of this initiative are the adaptive reuse of heritage buildings on three government sites: the Central Market (a single building occupying an entire city block); the Central Police Station Compound (involving a cluster of 16 buildings) (Figure 11.5); and the former Police Married Quarters (a cluster of three buildings). As of January 2015, the Central Market is undergoing pre-construction preparation for adaptive reuse as a mall for small local shops and restaurants, while the Central Police Station Compound is expected to open later in the year as a public venue for events and exhibitions related to contemporary art and built heritage conservation. The Police Married Quarters, now known as the PMQ, opened in 2014 as a hub showcasing and selling products by young local designers.

The successful completion of projects under the Revitalisation Scheme and Conserving Central initiative demonstrate the critical importance of integrating built heritage with development in a fast-changing urban environment, particularly in terms of the cultural, social and especially economic benefits that can be brought to the community. As the operators of all of these projects are expected to attain financial self-sustainability, such a demonstration of economic viability will help dispel the perception that conservation projects are financial burdens borne by the government with taxpayers' money. This is in line with Chief Executive Tsang's

Figure 11.5 One of the cluster of 16 buildings in the Central Police Station Compound, pictured in 2011, shortly before conservation work began under the Conserving Central initiative.

Source: Lee Ho Yin.

argument that conservation should be linked with Hong Kong's urban development that he made in the introduction to the Conserving Central initiative in his 2009–10 Policy Address:

> The concept of 'Progressive Development' that I advocate emphasizes the need to strike a balance between economic development and cultural conservation. The community has responded positively to our conservation measures. This reaffirms my belief that Central [District] has unique historical and cultural features suited to sustainable development that have yet to be realized.
>
> (Office of the Chief Executive 2009: paragraph 54)

Conclusion: what the future holds for urban conservation in Hong Kong

Although the Development Bureau's Revitalisation Scheme and Conserving Central initiatives have yet to reach their full potential, the sustained effort to conserve a cross-section of urban heritage assets remains a government priority. Such effort is not without challenges, as cautioned by Carrie Lam:

> Similar to other international metropolises, Hong Kong is facing enormous pressure brought about by continuous economic development. While we truly believe that sustainable urban development and conservation of our cultural heritage are not mutually exclusive, striking a right balance between them presents a never-ending challenge.
>
> (Lam 2014)

Lam's statement reinforces the point that urban conservation in Hong Kong has progressed from a zero sum game to a mutually win-win partnership between conservationists and urban developers. Even though this relationship is new, the accomplishments achieved so far point towards greater integration in future. As the authors were finishing this chapter in early January 2015, the Antiquities Advisory Board – the highest-level statutory body that advises the government on the conservation of Hong Kong's built heritage – released a landmark report on the review of the 2007 conservation policy (see Government of Hong Kong 2015).[14]

A number of recommendations are made in the report, three of which are particularly relevant to the government's committed effort in nurturing the fledgling arranged marriage between urban conservation and development. The first recommendation calls on the government to encourage private owners of heritage buildings to 'preserve, revitalise and maintain' them through such prevailing incentives as relaxation of plot ratio and land exchange, *but* using a more systematic and well-publicised mechanism that addresses scale, building conditions and heritage value. The second recommendation asks for the government to set up a grading system for heritage buildings that comes with statutory protection, a replacement for the current system that classifies heritage buildings in three grades without such protection. The third recommendation calls for the government to explore the conservation of building clusters, especially those with unique heritage value. These recommendations are welcome progressive steps in insuring that the relationship between conservation and development is a mutually beneficial one – and especially beneficial to the future development of Hong Kong's urban built environment.

As pointed out as far back as 1999 by David Lung, a former Chairman of the Antiquities Advisory Board and an endowed Professor of the Built Environment at the University of Hong Kong, the enabling factor for urban conservation in Hong Kong is not cultural development, but urban land policy and development (Lung 1999: 7). For built heritage conservation in Hong Kong to be compatible with the sustainable urban development agenda, the former has to be integrated with real estate development through the urban land conversion process. This land conversion process, as explained by Chau Kwong-wing, Chair Professor of Real Estate and Construction at the University of Hong Kong, is the process of changing the nature and characteristics of land and real estate property for the benefits of the landowner, user, government or society (personal communication with Lee Ho-Yin, December 2014). At a more detailed level, the concept of sustainable urban development can be integrated with urban conservation by regarding built heritage not as monuments and museums but as reusable land resources. This means that urban conservation should be employed as a means of extending the life cycle of heritage buildings, starting from land acquisition and preparation to building construction, building management and maintenance and subsequent adaptive reuse. By this means, urban conservation can be readily understood as a sustainable form of urban property development – one that returns value to existing properties without the demolition of existing buildings and destruction of existing communities.

Notes

1   The full name of the document is Joint Declaration of the Government of the United Kingdom of Great Britain and Northern Ireland and the Government of the People's Republic of China on the Question of Hong Kong. It is accessible on the website of the Hong Kong Legislative Council. Available at: http://www.legislation.gov.hk/blis_ind. nsf/CurAllEngDoc/034B10AF5D3058DB482575EE000EDB9F?OpenDocument.

2   Even though it is explained on the government website cited in note 1 that

> virtually all land in Hong Kong is leased or otherwise held from the Government of the HKSAR . . . leases were for terms of 75, 99 or 999 years, subsequently standardised in the urban areas of Hong Kong Island and Kowloon to a term of 75 years', the auction for land grant is misleadingly referred to as a 'land sale'.

3   The exact number of Chinese emigrants is in doubt. According to Chen Bingan (quoted in He 2013),

> some mainland media . . . say that about 560,000 residents [across China] . . . escaped to Hong Kong between 1949 and 1974 . . . Some Hong Kong media put the

figure at about 700,000 people. But I found, by spending two decades interviewing refugees and researching a large amount of historical materials scattered throughout the country, the real figure to be two to three times higher.

4 Under the Hong Kong Act 1985, British Dependent Territories Citizens in Hong Kong (the vast majority of the Hong Kong Chinese) could become British Nationals (Overseas) in the run up to the 1997 Handover. This category of British nationality does not grant right of abode or citizenship in the United Kingdom and it was a means to prevent a flood of Hong Kong immigrants into that country.

5 Section 3 of the Antiquities and Monuments Ordinance states that

the Authority, after consultation with the Board and with the approval of the Chief Executive, by notice in the Gazette, [may] declare any place, building, site or structure, which the Authority considers to be of public interest by reason of its historical, archaeological or paleontological significance, to be a monument, historical building or archaeological or paleontological site or structure.

6 It is likely that the ordinance was also influenced by The Venice Charter (1964), which focuses on historic monuments. However, a close reading of the charter reveals that 'more modest works of the past which have acquired cultural significance' should also be protected (The Venice Charter 1964, Definitions, Article 1).

7 This was first mentioned in the 1998 Policy Address delivered by Tung Chee-wah, Hong Kong's first Chief Executive (the post-colonial equivalent to the Governor of Hong Kong) on 7 October 1998. In Paragraph 124 of the 1998 Policy Address, Tung confirms that 'To foster a sense of belonging and identity, we need to promote our heritage, which is a valuable cultural legacy. This involves the protection of historic buildings. . .'.

8 It is notable that in a government statistical survey of internet users in 2000 (Census and Statistics Department 2013: FA8, Table 5), it was found that the most frequent users of the internet were people in the two youngest age groups, 10 to 14 years old and 15 to 24 years old, which cover the post-80s generation. This strongly indicates that the attitude and values of the post-80s generation factored significantly in this internet voting event.

9 The 50 shortlisted items are reported in the 8 September 2004 edition of the local Chinese newspaper, *Apple Daily*, which can be viewed at http://hk.apple.nextmedia.com/supplement/culture/art/20040908/4291999 (accessed 30 June 2015). The top-ten list is featured in the 28 September 2004 edition of this newspaper, which can be viewed at http://hk.apple.nextmedia.com/news/art/20040928/4336805 (accessed 30 June 2015).

10 The ferocity of the campaign can be seen in the titles of some local newspaper articles: 'A Community Fights for Its Soul' (Yung 2005); 'Lee Tung Protesters to Step Up Action' (Anonymous 2007a); 'Urban Renewal Chief Chased by "Wedding Card Street" Protesters' (Anonymous 2007b); and 'Hunger Strike Fails to Save Street' (anonymous 2007c).

11 See the LegCo paper by Housing, Planning and Lands Bureau (2007: Annex B, 7), in which it is stated that Annie Tam, the Deputy Secretary (Planning and Lands) of the Housing, Planning and Lands Bureau,

clarified that the works covered by CRIII [Central Reclamation Phase III, the final phase of planned waterfront reclamation in the Central District of Hong Kong Island, which involved the demolition of the Star Ferry Pier and Queen's Pier] were set out clearly in the funding submission to LegCo in 2002.

12 See http://www.policyaddress.gov.hk/07-08/eng/p49.html (accessed 30 June 2015), where the policy statements on urban conservation are covered in paragraphs 49–56.

For the full policy document, see the LegCo Paper DEVB(CR)(W) 1-55/68/01 (Development Bureau 2007).

13 In 2012, under a new administration headed by Chief Executive Leung Chun-ying, Carrie Lam became the Chief Secretary for Administration, the second most senior government official.

14 From 2013 to 2014, the authors led staff from the University of Hong Kong's Architectural Conservation Programme and the Chinese University of Hong Kong's Centre for Architectural Heritage Research in the preparation of a report on the built heritage conservation policies of eight countries. The report was used by the Antiquities Advisory Board as a reference for its policy review.

Bibliography

Anonymous (2007a). Lee Tung protesters to step up action. *Hong Kong Standard*, 7 December 2007.

Anonymous (2007b). Urban Renewal Chief chased by 'Wedding Card Street' protesters. *South China Morning Post*, 25 December 2007.

Anonymous (2007c). Hunger strike fails to save street. *Hong Kong Standard*, 28 December 2007.

Australia ICOMOS (2013). *The Burra Charter: The Australia ICOMOS Charter for Places of Cultural Significance*. Melbourne: Australia ICOMOS Incorporated, revised edition.

Barber, L. (2014). (Re)Making heritage policy in Hong Kong: a relational politics of global knowledge and local innovation. *Urban Studies*, 51(6), 1179–95.

Chen, B. (2013). *The Great Exodus to Hong Kong* (in Chinese). Hong Kong: Hong Kong Open Page Publishing.

Census and Statistics Department (2013). Usage of personal computers and internet services by Hong Kong residents, 2000 to 2012. *Hong Kong Monthly Digest of Statistics*, May, FA1–13.

Census and Statistics Department (1996). Summary result of the 1996 population by-census. *Hong Kong Monthly Digest of Statistics*, December, FB2.

Chai, K.W. (2009). Central Star Ferry Pier: Policy, Politics and Protest in the Making of Heritage in Hong Kong. MSc (Conservation) Dissertation. Hong Kong: The University of Hong Kong.

Chan, Y.F. (2008). *The Queen's Pier Incident*. Hong Kong: Longman Hong Kong Education.

Cheng, S.Y.J. (ed.) (2014). *New Trends of Political Participation in Hong Kong*. Hong Kong: City University of Hong Kong Press.

Development Bureau (2007). *Legislative Council Brief: Heritage Conservation Policy*. DEVB(CR)(W) 1-55/68/01, October 2007.

Development Bureau (2010). *Conserving Central*. Discussion paper for the Legislative Council Panel on Development, CB(1)1666/09-10(05), April 2010.

DiStefano, L., Lee, H.Y. and Cummer, K. (2011). Heritage: A Driver of Development – Hong Kong Style Conservation. Paper presented at the ICOMOS 17th General Assembly and Scientific Symposium, 27 November to 2 December. Paris: UNESCO Headquarters.

Fan, S.C. (1974). *The Population of Hong Kong*. Hong Kong: Committee for International Coordination of National Research in Demography, United Nations.

Government of Hong Kong (2015). *Antiquities Advisory Board Releases Report on Policy Review on Conservation of Built Heritage*. Government Press Release, 9 January 2015.

He, H. (2013). Forgotten stories of the great escape to Hong Kong. *South China Morning Post*, 13 January 2013.

Home Affairs Bureau (2004). *Review of Built Heritage Conservation Policy: Consultation Document*. Hong Kong: Home Affairs Bureau.

Hong Kong Legislative Council (1996). *Hong Kong Hansard*. HC Deb 18 December, 431, cc1951–2.

Housing, Planning and Lands Bureau (2007). Annex B: notes of the Town Hall meeting on the preservation of the Queen's Pier. In: *Proposals for Preservation of Queen's Pier in Central and the Way Forward*. Paper for the (Hong Kong) Legislative Council Panel on Planning, Lands and Work, CB(1)1411/06-07(03), April 2007.

Hughes, R. (1968). *Hong Kong: Borrowed Place, Borrowed Time*. London: Deutsch.

International Council on Monuments and Sites (1964). *The Venice Charter*. Available at: www.icomos.org/charters/venice_e.pdf (accessed 6 February 2015).

Kan, F. and Vickers, E. (2002). One Hong Kong, two histories: 'History' and 'Chinese History' in the Hong Kong school curriculum. *Comparative Education*, 38(1), 73–89.

Lai, C. (2006). Star Ferry standoff as protesters break in to stop pier's demolition. *South China Morning Post*, 13 December 2006.

Lam, C. (2014). *Speech by CS [Chief Secretary] at Opening Ceremony of International Institute for Conservation of Historic and Artistic Works 2014 HK Congress*. Government press release, 22 September 2014. Available at: http://www.info.gov.hk/gia/general/201409/22/P201409220557.htm (accessed 6 February 2015).

Lee, H.Y. (2007). Welcome embrace of a living city. *South China Morning Post*, 11 October 2007.

Lee, H.Y. and DiStefano, L. (2007a). Urbanism and conservation on the Victoria harbour-front. *SPACE*, 447(August), 75–7.

Lee, H.Y. and DiStefano, L. (2007b). Architectural Conservation Program (ACP): the concurrent development of conservation perception and conservation education in a city of change. *HKIA Journal*, 50(3rd Quarter), 52–5.

Lee, H.Y. and DiStefano, L. (2014). Purposeful repurposing: adaptive reuse of Hong Kong's heritage buildings. In: *Hong Kong: Our Smart City in the Next 30 Years*. Hong Kong: The Hong Kong Institute of Surveyors, 22–5.

Legislative Council Secretariat (2009). *Panel on Development, Meeting on 24 February 2009: Background Brief on Revitalising Historic Buildings Through Partnership Scheme*. Legislative Council Paper CB(1)816/08-09(04), 17 February 2009.

Leung, A. and Wu, H. (2007). Conservationists' last battle cry: 'there will be an end for Queen's Pier, but the end is not today'. *South China Morning Post*, 2 August 2007.

Leung, Y.W.Y. (2010). The Queen's Pier Saga: Unveiling the Inconvenient Truth of Heritage Conservation Legislation in Hong Kong. MSc (Conservation) Dissertation. Hong Kong: The University of Hong Kong.

Lo, C.P. (1992). *Hong Kong*. London: Belhaven Press.

Lung, D (1999). Notes for Central Policy Unit Seminar on Conservation and Hong Kong's Future Development. Speech by David Lung at the CPU Seminar, 28 October 1999.

Mak, R.K.S. and Chan, C.S. (2013). Icons, culture and collective identity of postwar Hong Kong. *Intercultural Communication Studies*, 22(1), 158–73.

Office of the Chief Executive (2007a). *2007–8 Policy Address*. Hong Kong: Government of the Hong Kong Special Administrative Region. Available at: http://www.policyaddress.gov.hk/07-08/eng/p49.html (accessed 6 February 2015).

Office of the Chief Executive (2007b). *2007–8 Policy Address*. Hong Kong: Government of the Hong Kong Special Administrative Region. Available at: http://www.policyaddress. gov.hk/07-08/eng/p51.html (accessed 6 February 2015).

Office of the Chief Executive (2009). *2009–10 Policy Address*. Hong Kong: Government of the Hong Kong Special Administrative Region. Available at: http://www.policyaddress. gov.hk/09-10/eng/p55a.html (accessed 6 February 2015).

Pryor, E.G. (1975). The great plague of Hong Kong. *Journal of the Hong Kong Branch Royal Asiatic Society*, 15, 61–70.

Tsui, R. (2007). Money isn't everything. *South China Morning Post*, 30 September 2007.

UNESCO (2011). *Recommendation on the Historic Urban Landscape, including a Glossary of Definitions*. UNESCO Legal Instruments, 10 November 2011. Online. Available at: http://portal.unesco.org/en/ev.php-URL_ID=48857&URL_DO=DO_TOPIC&URL_ SECTION=201.html (accessed 6 February 2015).

Wu, X. (2010). *Hong Kong's Post-80s Generations: Profiles and Predicaments*. Hong Kong: Report commissioned by the Central Policy Unit of the Government of the Hong Kong Special Administrative Region, prepared by the Centre for Applied Social and Economic Research, The Hong Kong University of Science and Technology.

Yung, C. (2005). A community fights for its soul. *South China Morning Post*, 11 July 2005.

Chapter 12

Entrepreneurial heritage

Historic urban landscapes and the politics of "comprehensive development" in post-Soviet Cuba

Matthew J. Hill and Maki Tanaka

This chapter examines how the transformation in UNESCO's policy towards urban conservation—from a narrow emphasis on architectural conservation to a broader focus on urban heritage management—plays out in the context of Old Havana, a UNESCO World Heritage site. In particular, we argue that this policy shift in the Cuban case gives rise to a form of governance that encourages the creation of a 'new' type of *hombre nuevo* (new socialist man) or *hombre novisimo* through the disciplining and shaping of the participation in the cultural production of heritage (cf. Frederik 2006). This new form of governance is particularly pronounced in the Cuban context given the centralization of power in a single, entrepreneurial sub-state actor, the Office of the City Historian of Havana (OHCH), which manages the territory of Old Havana and its population on behalf of the Cuban state. Moreover, the fact that the state controls all of the patrimony in Cuba further accounts for the OHCH's ability to govern and dispose of territory and population in ways that are complicated in liberal polities. In a liberal framework, public institutions must negotiate with the demands of private developers and property owners and institutionalized forms of public accountability. The Cuban case is particularly interesting given the fact that historic centers, such as Old Havana, play an increasingly important role in Cuba's tourism-oriented development strategy, together with the survival of quasi-socialist institutions in the post-Soviet period (cf. Colantonio and Potter 2006). Francesco Bandarin and Ron van Oers' book (2012), on the historic urban landscape, testifies to the importance of the Old Havana case through a case study that depicts the Old Havana experiment in combining urban landscape conservation with a dynamic form of urban development that is officially known as "comprehensive development" (*desarrollo integral*).

In developing our argument about the entrepreneurial nature of governance in Old Havana, we seek to contribute to recent discussions about heritage as a form of governmentality (De Cesari 2010) and the use of national culture as a resource for socio-economic development (Yúdice 2003; Scher 2011). In Cuba, the commodification of built heritage as a resource coincides with the replacement of the former command economy with a post-Soviet service economy based on tourism and the competitive marketing of cultural goods, whether historic centers, beaches, cigars, rum, natural landscapes, or even socialism itself. Primacy in the Cuban state development strategy then is increasingly given to culture, which comes to operate on social relations through its association with development, the economy, and society (Yúdice 2003; Keane 2005: 149; Hernandez-Reguant 2009; cf. Scher 2011). As Philip Scher has argued (2011), the growing reliance of Caribbean states on the commodification of cultural forms, such as Carnival, as an economic development strategy increasingly subjects those forms and their practitioners to "cultural intervention" and "institutional oversight" by the state that he refers to as "biopower" (Scher 2011: 9). In this chapter, we explore a similar shift, focusing on the way in which Old Havana as a historic urban landscape, when incorporated into dynamic urban heritage development processes, also becomes a site of biopolitical management of culture that we refer to below as "entrepreneurial heritage."[1]

We develop our argument in three parts. After first describing the shift from architectural conservation to historic urban landscape management in UNESCO's approach to historic cities, we then turn to the Cuban case, and describe a similar transformation in the orientation to urban conservation in the socialist and post-Soviet periods. We then move on to describe the creation of a unique, entrepreneurial sub-state actor in Old Havana that represents a uniquely Cuban strategy for urban heritage management, combining urban conservation with processes of urban planning and tourism-oriented economic development. Finally, we examine how this new form of urban heritage management plays out on the ground with the participation of the state, the local community, and individuals who are increasingly drawn into the heritage tourism economy. In so doing, we develop the notion of "entrepreneurial heritage" to describe the governmental aspects of the new heritage management regime in Old Havana, examining the way in which it organizes urban space and conduct in keeping with UNESCO and state aesthetics of outstanding universal value.

From architectural conservation to urban landscape management

> Historic Urban Landscape does not constitute a separate "heritage category". On the contrary, the concept is inscribed within the established concept of urban historic areas, while at the same time adding a new lens to the practice of urban conservation: a broader "territorial" view of heritage, accompanied by a greater consideration of the social and economic functions of an historic city, an approach to managing change that tries to cope with modern developments, and finally, a re-evaluation of modern contributions to historic values. It is a tool to project the ideas of urban conservation in the twenty-first century.
>
> Bandarin and van Oers (2012: 73)

After the Second World War, the Venice Charter (1964) took the important step of expanding the field of conservation from museum objects to architectural monuments. Nevertheless, its narrow focus on architectural conservation and prioritization of a self-contained idea of material authenticity overlooked the social context in which monuments gained significance. Moreover, its overwhelming emphasis on the restoration of "ancient" buildings as carriers of the "substance" of pastness gave monuments an inordinate priority over urban settings (Ashworth 2011: 6; Ruggles 2012: 8; Weiss 2014: 2). The World Heritage Convention (1972) did not explicitly address historic cities; yet, it referred not only to monuments, but also to groups of buildings that contained natural and cultural values (Ruggles 2012:9). Even so, it still defined those groups of monuments largely in static and aesthetic terms, and as territorially bounded. For instance, Article 1 of the World Heritage Convention defines cultural heritage as "architectural works" or "*groups of separate or connected buildings* which, because of their architecture, homogeneity or place in the landscape, are of *outstanding universal value* from the view of history, art or science."[2] In this respect, it implicitly presented the city as a "historic center" or "ensemble" of buildings separated from the broader urban context, and defined by outstanding, exceptional, and unique cultural expressions considered in danger of disappearing (Kirshenblatt-Gimblett 2006:186).[3]

The Washington Charter (1987) sought to improve upon these previous texts by addressing the fact that historic cities are composed of more than collections of material artifacts. It moved to viewing historic urban areas as complex, inhabited communities and urban settings plagued by problems with automobile traffic, aging infrastructures, and processes of economic restructuring (Ruggles 2012: 10; Bandarin and van Oers 2012: 48). In this respect, it attempted to resituate the practices of architectural conservation within the broader purview of government policy focused on "local area renovation" and urban renewal (Ashworth 2011: 10). Yet at the same time, the Washington Charter was still limited by its static view of social processes, dependency on sources of public funding, and an overreliance on a conservation plan and its implementation by the public sector (Bandarin and van Oers 2012: 49).

The Vienna Memorandum (2005) and the subsequent UNESCO Recommendation on the Historic Urban Landscape (2011) sought to address these shortcomings by integrating "historic urban landscapes" with dynamic processes of "social and economic" or "sustainable" development. By adopting the language of the "historic urban landscape," the authors of these charters dramatically expanded the field of urban conservation by incorporating the broader urban context into its purview. This context now included:

> [a site's] topography, geomorphology, and natural features; its built environment, both historic and contemporary; its infrastructure above and below ground; its open spaces and gardens; its land use patterns and spatial organization; its visual relationships; and all other elements of the urban structure. It also includes social and cultural practices and values, economic processes and the intangible dimensions of heritage as related to diversity and identity.
>
> (Bandarin and van Oers 2012: 212)

This much-expanded definition of the object of urban conservation, reconceptualized as "urban heritage management," represents an important shift towards what Bandarin and van Oers (2012: 63) call "*sustainable development*" in the governance of historic cities, as well as a broader vision of the nature of urban heritage" (our italics). Moreover, it takes a dynamic view of historic urban spaces, viewing change—social, economic, and physical—as "a variable to be managed and understood, not just as a source of contrast [i.e. with a static, unchanging past]" (Bandarin and van Oers 2012: 63). The goal of urban heritage management then is no longer to preserve stasis, but the management of change itself.

The historic urban landscape approach (which we refer to as HUL) then reconceptualizes urban conservation (or urban heritage management) as a "moving target" characterized by "an increasingly complex management environment" where "changes can occur at different intervals and different levels and with different magnitudes" (Bandarin and van Oers 2012: 143). As such, HUL complicates the challenges faced by the urban site manager by "expand[ing] . . . the territory under their surveillance . . . the number of stakeholders involved, and . . . the type of attributes that carry meaning and value" (Bandarin and van Oers 2012: 143). The successful management of this landscape requires "the forging of new partnerships, better institutional coordination, and more available resources, both technical and financial" (Bandarin and van Oers 2012: 143). Accordingly, the urban heritage manager must coordinate the activities of several actors. These include: *governments* that integrate urban heritage into national development policies; *local authorities* that prepare urban development plans; *public–private partnerships* (PPPs), where the private sector provides capital and the management know-how and the public sector ensures that the public benefits; *international specialists* in sustainable development; and *national and international NGOs* that disseminate tools and best practices (Bandarin and van Oers 2012: 121, 144).

In summary, HUL seeks to understand urban heritage as part of a "comprehensive system" that includes processes of urbanization, urban development, climate change, the shifting economies of cities, tourism, and changing perceptions of the urban heritage values to be protected (Bandarin and van Oers 2013: 75–111). Rather than try to control all of these variables, one could argue that it seeks to "graft an apparatus" on to these processes, arranging them, harnessing their fluctuations, and establishing connections with other "elements of reality" in such a way that it compensates, prevents or cancels out the undesirable element of that reality (Foucault 2007: 37). The HUL apparatus consists of a cluster of tools that allow such a modulated intervention. These include *regulatory systems* (e.g., ordinances, acts, decrees); *community engagement tools* (e.g., stakeholder analysis and mapping); *technical tools* (e.g., social and environmental impact assessments); and *financial tools* (e.g., development bank loans, micro-credit, finance mechanisms to support local enterprise) (Bandarin and van Oers 2012: 144–5). Bandarin and van Oers emphasize that the variety of "geo-cultural, institutional and political environments" prevent them from specifying the exact mix of roles and responsibilities required for HUL implementation and stress the interdependent nature of the policies and actions in the HUL toolkit. The HUL approach then treats urban heritage landscapes as "a field that doesn't admit to control," focusing instead on a series of "modulated interventions" into a field of "autonomous and mutually corrective decisions" (Collier 2009: 87).

From architectural conservation to urban heritage management: the Cuban case

The shift from architectural conservation to urban heritage management took place in three stages in Old Havana. During the first stage (1963 to 1976), urban conservation efforts focused on the preservation of isolated monuments from the colonial period following the conservation principles in the Venice Charter. An architect that Hill interviewed who was active on the National Monuments Commission (ca. 1963) during this period noted that the members of the Commission spent most of their time identifying, cataloguing, and studying historic buildings, and preventing them from being demolished due to their uninhabitable conditions. Given limited resources, the Commission carried out only a handful of restorations, focusing on monumental structures from the colonial period that were considered important because they were tied to an important historical figure or architectural style (F. López, personal interview, 30 May 2006, Havana, Cuba). These included the former palaces of the colonial governor and vice-governor (Palacios de los Capitaines Generales and Segundo Cabo), a military fortress (Fuerza Real), a monument to the founding of the city (El Templete), and a handful of palaces of former Spanish and Cuban nobility. All of these restorations were dedicated to cultural functions such as museums, libraries, or centers of visual art. These efforts focused on the conservation of colonial architecture because it was the oldest and considered the most significant representative of Cuban national identity. The late date of independence in Cuba (1902) meant that Cuba also had nearly 100 additional years of colonial architecture compared with its other Latin American counterparts.

During the second period of conservation (1976 to 1993), conservation efforts shifted to a broader territorial scale with the passage of Cuba's first conservation laws and the support of centralized state financing. This shift in official policy towards urban conservation took place in response to the failure of the 10 million ton sugar harvest (1970), which resulted in the government's search for new sources of national unity and pride in continuity with its past and the celebration of its heritage (cf. Tanaka 2011: 27). In response to these events, the government passed the first heritage protection laws (Nos. 1 and 2) in 1977, in the context of the broader administrative reorganization of the country, and established a registry of national landmarks and guidelines for their conservation and safeguarding (Comisión Provincial de Monumentos 1984: 8, 18; Fornet Gil 1997). One year later, Cuba's National Monuments Commission passed Resolution No. 3, declaring Havana *intra muros* (the portion of Old Havana contained inside of the city's old defensive walls) to be "Cultural Patrimony of the Nation," while the Department of Monuments, a division of the Office of Cultural Patrimony (*Dirección de Patrimonio*), undertook the first comprehensive study of the Historic District and drafted a set of proposals for its restoration (Capablanca 1983: 6; Arjona 1986: 104; Rigol Savio 1994). The Cuban state also approved the first five-year budget (1981 to 1986) of 13 million pesos for the restoration and conservation of the

Historic Center, an amount that would later be increased by an additional 4 million pesos in a second five-year budget (1986 to 1991) (Melero Lazo 2001: 4). Following on these measures, UNESCO's World Heritage Committee added Old Havana and its system of defensive fortifications to the World Heritage List in 1982.

The attempt to restore an entire ensemble of 20 colonial and republican era buildings together with the public space of one of the Old Havana's five original squares, the Plaza Vieja, represented the first steps towards a comprehensive approach to urban conservation. This project, carried out under the auspices of the National Center for the Conservation, Restoration and Museology (CENCREM), created in 1980 with a US$ 1 million UNESCO loan, sought to restore the plaza's colonial-era buildings, mostly badly dilapidated tenement houses (known in Cuba as *solares*), for use as social housing (Plan Maestro 2008: 8; Rigol Savio 1994). The Plaza Vieja became a test case for this new "integrated" restoration approach in the 1980s, which was subsequently extended to a broader plan of action for the entire historic center and incorporated into a proposed set of urban regulations for the old city in 1990 (Plan Maestro 2008: 9).[4] The shortcomings of this monumental approach in Old Havana included its overreliance on the drafting of numerous urban conservation plans and the limitations of centralized state financing. With 3,500 buildings, 40 percent of which were classified as in danger of imminent collapse, the estimate of the actual restoration cost by some estimates exceeded US$1 billion, far more than the roughly 30 million pesos committed by the state in two five-year plans in the 1980s.[5] Moreover, the restoration was plagued by the "overlapping state and local authorities" involved in the restoration—the Institute of Physical Planning, the Office of Cultural Patrimony, CENCREM, the Office of the City Historian of Havana (OHCH), and the municipal government (Hill 2004: 37). These limitations came to a head in 1993. In October of that year, due to a shortage of funds, an important eighteenth-century merchant's house, in the Plaza Vieja, the Colegio Santo Angel, suddenly collapsed in broad daylight while awaiting restoration (Hill 2007).

These events ushered in a third phase (1993 to present) in which urban conservation policy shifted to the "comprehensive" social, environmental, and economic development approach that is currently in force in Old Havana. Conservation on this scale required a shift to a "sustainable" development model in which the Cuban government empowered a single juridical actor, the OHCH, to carry out the restoration of the entire historic center on behalf of the Cuban people. This shift took place through the passage of Decree Law 143 (1993), which transformed the OHCH from a provincial cultural institution answerable to the local municipal government to a decentralized, "entrepreneurial" state agency subordinated directly to the Cuban Council of State (the highest level of government in Cuba). Decree 143 granted the OHCH the legal power to redevelop state properties in the historic center for use as hotels, restaurants, museums, and other commercial purposes, as well as to tax state companies in the area. This in turn enabled the OHCH to act as its own investor and self-finance the rehabilitation of Old Havana. The focus then in this period moved to the sustainability (i.e., continuity) of the restoration process through the creation of new structures, specifically OHCH-operated tourism and commercial real estate companies that could facilitate the generation of profits needed for further restoration.

The OHCH uses the term "comprehensive development" (*desarrollo integral*) to refer to the process of turning urban conservation into a sustainable development process. In an interview that Hill conducted with the Director of UNESCO's Regional Bureau of Culture for Latin America and the Caribbean about Old Havana, he emphasized that the lesson learned from the case of Old Havana was the need for such an integrated approach—the broader "territorial" and dynamic view of heritage as an urban process that takes into account what Bandarin and van Oers refer to as the "social and economic functions" of the historic city (Bandarin and van Oers 2012: 73). While Eusebio Leal, the City Historian and the head of OHCH, and the OHCH started with a focus on a number of individual conservation projects in the 1980s, the Director noted that they broadened the scope of their operations (after 1993), becoming more focused on the whole site, that is, a 2 square kilometer area with 3,500 buildings in various stages of deterioration and a population of over 70,000 inhabitants (H. Van Hooff, personal interview, June 2013, Havana, Cuba). This entailed a shift from a narrow, object-oriented focus on conserving isolated monuments to a broader outcomes and process focus, in which the heritage manager works to align a greater range of people, institutions, processes, and artifacts in a network or composition of forces. The key to this self-regulation is what Eusebio Leal has referred to as "sustaining the restoration and its economic demands with a productive structure . . . guided by culture" (Hill 2004: 31), or what Bandarin and van Oers refer to as "income generating development rooted in tradition" (Bandarin and van Oers 2012: 144). In both cases, culture and tradition play an important role in defining what counts as legitimate entrepreneurialism, and what does not.

Entrepreneurial heritage

In an influential article, Chiara De Cesari has talked about creative heritage as a form of "nonstate governmentality" or "governmentality from below" that takes on the role of state building in the context of the weak Palestinian state (De Cesari 2010). In her analysis, artistic endeavors, such as art biennales, play the important role of helping Palestinians imagine and perform a future Palestinian state, by recruiting them to care for their heritage and take on rehabilitation projects themselves. In the Cuban case, by contrast, where the one-party state (in particular, the OHCH) is a strong state, the performative aspect of heritage is more about generating a continuous stream of revenue, within the framework of "tradition," a form of self-regulation that we refer to as *entrepreneurial heritage*. The OHCH encourages entrepreneurialism, inviting various stakeholders' participation in to the socio-economic development of the historic city, so long as it conforms to the egalitarian and aesthetic standards of the OHCH, as well as UNESCO.[6] If it fails to fall into this category, it is not considered to be entrepreneurialism. In this respect, the heritage performed in Old Havana does not imagine the state, in a bottom-up fashion, so much as perpetuate the post-Soviet project through a more open field of heritage management.

What is entrepreneurial about this process is that the focus on crafting a present and possible future for socialism supersedes the emphasis on outstanding universal value and the monument-based, past-oriented approach that we would argue continues to operate through HUL—albeit with the freedom to adaptively reuse historic structures. In this new context, there is greater freedom to "fashion" a useful heritage out of the available materials (relics, memories, histories) in order to address contemporary needs and to create a future for socialism (Ashworth 2011: 11). While the OHCH remains committed to the conservation of architectural forms in keeping with UNESCO norms, it expands these activities in the context of a much broader domain of urban heritage management. In this new context, the OHCH seeks to regulate a more open field of entrepreneurial activity in which communities and individuals are taught to manage themselves through politics of "self-care" (Brown 2003). Part of this involves the creation of the conditions in which entrepreneurial activity can flourish as part of a necessary development strategy based on cultural heritage and tourism. This is why the OHCH as an urban heritage manager engages in a much broader range of social activities such as the operation of a maternity hospital, a center for children with Down syndrome, and infrastructure projects related to the sewerage system and the electrical grid.

Entrepreneurial heritage of the OHCH

Following the passage of Decree 143, the OHCH had to take charge of a much more complex management environment than existed in the 1980s, when conservation entities made plans for isolated buildings or small ensembles and waited for government financing to carry them out—an approach that also had a relatively small impact on the historic center. By contrast, in the late socialist context, the OHCH suddenly had to generate its own revenues, attract tourists, care for an aging population, deal with nagging infrastructure problems, create sources of employment, collect taxes, address problems of security, and solve an outsized housing problem, with roughly half the population living in over 900 badly dilapidated tenements, many of which lacked private toilets or running water (Nickel 1990). As a multi-faceted business enterprise, not only does the OHCH generate over US$100 million in gross revenues annually through its chain of branded hotels, restaurants, bars, museums, and shops; it also runs social welfare and cultural programs for the residents and beyond. Recently, the OHCH has even been investing in the infrastructure of Old Havana, replacing old electricity, gas, and water pipes.[7] The OHCH's scope of work is not limited to urban conservation, but extends to general governance of Old Havana (Figure 12.1).

The transformation of the previously mentioned Plaza Vieja that took place in the late 1990s, after the state placed the OHCH in charge of the restoration of Old Havana, illustrates the new emphasis on economic development through cultural

Figure 12.1 An example of the OHCH's infrastructure work in Old Havana in 2012 (photo by M. Hill).

heritage and tourism. In contrast to the previous attempt (in the 1980s) to restore the plaza, which sought to restore historic buildings for use as social housing, the OHCH (in the late 1990s) opted to integrate the plaza into a growing tourism network. This network comprised Old Havana's other main plazas (i.e., Catedral, Armas, and San Francisco) and their interconnecting streets, an area that the OHCH began to refer to as the "*kilometro de oro*" (Miracle Mile). To carry out this integration, the OHCH engaged in what Matt Hodges refers to as the "deworlding of artifacts from their local contexts and subsequent disclosure so that they can be consumed in the context of heritage tourism practices" (2009: 91).

An excellent example of this type of deworlding is the OHCH's decision to remove an underground parking structure that was originally constructed in the center of the plaza in the early 1950s, a few years prior to the Cuban revolution. In the late 1990s, the OHCH demolished the underground garage and the above-ground amphitheater. It made this decision both because the garage was considered to disrupt the traditional morphology of the plaza and due to its association with North American domination of Cuba during the republican period (1902 to 1959). The OHCH then covered the surface with polished paving stones and adorned it with a fountain, which it surrounded with a ten-foot-high iron fence. It then "pedestrianized" the square by installing heavy metal chains at the four corners of the plaza and cannon-ball-shaped bollards around the plaza's perimeter to prevent vehicular traffic (Figure 12.2).

Through this type of "disciplinary orchestration" of a "tacit network of signs," the OHCH reaffirmed the traditional origins of the plaza and Old Havana as one of Spain's last colonial possessions in the New World. In so doing, it also

Figure 12.2 The restored Plaza Vieja in 2006 with a fence around the fountain (photo by M. Hill).

succeeded in creating a "colonial nostalgia" (Bissell 2005) that attracted tourists and commercial investors to the plaza – such as the international retail chains Paul and Shark, Benetton, Paco Valente, and Pepe Jeans. The changes also helped the OHCH broker UNDP funds from a number of international donors (Spain, Austria, Belgium, Japan) to restore the remaining colonial-era buildings in the plaza for commercial, cultural, and a more limited social housing use. Ultimately, the commercial exploitation of the plaza resulted in the OHCH needing to relocate over half of its original residents to replacement housing on the city's outskirts. At the same time, it accommodated a smaller group of residents in more spacious social housing units that coexisted with revenue-generating commercial shops, hotels, and restaurants (Fornet Gil 2011).

Entrepreneurial heritage of the community

At the community level, entrepreneurial heritage consists of spontaneous activities by private individuals or civic groups—without state sponsorship. These activities arise in a community surrounded by heritage materials, which are likely to draw tourist attention. The activities may contribute to income generation, neighborhood revitalization (Brumann 2009), the articulation of a dominant group's identity (Hodges 2009), resistance to state planning agencies (Collins 2008), or even state building (De Cesari 2010). In a country such as Cuba, where the state author-ity is strong and neighborhoods are organized into mechanisms of vigilance, such spontaneous activities at the community level may be hard to observe. As a govern-ment official who Adrian Hearn interviewed noted, the Cuban state does not sup-port grassroots economic initiatives due to its "insecurity about local autonomy" and "economic self-sufficiency" (Hearn 2008: 52). The OHCH is an exception in this regard. Due to its decentralized system of administration, and autonomous financial management model, the OHCH is able to support "self-directed commu-nity projects" unlike other state entities (Hearn 2008: 91).

Hearn describes several such community development projects in Old Havana. Most of these involved Afro-Cuban religious groups that at least initially involved a community development orientation. In one such project, a *santero* (a priest of the Santería religion) used a community garden to teach neighborhood youth about Afro-Cuban cuisine and medicinal plants (Hearn 2008: 92). In another, a pair of local Afro-Cuban musicians established a weekly folkloric musical gathering in a tenement courtyard to showcase the talents of local rumba musicians and raise awareness about HIV and alcohol abuse (Hearn 2008: 233). Yet Hearn notes that both projects ultimately were sidetracked by commercial interests that detracted from their original community development goals.

Another such community development project in Old Havana derived from a previously unrecognized form of heritage. The neighborhood project, known as Arte Corte (the "art of haircutting"), was initiated by Gilberto Valladares, popularly known as "Papito," a charismatic community leader and barber with an artistic flair. Papito grew interested in the history of barbers and barbering techniques and devices, collecting old tools of the trade and other related objects, and eventually opening a private museum and salon. Papito also set out to train local youth and he had a vision of opening a barbering school to provide them with vocational skills and a means to generate income. Together with local hair stylists and artisans, Papito turned Santo Angel into a barbering heritage neighborhood, painting the facades of the buildings and placing artistic expressions in the streets. They also hold events such as "*el día del peluquero* the barber day" whereby hairstylists from all over the island join and demonstrate their professional skills. The spontaneity of this barrio and how they use the barbering heritage in order to invest in the local population represents a form of entrepreneurial heritage at the community level (Figure 12.3).

The vibrancy of this project attracted the attention of the OHCH. Papito's voluntary activism fits with Eusebio Leal's long-expressed concern that the local residents of Old Havana learn and appreciate the value of their own heritage. As the Havana historian is reported to have said: "I wish we had a hundred Papitos in Old Havana." The Arte Corte case study signals a shift from an architectural conservation approach to the built environment to a more open-ended heritage management approach. The latter entails a greater freedom to "fashion" a heritage from availa-ble materials, such as the local history of barbering and barbering implements, which can address the needs of community development. Rather than focusing

Figure 12.3 A mural in the Arte Corte neighborhood (photo by M. Tanaka).

strictly on the preservation of the built environment, the OHCH celebrates and manages community entrepreneurialism such as Papito's. The spontaneous transformation of public space in Old Havana is not penalized, but rather encouraged. In this manner, the OHCH promotes heritage-conscious subjects that act in accordance with the OHCH's vision. The OHCH, in fact, has provided assistance to the Arte Corte project by building a vocational school and a barbering-themed park in Santo Angel, placing its own logo on signs celebrating the project. While some might argue that the OHCH has coopted Papito's project, locals are quite proud to be recognized by the OHCH and they still call Arte Corte their own.

Entrepreneurial heritage of the individual

Since 1993, when the financing of the restoration shifted from the centralized state to an integral development model, more and more residents have been drawn into the heritage tourism project (Silverman 2002: 883). The government's liberalization of self-employment laws under Raul Castro has brought hundreds if not thousands of new entrepreneurs to the Old City (Hearn and Alfonso 2012). This includes artisans, book vendors, street artists, bicycle taxi drivers, musicians, folkloric groups, street vendors, and self-employed construction workers. The OHCH has itself supported this activity as a form of local economic development and even begun renting space for massage parlors, flower shops, and boutiques to local entrepreneurs. Between 2005 and 2011, the number of entrepreneurs in Old Havana multiplied from 2,500 to over 6,000. On the days when the OHCH opens to the public, employees are inundated with applications from residents seeking licenses to rent rooms, operate restaurants, or run galleries out of their homes. More recently, the

Figure 12.4 A Costumbrista posing for a photo in front of the Palacio de los Capitaines Generales, Old Havana, Cuba (photo by M. Tanaka).

OHCH has begun exploring the idea of renting space and equipment to private cooperatives of artisans such as cobblers.

The explosion of entrepreneurial activity has challenged the OHCH's ability to regulate individual forms of entrepreneurial practice so that they remain in keeping with the heritage aesthetic and the selfless dictates of *desarrollo integral*. In this respect, it seeks to manage entrepreneurial activity through the licensing of entrepreneurs as a means of controlling how residents engage with capital and the past in Old Havana. Perhaps the most visible individuals of these are *costumbristas*, who display themselves in colorful period costumes in the tourist area (Figure 12.4). These individual entrepreneurs are licensed and heavily taxed by the OHCH and they practice their businesses under certain rules and close watch by the state.

In addition to the *costumbristas*, Bandarin and van Oers celebrate the carnival troop that regularly performs in Old Havana's main tourist plazas as an example of intangible heritage (2012: 109). This group presents another example of "folkloric" practice established through the OHCH's licensing as a way to enhance the tourism interface in this heritage site. While the carnival group regularly performs for tips, if an unlicensed Cuban were to ask a tourist for a "gift," he or she might be stopped by the tourist police. Individual heritage entrepreneurs, such as the *costumbristas* or the carnival group, are perhaps most regulated by the state, as they must conduct their businesses within the legal framework or legally defined categories of the OHCH. In many ways, this is a form of heavily managed capitalism, largely so that the state can keep a tight grip on the private sector (Corrales 2004). But within the heritage district of Old Havana, the OHCH encourages entrepreneurial heritage so long as it is conducted in a "selfless" way, is in keeping with official heritage aesthetics, or community needs as in the Barrio Santo Angel, and ultimately, enhances the tourist experience in Old Havana.

Conclusion

The Cuban case illustrates the transition from a narrow approach to urban conservation focused on the preservation and transmission of an isolated group of monuments to a post-Soviet urban heritage management orientation, combining profit-making, planning, social development, community engagement, and urban conservation in a single entrepreneurial sub-state agency—the OHCH. We suggest that this new form of urban heritage management coincides with a type of governmentality that we have called entrepreneurial heritage. This style of management seeks to draw buildings, communities, and individuals and their bodily practices into a dynamic and transnational urban heritage landscape, largely on terms that are set by the OHCH itself. These terms include subordination to the logics of the OHCH's capture of tourism revenues (licensing, policing, and taxation), deference to officially sanctioned heritage aesthetics, and obedience to the selfless dictates of the "new" new socialist man (Frederik 2006). At the same time, the emphasis on fashioning a "usable" past out of the range of available materials has given rise to new forms of previously unrecognized heritage such as the intangible practices of haircutting. Such forms of heritage are accepted so long as they further the broader goals of egalitarian economic development. While some might view the OHCH's disciplinary orchestration of a "tacit network of antiquated signs" (Hodges 2009)—both at the level of buildings and bodily practices—as heavy-handed, they are viewed as an accepted trade-off to maintain Cuba's autonomy in the face of the Soviet collapse and the US economic embargo.

The Cuban case raises a larger set of issues about HUL itself, which we argue remains highly Eurocentric in its orientation towards urban conservation and its incorporation into dynamic urban development processes. When transplanted to poor, post-colonial countries such as Cuba, the focus of urban heritage management shifts. Rather than integrating urban conservation with urban development, urban conservation itself becomes the primary means of tourism-oriented, urban and economic development. This results in vast disparities in wealth, resources, and mobility between Cubans who work and reside in Old Havana, and the European and North American tourists who visit it in pursuit of "authentic" historic cityscapes and an intensively marketed "colonial nostalgia." Such historic urban landscapes represent one of the few ways for Cuba to enter the global economy and to capture much-needed hard currency reserves. At the same time, the OHCH, on behalf of the state, tries to manage this economic opening by capturing the value of global capitalism and tourism flows through its network of newly minted hotels, restaurants, and museums—a new form of decentralized centralization.

This dependency on tourism gives rise to a host of contradictions that are not fully envisioned by HUL. Steven Gregory (2014) captures some of these contradictions with the metaphor of the "devil behind the mirror," referring to the vagaries of uneven, tourism-based development in the neighboring Dominican Republic. In Cuba, this devil includes: spatial segregation between tourist and residential areas; racialization as blacks are excluded from working in hotels and more heavily policed in the increasingly "whitened" Old Havana; some residential displacement, as former palaces converted into tenements are refurbished for commercial uses in an ever-expanding tourism zone; and an expansion of people working as "hustlers" (*jineteros*) in the informal economy – selling cigars, acting as unofficial tour guides, seeking amorous relations with tourists, and many other forms of feeding (*picando*) off the tourist sector. The OHCH seeks to regulate and manage this economic opening through licensing, providing jobs and employment, operating schools and hospitals, repairing the urban infrastructure, and ultimately, defining what is appropriate conduct. But there are also inevitable costs for those who must increasingly work officially or informally within this disciplinary, urban heritage apparatus in order to "make ends meet" (*resolviendo*).

One could argue that the situation in Old Havana is not HUL, or is not consistent with the HUL model, as it involves some displacement, top-down orchestration of heritage aesthetics, and consultations with the community that are more about legitimating projects that have been decided in advance. But if this is the case, we would argue that HUL is truly only applicable in a narrow group of European cities due to its inability to fully grasp the range of informal urbanization processes and forms of economic dependency that characterize countries in the Global South such as Cuba (cf. Weiss 2014). In such contexts, entrepreneurial heritage, whether demolishing a parking structure, sanctioning haircutting as official heritage, or licensing *costumbristas*, serves the larger goal of maintaining Cuban exceptionalism in a post-socialist world, and reaffirming Cuba's commitment to solidarity and the egalitarian values of socialism in a reconfigured world economy. Further research will be required to better understand the forms that urban heritage management takes in other "developing" country contexts seeking to follow the HUL paradigm.

Notes

1   As Ploger notes, it was through cities, and in particular, historic urban cores, that societies first developed ideas about how to discipline life through urban space beginning in the 1800s (Ploger 2008: 52). Moreover, governments, in seeking to control many of the social problems of cities—poverty, illness, lack of hygiene, poor housing—discovered that forms of biopolitics (surveillance, registration, classification) made it possible to "clean, shape and order" cities and to create "healthy" populations (Ploger 2008: 64).

2   Italics ours. Available at: http://whc.unesco.org/en/conventiontext/ (accessed 30 June 2015).

3   In this respect, it continued to present the historic city as a "romanticized monumental place" characterized by the sense of unchanging permanence that Herzfeld has called "monumental time" in contrast to the "social time" of lived, everyday practices and their related urban forms (Franquesa 2011: 1027).

4   It also served as the basis of ongoing debates about the right level of population in Old Havana, with some planners arguing for the ability to accommodate the existing

population through better distribution and others arguing for the need to reduce population densities in order to provide adequate housing and use of the territory (Plan Maestro 2008: 9).

5 According to Jorge Pérez-López, the official Cuban exchange rate was 1 US dollar to 1 Cuban peso in the 1980s, but the unofficial rate was 6 pesos to 1 US dollar (Pérez-López 1995: 253).

6 This is similar to the situation in the "Levant," where what often counts as heritage are Western (post)colonial discourses that emphasize sites such as Petra, Jerash, or Wadi Rum and the Western archaeologists and explorers (e.g., Lawrence of Arabia) who "discovered" or "opened up" these places (Jacobs 2010: 319). As Jacobs notes, these Western models are imbued with a sense of "colonial nostalgia," "often found under imperialism, where people mourn the passing of what they themselves have transformed" (Jacobs 2010: 318).

7 The OHCH is unique in this regard. As a near-autonomous entity, created by the socialist state to facilitate entrepreneurship, it only reports to the Council of State. Such semi-autonomous status is unprecedented and singular in Cuba.

Bibliography

Arjona, M. (1986). *Patrimonio Cultural e Identidad*. Havana Editorial Letras Cubanas.

Ashworth, G. (2011). Preservation, conservation and heritage: approaches to the past in the present through the built environment. *Asian Anthropology*, 10(1), 1–18.

Bandarin, F. and van Oers, R. (2012). *The Historic Urban Landscape: Managing Heritage in an Urban Century*. Oxford: Wiley-Blackwell.

Bandarin, F. and van Oers, R. (eds) (2013). *Reconnecting the City: The Historic Urban Landscape Approach and the Future of Urban Heritage*. Oxford: John Wiley & Sons.

Bissell, W.C. (2005). Engaging colonial nostalgia. *Cultural Anthropology*, 20(2), 215–48.

Brown, W. (2003). Neo-liberalism and the end of liberal democracy. *Theory and Event*, 7(1).

Brumann, C. (2009). Outside the glass case: the social life of urban heritage in Kyoto. *American Ethnologist*, 36(2), 276–99.

Capablanca, E. (1983). *Habana Vieja. Anteproyecto de Restauración*. Havana: Departamento de Monumentos. Dirección de Patrimonio Cultural. Ministerio de Cultura. Republica de Cuba.

Colantonio, A. and Potter, R.B. (2006). The rise of urban tourism in Havana since 1989. *Geography*, 91(1), 23–33.

Collier, S.J. (2009). Topologies of power: Foucault's analysis of political government beyond "governmentality." *Theory, Culture and Society*, 26(6), 78–108.

Collins, J. (2008). "But what if I should need to defecate in your neighborhood madam?": Empire, redemption, and the "tradition of the oppressed" in a Brazilian heritage site. *Cultural Anthropology: Journal of the Society for Cultural Anthropology*, 23(2), 279–328.

Comisión Provincial de Monumentos (1984). *Principales legislaciones para la protección del patrimonio cultural*. I Simposio provincial de restauración y conservación de monumentos. Junio. Dirección Provincial de Cultura Poder Popular Ciudad Habana.

Corrales, J. (2004). The gatekeeper state: limited economic reforms and regime survival in Cuba, 1989–2002. *Latin American Research Review*, 39(2), 35–65.

De Cesari, C. (2010). Creative heritage: Palestinian heritage NGOs and defiant arts of government. *American Anthropologist*, 112(4), 625–37.

Fornet Gil, P. (1997). Gobierno y territorio: Cuba en dos tiempos. *Revista Interamericana de Planificación*, 39(14), 29–41.

Fornet Gil, P. (2011). Twenty-five years of transformations in the historic center of Havana: a case study of the Plaza Vieja. *Facilities*, 29 (7/8), 303–12.

Foucault, M. (2007). *Security, Territory, Population: Lectures at the Collège de France, 1977–78*. Trans. G. Burchell, ed. M. Senellart. New York: Palgrave Macmillan.

Franquesa, J. (2011). "We've lost our bearings": place, tourism, and the limits of the "mobility turn." *Antipode*, 43(4), 1012–33.

Frederik, L. (2006). Cuba's national characters: setting the stage for the *hombre novísimo*. *Journal of Latin American Anthropology*, 10(2), 401–36.

Gregory, S. (2014). *The Devil behind the Mirror: Globalization and Politics in the Dominican Republic*. Berkeley: University of California Press.

Hearn, A.H. (2008). *Cuba: Religion, Social Capital, and Development*. Raleigh: Duke University Press.

Hearn, A.H. and Alfonso, F.J. (2012). Havana: from local experiment to national reform. *Singapore Journal of Tropical Geography*, 33(2), 226–40.

Hernandez-Reguant, A. (2009). *Cuba in the Special Period: Culture and Ideology in the 1990s*. Basingstoke: Palgrave Macmillan.

Hill, M.J. (2004). Globalizing Havana: World Heritage and Urban Redevelopment in a Late Socialist City. Unpublished PhD thesis. Chicago: University of Chicago, UMI.

Hill, M.J. (2007). Reimagining Old Havana: world heritage and the production of scale in late socialist Cuba. In: S. Sassen (ed.), *Deciphering the Global: Its Scales, Spaces and Subjects*. New York and London: Routledge.

Hodges, M. (2009). Disciplining memory: heritage tourism and the temporalisation of the built environment in rural France. *International Journal of Heritage Studies*, 15(1), 76–99.

Horowitz, I.L. (1995). *Cuban Communism, 1959–1995*, 8th edn. New Brunswick: Transaction Publishers.

Jacobs, J. (2010). Re-branding the Levant: contested heritage and colonial modernities in Amman and Damascus. *Journal of Tourism and Cultural Change*, 8(4), 316–26.

James, J. (2012). Preservation and national belonging in eastern Germany heritage fetishism and redeeming Germanness. In: *Palgrave Macmillan Memory Studies*. New York: Palgrave Macmillan.

Keane, M. (2005). Review of the expediency of culture: uses of culture in the global era. *Continuum: Journal of Media & Cultural Studies*, 19(1), 149–52.

Kirshenblatt-Gimblett, B. (2006). World heritage and cultural economics. In: I. Karp, C. Krantz, L. Szwaja and T. Ybarra-Frausto (eds), *Museum Frictions: Public Cultures/ Global Transformations*. Durham, NC and London: Duke University Press.

Melero Lazo, N. (2001). *Experiencia Cubana en la Restauración del Patrimonio Arquitectónico*. Havana: Centro Nacional de Conservación, Restauración y Museología.

Nickel, A. (1990). El casco histórico de La Habana: la situación de vivienda y los conceptos de renovación urbana en La Habana. *Revista Geográfica*, 112, 75–90.

Pérez-López, J. (1995). Cuba's underground economy. In: I.L. Horowitz (ed.), *Cuban Communism, 1959–1995*, 8th edn. New Brunswick: Transaction Publishers, pp. 245–70.

Plan Maestro, Oficina del Historiador (2008). Historia de una Plaza en Movimiento: del Parque Habana a la Plaza Vieja. Havana: unpublished manuscript.

Ploger, J. (2008). Foucault's dispositif and the city. *Planning Theory*, 7(1), 51–70.

Rigol Savio, I. (1994). Rehabilitación de la Plaza Vieja de la Ciudad de la Habana. In *Rehabilitación Integral en Áreas o Sitios Históricos Latinoamericanos*. Ecuador: Abya-Yala.

Ruggles, D. F. (2012). *On Location: Heritage Cities and Sites*. New York: Springer.

Scher, P.W. (2011). Heritage tourism in the Caribbean: the politics of culture after neoliberalism. *Bulletin of Latin American Research*, 30(1), 7–20.

Silverman, H. (2002). Touring ancient times: the present and presented past in contemporary Peru. *American Anthropologist*, 104(3), 881–902.

Tanaka, M. (2011). *Heritage Modern: Cityscape of the Late Socialist Political Economy in Trinidad, Cuba*. Berkeley: University of California.

Weiss, L.M. (2014). Informal settlements and urban heritage landscapes in South Africa. *Journal of Social Archaeology*, 14(1), 3–25.

Yúdice, G. (2003). *The Expediency of Culture: Uses of Culture in the Global Era*. Durham, NC and London: Duke University Press.

Part III

Grassroots heritage and bottom-up approaches

Chapter 13

The sustainable conservation of urban heritage

A concern of all social actors

Eduardo Rojas

The conservation of the material urban heritage is gaining relevance in the management of cities all over the world.[1] Individuals, organisations of civil society and latterly governments are concerned for the loss of many irreplaceable buildings and places where significant events took place. These are fine examples of the architecture or town building practices of the past that hold social or religious significance for society. Communities in many regions of the world mobilise to prevent the loss of their material heritage due to the re-emergence of the depredatory real estate developments that in the second half of the twentieth century demolished significant monuments, neighbourhoods and areas of historic, aesthetic or social significance to satisfy the demand of the rapidly expanding population and economic activities of the cities.

Conservation practitioners have perfected their abilities to safeguard the urban heritage through research, evaluation of conservation experiences and international agreements on good practices and principles that are distilled in research documents and charters. Most of the academic work and debate centres on the reasons to conserve the urban heritage and the best technical methods for getting good results. The lessons learned are in use worldwide, bringing great benefits to the conservation effort. However, less attention is paid to the complex governance issues posed by the heritage conservation processes that have greatly increased in recent years due to the expanded set of social actors concerned for the urban heritage. In addition, there is the growing acceptance of the adaptive rehabilitation of heritage properties to contemporary uses – a form of intervention that is proving more effective in ensuring sustainable results than the full preservation of the physical and use characteristics of the properties advocated by traditional practices. The present chapter aims at contributing to the understanding of the governance issues posed by the sustainable conservation of the material urban heritage through its adaptive rehabilitation for contemporary uses. The analysis focuses in particular on the role of the different stakeholders participating in the process, their contributions and conflicts and the institutional arrangements to solve them.

Based on the relevant literature and the practical experience of the author, the study discusses these issues following Bell's definition: 'governance is about the use of institutions and structures of authority to allocate resources and coordinate or control activities in society' (Bell 2002: 1). Consequently, this chapter explores three major areas of concern: the roles and conflicts of the *social actors* interested in the conservation of the urban heritage; the *structures of authority* that can be brought to bear in coordinating or controlling their actions; and the *institutional arrangements* that are most suited to exercising the structures of authority and allocating the resources devoted to the task.

Social actors concerned for the urban heritage

Actors in the conservation of the urban heritage

People care for what bring them benefits so individuals and communities are moved to conserve the material urban heritage – the stock of public spaces, urban infra-structures and buildings inherited by a community – because they appreciate the benefits that it brings to them. Communities are prepared to spend resources – knowledge, skills and money – to ensure that this form of heritage continues to exist so that their members can enjoy the benefits that it generates. The value of the urban heritage for society is now better understood thanks to advances in the economics of cultural heritage (Peacock 1998; Throsby 2007, 2010, 2012; Peacock and Rizzo 2008; Licciardi and Amirtahmasebi 2012), a branch of economics that conceptualises the heritage as capital. Cultural capital provides socio-cultural ser-vices to society that are central to the formation of human and social capital. Physi-cal capital supports social activities and is capable of producing flows of economic benefits as an input for production and exchange (Throsby 2012). Both forms of heritage are linked as the physical capital provides support to many of the urban expressions of the cultural capital (Bandarin and van Oers 2012). The significance of the urban heritage for the social and economic development of the communities appears in the form of flows of socio-cultural and economic benefits received by different social actors individually or as members of a community.

One of the consequences of this expanded view of the importance of urban heritage is that its conservation is no longer the preserve of the cultural elite or a small group of philanthropists. In most countries, governments are also involved in conserving monuments, and in some advanced marked economies, a much wider variety of social actors – public and private – are involved. The above trends are the result of several processes. There is a wider awareness in society about the multiple *socio-cultural* and *economic* values of the urban heritage (Throsby 2012). Scholars, philanthropists and organisations of the civil society concerned with culture are currently interested, not only in the traditional *religious, historic* or *aes-thetic* values of monuments, but also in a broader range of socio-cultural values. These include the *social* and *symbolic* values of buildings and public spaces in cities and their contributions to social cohesion, the transmission of knowledge and the preservation of social capital. In most countries, governments are driven by their constituencies to ensure that parts of the urban heritage are conserved given their *bequest* or *existence* values. In advanced market economies, groups of households, entrepreneurs and firms are finding it convenient to live and trade in urban heritage areas, creating a demand that supports a growing real estate business centred on the adaptive rehabilitation of heritage properties for contemporary uses. This is a movement that materialises the *economic use* value of the heritage. It must be noted that this level of involvement of the private sector is still lacking in most developing countries.[2]

As there are new social actors playing active roles in the conservation effort, there are also other actors that oppose the conservation of some components of the urban heritage – particularly private buildings – arguing that conservation retards or impedes the development of cities. The argument is that it is better for cities to use the land occupied by heritage buildings for their best and highest use according to what is demanded in the real estate markets. This would secure the provision of residential, manufacturing, office, retail and recreation space at the lowest possible cost to consumers (Glaeser 2011). In parallel, a reaction to the activities of real estate developers is emerging in communities that are defending their lifestyle, which is threatened by contemporary urban development, and they pursue the conservation of the material heritage of their neighbourhoods as the physical support of their social practices and uses.

In a few cases, the conflicting views of these stakeholders are solved through dialogue and agreements pertaining to the adaptive rehabilitation of heritage sites for contemporary uses. In most cases, however, the unsolved conflicts lead to stagnation and paralysis. In the worst cases, unscrupulous developers opt for the demolition of the heritage buildings to develop the land, relying on the slowness and leniency of the heritage conservation enforcement mechanisms.

Stakeholders in the evolution of the concern for the urban heritage

In countries that are actively conserving the urban heritage the variety of social actors interested in its conservation (herein referred to as stakeholders) increases. In addition to those that traditionally promote the conservation of the urban heritage – members of the cultural elite, scholars, philanthropists, conservation boards and international organisations – there are other stakeholders – such as property owners, real estate investors, informal producers and local users – that at different points in time, and under different incentives, can either promote the conservation effort or oppose it.

As the variety of stakeholders increase so do the opportunities for cooperation and conflict turn the governance of the conservation process into a more complex exercise. A review of the evolution of the process sheds light on to these issues. The analysis that follows expands a schema originally proposed by Rojas and de Moura Castro (1999) that tracks the evolution in the approaches to urban heritage conservation practice at national level and identifies three stages. The first stage is when the conservation of the urban heritage is essentially the 'concern of the elites' centred mainly in preventing the loss of monuments holding historic, aesthetic or religious socio-cultural values. In this phase, most cities do not have a strong institutional framework for action, nor have they adequate structures of authority to coordinate the actions of other stakeholders and they lack resources to deal with the problems affecting the whole of the heritage area. The resulting interventions are essentially isolated actions to preserve specific monuments with funds coming from the philanthropy or sporadic contributions from the national government. In certain cases, organisations of the civil society and international organisations concerned with cultural issues, such as UNESCO, also participate, particularly when the urban heritage area is proposed for inclusion into the World Heritage List.

A second stage emerges when 'governments intervene' to ensure that part of the urban heritage is conserved for future generations. In this stage, there is a broader awareness about the economic non-use values of the urban heritage – the existence and inheritance values described by Throsby (2012) – adding impetus to the preservation effort. A characteristic of this stage is that national governments set up structures of authority by enacting conservation legislation, establish national institutions to list and protect the heritage, and devote resources to its conservation. Progress is observable in the wider scope of the conservation effort, although there is always a shortage of resources, as government funds are needed for many others causes.

The third stage identified by the authors is when the urban heritage becomes the 'concern of all social actors' and engages the interest and resources of a wide spectrum of stakeholders (Rojas 2002). This stage benefits from the interest of some groups in society to live and trade in the urban heritage areas, a trend that materialises in the economic use value of the heritage (Throsby 2012) and supports private investment for the adaptive rehabilitation of heritage properties for contemporary uses (Rojas 2012). Table 13.1 presents a synthesis of the three phases indicating the heritage values and stakeholders at play.

Mapping stakeholders' interactions

The variety of stakeholders involved in the third stage makes the governance of the process more complex as the opportunities for conflicts increase, as do the opportunities for cooperation and partnerships. Conflicts mostly originate in the stance of the stakeholders towards conservation. There are stakeholders who *support* the conservation of the urban heritage wholeheartedly. This is the case with individuals committed to the development of culture and its related artefacts and scholars or members of the cultural elite acting individually or as members of organisations of the civil society. Among the government-sponsored institutions, the conservation boards have as their central function the conservation of the urban heritage. At the opposite end of the spectrum are groups that mostly *oppose* the conservation efforts including landowners and real estate investors who seek to maximise the short-term gains of re-developing heritage properties that are deemed functionally obsolete and that are valuable for the location of the land where they sit. These two groups are likely to be in conflict in a debate about *why* conserve the urban heritage and *what* to conserve.

Table 13.1 Stages in the conservation of the urban heritage

Stage		Initial stage Deteriorated heritage	Stage 1 Concern of the elite	Stage 2 Government intervention	Stage 3 Concern of all social actors
Description		Urban heritage areas deteriorated as a result of functional and physical obsolescence	Monuments preserved through sporadic interventions	Legislation and institutions to list and protect monuments and urban heritage areas. Sporadic interventions	In addition to the actions in Stage 2, the heritage is put to contemporary uses with social or market demand
Values at play	Sociocultural	None	Historic Aesthetic Religious	Historic Aesthetic Religious Social	Historic Aesthetic Religious Social
	Economic	None		Bequest Existence	Bequest Existence Direct use Indirect use
Stakeholders	Government		National	National Regional Conservation boards	National Regional Conservation boards Local
	Private sector	Informal producers Local users	Informal producers Local users Cultural elite Scholars Philanthropists	Informal producers Local users Cultural elite Scholars Philanthropist	Informal producers Local users Cultural elite Scholars Philanthropist Real estate investors Land and property owners Formal entrepreneurs Households Interested individuals Tourists
	Third sector		Civil-society organizations International organisations	Civil-society organizations International organisations NGOs Community organisations	Civil-society organizations International organisations NGOs Community organisations

Source: author elaboration based on Rojas and de Moura Castro (1999) and Rojas (2002).

Other stakeholders may favour or reject the conservation of the heritage depending on the circumstances. This is the case of neighbourhood associations that promote the heritage designation of their neighbourhoods as a mechanism to safeguard their ways of life threatened by predatory real estate developments. Local users of the heritage area may favour conservation activities that improve the accessibility and quality of public spaces in the heritage area, thus improving their use experience; but they can also oppose the conservation effort if they feel that it expels traders and service providers that cater for their needs. Moving undecided or opposing stakeholders into supporting the conservation effort – or at least into passive tolerance – depends on the type of conservation interventions and the measures to mitigate the ill-effects of the conservation on them. One case in point is allowing property owners and real estate investors to adapt heritage buildings to contemporary uses – including the addition of modern amenities – that greatly contribute to the acceptance of the conservation process among this group of stakeholders.

Two stakeholder-related aspects are also significant: the extent of the stakeholders' permanent interests in the heritage site and the resources – political support, technical expertise and financial – that they commit to the task. In the first dimension, it is useful to distinguish three classes of stakeholder. *Core stakeholders* include individuals, groups or institutions that are fully and permanently invested in the urban heritage site. *Committed stakeholders* have a specific concern for the heritage area, thus being devoted to the site, alas, only temporarily. *Peripheral stakeholders* have a marginal interest in the urban heritage area and only make sporadic contributions. The second dimension focuses on the stakeholders' contributions to the conservation process. Three classes of stakeholders are of interest: *promoters* of the preservation of the heritage site; *financers* supplying the resources needed to actively conserve heritage; and *beneficiaries*, those who receive the flows of benefits. In addition to beneficiaries of the conservation process, there are also stakeholders who suffer some sense of loss as a result of the conservation process. This is the case of low-income renters impacted by the gentrification of a heritage area. Individual stakeholders can fit into one or several of these above-listed categories depending on roles that they play in the conservation process.[3]

Rojas (2012) argues that the sustainability of the conservation process increases when there is ample presence of core and committed stakeholders who simultaneously play the roles of promoters, financiers and beneficiaries. A major advantage of the third stage is that there are a variety of social actors engaged in the process as either core or committed stakeholders acting as promoters and financers and directly receiving the benefits.

The pre-eminence of local actors

Under the paradigm of the third stage in the evolution of the conservation process, the majority of the stakeholders involved are local actors. They include local government, land and property owners, formal and informal entrepreneurs, residents, local users and community organisations. In market economies, local stakeholders and those who are attracted to live and invest in the heritage areas provide the bulk of the resources that go into the adaptive rehabilitation and conservation of the heritage buildings. The government – national, regional or local – does not have sufficient resources to rehabilitate or conserve an entire urban heritage area, no matter how committed. Local stakeholders also bear the bulk of the costs of the conservation of the heritage in the form of restrictions to the use of their properties in their present condition or as the opportunity cost of not being able to develop them to the best and highest use demanded in the real estate market. Furthermore, the residents and local users bear the negative effects of the conservation process on their quality of life – particularly the lack of modern urban amenities – although in cities of the developing world, the historic centres have better basic infrastructure than the poor neighbourhoods of the city.[4] Local community organisations are often the driving force in promoting the conservation of the material heritage of their neighbourhoods, mostly to avoid undesirable developments that threaten their quality of life.

The arguments presented in the previous section substantiate the assertion that even in the cases when other stakeholders lead the conservation process (the national or regional government or an organisation of the civil society), there is the need to work in close consultation with local stakeholders incorporating their views in the planning and implementation of the interventions. Contrary to what is common in the first and second stages – characterised by top-down decisions imposed on the local stakeholders – the governance process in the third stage needs to rest on widely subscribed agreements on what to conserve and by which means.

What to conserve and why: the foundation of the structures of authority to guide the conservation process

Identifying the values of the urban heritage

What to conserve in an urban area depends on its heritage values. Heritage sites can hold a multiplicity of values. A building can be the place where historic events took place, thus having historic value for the community and scientific value for historians. Additionally, the same building can be an outstanding example of the architecture of a given period, thus holding also aesthetic values for art historians in addition to its scientific value. Also, a building can be a landmark in the city or neighbourhood holding a symbolic value for the community. If the building is a place of prayer, it may hold religious values for some members of the community. Similarly, a historic centre can be an example of the way cities were built and by preserving its original features gains historic and scientific value.[5] Also significant is the authenticity of what exists in these urban heritage areas – a quality that becomes a value.[6]

Two interrelated processes enhance the appreciation of the socio-cultural values of the heritage: scholarly research in the form of studies by historians, art historians, sociologists, anthropologists and specialists in other related fields and the dissemination of this knowledge through the education system, the mass media and the open discussion in the communities. Awareness about the socio-cultural values of the urban heritage drives the formation of its economic use values. Well-grounded knowledge on the significance of the socio-cultural values contributes to building the agreement among members of the community on the need to conserve the urban heritage and, in turn, the motivation for the government's concern for the economic non-use values of existence and bequest. In many cities of advanced market economies, urban heritage areas are attractive for segments of the real estate market that attach significance to their historic, aesthetic or symbolic values and are prepared to pay a premium to live, work or trade there. Moreover, a great majority of the urban heritage areas in large and medium-sized cities enjoy exceptionally good locations in relation to the city's concentrations of high quality employment and services when they themselves do not concentrate these activities.

The importance assigned to the socio-cultural and economic use values of the heritage would naturally differ among stakeholders. Some will consider one value more significant than the other and most will differ on the combination of values they assign to a given building or public space. This lack of coincidence is unavoidable and may not be too damaging as long as it does not lead to insurmountable conflicts. The recognition of the multiple values strengthens the unity of the social actors favouring its conservation and putting the heritage properties to contemporary uses provides avenues for the pro-development stakeholders to obtain returns from their properties at the time they comply with the conservation regulations.

The urban heritage: a liability or a development asset?

Many developing countries are still in the first stage of the evolution of the conservation of the urban heritage, notwithstanding that in the last decades of the twentieth century there was an increase in the number of countries that moved to the second phase. The most common actions in the second stage of the process are for the government to set up specialised institutions to identify monuments, declare them under protection and enforce legislation to ensure that the existence and bequest values of the listed heritage are preserved. The responsibility of the conservation of the heritage in private hands is left to its owners, essentially by requiring them to conserve the properties and allowing only the modifications and uses dictated by the official institutions. In addition, the conservation regulations charge the government with the responsibility of maintaining public heritage properties. This approach turns the urban heritage into an *urban and financial liability* for the property owners and communities who see their opportunities of developing the buildings and lands of the heritage area restricted (usually outside what is financially viable) and force spending scarce public resources for the up-keep of the public monuments (Rojas 2012).

In the third phase of the urban heritage conservation process, the volume and stability of the resources devoted to the conservation of the urban heritage increases with the diversification of the social actors interested in the conservation of the variety of values of the urban heritage, in particular, by the materialisation of the economic use values that emerge from allowing the adaptive rehabilitation of the properties for contemporary uses. Under these conditions, the urban heritage turns into an *asset for the social and economic development* of the communities, allowing the design and implementation of more inclusive and sustainable preservation and development processes (Rojas 2012).

The shared vision for the urban heritage area

A critical condition to coordinate the activities of a community towards the conservation of their urban heritage is that their members agree on *what* to conserve and *why*. It is necessary for the stakeholders – whose interests might collide in very fundamental ways – to agree on a common vision for the future of the heritage area. This agreement legitimises instituting structures of authority to control the activities of the social actors, coordinate their contributions and sustain a strong commitment on the communities to allocate public resources to the task. The agreed vision provides the foundations for the formulation and enactment of a conservation plan, the legal instrument authorising the government to intervene. In reaching these agreements, the communities would greatly benefit from the use of methodologies long developed by strategic city planning (Fernández Güell 1997). The stakeholders would find common grounds – or at least solid basis for compromise – in the more flexible approach to conservation used in the third stage that promotes the adaptive rehabilitation of the heritage properties within their *carrying capacity*: that is, adapting them to contemporary uses while preserving the characteristics that give them their heritage value.[7]

Structures of authority for conserving the urban heritage

The city development plan and the conservation
of the urban heritage

To turn the shared vision about the future of the urban heritage area into collective action, it is necessary to develop structures of authority to control and coordinate the actions of the different social actors. There are *soft* (non-legally binding) and *hard* (mandatory) structures of authority. The practice of conservation has many soft structures of authority in the form of the accumulated knowledge in the practitioners and the guidelines and recommendations included in the numerous charters and conventions adopted by the international and national conservation associations. They provide guidance but they are not legally binding for the social actors. They are not discussed in detail in this work, which will focus on the hard and formal structures of authority.[8]

The most common form of hard structure of authority is the heritage conservation regulations applied on urban heritage areas when they are declared under protection by the conservation boards or other government agencies that, in most cases, are under the supervision of cultural institutions of the national government. These are the tools of choice of the second stage of evolution in the governance of the conservation of the urban heritage and are typically enforced by national or regional entities quite removed from the day-to-day management of the city. Commonly, local stakeholders are not consulted in the design of the regulations that, in most cases, strive to conserve the urban heritage, allowing little room for adaptation to contemporary needs. Furthermore, these regulations are usually poorly coordinated with the city's urban development plans that are the responsibility of the local governments.

In moving to the third stage, the governance of the process requires hard structures of authority that are accepted by the social actors. These structures are akin to a *social contract* where all actors willingly accept the authority that controls and coordinates their activities. The heritage conservation regulations are more likely to be obeyed by the social actors if they are designed and approved with their full involvement and when they reflect the agreements they reached concerning the future of the heritage area. Additionally, for the regulations to be effective, the social actors must trust the technical capacity and probity of the institutions charged with the formulation and enforcement of these structures of authority.

In the urban field, the most significant structure of authority that guides the urban development process is the city development plan whose role in market economies is 'to intervene in market processes to achieve certain broader aims' (Newman and Thornley 1996: 4). A democratically approved plan is a social contract that spells out the community's long-term objectives for the city and the means to attain them. There is ample experience of conflicts in implementing conservation regulations when designed and enforced by cultural institutions removed from the management of the city. The conservation of the urban heritage would be better served if the pertinent regulations and implementation mechanisms were part of the city development plan and its investment proposals; that is, they make a *conservation component* of the city development plan. A well-defined and democratically approved heritage conservation component in the city development plan also provides prospective investors in the heritage areas with a stable regulatory environment that reduces the uncertainties that emerge when the decisions are made by national institutions and often on 'ad-hoc' basis.

Frequently, cities do not have efficient structures of authority and institutions to coordinate and control the activities of the different stakeholders to ensure the attainment of socially acceptable goals defined in a democratically approved conservation component of a city development plan. It is common in developing countries – and in some developed countries as well – that the decision-making process concerning the management of urban development is opaque and plagued with corrupted practices. In these circumstances, developers tend to have the upper hand over the concerns of the conservation groups or the communities in obtaining planning approval for projects that may violate the conservation regulations. It is also common that the penalties for non-compliance with the plan are either insignificant or hard to enforce having little deterrent effect on determined landowners or land developers. Preventing the loss of heritage under these circumstances is hard and contentious. Lacking voluntary cooperation to comply with the plan on the part of landowners and real estate developers, pressure from the local communities and advocacy groups with presence in the mass media may move elected and designated officials in the local government to stop such practices. The sad reality is that there are many countries where these pressure mechanisms rarely work and frequently significant pieces of the urban heritage are lost to speculative and predatory real estate projects. In the best of circumstances – that is, when there is awareness about the values of the heritage, an explicit agreement on the conservation measures among stakeholders and flexibility in the regulatory framework to allow the adaptive rehabilitation of the heritage assets – the opportunities for profitable adaptation of the urban heritage to new uses may mitigate the pressures exercised by predatory developers to demolish heritage properties in order to put the land to its highest and most profitable (short-term) uses.

The urban heritage conservation component of the city development plan

The heritage conservation component of the city development plan defines the physical limits of the urban areas containing heritage values and that are subject to conservation, and the planning and conservation regulations establishing the level of protection required by the buildings and public spaces of the area. Additionally, the plan establishes the procedures for reviewing and approving adaptive rehabilitation proposals affecting them, the incentives and support provided by the government to induce or facilitate compliance by the stakeholders with the conservation regulations and the legal and financial consequences of non-compliance.

When heritage areas suffer from abandonment due to functional or physical obsolescence, the plan also needs to include the actions required to revitalise the areas, including improvements in infrastructures and public spaces, better accessibility and improved urban services. In the cases when the heritage area deteriorates due to over-use by unsuitable uses, the plan needs to include the actions required to re-establish a sustainable equilibrium between uses and the area's capacity to accommodate urban activities. The need to address these issues is the reason for my assertion that the planning and implementation process for the conservation of urban heritage areas should combine the concepts and methods of historic conservation with those of urban rehabilitation (Rojas 2012).

Gentrification: the displacement of vulnerable groups and the loss of diversity

Urban heritage areas under active rehabilitation tend to become attractive to new uses and users. Gentrification – the expulsion of existing in habitants and users (mostly vulnerable groups) by newcomers – is a common occurrence that is difficult to prevent and may only be mitigated with government interventions. Two groups are particularly vulnerable: households and craft persons renting low-cost housing or production space in deteriorated heritage buildings and informal street traders that are displaced by the rehabilitation of public spaces. The conservation component of the city development plan needs to contain mitigation measures for gentrification; principally, the provision of affordable rental space for low-income households and craft persons and facilities for informal traders to continue operating – hopefully more efficiently and profitably – in the rehabilitated public spaces.

Another trend observable in urban heritage areas undergoing active rehabilitation is the loss of diversity as the gentrification process takes hold. The most profitable uses tend to displace others, making the area lose a variety of uses and users, a phenomenon that occurs when:

> the winners in the competition for space will represent only a narrow segment of the many uses that together created success. Whichever one or few uses have emerged as the most profitable in the locality will be repeated and repeated, crowding out and overwhelming the less profitable forms of use.
>
> (Jacobs 1961: 243)

The conservation component of the city development plan needs to acknowledge this trend and mitigate its most damaging effects. Possible measures include set allocations of space for given uses (for instance, bars and restaurants whose profitability per square metre exceeds most other urban activities) or protection measures (for instance, reduced patents or real estate taxes) for uses needed by the community (corner stores, laundry shops and hardware stores) to prevent them from exiting the urban heritage area.

Heritage conservation regulations in the city development plan

The conservation regulations are important determinants of the capacity of the heritage properties to take on contemporary activities. The level of protection assigned to a property that must fit within its carrying capacity imposes a limit on its ability to accommodate new activities. The common practice in countries that are still in the second stage of evolution in the governance of the conservation process is to apply the same level of protection to all buildings and public spaces in the designated urban heritage area. This approach greatly reduces the opportunities for adaptive rehabilitation. In the third stage, conservation regulations must carefully discriminate among the heritage properties to apply the necessary levels of protection. Full conservation preventing any alterations and allowing only restoration work is required only for outstanding monuments holding such a variety of socio-cultural values that they cannot be altered without losing some or several of them. In most urban heritage areas, there are usually a small number of properties requiring such a high degree of protection. For monuments of significance that do not fall in the previous category, the regulations should allow minor changes to facilitate the new uses. The rest of the buildings and public spaces – that in most urban heritage areas are the majority of the properties – need an intermediate level of protection.

Five general levels of conservation are commonly used lying on a continuum, from the *full conservation* required by monuments of significance at one end to *contextual restrictions* imposed on new construction to fit into the cityscape of the heritage site at the other. The intermediate levels of conservation include *rigorous*, *typological* or *contextual* conservation and they allow greater degrees of freedom for the adaptive rehabilitation of the heritage properties. Table 13.2 contains a synthesis of the different types of conservation, the interventions allowed in each type and the heritage properties likely to benefit from this level of conservation. They are particularly important for properties whose main contribution to the heritage are as examples of a particular building typology, that is 'any group of buildings with some characteristics, or a series of characteristics in common' (Caniggia and Maffei 2001: 52). The regulations can allow modifications to the interior design as long as they maintain the characteristics that define the typology.[9]

Table 13.2 Guidelines for determining the type of protection required by urban heritage assets

Type of conservation	Permitted interventions	Type of urban heritage assets
Full conservation	Full preservation of existing features. In qualified cases, reconstruction	Monuments of international, national, regional, and local importance
Rigorous conservation	Minor adaptive interventions	Monuments, emblematic buildings, and public spaces, the most significant features of which require preservation to retain their socio-cultural values
Typological conservation	Adaptive interventions within clearly established design guidelines	Buildings and public spaces that are authentic expressions of a typology. Adaptive rehabilitation interventions must retain the key characteristics of the type (bulk, inner courtyards, gables, facade features, etc.)
Contextual conservation	Adaptive interventions may change the interior distribution and uses of the buildings	Buildings that contribute to the urban landscape of the heritage area. Adaptive rehabilitation interventions must retain the characteristics of the type that contributes to the urban landscape (bulk, facade, roof)
Contextual new construction	New construction conforming to design guidelines	Empty lots or irrecoverable ruins. New buildings can be erected following strict design guidelines that ensure that the new construction is compatible with the heritage of the area

Source: author elaboration based on Rojas (2014).

In these cases, the regulations could allow significant internal modifications and additions as long as they do not make the properties lose the characteristics that are their contribution to the heritage character of the urban area.

The development of the empty lots in an urban heritage area provides opportunities to attract new residents and users offering developed space with modern amenities. Unused government land offers the city an opportunity to build new urban amenities that would make the area more attractive. Contemporary buildings can be inserted in urban heritage areas without major conflicts if their bulk, alignment and facades adjust to the urban context and contribute to the richness of the cityscape.

Institutional arrangements for implementing the conservation component of the city plan

Controlling and coordinating the activities of stakeholders

The implementation of the conservation component of the city plan needs two types of institutional arrangements. First, institutions capable of controlling the activities of the stakeholders so that they align with the long-term vision agreed for the heritage area and comply with the adaptive rehabilitation regulations included in the plan. Second, institutional structures capable of promoting the cooperation among the stakeholders so that they pool their resources – knowledge, skills, financing – effectively and ideally become joint partners in the sustainable conservation of the urban heritage area.

Cities with a strong institutional structure for urban management can rely on the development control section of their planning offices to oversee compliance with the conservation component of the city development plan. However, the control of development in a heritage area under the approach suggested in this chapter requires delicate negotiations with developers concerning technical issues that are significantly different from the regular decisions involved in the implementation of standard regulations applied to new buildings. This fact prompts many cities to establish dedicated sections in the planning offices to manage the heritage areas. They concentrate the city government's technical expertise on urban heritage conservation with the capacity to review, comment and negotiate adaptive rehabilitation proposals put forward by landowners and developers. As the approval of these initiatives often needs waivers from other city departments – environmental control, health or fire protection – the heritage offices often act as unified windows to process all the approvals required from the city.

Cities lacking a strong institutional structure for urban planning and development control may have to adopt ad-hoc arrangements. An effective strategy is to designate the urban heritage areas as *special districts* and establish dedicated administrative units to manage all city-related business in these districts. Special districts tend to be dysfunctional with the bureaucratic structure of city governments and can create internal frictions. Strong support from the major and the elected officials is a way to minimise these problems. The downside of this high-profile support for the agency is that it makes it vulnerable to the volatility of city politics.[10]

In deteriorated urban heritage areas – either due to abandonment or to over-utilisation – there is the need to coordinate the activities of private and public agents to reverse the deterioration process. The decisions of all the individual actors are affected by the decisions of the others creating a coordination issue that if not solved can lead to paralysis. Although all property owners would benefit by the adaptive rehabilitation of their properties for contemporary uses with demand in the markets, the returns on their investment diminish due to the deteriorated state of the surrounding properties. From the point of view of the property owner, it is more convenient to be the last to invest, obtaining higher rents from the start and avoiding the risk that the area will not rehabilitate.

A review of successful experiences in the rehabilitation of deteriorated urban areas indicates that an institutional structure capable of promoting cooperation among stakeholders needs to satisfy the following set of conditions:

- Provide assurances to the stakeholders that the sequencing of public and private actions agreed in the plan would take place as planned.
- Channel the actions of the different stakeholders into the types of activities for which they have the greatest comparative advantage: entrepreneurs opening new business, private developers undertaking real estate investments, the government improving the infrastructure and public spaces in addition to providing a stable regulatory environment and expedient review and approval of development proposals.
- Assign the risks inherent in urban heritage conservation to those who are best suited to handle them and who have the most interest in assuming these risks in view of the potential benefits that they might generate.

The financing arrangements must be capable of enabling all those involved in contributing in proportion to the benefits received and in accordance with their particular interests (Rojas 2004).

One institutional arrangement that performs these tasks is public–private partnerships (PPPs), where the *private partner* encompasses not only the private developer or construction partner but also the numerous private property owners and users (Amirtahmasebi 2010). Cheong (2014) distinguishes between *weak* and *strong partnerships* depending on their governance structure. A weak partnership exists when the majority of decision rights, risks, costs and responsibilities are concentrated in one partner within the partnership and strong partnerships when these are shared amongst partners. The author stresses that these classifications are not evaluative interpretations of a partnership's success or failure, but instead they highlight the importance of the power-sharing structure in these institutional arrangements. Moreover, Cheong (2014: 13) stresses that

a weak PPP may be highly effective in economic conditions with limited access to stable markets, while a strong PPP may be ineffective if the partners are unable to effectively tolerate and share the necessary amounts of risk or responsibility.

This author indicates that mixed-capital companies more correctly align the interests of the different stakeholders. They are increasingly used for financing and managing the risks and responsibilities in urban regeneration projects – particularly those that channel public and private resources.

Financing the conservation of the urban heritage

The heritage conservation component of the city development plan should specify the sources of funds for implementing the different interventions including the resources to finance the compensations that are due to the stakeholders affected by the heritage conservation proposals. The financing arrangements must be capable of enabling all those involved to contribute in proportion to the benefits received and in accordance with their particular interests. Following the traditional public finance theory, taxpayer funds would pay for public goods and urban infrastructures and the funds of real estate developers would finance profit-making investments. The financing arrangements must also open opportunities for private philanthropic institutions or individuals to find investment niches that satisfy their charitable and public relations objectives.

In the conservation of the urban heritage, there is a role for transfers among levels of government or between the government and private stakeholders. A well-conserved urban heritage area that is declared of interest for the community has an element of a public good. All members of the community can enjoy the conserved urban structure of the area, the harmony of the streetscape and the beauty of the architectural pieces that it contains and access to their enjoyment cannot be restricted or made subject to payment of any sort. When this is the case, it makes sense that the national or regional government that declared the area as protected heritage contribute to its conservation, transferring resources to the local government for its upkeep or to compensate private property owners for the extra expenses incurred in rehabilitating and maintaining the heritage properties according to the standards set by the conservation plan.

The financing mechanisms should allocate funds to compensate the individuals or groups negatively affected by the interventions. These can range from direct monetary compensations for loss of fair market value of the properties to allowances for the transfer of unused development rights in the conserved properties. The counterbalance of these entitlements is the capture by the city government of the increase in value of the properties due to government interventions. Part of this value can be captured through real estate taxes, betterment levies or capital gains taxes (Ingram and Hong 2012; Smolka 2013).

In many developing countries, cities do not have significant taxation capacity nor are they able to effectively collect all the taxes. This makes tax-based instruments less effective. Cities facing this problem must rely on higher-level government transfers to finance their conservation-related investments. Lower per capita income and under-developed financial markets reduce the demand for rehabilitated space in general, and in particular, in urban heritage areas where private investment faces greater uncertainties compared with greenfield developments in the expansion areas of the cites. This fact imposes a greater burden on the local government to initiate and sustain the urban heritage conservation process in the hope that private investors, households and local users will participate in the near future.

Summaries and conclusion

The analysis shows the relevance of the governance issues for the implementation of a values-based urban heritage conservation approach centred on the adaptive rehabilitation of urban heritage sites to uses with community-relevant, social or market demand. The discussion highlighted the advantages of this approach for the sustainable conservation of urban heritage areas and the operational and institutional complexities involved in managing the interests and contributions of an expanded and diversified set of core and committed stakeholders interested in taking advantage of the economic use values of the site. This operates in parallel and often cooperating with stakeholders promoting the conservation of the wide range of socio-cultural values held by urban heritage areas. The analysis substantiates the need for efficient structures of authority and institutions to control and coordinate the interventions of the expanded set of stakeholders to ensure that they contribute to attaining the conservation goals defined in a democratically approved plan. Furthermore, it argued that the best setting for the structures of authority is within the city development plan and its implementing agencies. The study also advocates for establishing mixed public–private institutional arrangements to coordinate the contributions of the different stakeholders and allocate their inputs (financial, knowledge and implementation capacity) to the activities where they can contribute the most to the social objective of conserving the heritage on a sustainable basis.

The analysis highlighted two general rules that improve the chances of the urban heritage conservation process to coordinate effectively the efforts of all the stakeholders. The institutional arrangements must always be capable of assigning the different tasks involved in the conservation effort to the stakeholders best capable of handling them. In addition, they should promote close public–private cooperation in sharing the costs and benefits of the conservation process – a strategy that can overcome the limitations of pure government intervention (lack of resources to conserve all the urban heritage) and of elite-driven interventions (sporadic intervention efforts focused on monuments).

The analysis documented the significance of six factors for the governance of the urban heritage preservation process.

1   The diversity of the socio-cultural and economic-use values that are the drivers of the efforts of the community to preserve urban heritage sites;
2   The diversity of stakeholders involved in the process including public, private and third-sector actors;
3   The commitment of the stakeholders to the heritage area, whether they have permanent or intermittent interests in the site;

4   The roles played by the stakeholders in the preservation process, whether they act as promoters, financiers or beneficiaries or different combinations of them;

5   The institutional arrangements that coordinate the contributions of the different stakeholders, particularly by promoting public–private cooperation and the sharing of costs and benefits;

6   The social validity of the structures of authority and institutions that regulate private investments and allocate public resources.

The study encourages all parties involved in the design and implementation of a conservation programme for an urban heritage area to pay attention to these factors and design governance structures that promote the materialisation of the whole spectrum of values held by the urban heritage areas, and in addition, to allow all stakeholders to become core actors in the process, contributing to the promotion and financing of the programmes and becoming direct beneficiaries.

The government must place the urban heritage conservation governance mechanisms firmly within the city's urban development governance institutions. In governance contexts with weak structures of authority and limited institutions, a possible solution is to establish strong ad-hoc dedicated management arrangements for urban heritage areas designated as special districts. Although this is an extreme method to deal with the governance weakness of some cities, it finds justification in the fact that urban heritage properties when lost cannot be replaced.

Notes

1   This analysis centres on the material heritage of cities. Whenever relevant, the text will mention the different forms of human and social capital of cities.

2   David Throsby (2012) provides detailed definitions for all these socio-cultural and economic values.

3   For instance, a local government (municipality or district) can be a promoter of the preservation process when it is lobbying the regional or national governments for listing a heritage site and for securing resources for its upkeep. The same entity will be a financing stakeholder if it contributes resources to the preservation effort. Similarly, a community can be just a passive beneficiary of the preservation effort if the process is led by other stakeholders and financed by yet another group. Conversely, more proactive communities can act as promoters of the conservation efforts and, if they contribute, they will also adopt the role of a financing stakeholder.

4   A case in point is the provision of parks, playgrounds and other recreational amenities demanded by the households. These are very limited in historic centres and local residents are forced to live with a diminishing supply of these amenities, at least in relation to the upscale suburban areas. Another example is the vehicular access to the heritage areas. Local users of these areas find it difficult to reach their destinations by car due to congestion on the usually narrow streets and lack of parking facilities. This also puts traders and entrepreneurs of the heritage areas at a disadvantage in comparison with their counterparts in new shopping districts and malls in the periphery.

5   Good examples are the historic centres of Latin American cities established during the Spanish colonial rule. They were laid out using a similar and well-defined urban

structure based on a gridiron pattern of streets that creates regular city blocks within which the most significant urban uses (government offices, churches, convents, universities, army barracks, jail, etc.) are placed in similar pre-determined locations and the distribution of residential lots in all cities followed similar rules related to the social position of the residents (CEHOPU-CEDEX 1997).

6 The factors taken into consideration by UNESCO to include historic centres in the World Heritage List reflect this approach, as there is a pre-eminence of the socio-cultural historic and aesthetic values of the heritage in the set leading to listing the historic centres (UNESCO 2015).

7 Obviously, the adaptive potential of these properties would always be less – in terms of developable square metres – than new construction developed at the maximum allowed by the local land use and building regulations. Tung (2001) extensively discusses these conflicts in his analysis of the politics of preservation in New York.

8 A recent US ICOMOS Symposium, 'The Venice Chart After Fifty', held on 2–3 April 2014, cosponsored by The Graduate Program in Historic Preservation of the School of Design at the University of Pennsylvania, reviewed the evolution of the concepts and practice of historic conservation through the analysis of the many documents adopted by international organisations since the formulation of the Venice Charter in 1964. The works discussed at the Symposium are published in a special issue of the journal *Change Over Time*, 4.2, Fall, 2014. Available at: http://cot.pennpress.org/home/ (accessed 1 July 2015).

9 The one- or two-storey and three-yard-structured urban manor house is another widespread building type in Latin America. This building type is typically constructed with adobe walls and tile roofs, adobe and tile being the prevailing construction materials in most geographical locations. As a rule, this house type was designed to have numerous rooms, with undifferentiated uses (with the possible exception of the salon or dining room, two spaces that were always larger and outfitted with better finishes than were the rest of the rooms). These urban manor houses all share a similar arrangement of spaces: the family's commercial activities around the front yard, the private rooms group around the second yard and the services, situated in direct relation to the orchard and the water canal for irrigation and disposal of waste, which runs along the end of the city lot, in the third yard.

10 Cities in developing countries confronted with the need to control development in sensitive urban heritage areas often resort to international assistance to bring into the process the necessary expertise but also to provide more stability to the ad-hoc institutional arrangements that act as the counterparts of the international technical experts.

References

Amirtahmasebi, R. (2010). *Public–Private Partnerships in Urban Regeneration and Cultural Heritage Projects*. Washington, D.C.: The World Bank.

Bandarin, F. and van Oers, R. (2012). *The Historic Landscape. Managing Heritage in an Urban Century*. Chichester: Wiley-Blackwell.

Bell, S. (ed.) (2002). *Economic Governance and Institutional Dynamics*. Melbourne: Oxford University Press.

Caniggia, J.F. and G.L. Maffei. (2001). *Architectural Composition and Building Typology. Interpreting Basic Building*. Florence: Alinea.

CEHOPU-CEDEX. (1997). *La Ciudad Hispanoamericana: El Sueño de un Orden*. Madrid: Centro de Estudios de Obras Públicas y Urbanismo (CEHOPU) y Centro de Estudios de Experimentación de Obras Púbicas (CEDEX).

Cheong, C. (2014). Instruments for urban regeneration: mixed capital companies. Unpublished paper. Philadelphia: Historic Preservation Program, School of Design, University of Pennsylvania.

Fernández Güell, J.M. (1997). *Planificación Estratégica de Ciudades.* Barcelona: Editorial Gustavo Gili.

Glaeser, E. (2011). *The Triumph of the City.* New York: Penguin.

Ingram, G. and Hong, Y. (eds) (2012). *Value Capture and Land Policy.* Boston: Lincoln Institute of Land Policy.

Jacobs, J. (1961). *The Death and Life of Great American Cities.* New York: Vintage Books.

Licciardi, G. and Amirtahmasebi, R. (eds) (2012). *The Economics of Uniqueness: Investing in Historic Cores and Cultural Heritage Assets for Sustainable Development.* Washington, D.C.: The World Bank.

Newman, P. and Thornley, A. (1996). *Urban Planning in Europe: International Competition, National Systems, and Planning Projects.* London: Routledge.

Peacock, A. (ed.) (1998). *Does the Past Have a Future?* London: Institute of Economic Affairs.

Peacock, A. and Rizzo, I. (2008). *The Heritage Game; Economics, Policy and Practice.* Oxford: Oxford University Press.

Rojas, E. (2002). *Urban Heritage Conservation in Latin America and the Caribbean: A Task for All Social Actors.* Washington, D.C.: Inter-American Development Bank. Available at: http://publications.iadb.org/handle/11319/1163?scope=123456789/1&thumbnail=false&order=desc&rpp=5&sort_by=score&page=4&group_by=none&etal=0&filter type_0=author&filter_0=Rojas%2C+Eduardo&filter_relational_operator_0=equals (accessed 1 July 2015).

Rojas, E. (2004). *Volver al Centro: La Recuperación de Áreas Urbanas Centrales.* Washington, D.C.: Banco Interamericano de Desarrollo.

Rojas, E. (2012). Governance in historic city core regeneration projects. In: G. Licciardi and R. Amirtahmasebi (eds), *The Economics of Uniqueness: Investing in Historic Cores and Cultural Heritage Assets for Sustainable Development.* Washington, D.C.: The World Bank, pp. 143–81.

Rojas, E. and de Moura Castro, C. (1999). *Lending for Urban Heritage Conservation: Issues and Opportunities*, Document SOC-105. Washington, D.C.: Inter-American Development Bank. Available at: http://www.iadb.org/en/publications/publication-detail,7101.html?id=4534&dcLanguage=en&dcType=Technical%20Notes&doctype=&docTypeID=AllPublic&searchLang=&keywords=Rojas%20and%20Moura%20Castro&selectList=All&topicDetail=0&tagDetail=0&jelcodeDetail=0&publicationCover=0 (accessed 1 July 2015).

Smolka, M. (2013). *Implementing Value Capture in Latin America: Policies and Tools for Urban Development.* Boston: Lincoln Institute of Land Policy.

Throsby, D. (2007). Overview of heritage and economics: some basic concepts. In: M. Martinez, F. Descamps and K. Louw (eds), *Proceedings. World Congress of the Organization of World Heritage Cities.* Kazan, Russian Federation, 19–23 June 2009. Los Angeles: The Getty Conservation Institute.

Throsby, D. (2010). *The Economics of Cultural Policy.* Cambridge: Cambridge University Press.

Throsby, D. (2012). Heritage economics: a conceptual approach. In: G. Licciardi and R. Amirtahmasebi (eds), *The Economics of Uniqueness: Investing in Historic Cores and*

Cultural Heritage Assets for Sustainable Development. Washington, D.C.: The World Bank, pp. 45–73.

Tung, A. (2001). *Preserving the World's Great Cities: The Destruction and Renewal of the Historic Metropolis*. New York: Three Rivers Press.

United Nations Educational, Scientific and Cultural Organization (UNESCO) (2015). *UNESCO World Heritage List*. Available at: http://whc.unesco.org/en/list (accessed 26 January 2015).

Chapter 14

Whose heritage?

Conflicting narratives and top-down and bottom-up approaches to heritage management in Yangon, Myanmar

William Logan

Cultural heritage plays a key role in societies and cities undergoing dramatic political, economic and social change (Logan 2005–6, 2014a). At the most obvious level, cultural heritage places, objects and practices are economic assets that underlie job creation, income generation and local and national economies. Cultural heritage also underlies community, city and national identity and all governments intervene to protect it to a greater or lesser extent. Much government involvement in cultural heritage protection is politically motivated and, beyond safeguarding the heritage, can have other impacts, both benign and malign. National governments use cultural heritage as part of their nation-building strategies, encouraging the citizens to accept a common narrative of the nation's past and to join forces in developing the nation into the future. National governments use a World Heritage listing to gain global recognition of the national culture and successful inscription brings them political credit within the nation. At a more local level, city administrations use cultural heritage to promote the distinctiveness of their particular cities, increase their cities' visibility among would-be investors and developers and improve their cities' position on national and international city hierarchies.

Therefore, the protection of cultural heritage is not simply a technical matter, as some in the heritage conservation field have seen it, nor even merely about management technique (Logan 2013). It is a form of cultural politics, usually linked to ideological ways of seeing the world, and nearly always complex and contested. Heritage is what we make today of things surviving from the past. In this sense, heritage is about not the past, but the present and future. It is a mental construct that is formed as the result of processes that are essentially political in that they involve decision-making about scarce resources, are based on unequal power relations and distribute benefits unequally. Cultural heritage is used and misused, even abused by those with the power to do so. It can be used to manipulate people and governments commonly use it to shape public opinion or to try to weld disparate ethnic and social groups into more cohesive and harmonious national entities. These manipulative activities may be benign if they promote tolerant states and societies based on human rights. However, in too many cases, governments have used selective versions of the 'national cultural heritage' to force minority groups to adopt the dominant culture, effectively wiping out their own cultural identity, and to generate support for government aggression against neighbours or, indeed, in far-distant war zones.

Understood in this way, heritage interventions and the field of heritage studies always involve fundamental philosophical and ethical questions: Why are we protecting heritage? Which and whose heritage? Who does heritage protection benefit? Who gave authority to protect? Are the local people whose heritage is being 'protected' involved? Does the protection of local people's heritage acknowledge their cultural and other human rights? How does it fit with sustainability? Seen this way, cultural heritage and its protection plays a critically important social, economic and political role in nations, states and cities, especially those undergoing rapid transformation.

Rather than engaging local communities in meaningful ways, the processes of cultural heritage identification and management are most commonly top-down in character. Laurajane Smith (2006) has given the term 'authorised heritage discourse' (AHD) to the set of professional arguments and practices that support such top-down processes. Although this has become something of a buzz term among graduate students and scholars in heritage studies, it has certainly led to a growing interest in finding ways to break away from this top-down model and to develop and use bottom-up approaches. The impact of the AHD discourse on practitioners is less clear; indeed, a few scholars have expressed a concern that the AHD, as a symptom of over-theorisation of heritage studies, may lead to a widening gap between theory and practice (e.g. Witcomb and Buckley 2013).

Nevertheless, the AHD and top-down/bottom-up notions have been taken up by a number of global, national and local government heritage agencies. This can be seen, for example, in the work of UNESCO, the principal global heritage agency, through its World Heritage, Intangible Heritage and Memory of the World programmes. In 2003, the Dutch National Commission for UNESCO hosted a conference in Amsterdam on the theme of 'linking universal and local values' (see de Merode *et al.* 2004). An outcome of the conference was adoption of the view that heritage protection does not depend alone on top-down interventions by governments or the expert actions of heritage industry professionals but must involve local communities. UNESCO now argues that it is imperative that the values and practices of the local communities, together with traditional management systems, are fully understood, respected, encouraged and accommodated in management plans if the heritage resources are to be sustained into the future (de Merode *et al.* 2004: 9). These changes do not go far enough or fast enough according to the United Nations Permanent Forum on Indigenous Issues (UNPFII) (Logan 2014b). The world's indigenous peoples have learnt to make use of rights discourses in their bid to bring about change in the World Heritage system, notably through their insistence on free, prior and informed consent before their heritage places are nominated by States Parties to the World Heritage list. This is a clear example of the bottom wanting to reclaim stewardship of those places and reassert their way of life, dignity and identity.

As a vehicle for exploring the top-down versus bottom-up issue, this chapter uses a case study of heritage identification and management in the Southeast Asian state of Myanmar (Burma), a developing country that is undergoing transition from 50 years of extreme isolation under a military junta to more democratic governance and reconnection with the global economy. The chapter shows the existence of conflicting views of what heritage is significant within Myanmar and explores the reasons for this. As might be expected, wide differences can be seen between the authorised heritage of the national government, based in the capital Naypyidaw, and the unauthorised heritage of local communities. The complex and changing governance structure in Myanmar leads, however, to conflicting authorised heritage at regional and city levels. The chapter highlights the divergence between the national view of what is significant and that of Yangon (Rangoon), the former capital, still the largest city and a region in the current governance structure. In this respect, authorities in Yangon are effectively rejecting the top-down Naypyidaw narrative and proposing a different, bottom-up heritage.

The multi-ethnic character of Myanmar also leads to a variety of local unauthorised heritages. The chapter refers to efforts currently under way to draw the local into the national narrative (especially through a new intangible cultural heritage programme) and the Yangon counter-narrative (especially through work being done by the Yangon Heritage Trust to develop a conservation management plan that recognises the impacts of ethnic diversity on the city). This Myanmar case study shows that the AHD concept can be used in complex and conflicting ways within a single state and that a detailed understanding of governance, scale and time is required in order to come to terms with the full set of heritage hopes and projects in the context of a rapidly transforming city.

Rapid transformation of Myanmar and Yangon

Since 2011, the Myanmar nation, people and cities have been undergoing a rapid and fundamental transformation (Logan 2015). Most of the changes are for the good – the burgeoning democratisation processes, considerable freedom of the press, the return of land confiscated by the military and even a growing readiness to confront human rights issues – but they remain fragile and much depends on the outcome of the presidential election scheduled for November 2015. This is a critical event when Myanmar may move forward towards more democratic government or, if the hard-line conservative generals resurface, it may slide backwards into more repression and renewed isolation. The official Myanmar and Yangon narratives will reflect the result of the election and set a new context for heritage interpretation and protection in the country and city.

At the 2014 census Myanmar's largest city, Yangon, had a population of 5.2 million, compared with Naypyidaw's 1.15 million (Heijmans 2014). Although the capital city functions have been shifted over the past ten years from Yangon to the new capital city, Naypyidaw, Yangon remains the dominant population and economic centre. In fact, Yangon's time as the capital of the territory now called Myanmar was brief: it was a colonial capital from 1937 to 1948 and capital of the independent country from 1948 to 2005, a status it enjoyed until the military junta decided to create a new capital at Naypyidaw in November 2005. Nevertheless, while no longer the capital city, Yangon still has the aura of one and for many Myanmar citizens, particularly from among the Burman majority, it remains the country's emotional heart.

Yangon's physical heritage is largely built – ancient religious monuments and a late nineteenth- and early twentieth-century town plan and buildings located in today's downtown. The magnificent Shwedagon is the heritage centrepiece in its setting of hills and gardens, although the Sule Pagoda is an impressive feature of the downtown area. One of the very few positive effects of Myanmar's half-century of extreme isolation and trade and investment sanctions was the survival of Yangon's rich stock of late nineteenth- to early twentieth-century buildings. This colonial-era heritage is in desperate need of repair and since the re-opening of Myanmar to foreign capital investment and tourism, it faces a sudden surge in development pressure. Foreign investment is reported to have increased from over US$900 million in 2010 to a predicted US$5 billion in 2015 (*The Economist* 2015), while international tourist arrivals through Yangon have grown from 295,174 in 2011 to 803,014 in 2013 (Feng 2011; Zaw Win Than 2014).

Conflicting and contested narratives

The speed of change in Myanmar and Yangon means that President Thein Sein and both the national and Yangon city governments are currently eager to draw on the so-called developed countries for sources of advice on a full range of policy matters, including urban heritage management. Sensitive interventions are required on the part of foreign advisors if the country's and city's heritage elements and the rights of local communities are to be respected. Muddying the waters is the existence of two competing official narratives – one national and one restricted to Yangon – as well as numerous regional and local unofficial narratives that are largely based on ethnicity and that lead to different views about what cultural heritage elements are significant and why.

Ethnicity not only creates diverse heritages but also underlies the way in which Myanmar is governed. Myanmar officially recognises 135 ethnic groups within its total population of 54 million. The major ethnic groups are distributed in separate areas and they form the geographical basis of governance in the Union. The Burmans dominate demographically (two-thirds of total population) as well as economically and politically. They are concentrated in seven administrative units, called Regions (formerly Divisions), covering the Irrawaddy River valley and the coastal strips. Their historic homeland was in the central dry zone towards Mandalay and the new capital, Naypyidaw, and their language, Burmese, is of the Tibeto-Burman group. The Shan are the next largest group numerically and in terms of geographical spread. Their language is of the same group as Dai, Thai and Lao, although most Shan, apart from those in the extreme east, are now more closely allied to the Burmans and use Burmese. Shan State itself in fact houses eight ethnic groups – Shan, Wa, even Hmong around Lashio. The other six States with major ethnic groups can be seen in Figure 14.1: Mon, Kayin (Karen), Kayah, Kachin, Chin and

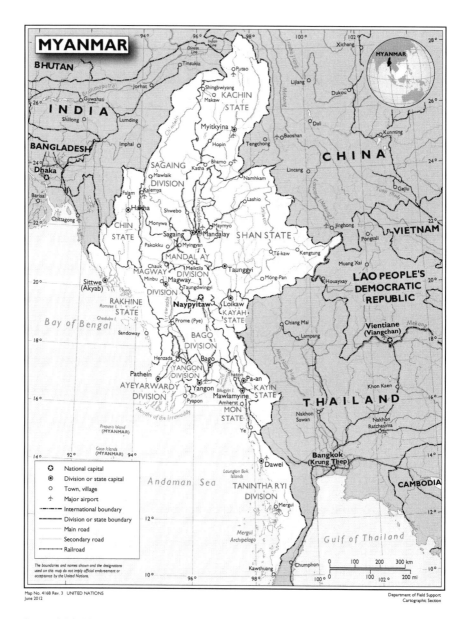

Figure 14.1 Map of Myanmar, June 2012 (courtesy of the UN; Map No. 4168 Rev.3, June 2012). Available at: http://www.un.org/Depts/Cartographic/map/profile/myanmar.pdf (accessed 1 July 2015).

Rakhine. The States and Regions, despite the terminology distinguishing histori-cally 'ethnic' states from majority Burman regions, are constitutionally equivalent (Nixon *et al.* 2013: 9).[1]

The clumsiness of Myanmar's official name – Republic of the Union of Myanmar – results from two long-held and continuing ambitions: rejection in 1948 of the British crown and Commonwealth status and the need to hold together seven Burman-dominated Regions and seven semi-autonomous ethnic minority-dominated States. In order to prevent the country's disintegration, the Myanmar government promotes a nation-building narrative that, although not overtly anti-colonial, calls upon all ethnic groups – usually referred to as 'nationalities' – to uphold a patriotic 'Union Spirit'. Nowhere is this better seen than in the National Museum of Myanmar in Yangon. The museum's lower floors showcase the national narrative with displays of the royal Lion Throne from Mandalay, regalia and other treasures from past Burman kingdoms and relics from Buddhist pago-das and monasteries, while displays of costumes and other artefacts produced by Myanmar's ethnic minorities are featured on the fourth floor. In one corner of the fourth floor is the 'Twelve National Objectives and Nation-Building Endeavours Showroom', which exhorts citizens to uphold 'true patriotism' (Figure 14.2). Alongside maps, diagrams and photographs of completed and proposed major infrastructure developments are lists of 'four political objectives', 'four eco-nomic objectives' and 'four social objectives'. The role of heritage in nation building is clearly seen in the social objective to 'uplift . . . national prestige and integrity and preservation and safeguarding of cultural heritage and national character' (Figure 14.3).

Figure 14.2 'True patriotism' notice at the entrance to the nation-building exhibition hall, National Museum of Myanmar.

Source: R. Mann.

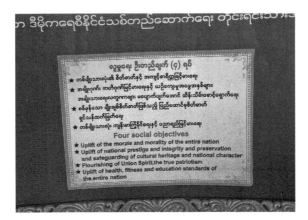

Figure 14.3 The 'four social objectives' of Myanmar's nation-building project.
Source: R. Mann.

One can argue that such overtness is advantageous: at least the official message is out there, clearly articulated for all citizens to hear, whereas in many countries the message lies buried, unstated and unchallenged. Of course, in Myanmar under the generals, the message is also not challenged: to challenge it openly would be construed as a rebellious and treasonable act. This makes the message no more than slogan making and divorced from nation building at the implementation level.

Across the Burman Regions, the generals have engaged in 'restoring' Buddhist archaeological structures and building new pagodas, as at Naypyidaw (Figure 14.4) and in the Shwedagon complex. While such activity has a basis in Buddhist merit making, some researchers have argued that such activities amounted to an appropriation by the military of the country's Buddhist heritage, undertaken to bolster the regime's legitimacy (see Philp and Mercer 2002; Than Than Nwe and Philp 2002; Philp 2010; Fong 2014: 35). Cut off from seeking best international advice, the reconstruction work by the Myanmar government at Bagan in the late 1990s to early 2000s was amateurish and damaged the heritage in ways that will cause difficulties when Myanmar submits the site for UNESCO World Heritage listing in the next few years (Fong 2014: 29–31).

The national narrative focused on the royal past and Buddhism operates as an authorised heritage discourse that is imposed on the country in a top-down manner. This focus is seen in the only piece of cultural heritage legislation existing in Myanmar, the Protection and Preservation of Cultural Heritage Regions Law, 1998, which is heavily oriented towards monuments of the Buddhist heritage, such as Bagan. Similarly Myanmar's World Heritage list nomination activity shows the same bias, as did its Tentative List until a revision in February 2014.[2]

Figure 14.4 Pagoda building for merit making, Uppatasanti pagoda, Naypyidaw, October 2013.

Source: W. Logan.

While it is perhaps paradoxical that a military regime with strong socialist leanings should have adopted such a focus on monarchy and Buddhism, this choice reflects Burman attitudes well and is a pragmatically useful one.[3] All governments cultivate narratives and make use of heritage for political purposes and it is understandable, given the multi-ethnic character of Myanmar, that its national government would do the same as a means to enhance social cohesion and ensure political stability. It is indeed praiseworthy, providing that the society and polity created are inclusive and respectful of ethnic minority cultures and provide the dignity they warrant under international human rights law, including the United Nations' Universal Declaration of Human Rights, whose adoption, by the way, Myanmar (then Burma) supported in 1948.

Regrettably, under the military regime, scant attention was paid to the political, economic and cultural rights of the ethnic minorities in the various states. Even with the liberalisation under President Thein since 2011, none of the current leaders, including opposition leader Aung San Suu Kyi, have yet spoken out in favour of protecting the cultures and cultural heritage of the ethnic minorities. The Protection and Preservation of Cultural Heritage Regions Law empowers the Department of Archaeology in the Ministry of Culture to run Myanmar's cultural heritage management system, a system that is both highly conservative in its approach and grossly under-resourced. The Law makes no reference to minority cultures, except by inference when it defines cultural heritage as ancient monuments or sites that require protection by reason of their historical, cultural, artistic or *anthropological* value (my emphasis). The cultural heritage of the ethnic minorities is essentially intangible rather than monumental but the Law makes no mention of intangible heritage or, indeed, of human or cultural rights. This has meant that the minorities have had to find other ways of safeguarding their heritage. The Shan, for instance, have established a network of Associations of Literature and Culture across Shan State and in Yangon and Mandalay that run cultural discussion groups and lobby for the teaching of Shan-language in schools and publication of appropriate teaching materials. Shan-language teacher training takes place in monastery premises under the guise of Buddhism courses. Civil society alternatives to government intervention in heritage matters have been less numerous and active in other states.

The situation changed in 2014 when the Myanmar government decided to move towards ratifying the Convention for the Safeguarding of the Intangible Cultural Heritage (UNESCO 2003). As a preliminary to ratification, a major national project began early in the year to identify, collect, catalogue and document the cultural practices of ethnic groups across all states of the Union. These moves in the intangible heritage field are immediately and fundamentally important. While not dismissing the powerful ethnic politics that underlies the Myanmar state and its functioning, my recent field research (November 2014) in Yangon, Mandalay and northern Shan State saw the potential of this project to open up new lines of dialogue between Myanmar's various ethnic groups and to strengthen human rights within the country. The UNESCO Bangkok Office has been giving support to the project, beginning with a national fieldwork workshop in Mandalay in May 2014, the same month that Myanmar formally ratified the convention. If the project is going to succeed, it will need to engage the local communities from the outset and throughout and extend from the identification and recording of cultural practices to their transmission to younger generations. So far, there appears to be little consideration of, or funding for, transmitting traditional skills through the education system, although the national Ministry of Education is collaborating with the Ministry of Culture to start teaching eight ethnic languages in relevant parts of the country in 2015 or 2016 (interview with U Nyi Moon, Director Department of Archaeology and National Museums, Lashio, 12 May 2014).

The Yangon narrative

As previously indicated, Yangon sits uncomfortably in relation to the national narrative. Yangon's heritage, of course, includes religious places such as the Shwedagon, Sule and Botahtaung pagodas and some early monastic complexes, set among hills and lakes but now engulfed by urban settlement. However, its other significant heritage derives from the late nineteenth and early twentieth century when Yangon was the chief trading city in the Burmese section of British India, that is, before it became capital of the separate British colony of Burma. The British influence is seen in Yangon's town plan and downtown architecture (Figure 14.5), although locals correctly insist that the city was built physically through the toil of Asians, mostly immigrant Indians in fact, as the Burmans refused to do it. The British also set the framework of multicultural Yangon with its rich intangible cultural heritage by encouraging the immigration of Indians and Chinese.

Figure 14.5 Early twentieth-century colonial architecture in Yangon's downtown.
Source: W. Logan.

This alternative heritage needs to be handled sensitively within the Myanmar political context. Although many postcolonial states are reviewing their colonial legacy (Logan and Howe 2002: 249; Aygen and Logan 2015: 410–25), there is, nevertheless, a lingering anti-colonial sentiment across Myanmar. The generals have a particular anxiety about Yangon partly based on its foreignness and partly on the city being the site of political dissent (Kean 2010; Logan 2015: 294). Despite this, most of the generals live in Yangon rather than in the sterile new capital and they expect Yangon to develop as a major economic centre. In the early 1990s, a short-lived regime relaxation led to the city's first high-rise buildings and hundreds of demolitions of pre-1960 buildings occurred across the 1990s and 2000s (Thant Myint-U 2014).

There is clearly an urgent need for urban heritage protection and management in Yangon. The existing legislative and planning frameworks are inadequate, however. The Protection and Preservation of Cultural Heritage Regions Law, 1998, 'has no capacity to deal with the dynamic and lived-in urban heritage of Yangon under constant pressure from development' (Yangon Heritage Trust 2014: 3) and the city government – the Yangon City Development Committee (YCDC) – has a very small staff with minimal qualifications and experience in heritage matters. In the absence of a specific government authority adequately funded and staffed to conserve the city's historic places, a non-government organisation – the Yangon Heritage Trust (YHT) – has stepped in with support of President Thein Sein. Founded in 2012 by historian Dr Thant Myint-U, the influential grandson of U Thant, the United Nations Secretary General from 1961 to 1971, the Trust's mission is to protect and promote Yangon's urban heritage within a cohesive urban plan. It advocates Yangon's heritage protection through official channels and the media, advises the YCDC and developers on heritage issues and undertakes preservation projects, studies, conferences and training. This is an unusual role and ultimately untenable.

Currently, however, it is the best hope for Yangon's heritage. The Trust has achieved a number of successes in the short time of its existence. In the planning sphere it drew up a heritage law in mid-2013 at the request of the President's Office; this is currently being reviewed by the government. It has developed a proposed downtown conservation area scheme and suggested a set of height controls. It has provided critical comment on a master plan funded by the Japanese International Cooperation Agency (JICA), describing it as 'primarily an infrastructure plan . . . [that] does not incorporate what is unique about our city and offer a comprehensive vision for future' (Thant Myint-U 2014). In terms of building conservation, it is remarkable that there have been very few new demolitions of pre-1960 buildings since the Trust was established and a few inappropriate new developments have been stopped (Thant Myint-U 2014). It has successfully advocated the adaptive re-use of historic buildings in the downtown area, such as the former New Law Courts, which is currently being restored for use as a five-star hotel. A Conservation Management Plan has been completed by the Edinburgh firm of Simpson and Brown for the Secretariat complex and renovation will proceed. Meanwhile, a programme of attaching blue plaques to notable historic buildings is under way.

There is no doubt that Thant Myint-U's family background and connections have been advantageous in positioning the Trust in Yangon's planning and heritage management. It is also clear that, to an extent, the Trust reflects the views of Yangon's Burman social elite and, in governance terms, may not be entirely 'bottom-up'. Nevertheless, Thant Myint-U previously worked in peacekeeping and he has a strong continuing personal interest in human rights. He is on record as saying that the

> last big challenge is for the poor in this city. I think one thing is to protect the old architecture, one thing is to make the city work for business, but it also has to work for ordinary people. The trick is to combine all of these things . . .
>
> (quoted in Kyaw Zwa Moe 2013)

The Trust is fully aware of the need for bottom-up input into its processes and sees community engagement as essential in building a rationale based in notions of rights for its interventions as well as in maintaining and enhancing Yangon as a harmonious richly multi-cultural city. One of the five paragraphs in its mission statement addresses the local community:

> Yangon's importance is as much about its people as its buildings. The vibrant and dynamic street economies, diversity of traditions and cultures, and the evolving life of the city is something YHT wants to see included in its future.

The Trust's view is that 'Yangon is for all' and it is directing some effort towards 'inviting the local community to share in the vision that YHT has for the future of Yangon and allowing them to influence and contribute to the shaping of that vision' (Yangon Heritage Trust 2014: 4). It is keen to include the views of local Indian and Chinese communities, as well as other ethnic minorities who have moved in from the outlying States, in its decision-making processes. Whether this effort will be successful ultimately has yet to be seen, although difficulties are already being identified.

The Trust's first major attempt at engaging with locals about their heritage is a project funded by New Zealand but managed and implemented by the Trust. Currently underway (mid-2015), the project invites local people to identify what they consider significant within the built environment in which they live. The Trust has brought together a cross-section of locals in terms of age and gender and is providing them with a Polaroid camera to photograph what they value in the street and what they do not value. The local people will also give some written explanation about their choices. These results will then be collated and analysed for publication in a formal report, as well as in more accessible publications for local community readers and for presentation at a street festival.

Another project that engages with the community is through a 'Livelihood' study being conducted by Jayde Lin Roberts, a built environment and Burma studies scholar based at the University of Tasmania (Roberts 2015). This is the second study in a European Union-funded capacity-building project for the YCDC Urban Planning Unit and is co-sponsored by the YHT. The study looked at the livelihood dimensions of three downtown street blocks that were previously examined in the Trust's Built Form Study – 26th Street (Lower Block), Latha Street (Lower Block) and Bogalay Street (Upper Block), all part of the grid designed and built by the colonial authorities after 1852. In her 2015 report, Roberts notes that while the meaning of the term 'Livelihood' would seem to be simple, in fact:

> in our common sense application of the word, we often forget about the complex interconnections that enable us to live securely, that is: 1) to earn a sufficient income to support ourselves and our families, 2) to access goods and services, and 3) to feel at home.
>
> (Roberts 2015: n.p.)

This is a broad use of the term but one that ties in well with the Trust's mission statement and its recognition that the intangible heritage of the local community – the street life, occupational skills, festivals, religious activities, praying at nat (spirit) shrines – make an indispensable contribution, alongside historic buildings, to Yangon's rich culture.

The three blocks were chosen as providing a mix of functions from residential to commercial and religious and representing different cultures: 26th Street is a predominantly Indian community, Latha Street is part of Yangon's China Town, while Bogalay Zay Street has numerous architecturally intact historic buildings that have retained their original social function, such as the Young Women's Christian Association building (Kyaw Phyo Tha, 2014). However, use of the study to build a better understanding of how residents view new urban development and heritage conservation may be limited because of the small sample size and the particularity of the blocks. Latha Street, for example, was home to some of downtown's wealthiest citizens before they moved out to Golden Valley; they are now absentee owners who do not need to sell their downtown properties as they do not need the money (Roberts, pers. comm., 13 March 2015).

Another way in which the Trust seeks to connect with the community is through the print and electronic media, including through the *Myanmar Times* newspaper and *Irrawaddy* magazine, both of which are available in Burmese and English and widely available. Whether it gets its message across to the poorer sections of the downtown communities is uncertain. Most Burma scholars say that Burmese people are avid readers but there may be a gap in the lack of alignment between the Trust's message and the concerns of everyday residents (Roberts, pers. comm., 21 March 2015).

The Trust's statements embody sincere intentions but there is huge gap between intentions and the reality of the situation in which the Trust is operating. The prevailing climate is one of neo-liberalism, which encourages privatisation and minimum control on new development. Money will talk. To take a recent example, in late January 2015, in response to growing public concern over proximity to the Shwedagon pagoda, government authorities suspended five large construction projects of the proposed Dagon City, which sits on former military land in Dagon township north of Yangon's downtown (Myat Nyein Aye and Mullins 2015). YCDC and Myanmar Investment Commission officials were to consider the impact the proposed 12-storey buildings would have on the skyline and the city's cultural heritage. The height of the proposed project appears to have been a key issue. The public's concern had been largely expressed through social media, as had the positive response to the suspension, including from Thant Myint-U. However, two weeks later it was announced in the press that the project was going ahead (Kyaw Phyo Tha 2015).

It is said that, in addition to the neo-liberal context, the Yangon Heritage Trust must always talk the way that the generals like to hear, which is conservatively. This puts a brake on what the Trust will be able to do. Alongside the Yangon Heritage Trust are other civil society groups working to relieve poverty (e.g. Free Funeral Service Society[4]), improve women's conditions (e.g. Myanmar Women's Affairs Association) and promote good planning, architecture and heritage (e.g. Association of Myanmar Architects), but these are not well connected and ways need to be found to bring them together into bigger, more powerful groups or networks. At the Union level, a set of Development Support Committees (DSCs) was created in 2011 in townships, both rural and urban, across the country (Yen Snaing, 2013). This refers to the lowest level of government in Myanmar, where the formerly government-appointed 'village-tract officers' were changed to elected 'village elders'. This was a top-down initiative apparently originating in the President's

Office, but hailed nevertheless as a sign of Myanmar's move towards democratic governance (Robertson 2013). Some commentators see them as operating sub-optimally, partly due to the lack of clear guidelines on what they are meant to do and partly because of the reticence of committee members in meetings due to the uncertain political situation in Myanmar and the danger of 'elite capture' (Robertson 2013). Even in Yangon, the DSCs appear to be working poorly as a community voice, although the Chinese community may be an exception (Roberts, pers. comm., 13 March 2015).

Generally speaking, there seems to be insufficient expertise and inadequate government structures to allow a local voice to be heard and incorporated into planning matters and the identification and management of heritage in Yangon. Even Thant Myint-U has expressed doubt about whether the Yangon Heritage Trust can 'come up with a scheme that will benefit the poor and middle-income people living downtown and keep old communities intact' and sees the need for very strong public support if this is to be achieved (Kyaw Zwa Moe 2013). If these contextual constraints overwhelm the Trust, it may find its remit narrowed to making the downtown and other central neighbourhoods more liveable for the people who live there; that is, to clean up the streets and alleys, make the city more walkable by reinstating footpaths and improve restaurant hygiene (Thant Myint-U 2014). Even so, this will not be an insignificant achievement, improving the living envi-ronment and generating more income for the local people, making Yangon more attractive to tourists and giving it a competitive edge in winning international business investments. But, as the Trust director, Moe Moe Lwin, has observed (pers. comm., 14 May 2014), even if the Trust's main ambitions are fulfilled – to see a legislative framework put in place and the YCDC develop its own heritage expertise – the Trust's role, nevertheless, is bound to change with time.

Conclusion

These are early days but Yangon is already making surprisingly good progress in managing the developmental pressures faced by the city's urban heritage. We have yet to see if more inclusive ways of identifying and managing heritage and a more sustainable balance between heritage protection and new development can be achieved in Yangon than has been possible in many other cities in Asia. It is likely that local people's voices in Yangon will not be heard on heritage issues except through progressive, if elite, civil society organisations such as the Trust, an essen-tially Burman civil organisation that seeks to act on behalf of more local, often ethnically based communities and that effectively represents top-down heritage management. In Myanmar as elsewhere, opportunities for bottom-up approaches to urban heritage management are limited – possibly inevitably so, if we are talk-ing about the development of effective, efficient and fair planning systems in which decisions are made openly and decision-makers are accountable to the citi-zenry through democratic processes. Opportunities do currently exist in Yangon for grassroots political protest (Figure 14.6); indeed, we should try to keep such

Figure 14.6 Land seizure protest site, downtown Yangon, November 2014.
Source: W. Logan.

one-off opportunities open and extend them into the planning and heritage arena. They can help shift opinions and policies but they are not yet, however, a recipe for creating systems.

While a top-down approach operates so far in Yangon in relation to the local, especially ethnic minority communities, at the larger scale Yangon acts in a bottom-up manner to resist the narrowness of the state's official view of heritage. The Yangon narrative and the Myanmar state narrative clearly do not fit well together, but they co-exist because they operate at different governmental levels – Union and Regional. The former is imposed top-down over all of Myanmar; the latter is upheld from below. This duality may change if conceptions of heritage are recast as Myanmar's political regime changes. On the one hand, the move to establish human rights may lead to a more inclusive view of heritage, particularly in relation to the country's ethnic minorities and their intangible heritage. On the other hand, the November 2015 presidential election will also be crucial, perhaps sending the country back into the grip of the more conservative generals.

This does not mean, of course, that there is not or cannot in future be considerable grassroots heritage conservation activity by the people and communities themselves. Agency in the heritage field is not restricted to governments and their bureaucracies alone. As with the ethnic groups in Shan State referred to in this chapter, so, too, in Yangon, there is considerable grassroots activity aimed at conserving the built and safeguarding the intangible heritage. Nor is the significant heritage confined to the downtown. The Shwedagon pagoda is certainly of World Heritage list quality and the Inya and Kandawgyi lakes and the riverfronts on three sides of the city, all have great environmental and cultural value. An impressive example of urban heritage that both depends on grassroots activity and is located outside Yangon's downtown is the K'uanyin T'ing (Guanyin Temple), a temple complex whose significance is explored in Jayde Roberts's book on Yangon's Chinese community (Roberts, forthcoming). Built in 1861 and rebuilt after a fire in the late 1890s, Hokkien Sino-Burmese families originating in Fujian see it as an auspicious convergence of three forces – blessings from the gods, their own good works and protective *chi* or energy from the temple's physical location. As stated by Roberts: 'these forces properly aligned' are regarded as a 'manifestation of their good work and their rightful claim to inhabit that space, to belong to Rangoon' (Roberts, forthcoming).

There are many authorised heritage discourses in Myanmar, working at different political and administrative levels and with varying degrees of control over the heritage agenda. The Myanmar case shows that much discussion of the AHD concept is oversimplified and that the reality is messier and less amenable to generalisation than often assumed. There is, of course, always a danger of one heritage narrative being favoured and others neglected. Ultimately, to reach an inclusive approach to heritage, it is necessary to rely on democratic decision-making processes in which the voices of minorities are respected by the majority. Regrettably, such a political system is hard to achieve and it does not exist in many parts of the world. Currently at least, Myanmar is trying and it is to be hoped that the presidential election in late 2015 will not upset the current upward trajectory.

Notes

1   In addition, there are five self-administered territories – the zones of Naga in Sagaing Region, and Danu, Pa-O, Palaung and Kokaung in Shan State – and the Self-Administered Division of Wa, also in Shan State. These have a constitutional status similar to that of a Region or State, and they can form their own indirectly elected and appointed 'leading bodies', headed by a chairperson (Nixon *et al.* 2013: 9). The Union Territory of Naypyidaw is administered by an appointed council under the authority of the President.
2   Myanmar won its first World Heritage inscription – Pyu Ancient Cities – at the 2014 meeting of the World Heritage Committee and has 14 places on its Tentative List.
3   Note the similar case in Vietnam described by Long (2003), where the socialist government chose the Complex of Hue Monuments as its first nomination to the World Heritage list despite Hue's imperial and feudal background.
4   The Free Funeral Services Society was established in 2001, initially to assist poor Yangon residents in meeting funeral costs. More than 100,000 funerals have been funded since 2001 and a free health clinic was opened in 2006 (see Free Funeral Services Society 2010).

References

Aygen, Z. and Logan, W. (2015). Heritage and in the 'Asian century': responding to geopolitical change. In: W. Logan, M. Nic Craith and U. Kockel (eds), *A Companion to Heritage Studies*. New York: Wiley, pp. 410–25.

The Economist (2015). The square mile: Myanmar's commercial capital. 31 January 2015. Available at: http://www.economist.com/news/asia/21641296-after-years-stagnation myanmars-biggest-city-developing-last-square-mile (accessed 4 February 2015).

Feng, Y. (2011). Myanmar continues efforts in developing tourism. *Xinhua*, 1 June 2011. Available at: http://news.xinhuanet.com/english2010/world/2011-06/01/c_13905950.htm (accessed 4 February 2015).

Fong, K. (2014). Imagining Yangon: assembling heritage, national identity and modern futures. *Historic Environment*, 26(3), 26–38.

Free Funeral Services Society (2010). Free Funeral Services Society Yangon (F.F.S.S). *Facebook*, 7 January 2010. Available at: https://www.facebook.com/note.php?note_id= 229176432913 (accessed 20 March 2015).

Heijmans, P. (2014). Myanmar's controversial census. *The Diplomat*, 2 September 2014. Available at: http://thediplomat.com/2014/09/myanmars-controversial-census/ (accessed 19 January 2015).

Kean, T. (2010). No longer the capital of Burma: Yangon today. *East Asia Forum*, 25 May 2010. Available at: http://www.eastasiaforum.org/2010/05/25/no-longer-the-capital-of-burma-yangon-today/ (accessed 30 March 2013).

Kyaw Phyo Tha (2014). Yangon Heritage Trust to survey how residents benefit from conservation. *The Irrawaddy*, 7 August 2014. Available at: http://www.irrawaddy.org/burma/yangon-heritage-trust-survey-residents-benefit-conservation.html (accessed 27 November 2014).

Kyaw Phyo Tha (2015). Dagon City 'will resume', amid calls for planning overhaul. *The Irrawaddy*, 13 February 2015. Available at: https://www.google.com.au/?gws_rd=ssl#q= development+near+Shwedagon+to+go+ahead (accessed 20 March 2015).

Kyaw Zwa Moe (2013). 'People have to see what we are talking about'. *The Irrawaddy*, 12 October 2013. Available at: http://www.irrawaddy.org/magazine/people-see-talking. html (accessed 27 November 2014).

Logan, W. (2005–6). The cultural role of capital cities: Hanoi and Hue, Vietnam. *Pacific Affairs*, 78(4), 559–75.

Logan, W. (2013). Learning to engage with human rights in heritage education. In M.T. Albert, R. Bernecker and B. Rudolff (eds), *Understanding Heritage: Perspectives in Heritage Studies*. Frankfurt am Main: IKO – Verlag für Interkulturelle Kommunikation, pp. 35–48.

Logan, W. (2014a). Making the most of heritage in Hanoi, Vietnam. *Historic Environment*, 26(3), 62–72.

Logan, W. (2014b). Heritage rights: avoidance and reinforcement. *Heritage and Society*, 7(2), 156–69.

Logan, W. (2015). Heritage in times of rapid transformation: a tale of two cities – Yangon and Hanoi. In: G. Bracken (ed.), *Asian Cities: Colonial to Global*. Amsterdam: Amsterdam University Press, pp. 279–300.

Logan, W. and Howe, R. (2002). Protecting Asia's urban heritage: the way forward. In W. Logan (ed.), *The Disappearing 'Asian' City: Protecting Asia's Urban Heritage in a Globalizing World*. Hong Kong, Oxford University Press, pp. 245–56.

Long, C. (2003). Feudalism in the service of revolutions: reclaiming heritage in Hue. *Critical Asian Studies*, 35(4), 535–58.

de Merode, E., Smeets, R. and Westrik, C. (eds) (2004). *Linking Universal and Local Values: Managing a Sustainable Future for World Heritage*, World Heritage Paper No. 13. Paris: UNESCO World Heritage Centre.

Myanmar Government (1998). *The Protection and Preservation of Cultural Heritage Regions Law* (The State Peace and Development Council Law No. 9/1998, 10 September 1998). Available at: http://www.unesco.org/culture/natlaws/media/pdf/birmanie/birmanie_law_10_09_1998_rngl_orof.pdf (accessed 20 March 2015).

Myat Nyein Aye and Mullins, J. (2015). Five projects near Shwedagon are temporarily suspended. *Myanmar Times*, 8 February 2015. Available at: http://www.mmtimes.com/index.php/business/13022-five-projects-near-shwedagon-are-suspended-local-media.html (accessed 20 March 2015).

Nixon, H., Joelene, C., Kyi Pyar Chit Saw, Thet Aung Lynn and Matthew, A. (2013). *State and Region Governments in Myanmar*. Yangon: CESD-MDRI and The Asia Foundation (online). Available: https://asiafoundation.org/resources/pdfs/StateandRegionGovernmentsin MyanmarCESDTAF.PDF (accessed 4 February 2015).

Philp, J. (2010). The political appropriation of Burma's cultural heritage and its implications for human rights. In: M. Langfield, W. Logan and M. Nic Craith (eds), *Cultural Diversity, Heritage and Human Rights*. London: Routledge, pp. 83–100.

Philp, J. and Mercer, D. (2002). Politicised pagodas and veiled resistance: contested urban space in Burma. *Urban Studies*, 39, 1587–610.

Roberts, J.L. (2015). *Urban Livelihoods in Specific Yangon Neighbourhoods and the Economics of Heritage Protection Study*, internal report. Yangon: European Union and Yangon Heritage Trust.

Roberts, J.L. (forthcoming). *The Chinese in Rangoon: Making a Place for Themselves in a Post-Colonial Capital*. Seattle: University of Washington Press.

Robertson, B. (2013). A vital, little-known cog in Myanmar's reform process. *Myanmar Times*, 27 October 2013. Available at: http://www.mmtimes.com/index.php/opinion/8606-a-vital-little-known-cog-in-myanmar-s-reform-process.html (accessed 20 March 2015).

Smith, L. (2006). *Uses of Heritage*. London: Routledge.

Than Than Nwe and Philp, J. (2002). Yangon, Myanmar: the reinvention of heritage. In: W. Logan (ed.), *The Disappearing 'Asian' City: Protecting Asia's Urban Heritage in a Globalizing World*. Hong Kong: Oxford University Press, pp. 147–65.

Thant Myint-U (2014). Polishing Myanmar's colonial gem. *The Irrawaddy*, 14 October 2014. Available at: http://www.irrawaddy.org/contributor/polishing-myanmars-colonial-gem.html (accessed 27 November 2014).

UNESCO (2003). *Convention for the Safeguarding of the Intangible Cultural Heritage*. Paris: UNESCO. Available at: http://www.unesco.org/culture/ich/ (accessed 4 February 2015).

United Nations (1948). *Universal Declaration of Human Rights*. New York: United Nations. Available at: http://www.un.org/en/documents/udhr/ (accessed 3 February 2015).

Witcomb, A. and Buckley, K. (2013). Engaging in the future of 'critical heritage studies': looking back in order to look forward. *International Journal of Heritage Studies*, 19(6), 562–78.

Yangon Heritage Trust (2014). *International Advisory Group Background Briefing*, confidential internal document. Yangon: Yangon Heritage Trust.

Yen Snaing (2013). In township development, civil society seeks a voice. *The Irrawaddy*, 26 December 2013. Available at: http://www.irrawaddy.org/burma/township-development-civil-society-seeks-voice.html (accessed 20 March 2015).

Zaw Win Than (2014). Growing pains as Myanmar hits 2 million visitor mark. *Myanmar Times*, 24 February 2014. Available at: http://www.mmtimes.com/index.php/lifestyle/travel/9679-industry-concerns-over-tourism-growth.html (accessed 4 February 2015).

Chapter 15

Living heritage, community participation and sustainability

Redefining development strategies in the Hoi An Ancient Town World Heritage property, Vietnam

Pham Thi Thanh Huong

At the international level, it was only in the early 2000s that the living heritage approach was developed by the International Centre for the Study of the Preservation and Restoration of Cultural Property (ICCROM) as a tool enabling the capture of key issues in the conservation and management of urban settlements. This new approach, which flowed out of numerous ICCROM development projects and studies focusing on communities and their connections with heritage, such as the integrated territorial and urban conservation (ITUC) programme in the mid-1990s, opened up a new dimension of heritage. It shifted the focus of heritage conservation practice from materials to the role of heritage in the lives of the people to whom it belonged (Poulios 2014). This new approach succeeded in embracing the living dimension or the continuity of heritage (De Caro and Wijesuriya 2012) and challenged the conventional Western material fabric approach that insisted on intact preservation, consequently, reinforcing the discontinuity between the past and present generations.

Strategic innovation often emanates from practices at local level. The municipal authorities of Hoi An City[1] issued a policy entitled 'Building Hoi An towards a Cultural City' in July 1999, only five months before the Ancient Quarter at the town's heart was inscribed on the World Heritage List. Although the living heritage approach was still vague at that time, the policy revealed a remarkable effort by the authorities and local people to develop Hoi An into 'a Cultural, Ecological and Tourism City where the eco-socio development would harmonize well with heritage preservation and promotion, making the City a unique Cultural City of Vietnam' (Hoi An People's Committee 2014).

Yet within that early context of dealing with a World Heritage site in Vietnam, the concepts of material-based, value-based and living heritage approaches were not clearly defined. Indeed, these notions were not well understood by heritage practitioners and officials across the country. However, huge efforts were made to differentiate this property from its sister heritage sites in central Vietnam, namely, Hue Complex of Monuments (inscribed 1993) and My Son sanctuary (inscribed 1999), both of which were focused on monument preservation and isolated from living communities. By contrast, Hoi An's inscribed area of 30 ha lay within a town of 77,000 people and most of its heritage elements – 929 out of 1,254 heritage

BẢN ĐỒ ĐIỀU CHỈNH KHOANH VÙNG BẢO VỆ KHU PHỐ CỔ HỘI AN

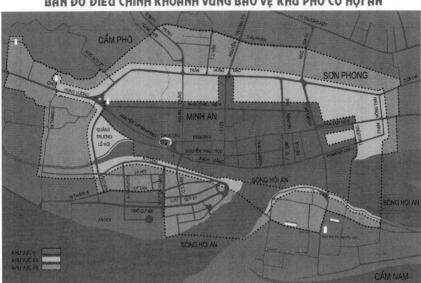

Figure 15.1 Revised map of Hoi An protection zones, 2015.
Source: Hoi An Centre for Heritage Management and Preservation.

buildings – were privately owned whilst the remaining properties belonged to community groups or associations (UNESCO 2008: 31). In the literal sense of a 'lived-in' heritage town (Galla 2012), the living aspects of the Hoi An property forced the municipal authorities, including site managers, to go beyond the conservation of the built structures that contributed to the site's outstanding universal value and underline the importance of involving the local community in management and preservation of Hoi An's heritage (Figure 15.1).

Like many other countries, Vietnam has benefited from the World Heritage listing of Hoi An and other sites (Johnson and Barry 1995; Frey and Steiner 2011; Bertacchini and Saccone 2012; Logan 2015). Having paid special attention to the living aspects of Hoi An's urban heritage, the municipal authorities were successful in both attracting international resources for heritage protection and marketing the site as a cultural tourism destination. The town became one of the demonstration projects for sustainable poverty reduction (Galla 2012). With tourist arrivals and average annual tourism revenue increasing ten times by the end of the first decade after inscription (UNESCO 2008), different groups of local residents, government entities and social organisations became engaged in the socio-economic, cultural development and improvement of living standards (Hoi An People's Committee 2014). The positive progress of the town that had allowed it to emerge as one of the main visitor attractions in the region was quietly diverting attention from a number of pressures that came out later, particularly when the higher levels of energy consumption due to the increased population and volumes of visitors put the limited natural resources at risk. Further, a rupture emerged between the residents in the World Heritage-inscribed property – the 'core community' that benefits most from the heritage – and the wider Hoi An community, which had been rarely mentioned in the connection with the town but which was, in fact, experiencing serious negative impacts on its living conditions.

This chapter seeks to examine how the perceptions of living heritage were shaped and to what extent the living heritage approach in combination with greater community participation contributed to heritage management and preservation and to easing tension between the occupants of the World Heritage property and those in the wider Hoi An City. The new approach adopted by the Hoi An authorities has important implications for the sustainable development of the town's urban heritage. Much of the past literature on living heritage has emphasised the management of the heritage itself, whereas Hoi An heritage town provides a useful subject of research because it combines successful preservation of historic monuments and social and economic development, particularly in relation to tourism and poverty reduction (ICOMOS and UNESCO 2009; Galla 2012). This chapter seeks to fill a gap in the heritage literature and to add new insights into the relationships between living heritage, community participation and sustainable development.

Living heritage approach in a 'lived-in' heritage city

Hoi An Ancient Town was added to the global collection of World Heritage in 1999 for representing 'an outstanding material manifestation of the fusion of cultures over time in an international commercial port' (*criterion ii*) and 'an exceptionally well-preserved example of a traditional Asian trading port' (*criterion v*) (UNESCO 1999). The historic town, which dates from the sixteenth century, provides vigorous evidence of economic and cultural exchanges between Vietnam and the world, especially Japan, China, India and several European countries. This is seen in the intact survival of over 1,300 monuments that take a variety of architectural forms, including residential houses, family chapels for worshipping ancestors, village communal houses, pagodas, temples, tombs, bridges, water wells, markets and assembly halls (UNESCO 1999).

The Government of Vietnam's statement at the time of nomination that these monuments had been 'completely and assiduously preserved' reflected an over-optimistic view of heritage preservation that was heavily influenced by the material fabric-based approach to preservation and failed to acknowledge the ambiguous definition of ownership, land titles and land-related rights that characterised the early transition stage of social and economic reform in Vietnam. The nomination document indicated that the entire town was 'State property' and 'effectively protected by a number of relevant laws' and claimed that there was no pressure to replace older buildings with new ones using modern materials such as concrete and corrugated iron (UNESCO 1999). Despite the particularity of Vietnam's legal framework and economic situation, this local perception shared much in common with the international definition of historic towns and urban areas at that time, which, in the World Heritage context, were usually defined as a group of buildings (Jokilehto 2010). However, what happened to this once quiet town was completely unpredictable, particularly the rampant growth in tourist arrivals that jumped 106 per cent within the first two years after its inscription. The blossoming of retail services, the increase in average income, the need to alter the balance between living and commercial space in the old houses and, finally, the gentrification of the inscribed town – a common phenomenon in many cities around the world – started to reshape this small town (UNESCO 2008). Facing these unforeseen changes, many local residents and municipal authorities admitted that the 'intact preservation' of the town was once mostly due to the difficult economic situation faced by the country in its non-market economy period when Hoi An was largely devoid of development pressures.

Local residents of Hoi An have been living and working for generations in the old houses that now became reconceived as heritage and they have continuously reorganised their living space over time. Whilst there was little renovation in the past, the better incomes and changes in structures of livelihoods that followed inscription accelerated their need to renew living arrangements. Alteration of spaces within the historic buildings has been embraced by the local people to an extent that challenges and even confronts the 'intact preservation' principle set out in the material fabric-based approach that limits the use of heritage structures in order to ensure their protection (ICOMOS 1964) (Figure 15.2). Such an

Figure 15.2 Tan Ky old house, one of the private residential properties in the city's top priority preservation category, 2011.

Source: Mai Thanh Chuong.

approach assumes that current human practices could be harmful to the historic fabric and prevent the transmission of the heritage of the past into the future (Poulios 2014). The connection between the community and heritage has been undervalued in this approach and the contribution of the present generation in enriching the heritage has not been adequately recognised. In the context of Hoi An, the imposed system of laws and regulations on heritage preservation that emphasised all the "do nots" was considered by local residents to be a disadvantage of living in the old quarter.

The early response by municipal authorities was to invest in public facilities and services outside of the old quarter with the intention of attracting the residents away from it (UNESCO 2008). Unsurprisingly, the consequence showed much in common with the Angkor World Heritage site in Cambodia where the monks and local residents were given restricted access to the site or relocated from it in order to develop tourism (Miura 2005). The site was regarded as 'dead' heritage of the past due to a colonial and dated vision focusing on architectural preservation (Winter 2004: 4). The old quarter of Hoi An similarly lost many of its original residents and none of the admittedly attractive new restaurants, cafés and shops have much to do with tradition (UNESCO 2008). Although the approach in heritage preservation focusing on the protection of fabric once contributed to the rescue of monuments (Layton 1989, cited in Poulios 2014), in those sites with living communities, such as Hoi An, it led to broken relationships between the heritage and communities. The site would lose more than isolated relics, as has occurred at Angkor, Borobodur and My Son sanctuary, as its heritage is primarily attached to all the living aspects of families, clans, indeed, an entire commercial society, rather than an isolated religious area. The relocation of many local residents put at risk the key heritage values, including the authenticity of the town. In addition, the ancient town did not in fact entirely belong to the State and it could not be considered a 'State property' as was stated in the early description. Even if the permanent land ownership belongs constitutionally to the State, private land-use rights are legally recognised and are tantamount to property ownership. Family living space has been always subject to diverse household decision-making. In short, the preservation of many heritage elements in the Hoi An site cannot be conducted through top-down government regulation without the local residents' consent.

The rapid changes of the site in the early period after its inscription led to the realisation that policy reform in heritage preservation and in socio-economic development was needed. This is seen in the accumulation of political will to implement the 'Building Hoi An towards a Cultural City' policy. Although the policy was issued several months before the nomination of the Hoi An Ancient Town as a World Heritage site, resources were only allocated to implement it during the period 2001 to 2009 (Hoi An People's Committee 2014). The priorities of the policy were to develop the tourism sector and support families and clans to maintain and foster cultural activities, thereby improving their incomes, living standards and cultural enjoyment.

Although it was not clearly written down in any documents, the practices in heritage management of Hoi An reflected a transition in the approach from focusing on monuments to focusing on the living aspects of heritage. As pointed out by Ioanis Poulios (2014), the concept of living heritage employed in this World Heritage context is different from that of intangible heritage, which focuses primarily on intangible cultural practices and performances. Instead, it embraces both tangible and intangible heritage and deals with heritage components that exist in a living environment (Jigyasu 2013) and is inextricably linked to the concept of continuity (De Caro and Wijesuriya 2012). In the context of Hoi An, the local residents who have been living for generations in the old houses must not be considered threats to the existence of heritage. Without these residents, the functions of historic buildings would have been altered and the preservation of the townscape would be a failure despite huge efforts in restoring and protecting the building structures. The emphasis on valuing the heritage town in order to improve local people's incomes and living standards and harmonise the heritage preservation and promotion (tourism development) indicated a new dimension of the living heritage approach. Such an approach calls for the safeguarding of heritage while maintaining its connection with the present community, and sees the heritage being protected by, and for, the present community (De Caro and Wijesuriya 2012; Poulios 2014).

The living heritage approach is perhaps best reflected in the exceptional efforts made by Hoi An in its programme of 'Adaptive Re-use of Built Heritage'. Within the first decade after World Heritage inscription, approximately 200 heritage buildings were fully restored. Among these, 43 government-owned properties have been leased as residential, public and commercial spaces after restoration. Many of these old houses were occupied by lower-income families and they would otherwise have been sold to private investors from big cities, such as Hanoi, Ho Chi Minh City and Da Nang, as part of a gentrification process or real estate speculation. It deserves mention that the 'adaptive re-use' of these properties by local government resulted in over 50 per cent of houses leased as residential places at a reasonable rent, while the remaining properties were opened for public uses such as a kindergartens, residences for disadvantaged local students, public medical clinic and cultural services and traditional performance and tourism information offices. A small percentage have been leased as shops and restaurants (UNESCO 2008). With the revenue generated from leased properties being used to invest in public facilities and reinvested into conservation projects, the town has been referred to several times as an excellent example of heritage preservation in the Asia-Pacific region (UNESCO 2007, 2008, 2009; Galla 2012; Pascual 2014). In addition, about 1,125 privately owned heritage buildings were partially repaired or renovated by the owners under restoration permits. Many of these private properties were provided a partial subsidy because the cost of restoration was high relative to the owners' income levels. The financial assistance was calculated depending on the classification of the buildings, the heritage values, location and the financial situation of the owner. The financial assistance could be a grant or interest-free long-term loan. The restoration of the buildings could be conducted by the house owners or by government-appointed agencies in the case of properties purchased by the municipal government. However, the restoration works in either case must be supervised by the technicians at the Consultancy Office for Relics Restoration and Heritage Information that belongs to the Hoi An Centre for Heritage Management and Preservation.

The case of Hoi An illustrates the combination of conventional and new approaches to heritage conservation: the material fabric-based approach reflected in the government's initiative in purchasing endangered old houses and investment in those properties' restoration, and the living approach reflected in its adaptive re-use policy, which supported both the right of original residents to continue to live in their traditional places and improved the public facilities of the old quarter. Reversing the early post-inscription trend, Hoi An avoided the costly lessons often seen in Asian and African heritage sites where the local community has been physically removed from the core zones (Layton 1989; Miura 2005). Instead, the support given to local residents highlighted the revival and sustainable preservation of a heritage site in which a large number of antiquities were kept, traditional crafts were maintained and folk cuisine, habits, customs and festivities were fostered by the original community (Galla 2012).

What happened in this heritage town backs up the literature on the living heritage approach that sees the living dimension as one of the most important aspects of heritage in many cultures of Asia and Africa (ICOMOS and UNESCO 2009), especially where the specific community group that created and sustains the original function of heritage continues to occupy their traditional homes (De Caro and Wijesuriya 2012). The maintenance of the original community may not be the only prerequisite for sustainable heritage preservation but it is certainly the key one as the community retains the original connection with the heritage over time and still considers heritage an integral part of its contemporary life in terms of identity, pride, self-esteem, structure and well-being and sees caring for the heritage as its own inherent obligation (Poulios 2014). Furthermore, the local knowledge and capacity to reduce disaster vulnerability are themselves embedded in the community's cultural heritage, as indicated in the Hoi An Protocols for Best Conservation Practice in Asia, which was adopted by ICOMOS in 2005 (ICOMOS and UNESCO 2009).

Whilst the conventional approach in heritage preservation shows an extreme focus on the preservation of fabric and construction techniques and is an expert-driven approach (Jokilehto 1986, cited in Poulios 2014), the living heritage approach highlights custodianship by those whose traditional heritage it is and calls for these custodians to be empowered and assisted to carry out authentic conservation (ICOMOS and UNESCO 2009). This is, of course, clearly in line with the Nara Document on Authenticity (1994), which defines the roles and responsibility of the local community in heritage preservation in the following terms: 'Responsibility for cultural heritage and the management of it belongs, in the first place, to the cultural community that has generated it, and subsequently to that which cares for it' (ICOMOS 1994).

The local community, however, could not easily wield its knowledge to perform its custodian responsibility. In urban heritage contexts around the world, many lower-income households cannot afford the rising cost of living in their places (UNESCO 2008). This challenge calls for heritage preservation relying on the local community as under this economic pressure, many of their members choose to migrate out of the area. The local community in the sense of the 'core community', which had the original connection with the heritage, needs supportive policies to continue living in and caring for it. The Hoi An initiative has clearly demonstrated good practice in which the government's support policy prevented outside investors from purchasing the properties and helped local households with financial hardships to commit themselves to protecting the heritage of the ancient town (Galla 2012).

Community participation, the primary community and the concerned stakeholders

The living heritage approach, which is clearly a community-based approach (De Caro and Wijesuriya 2012; Poulios 2014), has been a prerequisite for enabling community participation in Hoi An Ancient Town because it supports local people in continuing to live in their heritage place. At the same time, however, this approach stimulates the primary community to take part in joint activities in the preservation and promotion of heritage by signalling direct benefits such as the sharing of the costs of renovation and improving incomes with new livelihoods using these properties in tourism. Once abandoned during Vietnam's long war period (1940–75), then stifled under the post-1975 centrally planned economy and confronted by famine during the 1980s, Hoi An's local economy suffered significant disadvantage in both agricultural and industrial resources. This was turned around when the municipal authorities decided to give strong support to the tourism and service sectors, particularly after the town was listed as a World Heritage site. Adapting the functions of the heritage buildings was given the green light from site managers, although renovation of the buildings still required a permit in a strict approval process.

Focusing on the livelihood of the living community thus valued World Heritage as a powerful tool in articulating both the town's sense of place and the community's identity, self-esteem and pride, as well as in promoting the heritage as cultural capital that could be used to alleviate poverty and generate economic and social development. A decade after the site's inscription, the achievements were clearly seen in the remarkable increase in average income, which was now higher than the national average and far greater than similar-sized cities in Vietnam, and consequently, in the proportion of poor residents being lower than the national average (UNESCO 2008: 36). Local people believed that this economic growth was stimulated by heritage tourism and the municipal authorities declared openly that the key to these achievements had been local community participation in both heritage conservation and tourism development (Le Van Giang 2013, Nguyen Chi Trung 2014).

Nevertheless, it should be noted that the community addressed in this context has been narrowed to the core community living in the old quarter with only some cases extended to the citizens of the wider city and that the perceived 'community participation' falls into the lower scales on the ladder of participation. In reference to the six-rung ladder of public participation from passive participation to self-mobilisation and connectedness (Pretty 1995, cited in Afenyo 2012), the participation of the Hoi An population has been largely Type 1 – passive, Type 2 – contributors and Type 3 – implementers because they mainly participated as beneficiaries and had limited control over the decision-making process. This contrasts with the usual definition of community participation within the context of development as an 'active process whereby beneficiaries influence the direction and execution of development projects rather than merely receive a share of project benefits' (World Bank 1987).

Highlighting these points is intended to emphasise that community participation in heritage preservation and tourism development in heritage places varies in space and time and is attached to national and local political and socio-economic situations. Likewise, the conditions needed for full community participation are often non-existent in the local communities due to numerous external and internal factors (Afenyo 2012) and multiple definitions of the concept have been developed to suit the specific aspirations of the proponents (Tosun 2000, cited in Afenyo 2012). This is quite unlike the situation in Western communities, where communities might be more familiar with public participation processes and where local actors become involved if they perceive opportunities to influence decision-making in order to gain personal benefit (Murphy 1985). Hierarchical structures in Asian societies may inhibit community participation in decision-making (Pedersen 2002). As Okazaki (2008: 512) puts it, practical participation requires both the right and the means.

In Hoi An, a 'Sustainable Conserving and Promoting Hoi An World Heritage' workshop has been organised and convened by the municipal government once or twice a year for the past 15 years. It is attended by hundreds of homeowners, heritage buildings caretakers and selected tour operators. After listening to the government's update on conservation activities, participants raise their opinions on issues related to their benefits and the adverse impacts of the conservation activities and tour operator behaviour. The government officials then provide feedback and take the participants' views into account in subsequent decision-making (UNESCO 2008). This practice indicated a limited level of participation of local people: the local people only provide their feedback on the topics of discussion that are picked up by the government or have their opinions heard on the projects that are already formulated. Moreover, hierarchical structures and cultural norms may make it difficult to elicit the opinions of certain groups (Pedersen 2002), thereby making true participation in formal meetings impossible. For example, local homeowners and relics caretakers who are overwhelmed by high-ranking government leaders and powerful tycoons in such formal events often hesitate to raise the particular issues or barriers they have to face in their ordinary life.

Consequently, the outcomes primarily reflect the opinions and priorities of the decision-makers (UNESCO 2008).

The limitation of community participation in Hoi An has also been reflected in the lack of facilitators. Many civil society organisations and associations that are usually active facilitators elsewhere are, in Vietnam, closely attached to the government and highly structured at all levels, similar to government structures throughout the country. In Hoi An, although some of these organisations, such as the Youth Union, have been active in a number of restoration projects, they normally act as implementers of government initiatives (UNESCO 2008) and cannot offer independent views in public participation meetings. Besides the municipal government and the primary community, there is a 'broader community group' involved in the life of the heritage, which, however, has been omitted in the management of the heritage town. Within an urban heritage context such as in Hoi An, the broader community has much closer connections to the heritage than the normal perception. This is because the outstanding values of the heritage town rely on its geographical location, the commercial relations and exchange of products and resources with neighbouring areas in the past, as well as contemporary interdependent relations on a cause-and-effect basis in terms of the exploitation of natural resources and disaster risk management.

A broader view of heritage impacts and sustainability

The Hoi An heritage town used to be perceived as an isolated protected area while the broader region around it was considered the location for economic development. This simple dichotomy faced unprecedented challenges after a decade of development (Figure 15.3). The population of the old quarter had changed little but the total population of the city as a whole increased from 77,000 in 1999 to 90,000 people in 2013 (Hoi An People's Committee 2014). Although this was not in itself a key threat to the heritage, it sat alongside other factors – the mushrooming of hospitality facilities in response to the manifold increases in visitor numbers, the ambitious tourism development targets at provincial level that considered tourism as a leading economic sector and the expansion of infrastructure works associated with development. In addition, there was the thirst for energy that led to the proliferation of hydropower plant projects in the province. In the upstream sections of Thu Bon River, 64 hydropower plant projects have been proposed, 44 of which were in operation by late 2009.

The Thu Bon, which was a sacred river during the Cham civilisation that flourished in what is now central Vietnam, became the important axis connecting Hoi An's international trading port and its hinterland sources of reputable forestry products during the sixteenth to eighteenth centuries. But Hoi An's location on the river, once the basis of its prosperity as a trading port, is now making it extremely vulnerable. The residents of Hoi An as well as the inhabitants in its sister World Heritage site – My Son sanctuary – struggled with the shortage of water and power supply in the dry season and with the doubled flood levels due to the storm

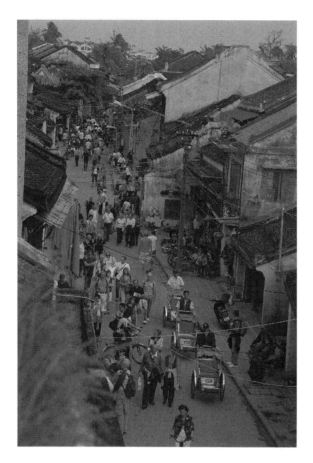

Figure 15.3 Hoi An Ancient Town from above, 2011.
Source: Mai Thanh Chuong.

water runoff in the rainy season. A record flood level in 2009 submerged the entire Ancient Quarter, including the iconic Japanese covered bridge, and it was a huge effort to save the fragile wooden structures (Figure 15.4). In addition to the disaster risks, the ambitious development targets with the quantity-based indicators focusing on growth rates paradoxically put at risk the quality of tourism experience in the region and physically affected the two World Heritage sites that have been the backbones of the tourism sector.

Additionally, the development strategy aiming at accelerating growth rates and a high-yield tourism market also led to the radical transformation of the outer area landscape, notably along the beach and dunes. Many traditional fishing villages have been moved from their places and sources of livelihood were lost without

Figure 15.4 Record flood level in Hoi An Ancient Town, 2009.
Source: Mai Thanh Chuong.

adequate compensation in order to provide space for the development of five star resorts and hotels (UNESCO, 2008). The Casuarina forest and green belt were massively chopped down for the construction of big hotels, exposing the coastal areas to high disaster risks, notably soil erosion and storms. These pressures are determined by the wider political and socio-economic contexts in which Hoi An and its greater region sit and the local authority and community sometimes have to live with strategies decided elsewhere. It is important to note that biological diversity and cultural diversity are closely and fundamentally inter-dependent, affecting one another in complex ways. As Rao (2012) argues, it follows that any local policy aiming to achieve sustainable development will necessarily have to consider and act upon both the bio-diversity and cultural diversity of the communities concerned. Similarly, the intention in preserving the heritage elements of the townscape must be to safeguard them not just as historical evidence but as a living system (ICOMOS and UNESCO 2009), taking into account all the reciprocal influences between the site, its primary lived-in community, the concerned stakeholders and the natural environment. This is very much in line with the consensus reached in the ICOMOS Washington Charter that the conservation of historic towns and other historic urban areas should be an integral part of coherent policies of economic and social development and of urban and regional planning at every level (ICOMOS 1987).

As the management and preservation of a living heritage is dependent on many factors, the tasks ought to involve multiple stakeholders, cross-sectoral planning and shared decision-making processes. In the case of Hoi An, the existing top-down planning process and the narrowed concept of 'development' risked undermining the values and even physical elements of World Heritage, and at the same time, led to conflict between conservation and development. It was time that the accelerated threats to the World Heritage questioned the goals of development strategies of the entire region because not only was the World Heritage town at risk but so were a myriad of livelihoods and valuable assets on the river downstream. Hence, it may be argued that the current conflict is not necessarily bad if it gives an opportunity for an exchange of interests, experiences and needs among stakeholders (Tjosvold 1996, cited in Okazaki 2008) and coordinated efforts are made to reset common goals, increasing the benefits for all (Timothy 2007, cited in Okazaki 2008).

A new strategy integrating culture and tourism with the redefined development goals and principles for Quang Nam Province was produced from a series of debates, working sessions and consultations attended by the public and private sector and implemented by a task force comprising all related government agencies from provincial to local level (Quang Nam People's Committee 2011). This integrated strategy, which aims at a sustainable development of the entire province, has been followed by a series of visitor management plans in all of the three protected areas, namely Hoi An Ancient Town, My Son sanctuary World Heritage site and Cham Island Biosphere Reserve. The strategy and plans seek to achieve economic development mostly with tourism activities in the protected areas and without destroying or undermining the assets on which the sites, as well as development in general, are based, not least the valuable cultural assets.

Although the concept of sustainable development is often overused yet poorly understood, it can be defined by what it specifically seeks to achieve and how it is measured (Kates *et al.* 2005). In this Quang Nam example, stakeholders shared the ultimate goals of improving local people's livelihoods and living standard in a sustainable way taking three pillars as a foundation for the new strategy:

- Pillar 1. Sustainable tourism development that conserves and enriches the region's cultural, social and environmental resources base.
- Pillar 2. Enhanced revenue generation with an equitable distribution of benefits and a focus on local livelihoods and poverty reduction.
- Pillar 3. Establishing the region as a high quality tourism destination featuring distinctive tourism products, services and experiences based on the region's outstanding cultural values.

Based on this foundation, the strategy aims to address nine key issues in the fields of linked culture and tourism:

- Heritage sustainability;
- Community engagement and participation in tourism and cultural conservation for poverty reduction and livelihood improvement;
- Environmental sustainability;
- Enhancement and development of cultural tourism products;
- Cultural tourism marketing and promotion;
- Information provision and interpretation communication strategy;

- Stakeholder coordination;
- Tourism human resource development;
- Coastal and marine area planning and development.

(Quang Nam People's Committee 2011)

Under these key areas, 63 key actions were proposed following a lengthy negotiation process attended by all related stakeholders from local to regional level. Among these actions, the priority placed on reassessing current planning targets to focus more on value rather than volume deserves mentioning. This has become a key principle for future decisions and planning, keeping hydro-electric dams in balance with tourism development and minimising the conversion of forestry and farming lands to other purposes. Some positive changes can be seen after two years of the strategy implementation with the notable decision of rejecting up to 20 hydro-power projects.

This case study reinforces Pedersen's view (2002) that where the policy development process is a joint exercise, a policy statement can unite people with different viewpoints and give direction to public and private tourism management. Achieving agreement on sustainable issues among the stakeholders in Hoi An had proved difficult given the poor coordination, but the efforts to achieve the cancellation of power plant projects, which needed central government approval in many cases, was much more painful. However, once the concerned stakeholders and particularly the key actor, the Quang Nam provincial government, are truly committed to preserve what they find valuable, they find ways to do it. Additionally, as much research has pointed out, sustainable development requires the participation of diverse stakeholders and perspectives with the ideal result being the reconciliation of different and opposing values and goals and the movement towards a new synthesis and subsequent coordination of mutual action to achieve multiple values (Kates *et al.* 2005). The local people here have much in common with people worldwide in their attempt to retain a sense of identity. During the negotiation for a new development strategy, World Heritage was placed on the scales with 'development growth targets' and people have become more fully aware that the World Heritage stands for their identity and needs to be conserved to inspire future development.

Conclusion

This study focused on the living heritage approach in an urban settlement and its application in redefining an effective development strategy for the Hoi An World Heritage property in its wider city and regional context. The findings suggest that the living heritage approach is clearly a prerequisite for community-based heritage preservation, a conclusion that is relevant to World Heritage sites across Asia. Adopting such an approach helps to support the continuity of the heritage, maintaining the value of legacy of the past in the present life of the local community and visitors. It enables the adaptation of heritage structures to new functions that generate resources needed for heritage preservation. It is also noteworthy that in Hoi An, the approach focusing on the local community was only the beginning for community participation in heritage management. The heavy focus on the core community had led to a rupture in the relationship between the heritage and the broader urban community outside the core area and undermined the heritage values as well as the role of heritage in the development process. World Heritage is indeed an inseparable part of Hoi An, but on a much broader social, economic and environmental scale than merely the area within the nominated boundaries. Its preservation is dependent on many factors and requires engaging multiple stakeholders in cross-sectoral planning and shared decision-making processes. However, World Heritage seen in its living environment can also be a key asset in redefining the goals for sustainable development. More research and published findings are needed both on a system of heritage impact assessment and on assessing the contribution of World Heritage in urban development.

Note

1   Hoi An is officially recognised in Vietnam as a City Type 2. Being smaller than the cities of Type 1, such as Hanoi and Ho Chi Minh City, Type 2 cities are placed under the provincial government – Quang Nam Provincial Government in Hoi An's case.

References

Afenyo, E.A. (2012). Community participation in ecotourism: evidence from Tafi Atome, Ghana. *African Journal of Hospitality, Tourism and Leisure*, 2(2), 1–12. Available at: http://www.ajhtl.com/uploads/7/1/6/3/7163688/article_3_vol__2_2_2012.pdf (accessed 18 November 2014).

Bertacchini, E. and Saccone, D. (2012). Towards a political economy of World Heritage. *Journal of Cultural Economics*, 36(4), 327–52.

De Caro, S. and Wijesuriya, G. (2012). Engaging communities – approaches to capacity building. In: UNESCO, *Involving Communities in World Heritage Conservation – Concepts and Actions in Asia*, Proceedings of the International Conference in Celebration of the 40th Anniversary of the World Heritage Convention. Byueo, Chungcheongnam-do: World Heritage Centre, pp. 35–42.

Frey, B.S. and Steiner, L. (2011). World Heritage List: does it make sense? *International Journal of Cultural Policy*, 17(5), 555–73.

Galla, A. (2012). World Heritage in poverty alleviation: Hoi An Ancient Town, Viet Nam. In: A. Galla (ed.), *World Heritage: Benefits Beyond Borders*. London: Cambridge University Press, pp. 107–20.

Hoi An People's Committee (1999). *Resolution no. 08/1999 dated 16 July 1999 of the Hoi An City People's Council on the Approval of the Policy Building Hoi An towards a Cultural City*. Hoi An: Archives of the Hoi An People's Committee Office. [In Vietnamese].

Hoi An People's Committee (2014). Building Hoi An towards a Cultural City. In: *UCLG Mexico City Culture 21 Application Form for the United Cities and Local Governments' International Award*. Hoi An: Archives of the Hoi An Centre for Heritage Preservation and Management.

ICOMOS (1964). *The Venice Charter: International Charter for the Conservation and Restoration of Monuments and Sites*. Venice: Second International Congress of Architects and Technicians of Historic Monuments. Available at: http://www.icomos.org/charters/venice_e.pdf (accessed 18 December 2014).

ICOMOS (1987). *Charter for the Conservation of Historic Towns and Urban Areas* ('Washington Charter 1987'). Washington D.C.: ICOMOS. Available at: http://www.international.icomos.org/charters/towns_e.pdf (accessed 19 December 2014).

ICOMOS (1994). *Nara Document on Authenticity*. Nara: ICOMOS. Available at: http://www.icomos.org/charters/nara-e.pdf (accessed 9 January 2015).

ICOMOS and UNESCO (2009). *Hoi An Protocols for Best Conservation Practice in Asia*. Bangkok: UNESCO Bangkok Regional Office.

Jigyasu, R. (2013). Integrated framework for cultural heritage risk management. In: UNESCO. *Proceedings of the Sub-Regional Workshop on Disaster Risk Preparedness and Management*. Yogyakarta: UNESCO and Ministry of Education and Culture of the Republic of Indonesia, pp. 11–21. Reprinted from Jigyasu, R. (2006). Integrated framework for cultural heritage risk management. *Journal of the National Institute of Disaster Management, New Delhi*, 1(1).

Johnson, P. and Barry, T. (1995). Heritage as a business. In: D.T. Herbert (ed.), *Heritage, Tourism and Society*. New York: Mansell, pp. 170–90.

Jokilehto, J. (1986). A History of Architectural Conservation: The Contribution of English, French, German and Italian Thought towards an International Approach to the Conservation of Cultural Property. DPhil thesis. York: Institute of Advanced Architectural Studies, University of York.

Jokilehto, J. (2010). Notes on the definition and safeguarding of HUL. *City and Time*, 4(3), 41–51. Available at: http://www.ceci-br.org/novo/revista/docs2010/C&T-2010-162.pdf (accessed 18 November 2014).

Kates, W.R., Parris, M.T. and Leiserowitz, A.A. (2005). What is sustainable development? Goals, indicators, values, and practice. *Environment: Science and Policy for Sustainable Development*, 47(3), 8–21.

Layton, R. (1989). Introduction: conflict in the archaeology of living traditions. In: Layton (ed.), *Conflict in the Archaeology of Living Traditions*. London: Unwin Hyman, pp. 1–21.

Le Van Giang (2013). The way forward for protecting Hoi An World Heritage (Hướng đi cho bảo tồn di sản Hội An). Interview by Phuong Hien, Information Gate of the Delegates of Quang Nam to the National Assembly and Provincial People's Council, 31 July 2013. Available at: http://qh-hdqna.gov.vn/Default.aspx?tabid=77&ctl=New&News=968&mid=436 (accessed 8 March 2015).

Logan, W. (2015). Making the most of heritage in Hanoi, Vietnam. *Historic Environment*, 26(3): 62–72.

Miura, K. (2005). Conservation of a 'living heritage site' – a contradiction in terms? A case study of Angkor World Heritage site. *Conservation and Management of Archaeological Sites*, 1(7), 3–18.

Murphy, E. (1985). *Tourism: A Community Approach*. New York: Methuen.

Nguyen Chi Trung (2014). Hoi An World Heritage: 15 years of sustainable conservation and promotion. *Heritage Conservation Newsletter*, 4(28), 3–9. (In Vietnamese: Di sản Văn hóa Thế giới Hội An, 15 năm bảo tồn và phát huy bền vững, Bản tin Bảo tồn Di sản số 04(28), 2014).

Okazaki, E. (2008). A community-based tourism model: its conception and use. *Journal of Sustainable Tourism*, 16(5), 511–29.

Pascual, J. (United Cities and Local Governments, Barcelona). Letter to: Le Van Giang (People's Committee of Hoi An City, Hoi An). In: *Report and Follow up of the International Award UCLG – Mexico City – Culture 21*, 23 June 2014. Archives of the Hoi An Centre for Heritage Preservation and Management.

Pedersen, A. (2002). *Managing Tourism at World Heritage Sites: A Practical Manual for World Heritage Site Managers*. Paris: UNESCO World Heritage Centre.

Pretty, J. (1995). The many interpretations of participation. *Focus*, 16, 4–5.

Poulios, I. (2014). Discussing strategy in heritage conservation – living heritage approach as an example of strategic innovation. *Journal of Cultural Heritage Management and Sustainable Development*, 4(1), 16–34.

Quang Nam People's Committee (2011). *Strategy Integrating Culture and Tourism for Sustainable Development*, attached to the Decision no.1219/2011 dated 18 April 2011. Tam Ky: Quang Nam People's Committee Office.

Rao, K. (2012). Pathways to sustainable development. In: A. Galla (ed.), *World Heritage: Benefits Beyond Borders*. London: Cambridge University Press, pp. 325–32.

Timothy, D.J. (2007). Empowerment and stakeholder participation in tourism destination communities. In: A. Church and T. Coles (eds), *Tourism, Power and Space*. London and New York: Routledge, pp. 199–216.

Tjosvold, D. (1996). Conflict management in a diverse world: a review essay of Caplan's understanding disputes: the politics of argument. *Human Relations*, 49(9), 1203–11.

Tosun, C. (2000). Limits to community participation in the tourism development process in developing countries. *Tourism Management*, 21(6), 613–33.

UNESCO (1999). *World Heritage Committee Nomination Documentation File 948: Hoi An Ancient Town*. Available at: http://whc.unesco.org/en/list/948 (accessed 28 December 2014).

UNESCO (2007). *Asia Conserved – Lessons Learnt from the UNESCO Asia-Pacific Heritage Awards for Culture Heritage Conservation 2000–2004*. Bangkok: UNESCO Bangkok, pp. 359–64.

UNESCO (2008). *The Effects of Tourism on Culture and the Environment in Asia and the Pacific – Impact*. Bangkok: UNESCO Bangkok.

UNESCO (2009). *UNESCO Asia-Pacific Heritage Awards Winners*. Available at: http://www.unescobkk.org/culture/wh/asia-pacific-heritage-awards/previous (accessed 9 January 2015).

Winter, T. (2004). Cultural heritage and tourism in Angkor, Cambodia: developing a theoretical dialogue. *Historic Environment*, 17(3), 3–8.

The World Bank (1987). *Community Participation in Development Projects; The World Bank Experience,* World Bank Discussion Paper 6. Washington, D.C.: The World Bank, pp. 1–37.

Chapter 16

Deep ecology and urban conservation principles for urban villages

Planning for Hauz Khas Village, Delhi City

Yamini Narayanan

India's cities, simultaneously rural and urban, ancient and modern, are edgy, vibrant spaces, with a unique sense of a living expression built up over several centuries. Cities such as Delhi, which is believed to be among the oldest living cities in the world, radiate historicity and modernity not only in architectural heritage and built form, but also through diverse – frequently conflicting – lifestyles, traditions, values and purpose. Delhi city, like the contemporary city elsewhere, is, to use Rykwert's terms, 'too fragmentary, too full of contrast and strife: it must therefore have many faces, not one' (Rykwert 2002: 7). However, Rykwert sees this very contrariness as in fact a 'positive virtue, not a fault at all, or even a problem'. Indeed, the 'contrary city' and its inherent capacity to challenge and resist 'any coherent, explicit image', maddening though it may be in its contradictions, presents endless possibilities for new, more equitable and ethical ways of conceptualising sustainable development, and indeed, living itself.

One of the starkest contrary qualities of Delhi city is its substantial village spaces located within the heart of the modern megalopolis with its world city aspirations. Many of these urban villages are located in historic precincts near iconic sites of the previous empires ruling the ancient city. Unlike village spaces that have been consciously created for ethno-tourism in many Indian cities (such as the Choki Dhani urban villages in Rajasthani cities or the Dakshina Chitra village-museums in urban Tamil Nadu), the villages in Delhi are real rural spaces within the city. Their agricultural and pasture lands have shrunk rapidly as the city swallowed up huge tracts of farming land to support its growth.

These historic-urban villages have become attractive in a rapidly modernising urban India, reflecting a sanitised creative bourgeois (re)making of a traditional Indian village as a selectively urbanised rural space. While urban villages more generally may continue to be perceived with disdain as stagnant spaces, historic-urban villages are attractive for their combination of heritage and rustic chic and as sites of elite consumption. As the city sprawls outwards, these villages often find themselves at the centre of the modern city, exposed and vulnerable to the growing march of capitalism, real estate hypergrowth and technologisation. The villages in the old historic cores also face the onslaught of ethno-tourism and ethno-consumption, both of which consciously seek the rural or rustic sense of place, as well as the memory of the city of another time, to consume. In all these cases, the villagers increasingly find themselves either without a voice in determining their own future, or in the position of having to reinvent themselves and their culture to present the most attractive and palatable aspects of village life for the consumption of the urban elite.

However, imposed social or cultural constructions of place that are not consistent with local frameworks for understanding place are of concern for the planning and protection of sustainable places (Beatley and Manning 1997). Delhi's urban villages – as with rural-urban sites anywhere in South Asia or the developing world – present the challenge of retaining a local sense of place while confronting at the same time the onslaught of modern capitalism. Identifying the distinctive elements that foster place attachments, familiarity and belonging 'concerns the connections between people and places, movement and urban form, nature and the built fabric, and the processes for ensuring successful villages, towns and cities' (CABE and DETR 2000). A planning framework that is attentive to the specific needs and elements of the urban village, and its unique sense of local place, is necessary in order to reverse the elite anthropocentric development of these spaces and the destruction of ecological diversity and rural cultures implicit therein.

In this chapter, I argue for a planning framework that uses deep ecology as value and urban conservation principles as strategy, to develop and manage heritage villages in cities in a manner that is responsive to the local sense of place. I suggest that inclusive planning may be best facilitated when it celebrates the *genius loci* or the inherent spirit of place, which urban conservation can protect through pragmatic strategies and deep ecology can celebrate through inclusive planning and participation. Deep ecology, a term coined by the Norwegian ecologist Arne Naess in the 1970s, is a body of environmental philosophy that emphasises the value of *all* nature forms regardless of their utility to humans. Deep ecology aims to reverse anthropocentrism of highly industrialised and urbanised societies and undertakes deeply existential critiques of humans' roles, specifically the role of elite humans privileged by neoliberal capitalist growth in perpetuating ecological crises.

A framework that supports the dismantling of elite anthropocentrism, I argue, is vital for the sustainable development of rural spaces within cities, especially in developing countries. This is especially vital for village spaces that have heritage value in the form of monuments, ecology or intangible cultural heritage and for villagers whose cultural and ecological resources are consciously sought for consumption and exploitation. A deep ecology framework for the planning of rural-urban-heritage spaces, I suggest, is compatible with the three dimensions of conservation for maintaining heritage sites proposed by Elnokaly and Elseragy (2013) – the socio-cultural, socio-physical and the environmental. Specifically, the development of such a framework can protect the following elements of historic urban-rural environments: the tangible heritage, the intangible heritage in the form of lifestyles, livelihoods, traditions and values attached to place, and the natural heritage surrounding historic sites and monuments. Deep ecology can thus enable historic, natural, social and cultural aspects to complicate notions of urban ecology.

Further, this addresses another consumption-related concern that development, which is 'often synonymous with the introduction of new technology, increased privatization and consumerism, environmental degradation and social atomization' (Narayanan 2015: 27), can destroy not only built but also intangible socio-cultural heritage. Deep ecology and urban conservation together can better respond to the argument rather than 'development' concepts such as 'rehabilitation', 'rebuilding' and 'renewal', and might better serve urban environmental protection, as well as social engagement and community participation in historic Indian cities (Brett-Crowther 1985; Naidu 1994). In this way, the chapter also addresses the noted under-theorisation of the multidisciplinary nature of urban ecology, where urban planning has neglected to draw upon historic urban innovations to creatively develop cities (Young 2009). Given the sheer scale of contemporary urban environments, especially the megacities and supercities of the global South, the 'mismatch' between the historic temporal and spatial realities and modern planning decisions has severely limited urban planning and compromised sustainable urban environments (Breuste and Qureshi 2011).

I use the case of the historic Hauz Khas Village in the Hauz Khas suburb[1] in south Delhi to demonstrate the multiple tensions regarding place perceptions and to argue for an application of the principles of deep ecology and conservation to the planning and development of socially equitable and ecologically sustainable rural spaces within the city. Hauz Khas Village in New Delhi is one of the best-preserved sites of the second incarnation of the ancient capital built by Aladdin Khilji in the thirteenth century. Villagers had maintained Hauz Khas's heritage for more than 700 years before the Delhi Development Authority formally took over the preservation and development of the area in 1954. Taking advantage of its historic environment, Hauz Khas is now an affluent suburb and the village itself is an elitist enclave of Delhi's celebrity fashion designers, Michelin star restaurants and art galleries. Hauz Khas also faces pressing issues of traffic congestion, the steady marginalisation and eviction of the villagers, the development of modernist constructions resulting in high living densities and one of the highest rates of air pollution in the city.

The chapter is structured as follows. I first provide a brief historical overview of the status and value of Delhi's Villages prior to the new role of the historic urban villages as sites of elite tourism and consumption. Next, I trace the different stages of the long history of Hauz Khas Village in particular, to its current re-making as an 'authentic village' for privileged urbanites. Last, I turn to a conceptual discussion linking the principles of deep ecology and urban conservation as a framework for planning urban villages.

The historic, stagnant and/or commercial statuses of Delhi's villages

Delhi is one of the most iconic heritage cities in the world. It has three World Heritage monuments – Red Fort, Humayun's Tomb and the Qutub Minar – 171 nationally significant monuments and a large number of state-level significant monuments. According to a survey by INTACH Delhi and the DDA in 1999, there are 1,208 heritage buildings, 27 Heritage Zones/precincts, and in each of these, they identified sites/monuments/areas worthy of conservation. There is currently strong lobbying from the Indian National Trust for Art and Cultural Heritage (INTACH) to declare Delhi a UNESCO World Heritage City.

Delhi's identity is by no means limited to its iconic or other built heritage. The city's distinctiveness is drawn as much from the agricultural farmlands that covered substantial tracts of the modern city, even as recently as two decades ago. Traditional family norms and kinship groups similar to agrarian rural areas are strongly pervasive in the metropolitan capital city. Links between natural and tangible heritage are 'compelling' (Krishna Menon 2010: 8) and they are most evident in the intangible heritage in the form of the traditional lifestyles and occupations. The villagers in the city continue to engage in primary occupations, such as farming and pottery, agriculture and animal husbandry, although the city is rapidly cannibalising the green spaces. In his work on Latin American cities, especially in Mexico, Oscar Lewis (1955: 31) describes such rural/traditional familial configuration of modern urban spaces as 'urbanization without breakdown in the traditional patterns' of social groups and employment.

In India, however, historic cities and spaces are considered 'urban "problems" and not cultural assets' (Krishna Menon 2010: 8) and investment in their development and preservation is usually guided by opportunistic motivations relating to tourism or retail. Overall, urban-historic villages, including the precincts surrounding historical monuments in the city, also badly need renovation and repair and they have fallen into a sad state of misuse and neglect because of centuries of official apathy. Aside from iconic historic sites, a lot of heritage is actually regarded as 'inconvenient impediments to new development' (Krishna Menon 2010: 2). With the undermining of tangible heritage, the intangible heritage of the city is also inevitably eroded through immigration, tourism and modernisation of the old neighbourhoods and the distinctive local food, arts and crafts spaces and rituals and customs fast give way to a more homogeneous and globalised culture and way of life. There is extraordinary disconnect between a sense and understanding that Delhi continues to be, in many ways, a medieval city, and the ambitious planning for the capital to be a modern, 'smart city', with a community that is interconnected by technology. Krishna Menon (2010: 2) writes, 'the significance of this extraordinary heritage is often contested by urban planners, city managers and even citizens who would rather gratuitously turn their gaze towards arriviste cities like Singapore, Shanghai and Dubai to make Delhi a "world-class city"'.

The simultaneous undermining of the city's heritage and the urbanisation of Delhi's villages started to occur in the most irreversible way after British colonisation. The transfer of the capital to Delhi in 1911 placed additional pressure on the city to urbanise and modernise. The privileging of the modern, albeit international/Euro-Western images and aspirations for the modern Indian city resulted in the decline of its older historic parts and its living precolonial, medieval character.

The racial discrimination that underpinned British policymaking never allowed for the conception of a democratic, equitable and locally relevant urban policy that took cognisance of its rural spaces for Delhi (Goel 2005) or other Indian cities. The British seized agricultural farmlands in the village settlements, whenever possible, to establish factories and set up their own capital north of Old Delhi in Civil Lines. The Partition of India in 1947 intensified spatial pressures; the newly independent state in Delhi was also forced to take over agricultural and rural holdings wherever possible in the city to rehome fleeing refugees from Pakistan. Land was also required for a number of projects such as the construction of airports and airstrips, sewerage treatment plants, cremation grounds and industries. If these pressures were not enough, large-scale immigration from the smaller towns and villages of India to the national capital started in the search for better employment opportunities, an ongoing trend that started in the 1950s and 1960s.

There are 362 villages in Delhi of which there are 135 urban villages and 227 rural villages (Singh 2013). When Delhi's Master Plan was inaugurated in 1962 (MPD-1962), the task of defining the city's villages within and beyond the Delhi metropolitan area was a priority. The MPD-1962 defined 'rural villages' as areas that were beyond 'urbanisable limits' in the foreseeable future until 1981 and identified 'urban villages' that had varying degrees of capacity to generate employment including through 'village-like' industries such as arts and handicrafts, weaving and handlooms, pottery, etc. The Plan proposed the idea of Metropolitan-Urban-Rural-Integration to investigate the possibility of an amalgamated urban/rural planning for the city. However, the 'slummification' of the villages started to become a significant concern, as their former agricultural lands became more densely populated, leading to thick congestion in the narrow alleyways and lanes. The villages surrounding historical monuments in the city badly need renovation and repair and they had fallen into a sad state of misuse and neglect because of centuries of official apathy. The villages started to lose their economic agency through farming and became dependent on metropolitan Delhi for their survival (Goel 2005). The resulting decay of the villages and the village economy was noted with some concern in a Mini Master Plan in 1985 (MMP-1985), which again emphasised the need for 'integrated development' of the urban and rural villages over an unspecified period of time but also failed to yield results in any substantial way.

The interest in Delhi's historic rural precincts came, not unpredictably in hindsight, from the city's elite, sophisticated consuming classes. As compared with Europe, middle- and upper-class India experienced urbanisation fatigue relatively late and it was not until as recently as the 1980s that the urban village within the megacity was revisited as an accessible and idyllic rural landscape for its possibility of escape, renewal and 'authenticity'. The urban elite came to slowly appreciate the heritage of a bygone, ostensibly more cultured and ecologically pure era, as well as rustic heritage; further, the possibility of actually enacting, albeit selectively, these lifestyles in real villages with valuable heritage sites was extremely attractive. The urban village in a historic precinct especially became regarded as an oasis and 'a fossil of old age [*sic*] civilisation amidst an elephantine urban mass scattered in steel and concrete' (Sen 2013: 251). The logistical convenience of the rural, idyllic village within the smart, modern city offered the best of two distinct worlds, times and spaces. In her extensive work on the elite consumption of urban villages in India and the UK, Emma Tarlo states:

> There is moreover an international tendency among elite groups who live in urban, industrialised environments, to idealise nature and the village. One manifestation of this trend . . . is to rediscover villages within cities. The particular appeal of the ideal of the village within the city is that it enables people to enjoy the same sort of village life and urban life, simultaneously, in one place.
>
> (Tarlo 1996: 34)

The historic urban villages started to experience a stratospheric leap in real estate development and investment, while villages in the city that were not attached to iconic heritage continued to struggle with infrastructural decay and blight. Notably, the village was not valuable as rural heritage in itself, but became priceless as part of a historic precinct. In Delhi's historic spaces, 'dressing up various aspects of the culture in the village idiom' (Tarlo 1996: 31) became a preoccupation of the moneyed, entrepreneurial classes in particular. This process of remaking the village involves extracting those palatable, aesthetic elements of the traditional village, which might also harken back to nationalist pride in the indigenous and own history. Consistent with these trends elsewhere, the aesthetic appeal of heritage also triggered a range of creative industries. Global tourism to heritage sites is a clear indication that heritage revives and encourages investment in almost all activities associated with the site, especially real estate and consumption (Nagy and Abu-Dayyeh 2002). The combination of carefully selected elements of heritage and modern consumption together creates the perfect rural-urban aesthetic environment for the consuming classes. Emma Tarlo's work on historic urban villages in Delhi and Nagy and Abu-Dayyeh's observations on similar themes from historic rural-urban Jordan both demonstrate that heritage and modern retail together make for a highly attractive environment for consumption, allowing the neat and carefully manipulated spatial intermingling of different worlds:

> When food, clothes, furniture and architecture are combined, as in the case of Hauz Khas Village, the result is the creation of a 'total ethnic environment'.
>
> (Tarlo 1996: 35)

> In the cafés we have described, heritage provides more than a temporal link between past and present. It links space – rural, urban, transnational – and spans the social boundaries of class and gender for café clientele.
>
> (Nagy and Abu-Dayyeh 2002: 17)

When living villages within the city are taken over as spaces of global consumption, the result is often an exclusion of the local people who are part of the living and built heritage. Issues of identity, power, struggles around space, usurpation and the loss in some cases of an entire way of life warn of an increasing separation of the economy and the local community (Urry 1995). The elite rediscovery and consumption of the ancient Hauz Khas Village in the late twentieth century exemplifies these struggles. It raises critical challenges for the sustainable integration of historic village precincts in Delhi – of which there are many – into the development of the megacity but it also provides the opportunity for alternative planning visions that are more responsive to local realities and histories.

Hauz Khas: the (re/un?)making of an 'authentic elite' urban village

At the end of the crowded dusty road leading into Hauz Khas Village, secluded from the commercial hum of the little thoroughfare, lies the remaining ruins of Hauz Khas, spanning at least two centuries and three empires of Delhi – the Khiljis of the thirteenth century and the Tuglaqs and the Lodis of the fourteenth-century. The congested road to Hauz Khas itself could be seen as a heritage site, riddled as it is with monuments from the later fourteenth-century Lodi era including tombs (Dadi-Poti) and natural heritage such as the Deer Park and a small forested area adjoining the park. This road to the almost concealed historic ruins is now also marked by the overt internationalisation of Delhi's bourgeois who own high-end fashion retail stores showcasing ethnic chic and Western-style bars and cafés featuring celebrity chefs who range from Iranian to French to German, in addition to carefully showcasing a selection of India's regional royal cuisine. Real village cows graze on peeling posters and the smattering of greenery that remains in the area.

Hauz Khas was first named Hauz-i-Ala'i after the large *hauz* or water tank that the great Khilji ruler Aladdin Khilji built in 1295 to store rainwater and water from the western Ridge. Khilji's successor, Qutub-ud-din Aibak, the legendary builder of the now World Heritage-listed Qutub Minar, expanded this city. It is presumed that Qutub's city lay within the Qutub complex based on the references to the area as 'shahr' (city) and on the considerable effort that has clearly gone into the fortification of the city (Chadha 2010). This old city did not go into decline. The emperor Firoz Shah of the Tuglaq dynasty, who ascended the throne in 1351, was a great lover of heritage monuments and revitalised the monument in 1353. He also built his beautiful tombed *madrassa* or the Madrasa-e-Firoz Shahi (College of Firoz Shah) and his own tomb on its banks. Living intangible heritage, religious, cultural and intellectual, thus flourished beneath the domed skyline of Hauz Khas. Villages surrounded the historic sites. The villagers usually had shopfronts in the lower storey of their houses or *havelis* and the living quarters were the second floors. Sometimes, the *havelis* had three or even four floors, depending on the size of the family. This was also a rich and fertile agricultural area; Ferishta (cited in Lewis and Lewis 1997: 125) describes the banks as a rich source of sugarcane, cucumbers, green melons and pumpkins.

The Hauz Khas ruins were declared protected monuments in 1914, shortly after the start of the First World War. Thus began the 'modern development' phase of the Hauz Khas precincts, which had been largely looked after by the villagers up to that point. Ironically, the 'protected' status of the Hauz Khas heritage meant that from this point onwards, the adjoining areas were constantly developed and changed, compromising almost irreversibly the state of non-interference and integrity that the site had hitherto largely enjoyed. The fateful swallowing up of the greenery had begun, which extended far around the Hauz Khas village precinct. After 1947, the rapidly expanding capital of independent India urgently needed more land, and the preservation of urban villages was not a priority. Between 1960 and 1967, the state completed the acquisition of agricultural lands of Hauz Khas and the affected landowners received compensation 'at the rate of 50 paise per sq. yard' (Goel 2005: 11). The impoverishment of the village community became vital to the growth of modern Delhi.

During the Emergency in 1979, the political interest in the preservation of the green cover threatened the lifestyles of the villagers. Sanjay Gandhi, and the erstwhile Delhi Governor K.C. Jha, proposed that the Hauz Khas area be converted into a greenbelt and parklands and that the villagers be removed and rehabilitated in modern housing. The plan had to be abandoned after widespread and hostile protests from the villagers. In 1981, the Hauz Khas Village was finally declared 'urban' when the remaining agricultural farmlands were formally taken over by the Delhi Development Authority (DDA). The DDA's Zonal Plan F-4 declared the entire Hauz Khas area to be a district of 300 acres, not including the Deer Park on its eastern end. Crucially, the decade also marked the interest, for the first time in Hauz Khas's history, of Delhi's elite middle and upper classes, rather than royalty.

It started to become apparent that 'ethnic' charm, which Hauz Khas Village exuded in spades, had a raging commercial potential. The first discerning entrepreneurs were the fashion designers for whom the combination of cheap rent in a well-located area, the historic charm and the rural idyllic environs provided an irresistible attraction to set up small business and ventures for ethnic clothing and apparel, arts and handicrafts. Specifically, high-profile designer Bina Ramani ushered in a whole new phase for Hauz Khas when she set up one of the first fashion retail outlets in the village precincts and introduced a culture of 'competitive professionalism' (Goel 2005: 13) in sleepy Hauz Khas. Lewis and Lewis write:

> The final death knell of the village and the villagers' traditional way of life was struck in the late 1980s with its 'boutiquification' and transformation into a smart shopping centre for Delhi's urban elite.
>
> (Lewis and Lewis 1997: 128)

However, the transformation did not entirely spell gloom and doom for the villagers; the land and rent value skyrocketed and many of the villagers began to sell, demolish or renovate their *havelis* for these boutique entrepreneurs. Those who remained in the area started to move their residences further inwards to make the space available for shopfronts, thus heralding the retreat of residential street life and the advancement of a commercial thoroughfare in the strip. Goel notes the differential impacts of the commercialisation of Hauz Khas on the villagers:

> [Some of them] built new houses replacing old ones. Some of them even bought luxury cars and sent their children to public schools. Some took to commercial professions. Some of the original old inhabitants remain plunged into depression on account of the new character of their village. For them the *chawpal* culture is missing. The gatherings and mutual friendly relationships which had been the cornerstone of the societal environment of the village have given way to formal meetings.
>
> (Goel 2005: 14)

Even so, the Hauz Khas commercialisation project was at least initially one of promise. It provided the hope of a historically and aesthetically sensitive way of planning, while locating the village and the villagers at the centre of the new development, rather than at the periphery. Pavan Varma writes for instance:

> With the infusion of money, the village stands transformed, but, I, must confess that the transformation is not entirely unappealing. The basic contours of the village profile have been preserved; in the pursuit of ethnic chic, Delhi's moneyed class has displayed a degree of taste quite uncharacteristic of it . . . In fact, for a city with such a rich architectural tradition, the real blot on the landscape is the terribly unimaginative nature of some of its modern constructions . . . When I am, for instance, in Hauz Khas, I find the elements in harmony and the entire setting has the authenticity of an indigenous tradition, where climate, heritage and local genius have blended to produce a cumulative aesthetic value.
>
> (Varma 1994)

In the initial phase of the ethnic remaking of Hauz Khas Village, some villagers, especially the landowning Jat Hindus who owned properties along the main road to the ruins, benefited enormously. The Muslims and low-caste Hindu Harijans (formerly untouchables) who owned land in the outer peripheries of the village were neglected, even though the distance from the centre was barely a few hundred metres (Kaur and Paul 2012). The advantages of new commercial development remained spatially and socially concentrated within the centre, even though the village precinct itself was small.

By 1991, the landmark year of economic liberation for India, the dream visions of the immense and unique potential for Hauz Khas had well and truly been destroyed; its 'dream-plan [had] gone askew'. Hauz Khas Village seemed to have reached the limits of its thwarted potential and it was variously slammed as 'monstrous', a 'big fraud', 'a deodorised, desanitised and cosmeticised Karol Bagh', a 'glorified Karol Bagh'. Referring to Hauz Khas as Karol Bagh was one of the worst insults one could throw at the historic site. Karol Bagh in West Delhi is the epitome of a modern urban village gone badly wrong, an unholy cocktail of infrastructural decay, blight, stagnation, over-congestion and pollution. The state was limited in its capacity to manipulate the development of Hauz Khas as its heritage marked it as a conservation zone. While this meant that the area retained its rural character for longer than other urban villages in Delhi, its population nevertheless grew rapidly. However, the conservation and environmental laws are dreadfully weak and pertain only to the monuments; slapdash cement constructions have mushroomed all over the traditional *havelis* in the village.

In the past five years, a new generation of entrepreneurs who are 'eccentric' by self-definition have launched new cafés and bars, such as the Kunzum Travel Café in the precinct, which seek to capitalise on the global trend of being organic and rustic (Kaur and Paul 2012). In a distinct departure, even from the 1980s and 90s, the café/bar trend has come to dominate Hauz Khas Village, even to the extent of perhaps diminishing the sense of place and the preservation of the monuments. New constructions openly disregard the by-laws of the Archaeological Society of India of leaving the surrounding 100 metres of protected heritage untouched; cafés can be found almost immediately adjoining the outer walls of the site. The retail shops were found to be flouting building norms and many restaurants and cafés in Hauz Khas were guilty of disposing of oil and kitchen waste directly on to the ground (Singh 2013).

The shock of new money pouring into the Hauz Khas precinct in the twenty-first century is distinctive from previous forms of invaders in its capacity to force-fully redefine the sense of place of the former village and its ruins. Tourism is also expected to increase exponentially in Delhi. There are concerns that if Delhi acquires World Heritage status, the autonomy of the state in decision-making will be reduced and it will place additional conservation and planning responsibilities on the state that it is barely delivering upon now. Such a status will also intensify pressure on already popular heritage sites in Delhi, such as Hauz Khas Village, with the real risk of exterminating once and for all, any authenticity associated with the site and offering instead, a pickled, museumised version of what has been hitherto substantially living rural heritage. As fodder for tourism marketing, the Hauz Khas precinct can become even more frozen as a carefully constructed historic rural-urban 'reality'.

The concept of 'sustainable development' has started to feature as a major theme in India's Master Planning policies for cities and it is informed by a three-fold focus on ecological preservation, heritage conservation and a growth-oriented economy. This conception of 'sustainable cities/development' has been criticised in the West for excluding the poor, minorities and women. In India, these issues are accentuated as they undermine the 'rights to the city' of the majority of urban citizens including its villagers. The last section briefly examined the potential for the application of deep ecology principles in an urban socio-political-cultural context for sustainable urban development that is cognisant of its rural and peri-urban areas. Planning's approaches to urban heritage in particular must plan for, and accommodate, the informal sector in India. Deep ecology can offer opportunities to deepen an inclusive sense of place, particularly for those at risk of social, economic and political marginalisation. In a teeming, diverse megacity, this is a core-planning asset for sustainable urban development.

Applying deep ecology to planning urban villages: the case of Hauz Khas Village

The elite remaking of Hauz Khas Village as an 'ideal' rural village in their own eyes is distinctive from the planning authorities' approach to villages, which was to demolish and rebuild a new, modern city altogether on their sites. Delhi's fashion and lifestyle entrepreneurs did, at the very least, seek to maximise and celebrate the rustic, historic sense of place – albeit highly selective elements – and predictably, this manipulation came with problems of marginalisation and social exclusion. The outcome in effect was to carefully subvert the democratic principles of deep ecology of letting *all* natural/historical elements remain; only the aesthetically palatable aspects of the historic and the rustic was to be excavated and celebrated.

However, planning that is attuned to a localised sense of place as identified and endorsed by the local inhabitants is regarded as one of the most important steps in developing sustainable places (Sepe 2013). In order to maintain the ecological and socio-cultural integrity of heritage sites and for social equity in multicultural sites, the essential qualities of local place must be identified, excavated and protected. Beatley and Manning (1997) identify 'sense of place as an important dimension of sustainable places, strengthening local identity, contributing to investment, and retaining communities'. How can deep ecology provide a framework for a new planning model that is inspired by indigenous urbanism in order to enable a more inclusive, ethical and effective basis for sustainable urbanism both in Hauz Khas and other urban historic sites in India?

Norwegian eco-philosopher Arne Naess's eight principles of deep ecology were inspired by Mahatma Gandhi's interpretation of *ahimsa* or non-violence. As summarised (and translated) by Lippe-Biesterfeld and van Tijn (2005: 212–13), these are: both human and non-human have innate value and the value of non-human lives is not to be determined solely by their usefulness to humans; diversity of natural life is a value in itself; humans do not have any right to risk this diversity, except to the extent that it serves their *needs* (rather than desires); the present nature of human relationships with the non-human world is one of exploitation; the flourishing of non-human life requires a decrease in human population; change in basic life conditions requires corresponding changes in institutional structures such as economical, technological and ideological; and 'the ideological change is mainly that of appreciating life quality (dwelling in situations of intrinsic value) . . . there will be a profound awareness of the difference between big and great'. Lastly, Naess says, the intention should be to leave all forms of life as undisturbed and unharmed as possible (Lippe-Biesterfeld and van Tijn 2005).

Naess's principles venerate all forms of natural life regardless of its 'value' to humans. However, cultural anthropologists have long pointed to the intimate intertwining of nature/culture and they have objected to their perception as separate notions. As such, advocates of deep ecology have also been highly concerned with the destruction of cultural diversity wrought by rapid growth and the associated exploitations of minorities, indigenous peoples and poor women. As deep ecologist Ruth Rosenhek (2011: 45) puts it,

> until we have social justice, we won't have justice for the Earth. Until we halt the ongoing cycle of violence, the exploitations of peoples worldwide for the sake of profit, greed and power, we will continue to do harm to the Earth, and hence to ourselves.

Notably, Naess (1989, translated by David Rothenberg) also takes particular care to distinguish between the anthropocentrism of the poor that is driven by lack of choice and survival motivations, and the anthropocentrism of the elite whose aggressive consumption choices spell disaster for social and environmental justice. Seen this way, concerns about human exploitation extend not only to non-human nature but also to oppressed humans. McLaughlin (1995: 30) is emphatic that deep ecology must extend to social justice in order to protect the ecological heritage of the past: 'there is no incompatibility between deep ecology and at least some progressive visions of human social justice'.

When this framework of non-violence is applied to modernist urban planning and conservation with its innate respect for *all* life forms and by extension, biocultural diversity and belief in their right to flourish, deep ecology can also deepen, so to speak, the notion of urban ecology. Urban ecology is the 'interaction of social and ecological systems within urbanized space and the impact that such interactions have on external systems' (Young 2009: 312). Socially diverse, historically layered complex urban forms can use the principles of deep ecology as an ethic philosophy as well as a strategy to conceptualise democratic and life-sustaining planning and development. As such, when the principles of deep ecology guide urban conservation which is 'a process of continuous yet controlled interventions in the environment' (Elnokaly and Elseragy 2013: 31), planning can, in addition to maintaining the environmental integrity of place, also preserve a historic sense of place that is as closely attuned to the local realities and histories as possible.

Deep ecology can provide a compatible framework for architectural, ecological and socio-cultural conservation of urban historic spaces based on its distinctive sense of place. It can safeguard the local place as much as possible from additional impositions on place and sense of place from various forms of modern consumerism, even as it is most definitively still located within the large and spatially diverse metropolis. While previous planning models have tended to either ignore rural spaces within the city as stagnant, or swallow them up and regurgitate them as an 'improved' modern artefact, deep ecology and conservation planning together may enable villages such as Hauz Khas to sustain themselves as urban villages seamlessly integrated within the modern metropolis, such as how Sen envisions:

the idea of an urban village is to see a massive city as a collection of neighbourhoods which are self-sustainable and where people can collectively own and share the neighbourhood while retaining the sense of being part of the bigger city. The idea of an urban village is thus a space that could keep the best of both, rural and urban, in a harmonious and symbiotic way.

(Sen 2013: 251)

The sensitivity to local place and the will to preserve its spirit of place enables the spatial flourishing of a vibrant 'contrary city' that Rykwert (2002) considered highly desirable, rather than a homogenised urban form and sense of place. Planning that considers sense of place, which deeply respects natural, as well as lower socio-economic human interests, as a universal ethic is likely to be highly compatible with other spaces within the city. In his work on the interconnected nature of diverse natural and cultural property in Delhi, Krishna Menon had noted:

While each component of Delhi's heritage is worthy of conservation for its own sake, it is the connections, overlaps and the creative energies that bind them which form the composite cultural heritage of the city. Understanding this will also help contributing to achieving sustainable urban form in future.

(Krishna Menon 2010: 4)

The development and application of such frameworks depends centrally on local participation and inclusive planning protocols. It remains the case, of course, that large numbers of the original villagers have already been displaced from Hauz Khas Village. Many of the new residents and 'villagers' are moneyed and influential elite classes. Rural-urban villages, more than other rural spaces in the city, are confronted with the challenge of a specific form of indigenous modernism where the sense of place is no longer the concern or preserve of the residents alone, but is also a commodity for ethno-tourism and consumption.

Deep ecology's intent to dethrone human interests, particularly elite priorities, is a fraught task that can only be achieved through dialogue and consensus. Colonisation of village land, farmlands and ancestral landholdings of the villagers in the precinct and rural lifestyles has been a constant strategy of the Delhi state, which has made repeated attempts to 'acquire' land from the areas surrounding the cluster of monuments in Hauz Khas. Muslim and low-caste Hindu Jat families have been particularly affected by the state and urban development's cavalier attitude towards their interests. Through its uncompromising commitment to democracy, deep ecology may productively serve as a guideline for two critical aspects particularly noted to be plaguing contemporary urban development (Hampton 2005), which are exemplified in the post-1947 making and remaking of Hauz Khas Village: identity and power relations, and the need, including economic rationale, for local community involvement in planning.

The major challenge for inclusive urban planning is to ensure that the project of inclusivity does not, ironically, become elitist (Narayanan 2015), and that the historical undermining of the agency of the villagers is carefully addressed. Greater grassroots democracy in the city's villages is one of the first steps to ensure that they bear the fruits, rather than the brunt, of neoliberalism. In order to redress the imbalance where the villagers have been left largely voiceless, and to successfully de-anthropomorphise, I suggest that deliberative, participatory, democratic processes need to be adopted in a manner that are underpinned by positive or affirmative discrimination.

First, the opportunity should be available for all villagers located in the village, as well as in the outer precincts of the village, to have the opportunity to select their development trajectory, identify the elements that comprise place for Hauz Khas Village and deliberate upon the possibilities for further growth with information and agency. The spaces for deliberation and negotiation need to occur where villagers feel empowered, which is more likely to be open public spaces in Hauz Khas itself, rather than in spaces that are alien and unfamiliar from their everyday life. Nearly 25 years ago, Mohan noted that vocabulary and the location of inclusive participatory planning workshops matter greatly in generating participation for determining visions and hopes for Indian cities:

> Perhaps if the same [seminar] is arranged around them, in their language, with their people initiating the discussion, they may feel like participating. So that the holding of seminars and discussions should be the other way round that rather than the Authorities initiating it, the public should do that. It is very necessary to quote examples where such projects are executed and for which the public is also aware so that during such discussions, one may really understand the entire problems [sic]. Even prior to the discussion, the participants be briefed, so that, healthy discussion could take place [sic]. Even a day earlier, the drawings, models could be displayed to make the public aware about the scheme.
>
> (Mohan 1992: 116)

Hauz Khas Village as recently as the 1990s embodied the village ideal of highly social and public streetscapes. Villagers adhered to a rural way of life, functioning with traditional community amenities such as the Panchayat (the village governance) hall, the *chaupar* or public square, shared open wells, small-scale shops that sold domestic goods and some traditional arts and handicrafts units (Lewis and Lewis 1997). These qualities of the village continue to live in living memory of the villagers, and be enacted, albeit in disembodied ways around the new growth (Lewis and Lewis 1997). These sites might serve as appropriate venues for deliberative workshops with the villagers who remain in the centre of village as well as those who have relocated to the outer peripheries of the rural precinct.

Second, the workshops and deliberations that occur over several phases must be carefully designed such that the complicated task of positive discrimination towards the diversity of village voices is successfully applied. Empowerment must occur such that the villagers have real agency and representation in influencing planning protocols and that elements of natural, cultural and built place are allowed to flourish. A conscious application of deep ecology to strategies of deliberation as well as conservation can ensure meaningful inclusivity and the empowerment of the original villagers and the development of Hauz Khas Village as a modern historical rural-urban heritage space.

Conclusions

In the past decade, heritage has been identified by key planning policies in India, such as the Jawaharlal Nehru National Urban Renewal Mission, as a vital theme for urban development, especially as almost all Indian cities can be regarded in varying degrees as historic. Considerable numbers of heritage sites are also located in village and/or older city precincts, and combined with their rural contexts, present a rich diversity of tangible and intangible heritage as factors for planning based on a localised sense of place. Urban historic residential village precincts are rife with intangible heritage such as customs and beliefs that frame lifestyles based on the geography, history and ecology of place (Elnokaly and Elseragy 2013). These reaffirm a sense of belonging to the residents, which is vital to the maintenance of sustainable places. The application of the tenets of deep ecology to urban development and conservation can be prioritised, leaving intact the interests of the historic village communities and planning growth and tourism in ways that do not compromise the essential elements of historic rural-urban place, while at the same time, bringing the benefits of modern urbanisation.

In a city poised for UNESCO World Heritage status, excavating Delhi's multi-faceted sense of rural place, especially in or near heritage sites, is urgent. Hauz Khas Village is a living historic precinct where different centuries spanning nearly 800 years continue to co-exist simultaneously every day. However, this vibrant historical and rural sense of place is being rapidly degraded. It is possible that with careful planning, deep ecology can make a more persuasive argument for rehabilitation and renewal of intangible, built and living heritage. It is also a framework that holds promise of social justice, poverty alleviation and understanding of the importance of sustaining and protecting village-scale economies within the larger city. Deep ecology can reinforce Hauz Khas as a 'living space' as there are clear links between the intangible, tangible and the natural heritage of the village. Considering deep ecology for inclusive urban policymaking can potentially offer one of the most realistic approaches for planning that takes into account the socio-cultural and historical elements of place, including the importance of retaining the rural dimensions of Indian urban life.

Note

1   Hauz Khas Village refers to the village precinct immediately adjoining the Hauz-i-Alai, the collection of tombs and monuments surrounding the *hauz* or the ancient water reservoir. The village is located within the larger Hauz Khas suburb, named for the *hauz*.

Bibliography

Beatley, T. and Manning, K. (1997). *The Ecology of Place: Planning for Environment, Economy and Community*. Washington, D.C.: Island Press.

Bhattacharya, V. (1977). *The Saga of Delhi*. New Delhi: Metropolitan Book Pvt. Ltd.

Brett-Crowther, M.R. (1985). Urban renewal in the Indian subcontinent. *The Round Table: The Commonwealth Journal of International Affairs*, 74(296), 348–59.

Breuste, J. and Qureshi, S. (2011). Urban sustainability, urban ecology and the Society for Urban Ecology (SURE). *Urban Ecosystems*, 14(3), 313–17.

CABE and DETR (2000). *By Design: Urban Design in the Planning System – Towards Better Practice*. London: Thomas Telford.

Chadha, R. (2010). The Delhi Sultanate. In: S. Liddle and A. Lopez (eds), *Delhi: A Living Heritage*. New Delhi: IGNCA and INTACH, pp. 24–33.

Clark, J. (1996). How wide is deep ecology? *Inquiry: An Interdisciplinary Journal of Philosophy*, 39(2), 189–201.

Elnokaly, A. and Elseragy, A. (2013). Sustainable heritage development: learning from urban conservation of heritage projects in non Western contexts. *European Journal of Sustainable Development*, 2(1), 31–56.

Goel, B. (2005). Hauz Khas and Peeran Garhi: A Study in the Urbanisation of Delhi Villages, 1911–1991. PhD thesis. New Delhi: Jamia Millia Islamia University.

Hampton, M.P. (2005). Heritage, local communities and economic development. *Annals of Tourism Research*, 32(3), 735–59.

Kaur, P. and Paul, S. (2012). From Hauz Khas to the Village. *The Sunday Guardian*, 15 April 2012. Available at: http://www.sunday-guardian.com/artbeat/from-hauz-khas-to-the-village (accessed 13 October 2014).

Krishna Menon, A.G. (2010). Introduction to the exhibition: Delhi: a living heritage. In: S. Liddle and A. Lopez (eds), *Delhi: A Living Heritage*. New Delhi: IGNCA and INTACH, pp. 2–15.

Lippe-Biesterfeld, I. and van Tijn, J. (2005). *Science, Soul and the Spirit of Nature: Leading Thinkers on Restoration of Man and Creation*. Rochester: Bear and Company.

Lewis, C. and Lewis, K. (1997). *Delhi's Historic Villages: A Photographic Evocation*. Delhi: Ravi Dayal Publisher.

Lewis, O. (1955). Peasant culture in India and Mexico. In: M. Marriot (ed.), *Village India*. Chicago: The American Anthropological Association, pp. 145–70.

McLaughlin, A. (1995). What is deep ecology? *Capitalism Nature Socialism*, 6(3), 25–30.

Mohan, I. (1992). *The World of Walled Cities*. New Delhi: Mittal Publications.

Naess, A. (1989). *Community, Ecology and Lifestyle: Outline of an Ecosophy*, trans. D. Rothenberg. Cambridge: Cambridge University Press.

Nagy, S. and Abu-Dayyeh, N. (2002). Village air for urban elites: heritage café complexes in Jordan. *Expedition Magazine*, 44(2), 11–16.

Naidu, R. (1994). A conceptual framework for the renewal of walled cities in India. *Ekistics*, 61(368/369), 298–306.

Narayanan, Y. (2015). *Religion, Heritage and the Sustainable City: Hinduism and Urbanisation in Jaipur*. London: Routledge.

Rosenhek, R. (2011). Deep ecology: a radical transformation of consciousness. *Biodiversity*, 5(4), 45–6.

Rykwert, J. (2002). *The Seduction of Place: The History and Future of the City*. New York: Vintage Books.

Sen, P. (2013). Journey from a city to an urban village: a study on India. *Journal of Settlements and Spatial Planning*, 4(2), 249–54.

Sepe, M. (2013). *Planning and Place in the City: Mapping Place Identity*. New York: Routledge.

Singh, K.B. (ed.) (1996). *People of India: Delhi*. Manohar: Anthropological Survey of India.

Singh, S. (2013). Capital needs a redevelopment plan to end the urban village mess. *Hindustan Times*, 30 September 2013. Available at: http://www.hindustantimes.com/comment/shivanisingh/capital-needs-a-redevelopment-plan-to-end-the-urban-village-mess/article1-1128903.aspx (accessed 18 September 2014).

Tarlo, E. (1996). Ethnic chic: the transformation of Hauz Khas Village. *India International Centre Quarterly*, 23(2), 30–59.

Urry, J. (1995). *Consuming Places*. London and New York: Routledge.

Varma, P. (1994). *Raghu Rai's Delhi*. New Delhi: Indus, HarperCollins.

Young, R.F. (2009). Interdisciplinary foundations of urban ecology. *Urban Ecosystems*, 12(3), 311–31.

Index